1995

Politics, Parties, and Elections in America

The Nelson-Hall Series in Political Science
Consulting Editor: Samuel C. Patterson
The Ohio State University

Politics, Parties, and Elections in America

Second Edition

John F. Bibby
The University of Wisconsin—
Milwaukee

Nelson-Hall Publishers
Chicago

Cover Painting: *The Reflecting Pond* by Mark McMahon

Library of Congress Cataloging-in-Publication Data

Bibby, John F.
Politics, parties, and elections in America / John F. Bibby. — 2nd ed.
p. cm.
Includes index.
ISBN 0-8304-1219-0
1. Political parties—United States. 2. Elections—United States. I. Title.
JK2261.B49 1992 91-20617
324.273—dc20 CIP

Manufactured in the United States of America

10 9 8 7 6 5 4 3 2 1

CONTENTS

CHAPTER 1

Parties and Politics in America: An Overview

The Nature of Politics
The Nature of Party
The Functions of Parties
- Serving as Intermediaries
- Nominating Candidates
- Contesting Elections and Channeling the Vote
- Organizing the Government
- Providing Public Accountability
- Managing Conflict

Parties as Competitors for Political Influence
Parties and Interest Groups: There Is a Difference!
- Parties Run Candidates under Their Own Labels
- Parties Have Broad Issue Concerns
- Parties Give Priority to Controlling the Personnel of Government
- Parties are Quasi-Public Organizations
- Parties Have a Unique Relationship to Their Clientele

Party Government and the Peaceful Transfer of Governmental Authority

Anyone who seriously studies American political parties soon is confronted with a series of seeming contradictions and confusing conditions.

On the One Hand	**On the Other Hand**
A majority of Americans surveyed agree with the statements that "Political parties do more to confuse the issues than provide a clear choice on them," and "It would be better if, in all elections, we put no party labels on the ballot."	Over two-thirds of the citizenry have a partisan identification with one of the major parties, and an additional 23 percent who claim to be independents admit to leaning to one of the parties.
A common complaint about American parties is that they are about as different from each other as Tweedledum and Tweedledee. That is, "there's not a dime's worth difference between them."	It does make a difference which party wins elections. The myriad of Great Society social welfare programs was possible only because of the Democrats' landslide victory in presidential and congressional elections of 1964. Similarly, Ronald Reagan's program of lower taxes, a reduced rate of government growth, and a defense build-up was possible because of Republican presidential victories in 1980 and 1984 and GOP Senate control from 1981 to 1986. The Reagan "revolution" ended when the Democrats retook control of the Senate in 1986.
With two-thirds of the electorate identifying with the Republican and Democratic parties, the two organizations have developed broadly based and relatively stable followings.	Few Americans have formally joined party organizations, worked for candidates, or contributed money to parties or candidates.
Only the nominees of the Republican and Democratic parties stand a reasonable chance to win the presidency, Congress, governorships, or state legislatures. Furthermore, these bodies are organized on a partisan basis with key power positions allocated to members of the majority party.	Elected public officials frequently deviate from the policy positions of their parties and demonstrate a marked sense of independence.

These seeming contradictions point up the unique character of American political parties. They count among their affiliates the vast majority of the voters. They nominate candidates and contest the major offices in the land. They staff formal organizational structures at the national level and in the 50 states. They organize the executive and legislative branches in Washington and the states. And they exert tremendous influence on governmental policy. Despite these signs of strength and pervasiveness, American parties have few formal members, are often undermanned and in financial straits, disunited in terms of policy direction, and fragmented in terms of power.

These puzzling aspects of American political parties dramatize many of the major concerns of this book:

- the unique character of political parties as institutions for aggregating political influence
- the functions performed by political parties within the American political system
- the relationship of parties to voters, candidates, officeholders, and interest groups
- the impact of parties on governmental policy
- the changing role of parties in the American political system

The Nature of Politics

What is politics? In common usage, it is the unseemly machinations of the ambitious and self serving to gain advantage over others; it is the subverting of the public welfare for group or partisan advantage; it is the never ending struggle between the Republicans and the Democrats; and it is what happens in government—in Washington or the statehouses of Sacramento, Harrisburg, Springfield, Baton Rouge, or Cheyenne. Generally, when one is accused of acting politically, there is a suspicion that less than wholesome activities are afoot.

But when these pejorative connotations are removed, the essence of politcs is *power*—the ability of one person to get another person to behave in a desired manner. Politics and the use of power inevitably involve *conflict* because what people want from life differs—they have different values—and because there is a scarcity of life's prized objectives (e.g., wealth, security, prestige, and power). In its most basic sense, then, politics is concerned with "Who Gets What, When, and How."[1]

Whether a political system works depends to a large degree upon whether society's inevitable political conflicts among competing interests can be resolved and managed via bargaining and compromise. If the processes of bargaining and compromise enable competing interests to get enough of what they want, it is possible for these interests to continue to cooperate and not disrupt the whole legal structure of government. Politics, therefore, can be viewed as a process of conflict management.

The political process, however, involves more than keeping the lid on the passions of social conflict. It is also the process through which individuals and groups organize and act collectively to achieve social goals—individual freedom, public health, quality education, national security, economic opportunity, clean air and water.

When politics is stripped of its unsavory normative connotations and viewed in its essentials, it can be seen as a basic social process involving (1) the acquisition, retention, and exercise of power; (2) the management of conflicts; and (3) collective action. In each of these aspects of politics, political parties play a central role. Parties help determine who governs, who wins or loses public policy disputes, and the extent of the win or loss.

The Nature of Party

In spite of their acknowledged impact on American government, political parties have proved to be elusive creatures for social commentators to define. One famous characterization was that of Edmund Burke, the British philosopher and member of Parliament, who in 1770 offered a classic ideologically oriented definition: "Party is a body of men united, for promoting by their joint endeavors the national interest, upon some particular principle in which they are all agreed."[2] Whatever relevance this conception of party had for eighteenth century England, it is clearly inappropriate for American political parties, which have never been noted for their ideological purity. Conservatives, moderates, and liberals are found in both the Republican and Democratic parties, albeit not in the same proportions. Furthermore, it is not uncommon for senators and representatives to vote in opposition to their party colleagues in excess of 40 percent of the time. Definitions stressing organizational structure (i.e., the existence of a hierarchy of organizations—county committees, state central committees, and national committees) are also inadequate because parties include masses of voters as well as dues-paying members, officials or staff, candidates, their supporters, and government officials.

A definition of parties better adapted to the modern American and Western democratic contexts is that provided by political scientist Leon D. Epstein: *"Any group, however loosely organized, seeking to elect governmental officeholders under a given label."*[3] This definition allows for the lack of ideological and policy unity so apparent in American parties. It also accommodates the wide variety of party organizations in the country, which range from the disciplined urban machines of the Mayor Richard J. Daley era in Chicago to the well-financed and professionally staffed Republican National Committee, to the under-financed and disorganized, but loyal, bands of volunteers who man local party organizations in regions where their party has virtually no chance of winning elections. The Epstein conception of party also takes into account two special aspects of parties: (1) their preoccupation with contesting elections, and (2) the fact that it is only parties that run candidates on their own labels.

As V.O. Key, Jr., pointed out, "the fundamental difficulty about the term 'political party' is that it is applied without discrimination to many groups and near groups."[4] He, therefore, urged students of parties to recognize them as tripartite social structures composed of the following elements:

the party in the electorate: voters with a sense of loyalty to and identification with the party
the party organization: party officials, committees, volunteer workers, and paid staff
the party in government: party candidates for governmental office and public officeholders at the local, state, and national levels.

American parties, therefore, are structures that contain a variety of components: from the weakly committed voter who usually supports the party's candidates to the dedicated activist with an ideological commitment who volunteers time and treasure; from the party boss seeking to run a disciplined patronage dispensing organization to the public official who, while elected on a party label, seeks to project an image independent of party. As Frank Sorauf has noted, the political party "embraces the widest range of involvement and commitment."[5]

The Functions of Parties

Serving as Intermediaries

Wherever free elections have been conducted on a continuing basis at the national or regional level, political parties exist. This basic fact is suggestive of the fundamental role of parties in a democratic society. They are intermediary or linkage mechanisms between the mass of the citizenry and their government. Parties function as institutions to bring scattered elements of the public together, to define objectives, and to work collectively to achieve those

Figure 1–1: The Tripartite Structure of American Political Parties

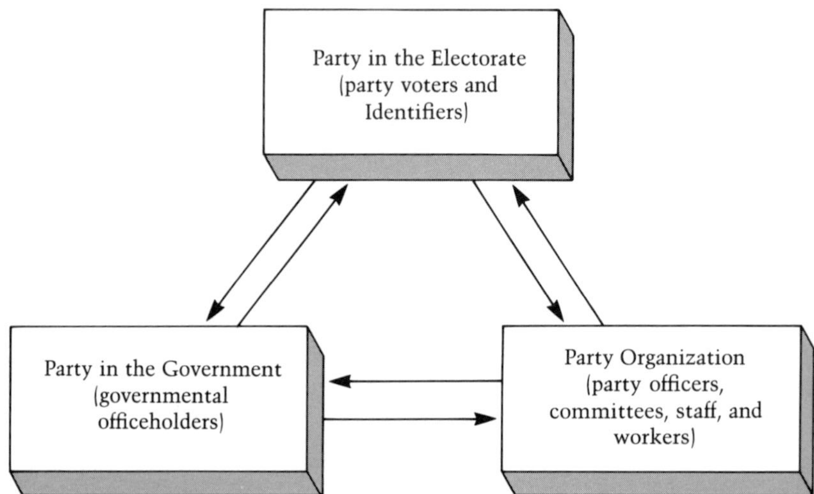

Source: Adapted from Frank J. Sorauf, *Party Politics in America*, 5th ed. (Boston, Mass.: Harper Collins, 1984), p. 9.

objectives through governmental policy. Parties, therefore, are involved in aggregating societal interests, recruiting leadership, compromising competing demands, contesting elections, and seeking to organize governments.

Parties developed as the old bases of governmental authority (e.g., divine right of kings) crumbled before the democratic revolutions of the eighteenth and nineteenth centuries and governments were seen as deriving their powers from the people. To legitimize their positions, leaders were compelled to appeal to the voters. Such appeals required the development of organizations to communicate with and mobilize the masses. V.O. Key, Jr., summarized the process of party development in the Western democracies as follows:

> As democractic theory spread, those dissatisfied with the old order rallied the masses . . . against the established holders of authority. In effect the outs played demagogue, lined up the unwashed in their support, and, at the elections, by superiority of numbers and organization they bested those dominant in government. Those who suffered such indignities were compelled in self defense to defer to the people, no matter how distasteful it was, and to form organizations to solicit electoral support.[6]

As will be discussed in the following chapter, the development of American parties generally follows the pattern Key outlined. America was the first nation to transfer executive power from one faction to another via an election (the election of 1800) and this feat was accomplished by a political party. The United States, thereby, became the first nation with modern political parties organized on a national basis with broad membership, in contrast to the parliamentary factions that existed in Great Britain.

Many political scientists believe that parties are the principal intermediary between the citizens and their government. E. E. Schattschneider, for example, opened his 1942 classic study with the assertion that "political parties created democracy and modern democracy is unthinkable save in terms of parties."[7] And more recently Samuel Huntington, in a cross-national study, observed that parties were distinctive institutions of the modern state whose function "is to organize participation, to aggregate interests, to serve as the link between social forces and the government."[8] Even if such statements overstate the role of parties, parties do permeate every aspect of national and state government and politics. As Sarah McCally Morehouse has reminded us, it is Republicans and Democrats who "make the major decisions regarding who pays and who receives."[9]

In their role as intermediaries, parties must compete with other institutions. They share the linkage functions with interest groups, which exist in infinite variety—labor unions; business and trade associations; professional organizations; racial, ethnic, and religious groups; single issue groups; ideological groups. The mass media, especially with the advent of television, also functions as an intermediary between government and the people. The party's place in the political system as an intermediary institution is illustrated in Figure 1–2.

Nominating Candidates

The determination of which names shall appear on the general election ballot—the narrowing of the voter's choice—is a critical stage in the electoral process. The nominating process controls the voter's range of choice and thus severely limits who is eligible for public office. For the candidate—both incumbent and challenger—the nomination is a hurdle that must be cleared if entry into elective politics is to be achieved. In the United States, all national and most major state elected officials are nominated by political parties. So crucial is the nomination process to the parties that Schattschneider concluded:

> Unless the party makes authoritative and effective nominations, it cannot stay in business . . . . The nature of the nominating procedure determines the nature of the party; he who can make nominations is the owner of the party.[10]

While interest groups, political action committees (PACs), pollsters, campaign consultants, and candidate organizations seek to influence nominating decisions, it is ultimately the party that makes nomina-

Figure 1–2: Political Parties as Intermediaries

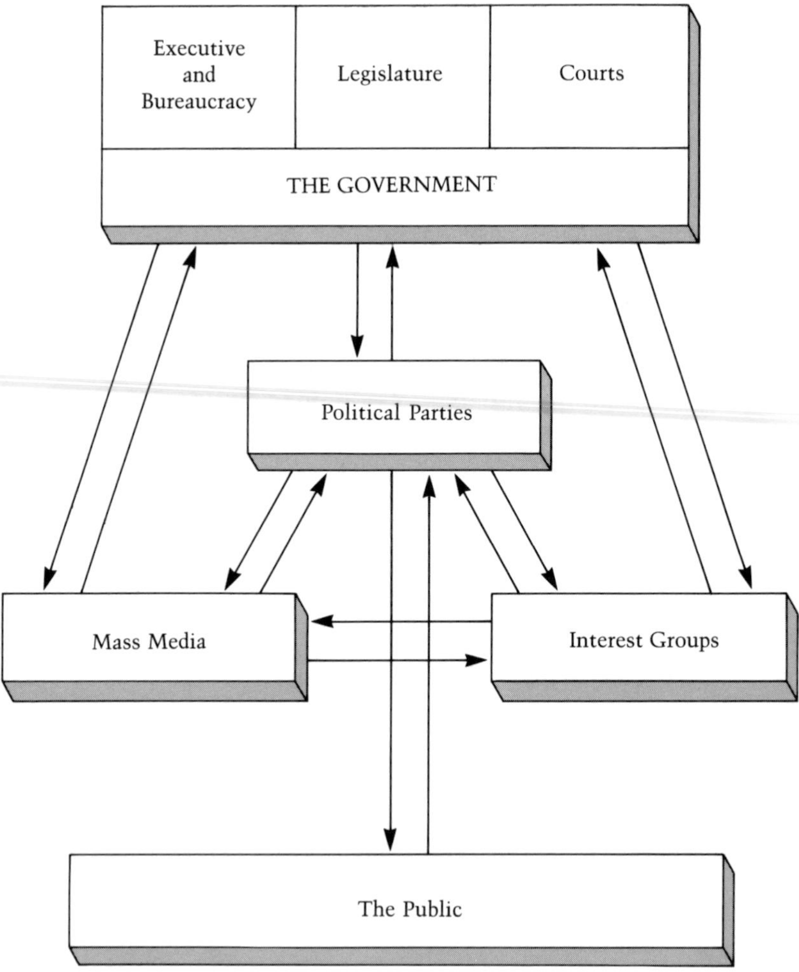

tions. And without a party nomination, the record demonstrates that it is virtually impossible to gain major elected office. No one has been elected president since the development of modern parties in the early 1800s without a partisan nomination. Following the 1990 elections, all members of the House and Senate except independent Representative Bernard Sanders (Vt.) were either Democrats or Republicans. Since 1942, only three persons have been elected governor as independents (James Longley of Maine in 1974, Walter Hickel of Alaska, and Lowell Weicker of Connecticut in 1990); and after the 1988 elections, only one state senator out of 1,944 (.0005 percent) and three state representatives among a national total of 5,454 (.0006 percent) were independents (excluding Nebraska's nonpartisan legislature).

The outcome of partisan nominations can dramatically influence a party's electoral prospects and its future course of development. For example, the Democrats' 1972 nomination of Senator George McGovern (S.D.), who was widely perceived to be way to the left of the average Democratic voter and American citizen, doomed the party to a landslide defeat and sowed the seeds for continuing divisiveness between liberals and moderates that has contributed to ensuing losses of the presidency.

Similarly, Senator Barry Goldwater's (Ariz.) capture of the 1964 Republican nomination led to the party's disastrous defeat, as the nominee was seen by voters to be substantially more conservative than they were. His nomination, however, signalled the growing conservative movement within the party. This movement helped develop the cadre of rank and file workers devoted to conservative ideology that made it possible for Ronald Reagan to challenge incumbent President Gerald R. Ford for the 1976 GOP nomination and then easily win the 1980 nomination. In nominating Ronald Reagan for president, the Republican party significantly altered the course of American history because he has been the first post-New Deal president to seriously attempt to limit the growth of government domestic programs and expenditures.

The impact of the nomination process upon the House of Representatives during the 1980s and 1990s has been striking. As the South became more competitive between the Republican and Democratic parties, conservatives increasingly were drawn to the GOP. At the same time, the Voting Rights Act of 1965 made it possible for black voters, who are overwhelmingly Democratic, to participate in the electoral process. The net effect of these changes was to make the Democratic party in the South more liberal than in the past and, therefore, it nominated congressional candidates who reflected the national party's policy orientation instead of the traditional southern conservative view. The nomination and election of substantial numbers of these moderate to liberal southern Democrats has given the Democratic party in the House increased unity in roll call votes and enabled it to enact much of its policy agenda.[11]

Control of the party nominating process has gradually shifted from the hands of the party organization to the party in the electorate. Nominations for congressional and state office since the 1920s have been made via the direct primary, in which party voters select the nominee. In presidential nominations, the party leadership's voice has similarly been diminished with the rise of the presidential primary as the principal method of selecting national convention delegates.

Contesting Elections and Channeling the Vote

In the general election stage, the parties mobilize the electorate and channel it normally either to the Democratic or Republican candidate. Given the physical size of the country, the masses of people involved, the diverse interests at stake, the number of states, the pace of social change, and the variety of political cultures, it is quite remarkable how successful the parties are in channeling the vote. Despite assertions of party decline and evidence of fewer Americans—especially young people—professing an identification with either party, the Republicans and Democrats can rely upon the partisan commitment of most voters to guide their election day choices. The parties, of course, cannot rely only on latent partisanship among the electorate. Partisans must be activated to turn out and actually vote; independents must be won; and opposition party identifiers must be wooed and at least temporarily converted. In these activities, parties play a central role, but they are not exclusively party tasks. These responsibilities are shared with interest groups, candidate organizations, various campaign technicians, and consultants.

Organizing the Government

For governmental institutions to operate with at least a modest degree of effectiveness, they require a division of labor, leadership, and rules; that is, they must be organized. The job of organizing government has fallen to the political parties. For example, Congress and most state legislatures are organized on a partisan basis. (Exceptions include the Nebraska nonpartisan legislature and some legislatures heavily dominated by one party.) Because of their current majority status, therefore, only Democrats now serve as Speaker of the House, President Pro Tempore of the Senate, committee chairmen, and subcommittee chairmen and thereby largely determine the agenda and decisions of the chamber. Similarly, the executive branch is also organized on a primarily partisan basis. Presidential appointments go almost exclusively to members of the president's party. Indeed, most policy making officers of the executive branch must gain a clearance from party officials at the national, state, and local levels prior to their appointment.

The constitutional separation of powers was intended by the Founding Fathers to encourage tension between the Congress and president so that neither branch would become too powerful and threaten individual liberties. However sound the Fathers' theory may have been, it is also clear that modern government requires legislative-executive coordination if societal needs and international obligations are to be met. An important source of such policy coordination is the tie of partisanship. Presidents tend to work primarily through their fellow partisans in Congress to achieve their policy goals. At the same time, leaders of the president's party in Congress, lacking formal power to control their party members, rely on the prestige and influence of the White House to exert leverage for party unity on roll call votes. Presidential influence on his congressional party is normally at its zenith during the first two years of the term, when his popularity is highest and fellow party members are seeking to enhance his record for the next election. The impact of presidential leadership can be impressive. For example, President Lyndon Johnson wielded heavy Democratic congressional majorities to enact his Great Society social welfare program after the 1964 election, and in 1981 Ronald Reagan worked through a Republican majority in the Senate to set a conservative agenda for Congress. Even a president whose party does not control the House or Senate counts upon the loyalty of fellow partisans in Congress to achieve his policy goals. President George Bush, for example, has relied upon Republican Senators to sustain his vetoes in order to achieve bargaining leverage on legislation with the Democratic congressional leaders. Of course, the president's ability to rely upon his fellow partisans in Congress varies with conditions—especially the popular support enjoyed by the president. When that support diminishes, so does his capacity to hold his party together in support of his programs in Congress.

Providing Public Accountability

Democratic governments derive their powers from the people. Fred I. Greenstein, therefore, has suggested a simple and workable definition of democracy as a political system in which "citizens have a relatively high degree of control over their leaders."[12] Parties provide voters with a means to hold public officials accountable for the actions of government. They, therefore, make a contribution to citizen control of government.

The contemporary political world is incredibly complex. The array of issues and candidates upon which the model citizen should be informed in a general election is almost mind-boggling. Political power in the United States is divided between the legislative, executive, and judicial branches and among national, state, and local governments. The voter, therefore, is expected to make informed choices for officials at all levels and in several branches of government. There are choices for offices from president to county registrar of deeds, and issues from U.S.–Soviet relations to the administration of county courts. Fortunately, the voter can respond to these tangled questions in terms of a few simple criteria and is not required to spend all available time studying politics.

Party labels enable voters to sort out this complexity and vote for the candidates of their preferred party—the party which they perceive to be closest to their interests. Because major elected officials each wear a party label—a type of political brand name—voters can also assign to the party in power either credit or, more likely, blame for the state of the union. Without party labels to sort out the candidates and issues, the average voter would be at sea with no compass for a guide.

Additionally, parties can contribute to citizen control of government because they are forced to advocate policies that will retain the support of their traditional constituencies, while at the same time seeking additional votes among the unaffiliated or the disaffected members of the opposition party. The very uncertainty of electoral outcomes works against parties becoming excessively complacent because retention of office requires a constant reassessment of public sentiments. As a result, parties and candidates spend millions of dollars in both election and nonelection years on public opinion surveys of voter sentiments.

The process of citizen control of government to which parties contribute is indirect, of course, and imperfect in nature. It is not a matter of voters instructing their leaders on the specific policies that they want the government to follow. Rather, periodic elections using party labels give the voters a chance to register their general reaction to a party's stewardship in office. For example, the 1980 presidential election has been generally interpreted as the voters rendering a negative verdict on the presidency of Jimmy Carter.[13] There is no evidence, however, that people who switched from the Democrats to the

Republican nominee, Ronald Reagan, in 1980 were voting for a specific governmental program. Rather, they were giving Reagan and the Republicans a chance to deal with the nation's problems. In 1984 and 1988, the voters again rendered their verdict—this time on the Republicans' stewardship of the presidency. In these elections, the judgment was generally favorable and the GOP lease on the White House was extended.

Managing Conflict

Because people vary in their goals and values and because what people want is often in short supply, conflict is inevitable in society. A stable governmental order, therefore, requires mechanisms for compromising competing group demands. Conflict must be managed and American parties have traditionally played a significant role in reconciling competing group demands.

Winning elections within a two-party system requires building broadly based coalitions. Inevitably elements of the coalition will have somewhat divergent objectives. For example, the dominant Democratic New Deal coalition forged by President Franklin D. Roosevelt during the 1930s contained such contentious elements as white Protestant southerners, blacks, northern urban Catholics, blue collar workers, Jews, and marginal farmers. The conflicts inherent in this alignment have been juggled with varying degrees of success since the 1930s. Within the Congress, for example, the Democrats have practiced the politics of "inclusive compromise" in which Democratic representatives from urban areas have supported farm price supports, while rural Democrats have voted for federally subsidized housing and urban development programs, and both groups have backed federal water projects for their party members from the arid Western states.[14] As this example suggests, within the American political system many group conflicts in society have been settled *within* the parties.

Parties as Competitors for Political Influence

As prominent as parties are in the American political order, they do not have the field to themselves. They must compete for political influence with candidate organizations, campaign consultants, interest groups, and the mass media. In recent years, the ability of parties to compete for a place in the campaign process has been weakened by the growing role of a professional corps of consultants and experts skilled in the latest campaign techniques and technologies. To a significant degree, these professional consultants operate outside the regular party organizations and are closely tied to the organizations of individual candidates. Even well financed and professionally staffed party organizations at the national, state, and local levels find it impossible to provide their candidates with all the technical assistance—media experts, pollsters, direct mail specialists, campaign managers—that they require. Recognizing the value of these specialists, the candidates, therefore, often seek to employ this type of talent using funds which have been raised independently of the parties. In the process, the candidates have become less dependent upon their party organizations at election time. This sense of independence from party is often reflected in the behavior of candidates after they have won public office.

Parties also face stiff competition from organized groups in terms of funding campaigns. Election costs are constantly and dramatically rising and the parties cannot fund (and are often forbidden by law from funding) all or even major shares of the costs of campaigns. Increasingly, interest groups, through political action committees (PACs), have come to play a larger role in funding candidates. Even the national government and the states are now competitors of the parties for a role in campaign finance. Since 1976, presidential campaigns have been funded primarily with taxpayer money and an increasing number of states have public funding programs designed to limit the role of the parties and PACs in elections.

The mass media, especially television, is also a competitor with the parties for political influence. To a large degree, political reality for most Americans is what they see on the network news programs anchored by Dan Rather, Tom Brokaw, or Peter Jennings. Americans get their news mainly from television. Television, therefore, has come to play a major role in politics and especially in presidential nomination contests.

By the 1970s the bulk of the national convention delegates were chosen in presidential primaries—mass elections that in 1988 attracted twenty-three million voters. In the sequence of presidential primaries that run from February to June of presidential election years, it is essential that a candidate establish the image of a winner, i.e., momentum. Being interpreted as the winner of an early primary is necessary to gain media coverage, achieve standing in the polls, and raise funds for the next in a long series of primaries. But as Austin Ranney has pointed out, "doing best in the early primaries is not simply a matter of getting more votes than the other candidates; it is getting substantially more votes than expected."[15] And it is the news media—especially television commentators—who decide what is expected. For example, in the 1972 New Hampshire primary, Democratic Senator Edmund Muskie (Maine) came in first with 46 percent of the votes compared to Senator George McGovern's (South Dakota) second place finish with 37 percent. But the media had previously announced that Muskie was expected to receive at least 50 percent of the vote in his neighboring state of New Hampshire. Therefore, McGovern, who had done better than expected, was declared the winner by the media. Muskie lost momentum and McGovern's campaign received a tremendous boost that carried him to the presidential nomination. Similarly, the media declared Jimmy Carter the winner of the 1976 Democratic primary in New Hampshire when he placed first in a multicandidate field with only 28 percent of the vote. With this "win," he was on his way to the nomination.

In effect, what has been happening in presidential politics is that the traditional role of screening the candidates is being shifted away from party leaders—governors, members of Congress, state and local party chairmen, and mayors—to the mass media and the participants in presidential primaries. It was the news media in 1988 that investigated and publicized former Senator Gary Hart's extramarital affairs on a yacht named "Monkey Business" and the voting public's negative reaction that submerged his front-running bid for the Democratic nomination. The party role in presidential nominations has not been eliminated, but the age of party leadership domination of presidential nominations has clearly passed. Television has become a powerful, competing intermediary institution.

Some observers viewing the rise of campaign consultants, PACs, and television have predicted a bleak future for American parties. There have even been apocalyptic visions of partyless politics. But the parties have demonstrated qualities of adaptability, durability, and resilience. As succeeding chapters will demonstrate, the three elements of the party retain significant influence: the party in the electorate retains the allegiance of over 60 percent of the voters who identify with one of the two major parties; the party in government dominates decision-making in the Congress; and there are signs of renewed strength in both national and state party organizations.

Parties and Interest Groups: There Is a Difference!

Interest groups engage in many of the same activities as political parties. They seek to influence nominations, elect favored candidates, influence the appointment of officials to the executive branch, and influence governmental decisions. While there are surface similarities, parties are unique institutions that can be distinguished from interest groups.

Parties Run Candidates under Their Own Labels

No matter how much interest groups may concern themselves with elections through endorsements and support of candidates in primaries and general elections, it is only the parties that run candidates on their own labels. There are no candidates for major office that run under the label of the AFL-CIO, U.S. Chamber of Commerce, NAACP, American Bar Association, or Methodist Church. Only parties assume responsibility for the candidates that run under their banners and act as agents of public accountability for the actions of their affiliated officeholders.

Parties Have Broad Issue Concerns

Interest groups reflect the concerns of persons who share a common viewpoint or set of attitudes and wish to further those interests through government policy. Normally these interests are quite narrow in scope, reflecting the special concerns of the membership and not the full gamut of governmental policies. The National Association of Home Builders, for example, is primarily concerned about federal housing policy and interest rates; the Tobacco Institute worries about regulation of smoking; the American Legion seeks benefits for former members of the armed forces and advocates a strong defense; the Wildlife Federation seeks sanctuary for wildlife through environmental protection, and so on. Most interest groups have clear priorities in terms of the issues to which they devote attention and they do not strain the unity of their organizations or their treasuries by getting involved in issues of only marginal interest to the membership. Even broadly based organizations like the AFL-CIO, which seeks to influence a wide range of governmental policies, have clear priorities that reflect the bread and butter concerns of union members.

Political parties, by contrast, take stands on the whole spectrum of issues with which government deals—foreign, fiscal, welfare, education, transportation, health, racial, environmental, science, energy, and social policy. No other political organization has a breadth of policy concerns comparable to that of political parties.

Parties Give Priority to Controlling the Personnel of Government

However broad the policy concerns of parties may be, they tend to give priority in the United States to winning elections. Parties want to control the personnel of government. To achieve this end, American parties have shown great flexibility in terms of their policy positions and willingness to accommodate a wide variety of different views in their midst. While Republican and Democratic members of Congress as a group show distinctly different voting patterns on major issues, it is also true that each party contains significant though differing proportions of conservatives, moderates, and liberals. Ideological purity takes a backseat to winning elections for American parties. By contrast, interest groups are concerned first and foremost with government policy. Most groups are concerned about who is elected or appointed only because of the policies these office holders will promulgate, not out of a desire to put fellow group members in public office. As a result, most interest groups support candidates in both parties whom they see as capable of advancing group aims.

Parties Are Quasi-Public Organizations

Interest groups like the American Bankers Association, American Farm Bureau Federation, the Teamsters, Common Cause, or the American Library Association are private associations. They operate under minimal governmental regulation and enjoy all the protections of the First Amendment. Parties are quite different organizations. In the United States they are heavily regulated by federal and especially state statutes. These statutes provide legal definitions of parties, mandate organizational structures and procedures, define membership, and specify how certain party functions like nominating candidates will be carried out. American parties are, therefore, quasi-public institutions, whereas interest groups are private associations.

Parties Have a Unique Relationship to Their Clientele

Parties have a unique relationship to their clientele—the party in the electorate. As Frank Sorauf has observed, other political organizations, like interest groups, seek to attract the support of persons beyond their membership, but such persons always remain outside the group. But the persons in the electorate being wooed by parties are permitted to take part through the direct primary in the most important activities of the party—the nomination of its candidates and the selection of its leadership. "The American party is an open, inclusive, and semipublic political organization composed of its own clientele, a tangible organization, and personnel in government. As such it stands alone and unique in the American political system."[16]

Party Government and the Peaceful Transfer of Governmental Authority

"Democracy involves a balance between the forces of conflict and consensus."[17] Institutional structures are needed to reflect and articulate the attitudes and demands of various elements of society. But conflict must be held within reasonable bounds if the political order is to have any stability and continuity. Structures for achieving agreement and consensus are required. As the discussion of party functions has demonstrated, parties are central to these seemingly conflicting requirements of a democratic order. They both reflect the conflicts in society and they are involved in the bargaining and negotiation needed to acheive conflict resolution.

As is discussed in Chapter 2, the party conflict has been institutionalized in the United States. Americans expect electoral contests between two parties, with the victorious party organizing the government, and the opposition party maintaining a steady barrage of criticism. Changes in the personnel of government are in reality shifts in party control of the presidency or Congress. This process of displacement from power via the election of partisan majorities, of course, is taken for granted by Americans. But it is, in fact, a fundamentally different way of replacing officeholders than the common practices of the not too distant past in Western nations. Party displacement of governments is "a substitute for revolt and insurrection and a new means for determining succession of authority."[18]

Governmental succession through changes in party control is possible only when the notion of the *loyal opposition* is accepted. Loyal opposition involves opposing and criticizing the policies of the government-of-the-day (those currently in office) and standing ready to take its place. But it also requires acceptance of the basic structure of the government and the processes under which it operates. In other words, acceptance of a loyal opposition party requires that those in power and their supporters recognize that to oppose the policies of the government is not treason and advocacy of revolution. In the United States, it took a long time to establish the principle that assaults on the government by the "outs" were to be expected and tolerated. In his Farewell Address, Washington, for example warned against a spirit of party that he feared would arouse the rabble against the government. And after the Federalists lost the election of 1800, they were so bitter that in the secret Hartford Convention (1814) they advocated the secession of the New England states from the Union, even though the country was at war. Wilfred Binkley has pointed out that from 1816 to the 1830s, most Americans believed that "there could be but one party—the Republicans—and that all of them belonged to it."[19] It was not until the 1840s that the "idea of loyal party opposition . . . [received] acceptance and approval from Americans."[20] Acceptance of the notion of loyal opposition made possible the institutionalization of party conflict which in turn made possible the achievement of public office for the "outs" by nonrevolutionary means.

Suggestions for Further Reading

Eldersveld, Samuel J. *Political Parties in American Society*. New York: Basic Books, 1982.

Epstein, Leon D. *Political Parties in the American Mold*. Madison: University of Wisconsin Press, 1986.

_______. *Political Parties in Western Democracies*. New York: Praeger, 1967.

Key, V. O., Jr. *Politics, Parties, and Pressure Groups*. 5th Edition. New York: Crowell, 1964.

Ranney, Austin, and Kendall, Willmoore. *Democracy and the American Party System*. New York: Harcourt, Brace, 1956.

Sorauf, Frank J., and Paul Allen Beck. *Party Politics in America*. 6th Edition. Boston: Scott/Foresman/Little, Brown, 1988.

Notes

1. Harold Lasswell, *Politics: Who Gets What, When, and How* (New York: McGraw-Hill, 1936).
2. Edmund Burke, "Thoughts on the Cause of Present Discontents," in *The Works of Edmund Burke* 1 (Boston: Little, Brown, 1871), p. 151.
3. Leon D. Epstein, *Political Parties in Western Democracies* (New York: Praeger, 1967), p. 9.
4. V. O. Key, Jr., *Politics, Parties, and Pressure Groups*, 5th edition (New York: Crowell, 1964), p. 163.
5. Frank J. Sorauf, *Party Politics in America*, 4th ed. (Boston: Little, Brown and Co., 1980), p. 10.
6. Key, *Politics, Parties, and Pressure Groups*, p. 201.
7. E. E. Schattschneider, *Party Government* (New York: Holt, Rinehart and Winston, 1942), p. 1.
8. Samuel Huntington, *Political Order in Changing Societies* (New Haven: Yale University Press, 1980), p. 91.
9. Sarah McCally Morehouse, *State Politics, Parties and Policy* (New York: Holt, Rinehart and Winston, 1981), p. 29.
10. Schattschneider, *Party Government*, p. 64.
11. David W. Rohde, "Something's Happening Here; What It Is Ain't Exactly Clear: Southern Democrats in the House of Representatives," in Morris

P. Fiorina and David W. Rohde (eds.), *Home Style and Washington Work: Studies in Congressional Politics* (Ann Arbor: University of Michigan Press, 1989), pp. 137–163.

12. Fred I. Greenstein, *The American Party System and the American People*, 2nd ed. (Englewood Cliffs, N.J.: Prentice-Hall, 1970), p. 2.
13. For an analysis of the Reagan-Carter contest, see William Schneider, "The November 4 Vote for President: What Did It Mean?" in Austin Ranney, ed., *The American Elections of 1980* (Washington, D.C.: American Enterprise Institute, 1982), pp. 212–262.
14. David Mayhew, *Party Loyalty among Congressmen: The Differences between Democrats and Republicans, 1947–1962* (Cambridge: Harvard University Press, 1966).
15. Austin Ranney, *Channels of Power: The Impact of Television on American Politics* (New York: Basic Books, 1983), p. 95.
16. Sorauf, *Party Politics*, p. 10.
17. Samuel J. Eldersveld, *Political Parties in American Society* (New York: Basic Books, 1982), p. 15.
18. Key, *Politics, Parties, and Pressure Groups*, p. 205.
19. Wilfred E. Binkley, *American Politial Parties: Their Natural History* (New York: Knopf, 1944), p. 152.
20. Austin Ranney and Willmoore Kendall, *Democracy and the American Party System* (New York: Harcourt, Brace, 1956), p. 110.

CHAPTER 2

The Party Battle in America

Organized partisanship was an unplanned development. In their plan for the Republic, the framers of the Constitution did not envision a president nominated by party conventions, partisan slates of presidential electors, or a Congress organized on the basis of partisanship. Early leaders like Washington, Hamilton, Madison, and Jefferson believed that parties would be divisive and undermine the public interest. Washington sounded the warning in his Farewell Address in 1796.

> [The Spirit of party] serves always to distract the Public Councils and enfeeble the Public administration. It agitates the Community with ill-founded jealousies and false alarms, kindles the animosity of one party against another, foments occasional riot and insurrection. It opens the door to foreign influence and corruption, which find a facilitated access to the government itself through the channels of party passions. . . .

Such misgivings about parties have remained a persistent element of the American political culture. Early in the twentieth century, when party conflict had been institutionalized, progressive reformers succeeded in imposing upon parties severe regulations which have stripped them of such functions as control of the nominating process. In the 1970s, Congress passed legislation that aided their rivals—the political action committees. A strong strain of apprehension about the role of political parties in the governing process continues to be found among the people. In 1984, a Harris survey found that by a 54 to 39 percent margin, Americans preferred to have the presidency and Congress controlled by different parties.[1] Thus from the beginning of the Republic to the present, political parties have functioned in an environment that is not altogether hospitable. American parties may have evolved into durable institutions that command substantial numbers of adherents, but the public retains a feeling of distrust, or at least suspicion.

The First Party System 1788–1824: Federalists, Republicans, and One Party Factionalism

American parties were born in the policy conflict between Hamilton and Jefferson during the Washington administration. As their disputes intensified, each turned to his supporters within the Congress and factional alliances between leaders of the executive and legislative branches developed. The emerging parties, therefore, developed out of national divisions, not state politics. It was, however, the Jeffersonians who first sought to broaden their operations beyond the nation's capital by endorsing candidates for Congress and presiden-

Table 2–1 Party Systems in American History

Party System	Dates	Competing Parties	Characteristics/Comments
First Party System	1788–1824	Federalists vs. Democratic-Republicans	Parties emerge in 1790s. One party factionalism within Democratic-Republican party after 1820.
Second Party System	1828–1854	Democrats vs. Whigs	Balanced two party competition, with Democrats the dominant party.
Third Party System	1856–1896	Republicans vs. Democrats	Republican dominance from 1862–1874; balanced two party competition from 1874–1896. Sectionalism in political conflict.
Fourth Party System	1896–1928	Republicans vs. Democrats	Republican dominance except for period of intraparty schism in 1912. Continued sectionalism.
Fifth Party System	1932–	Republicans vs. Democrats	Democratic dominance and formation of the New Deal coalition. After 1950s, New Deal coalition is weakened, sectionalism declines, competitive two party politics for president and statewide elections; divided party control of the national government becomes the norm with GOP holding the White House and the Democrats dominating Congress.

tial elector. Later they developed slates of candidates for state offices.[2] The Federalists, led by Hamilton and Adams, were forced to follow suit and compete for support within the mass electorate. The Federalists, however, were reluctant party organizers whose initial reaction to the party organizing activities of Jefferson's Democratic-Republicans was to bemoan their rivals' appeals to the public. As Hamilton noted, the Federalists "erred in relying so much on the rectitude and utility of their measures as to have neglected the cultivation of popular favor by fair and justifiable expedients."[3] Historians are in general agreement that the dramatic extension of party organizations at the local level in the election of 1800 and the aggressive organizing of the Democratic-Republicans in support of Jefferson contributed to his election over John Adams.[4] The nomination of presidential candidates by party caucuses in Congress is further evidence of the emergence of party organizations.

The Federalists were advocates of a positive national government capable of nation building and the protection of American business interests. In foreign affairs, they sided with the British against the revolutionary regime of France. In terms of electoral bases of support, the Federalists tended to be the established leadership strata in most of the states, while their challengers were Jeffersonians. Federalists were distinguished by being persons of old wealth, respectable occupations, and higher levels of formal education. By contrast, the Democratic-Republicans tended to draw support from less elite elements of society. They were fearful of the strong national government emerging under the Federalists and were protectors of agricultural interests. They were aligned with the French in foreign affairs.

Federalist electoral support suffered a precipitous decline after their defeat in 1800. This decline is related to their failure, as the party of the American elite, to respond in as timely a manner as the Democratic-Republicans to the popular and democratic style of politics that was developing.[5] After 1816, the Federalists disappeared as a national political party capable of contesting for the presidency and competed only in a few states such as Massachusetts and Delaware. The Jeffersonians were triumphant and the first era of partisan competition was over. The "Era of Good Feeling" which followed was a period of partyless politics characterized by factionalism among leaders all of whom claimed to be Republicans. Since all elected officials belonged to one party, it was impossible for President James Monroe to exercise any party discipline over Congress and coherent action by Congress became impossible to achieve.

Factionalism within the dominant Democratic-Republican party led to the collapse of the congressional caucus system of presidential nominations. Since there was no opposition party, the winner of the caucus nomination was assured of election. The congressional caucus, however, had never been popular. It was seen more and more as an undemocratic device as the franchise was extended to all white males due to the dropping of property owning restrictions on voting by the states. In 1824, when the congressional caucus nominated William Crawford for president, it was inevitable that other ambitious politicians would challenge Crawford in the general election. The 1824 election became a four way contest between Crawford, John Quincy Adams, Andrew Jackson, and Henry Clay. As a result, no candidate received a majority in the electoral college. The House of Representatives, after much bickering and maneuvering, finally chose Adams. His administration was characterized by intense intraparty conflict between his followers and those of Jackson. The "Era of Good Feeling" was at an end and the expanded electorate stood ready for political mobilization by political parties.

As Everett Carll Ladd has noted, this first party system was differentiated from those which have followed by the fact that neither Federalists nor Democratic-Republicans were born into families with these affiliations. There was no traditional party loyalties upon which to build electoral support and sustain parties. Political activists had not had their party identification passed on to them by parents and friends through reinforcing patterns of interaction.

> . . .The absence of inherited loyalties in the new party system of the first period, together with the rudimentary character of party organization and the prevailing tendency to see party as, at best, a necessary evil, made the new party growth relatively superficial. The roots of party simply did not run deep.[6]

The Second Party System, 1828–1854: Democrats Versus Whigs in Two Party Competitive Politics

Andrew Jackson, the popular hero of the Battle of New Orleans, defeated Adams in 1828 and gained reelection over Clay in 1832. These elections were fought in a transitional era of bifactional politics within the dominant Democratic-Republican party. Jackson and Adams in 1828 both used variations on the Republican name as their party labels as did Clay in 1832, when Jackson switched to the Democratic label. By 1834 the amalgam of forces and groups opposed to Jackson's policies had coalesced sufficiently to form an opposition party, the Whigs. An era of unusually close two party competition followed.

This Second Party System came into being during a period when American political life was democratized: slates of presidential electors were popularly elected; property qualifications for voting were dropped; and electoral participation increased dramatically. For example, voter turnout increased from 26.9 percent of eligible voters in 1824 to 78.9 percent in 1848.[7] Party nominating procedures were also opened to wider participation as the congressional caucus was replaced by the national convention.

In the two decades that followed Jackson's reelection in 1832, the Whigs and Democrats were engaged in an intense struggle for the newly expanded electorate. They engaged in popularized campaigning—torchlight parades, rallies, picnics, campaign songs, and slogans like "Tippecanoe and Tyler too." Both parties organized state and local parties and ran full slates of candidates under a party label. In this atmosphere of partisan mobilization, voters began to see themselves as either Whigs or Democrats.[8] Unlike the Federalists, who had been reluctant to court popular support, the Whigs did so with zeal. As the national minority party, one of their favorite techniques was to run military heroes with an appeal above party for president. They did this in four to six elections and were successful twice—in 1840 with William Henry Harrison and in 1848 with Zachary Taylor. In nine of eleven elections, however, the majority Democrats won control of the Congress.

Both the Democrats and the Whigs were truly national parties which engaged in relatively close competition not only at the national level but also in each region and in most states. For example, such old bastions of Jefferson's as Georgia, North Carolina, Louisiana, and Tennessee divided their support quite evenly between the Whigs and Democrats as did the Middle Atlantic states. Ladd has observed that in the 1836–1852 period, the "United States had less regional variation in voting than at any other time in history."[9] This lack of sectionalism in American politics was a tribute to the skills of Democratic and Whig leaders in balancing the interests of farmers, manufacturing and mercantile interests, nativists, immigrants, Catholics, and Protestants. Both parties were broad coalitions which sought backing throughout the country, with the Whigs attracting proportionately more support from manufacturing and trading interests, planters, and old Protestant stock, while the Democrats did well among newly enfranchised voters, western farmers, Catholics, and new immigrants.

The absence of highly salient issues that might have divided the nation along sectional lines also contributed to the ability of the two parties to compete in all regions. However, when the racial and slavery issues reached crisis proportions in the 1850s, the Whigs and Democrats were confronted with a nation divided along sectional lines. This national schism was reflected in the parties which split on a North-South axis because neither was able to satisfy both regions. America then entered its Third Party System.

The Third Party System, 1856–1896: Ascendant Republicans Versus Democrats

Culturally and economically the South became increasingly distinct from the rest of the nation during the 1840s and 1850s. While abolitionist sentiment gained support in the North, demonstrating the force of a compelling moral issue, the South continued to harbor the institution of slavery. In addition, the two regions' economies were developing quite differently. The South concentrated almost exclusively on agriculture, especially cotton, while the North was becoming more industrial, urban, and mixed in its ethnic composition. In addition, the population and wealth of the North were growing at a much more rapid rate than those of the South. These economic and cultural differences inevitably led to political conflicts over the direction of national policy. The sectional rivalries created by those differences came into their sharpest conflict because of the ceaseless westward expansion of the nation. Western settlement required the Congress and the parties to confront the issues of whether slavery would be permitted in the territories and whether the new states would be admitted as slave or free states. Any change in the number of free and slave states threatened to upset the delicate balance of power in the national government. Both the Whigs and Democrats were unable to reconcile the sectional conflicts within their ranks and as a result the electorate went through a major realignment in the 1850s and 1860s.

The Democrats' situation was made difficult by the powerful position occupied by its southern wing. In Congress, the Democrats were dominated by southerners determined to maintain the institution of slavery and protect the political position of the South by insisting that the balance of free and slave states not be upset when new states were admitted to the Union. The South was also strengthened by the two-thirds rule used by the Democratic national nominating conventions. This procedure guaranteed the South a veto over the selection of presidential nominees. As a result, the party could only agree to nominate weak "neutralist" or "doughface" candidates like Franklin Pierce (1852) and James Buchanan (1856). With weak presidents and a southern led Congress, it was not possible for the government to resolve the slavery issue.

In the midst of this sectional turmoil over the extension of slavery, the Whig party dissolved. The Whigs had traditionally been the party of national integration and accommodation between the North and South. But with the intensification of northern hostility toward slavery and heightened sectional sentiments in the South, the Whigs' position was undermined in both regions. Faced with declining electoral support, a schism between its northern and southern wings, and the emergence of the antislavery Republican party in the North, the Whig party ceased to be a major electoral force after the elections of 1854.[10]

There was a transition period toward two party competition between the Republicans and Democrats between 1854 and 1860. In the presidential election of 1856, the new Republican party—composed of abolitionists, Free Soilers, and dissident northern Whigs and Democrats—came in second to Democrats, as James Buchanan defeated General John C. Fremont. The remaining Whigs nominated former President Millard Fillmore under the American party banner and came in a dismal third. No candidate received a majority of the popular vote. The deterioration of the old party system continued in 1860. In the North, the election was a contest between the nominee of Northern Democrats, Stephen A. Douglas, and former Whig, Abraham Lincoln, the Republican nominee; while in the South, southern Democrat John C. Breckenridge contested a former southern Whig, John Bell. Again, no candidate received a popular vote majority, though Lincoln was able to gain 59.4 percent of the electoral vote with 39.8 percent of the popular vote.

The period of 1864–1874 was a period of Republican dominance. The successful prosecution of the Civil War identified the GOP with the Union, patriotism, and humanitarianism. But Republican strength did not rest on emotionalism alone. The party forged an alliance of farmers through the Homestead Act and free land in the West, business and labor through support for a high protective tariff, entrepreneurs through federal land grants to build transcontinental railroads linking the West and North (and bypassing the South), and veterans through pensions. By imposing Reconstruction upon the South, the post Civil War Radical Republicans in Congress sought to control the South through black votes and the support of carpetbaggers. Both parties were sectional parties. The GOP was dominant in the North and West, but it had little popular support in the South. The Democrats, by contrast, were a southern based party. The party's addiction to free trade did, however, give it some northern business allies among those who shared its views on trade.[11] In addition, the Democrats gained substantial support among Roman Catholic immigrants in cities of the North. After 1874 and the end of Reconstruction, the Republicans and Democrats started to compete on a more even basis up until 1896. They alternated control of the presidency and Congress, but the post Civil War period was primarily an era of Republican dominance in national political life.

In addition to the disappearance of the Whigs and the emergence of the Republicans as the dominant political party, two other significant developments came from the era of the Third Party System. One was the growth, particularly in the middle Atlantic and some midwestern states and cities, of patronage-based party organizations or machines that were extremely effective in controlling nominations and mobilizing party votes on election day.[12] Ironically, the Third Party System was also the era that ushered in the party machine weakening reform of the Australian ballot (ballots printed at government expense instead of party printed ballots, and provision for casting one's vote in secret). The Australian ballot movement gave the voter new independence from parties in making electoral choices. It was no longer public knowledge how people voted and using government provided ballots made it easier for citizens to split their ballots and vote for candidates of differing parties.

The Fourth Party System, 1896–1928: Republican Dominance Renewed

The period following the Civil War was a period of immense social and economic change with far-reaching consequences for electoral politics. It was a time when the United States ceased to be a primarily agrarian society and became an industrialized and urban nation. By 1890 more people were employed in manufacturing than in agriculture, and by the end of the 1920s only one family in four was involved in agriculture. On the eve of the Civil War, no American city had contained a million people, but by the close of the 1920s cities with a population in excess of a million inhabitants were becoming commonplace—New York, Chicago, Philadelphia, and Los Angeles. Transportation advances, like the completion of the great transcontinental railroads, linked the East and West and made the nation more interdependent. Rail mileage grew from 8,500 in 1850 to 193,000 in 1900. This was also the era of the rise of the corporation—mammoth enterprises like Standard Oil and U.S. Steel. The ethnic makeup of the population also changed as waves of immigrants entered the country from non-English speaking nations of Europe.

The economic and social revolution that was transforming America posed new problems for the political system. Radical agrarian movements swept the nation, e.g., the Grangers, Farmers' Alliance, and Greenbackers. Third party movements also formed. The most significant was the People's party (Populist) which in 1892 garnered over one million votes and twenty-two electoral votes on a radical platform that demanded the inflation of the currency through unlimited coinage of silver, nationalization of railroads and telephone/telegraph companies, and instituting an income tax. These movements reflected the economic dislocations that were occurring and agrarian discontent with the growing power of corporations and the frequently depressed state of the farm economy. The late 1800s also witnessed the rise of labor organizations which mirrored the discontent of urban workers with their status in the new industrial order.

Neither the dominant Republicans nor the "me too" Democrats were responsive initially to these popular protest movements. In 1896, however, the forces of agrarian radicalism captured the Democratic presidential nomination for William Jennings Bryan, whose platform was a challenge to the existing industrial order. A key plank in the Democrats' platform was a call for free and unlimited coinage of silver and gold at a ratio of sixteen to one. In adopting this position, the Democrats appropriated the principal program of the Populists and made a dramatic appeal to farmers, debtors, and western mining interests. The Democrats were also the party of a low tariff.

Seeking to bolster their post Civil War coalition, the Republicans countered by advocating the gold standard and opposition to the inflationary free coinage of silver; and they maintained their position as the party of the high protective tariff. Their stand on the silver issue cost them the support of western states, but the high protective tariff position brought them renewed support among urban workers, who blamed the depression of the 1890s on the low tariff policies of the Democratic Cleveland administration. William McKinley, the Republican candidate, was able to run on the themes of "Prosperity—Sound Money—Good Markets and Employment for Labor—A Full Dinner Bucket." Mark Hanna, the Ohio industrialist and skilled Republican campaign manager, also mobilized business interests terrified by Bryan and his policies to give generous and overwhelming support to the GOP cause.

The election of 1896 transformed the political landscape and realigned the electorate. The Republican coalition forged during and after the Civil War received an infusion of support, especially among urban dwellers of the Northeast. McKinley carried the nation's ten largest cities and increased the GOP vote in working, middle, and upper class wards. Byran was the sectional candidate of the agrarian South, the Plains, and the silver mining states of the West. He had little appeal to the industrializing East and Middle West, where the bulk of the population and electoral votes were located. V.O. Key has observed that the Democratic loss of 1896 "was so demoralizing and so thorough that the party made little headway in regrouping its forces until 1916."[13] Indeed, the Democrats elected only one president in the period between 1896 and 1928, and Woodrow Wilson's 1912 election was possible only because of a major schism within the dominant Republican coalition.

In that year, the festering internal Republican conflict between the traditional conservatives of the industrial-financial centers of the Northeast and the Progressive reformers of the Middle West and West broke wide open. Theodore Roosevelt, after failing to capture the GOP nomination from President William Howard Taft, ran as a candidate of the Progressive party. Roosevelt split the Republican vote and actually outpolled Taft in popular votes (27.4 percent to 23.2 percent). This division permitted a brief Democratic interlude under Wilson. After World War I, the fire was out of the progressive movement and Americans yearned for normalcy. In this postwar atmosphere, the Republicans asserted their dominance with impressive victories in 1920, 1924, and 1928. Although the Republicans won the election of 1928, the election returns gave evidence of expanding Democratic strength. The Democratic percentage of the popular vote jumped from 28.8 in 1924 to 40.8 in 1928, and the party's presidential ticket carried Massachusetts and Rhode Island, an indication of its approval to voters in Catholic, urban, and industrial centers. Democratic support was thus developing in the growing metropolitan and manufacturing centers, while the GOP tended to be dominant in northern and eastern rural precincts.[14]

The Fourth Party System was an era of diminished interparty competition. In the seven presidential elections after 1896, the average Republican share of the national two party vote was 57.7 percent, while the Democrats received 42.3 percent. In four of these elections the gap between the Republican and Democratic vote exceeded ten percentage points—the usual definition of a landslide. This was in sharp contrast to the evenness of competition between 1876 and 1896, when in 1880, 1884, and 1892, less than one percentage point separated the two parties' share of the popular vote for president. The post 1896 lack of competitiveness was also reflected in state elections. Regional voting patterns were sharply differentiated. The South, especially after the disenfranchisement of blacks via devices like the poll tax and white primary, became even more overwhelmingly Democratic. In the rest of the nation, however, the Republicans were dominant. In 22 states of the North and West, the Republicans received more than 60 percent of the vote on average in the presidential elections from 1896 to 1928.[15]

The Progressive reform movement of this period had a profound impact on American parties, even though the progressives never succeeded in forming a major party. It was during the Fourth Party System era that the direct primary was instituted as the principal method of nominating candidates. The primary weakened the capacity of parties to control the nominating process and enabled candidates to make direct appeals to the voters. The presidential primary was also born in this period. Another major change in the legal environment of parties was the imposition of governmental regulation, primarily by the states. Primary laws frequently regulated party organizational structure, and campaign finance was also brought within the purview of the law. Parties become quasipublic agencies subject to legislative control.[16]

The Fifth Party System, 1932–?: The Democratic New Deal Era and Beyond

President Herbert Hoover had been in office less than a year when the stock market crash signaled the beginning of the Great Depression of the 1930s. The election of 1932 was a major benchmark in American political history. It marked a realignment of the electorate from a Republican to a Democratic majority. The New Deal coalition that followed Franklin D. Roosevelt was formed. Like the old Republican coalition, the new Democratic majority was an amalgam of disparate and sometimes conflicting elements. White southerners, still wedded to the cause of white supremacy, were a core group, as were Catholic urban workers, mostly recent immigrant stock from eastern and southern Europe, who had been socialized to political life by the urban political machines. These Catholic voters had also been drawn to the Democratic banner by the antiprohibitionist candidacy of a coreligionist, Governor Al Smith of New York, in 1928. Blue collar workers, especially organized labor, rallied to support Roosevelt in the face of rising unemployment. Blacks forsook the party of Lincoln to back the Democrats, since the already economically depressed black society was severely rocked by the Depression. Jews, who heretofore had been predominantly Republican, also became identified with the Democratic party because of the Depression and Roosevelt's leadership against Nazi Germany. In addition, young people entering the ranks of the electorate in the 1930s and 1940s became Democrats. The Democrats were riding a wave of demographic change. Urban ethnics, Catholics, blue collar workers, and blacks were becoming a more and more significant proportion of the electorate; while the traditional Republican base of white Protestants, small town residents, farmers, and middle class businessmen constituted a shrinking share of population.

Franklin Roosevelt's election and his New Deal social welfare policies, which instituted an American version of the welfare state, had long-run weakening consequences for the traditional, patronage based, urban party organizations. New social insurance programs (like Social Security and unemployment compensation) were effectively insulated from patronage-type politics and served as models for later federal grant-in-aid programs that emphasized professionalism in state and local government.[17] The New Deal social welfare programs not only weakened the patronage base of the machines, they also took from the machines their traditional function of providing welfare services to the deprived urban populations.

The New Deal Democratic electoral coalition forged by Roosevelt proved to be an enduring alliance. Between 1932 and 1948, the Democrats won the White House all five times and only lost control of the Congress once in 1946. Divisions within the dominant coalition, however, appeared as early as the late 1930s when conservative southern Democratic representatives and senators began to dissent from Roosevelt's social welfare policies. The North-South split within the party became even more pronounced after 1948 and into the 1960s when northern Democratic leaders like Senator Hubert Humphrey (Minn.) led the party into taking a strong stand on civil rights issues.

Throughout the period since the 1930s, the Republican party has remained the minority party. At least twice after electoral disasters in 1936 and 1964, it was written off by political commentators as terminally ill. Its obituaries were prepared prematurely, however, because each time the party staged a timely comeback demonstrating the resiliency of two party competition in the United States. In 1952, Republicans used a strategy long favored by minority parties to help them win the presidency and Congress. Like the Whigs of 1840 and 1848, the GOP nominated a national hero, General Dwight D. Eisenhower, the charismatic commander of Allied forces in Europe during World War II. Running on the slogan "I like Ike," the Republicans made major inroads into all elements of the New Deal coalition, while holding the traditional Republican vote. Particularly noteworthy was Eisenhower's support in the heretofore solidly Democratic South, where he carried such states of the old Confederacy as Virginia, Texas, Florida, and Tennessee. The Eisenhower years proved to be a period of consolidation in American politics. The new Republican administration and Congress did not move to repeal the policies of the New Deal. Rather, they accepted the New Deal programs and made only minor modifications. With this Republican acceptance, the Roosevelt New Deal legacy ceased to be the divisive force in American politics that it had been. One of Eisenhower's Republican successors, Ronald Reagan, could even be heard praising and quoting Roosevelt in the 1980s.

Running on a theme of "Peace and Prosperity," Eisenhower swept to an even more overwhelming victory in 1956. The election, however, confirmed the continuing minority status of the GOP, which lost seats in the House and Senate despite the landslide election of the President. The normal Democratic majority reasserted itself in 1960 and 1964 with the elections of John F. Kennedy and Lyndon B. Johnson. The huge congressional majorities which Johnson carried into office with him in 1964 enabled the party to enact his Great Society program—a massive expansion of social welfare assistance, which was carried out largely through extensive grant-in-aid programs to state and local governments. Since their landslide win of 1964, however, the divisions within the Democratic party have intensified as the party has split over such issues as race relations, the Vietnam war, defense policy, crime and civil disorder, and social policy.

Many observers believe that starting in the mid 1960s America entered the post-New Deal era. The electoral alignments of the 1930s were still visible, but they were much less pronounced than in the past. Americans showed a marked tendency to be less influenced by party appeals. Party identification among the voters declined, especially among young people. Voters were more inclined to split their tickets between the two parties in any given election as party affiliation has come to have diminished influence on voter choice.[18] The class based distinctions between supporters of the two parties diminished as the Democrats competed more evenly with the GOP for the votes of middle class, professional, and business people. At the same time, the Republican vote among blue collar workers and even members of organized labor increased. And Republicans actually carried the white Catholic vote in 1980, 1984, and 1988. The electorate had become less predictable and capable of mobilization by either party. It was a highly volatile electorate subject to wide swings of sentiment from election to election.

This post-New Deal period has been a period of keen competition between the Republicans and Democrats for the presidency. In the ten elections since World War II, the GOP has won seven times and the Democrats four. Recent Republican presidential election successes—Richard Nixon's elections in 1968 and 1972 and the Ronald Reagan/George Bush victories of 1980, 1984, and 1988—plus GOP gains among socio-economic groups traditionally supportive of the Democratic party have even prompted speculation about the possibility of the country's entering a new Republican era. Republican presidential successes, however, have not carried over to other offices. The GOP has controlled both houses of Congress in only two of the years since Eisenhower's election in 1952, although it did gain majority status in the Senate after the 1980–1984 elections. In addition, the Democrats have been dominant in the nation's governorships and state legislatures.

Analyses of election returns from the 1980s and early 1990s reveal that the alignment of voters has changed since the 1930s when the New Deal coalition was assembled. White southerners, once a core Democratic support group, are becoming increasingly Republican. Catholics, and to a lesser degree blue collar workers, are showing greater susceptibility to Republican appeals. At the same time, black and Hispanic voters have become an increasingly important element of the Democratic party. Whether these shifts in voting patterns foreshadow an even more pronounced electoral realignment and the beginning of a Sixth American Party System remained unclear after the 1988 elections. Certainly, however, the coalitions of voters that support the two major parties have been substantially modified since the beginning of the Fifth American Party System in the 1930s.[19]

Some Lessons from Party History

Although this has been but an overview of party history in the United States, it does provide the main contours of party development and permit observations about the nature of the American party system.

The Two Party System: Some Explanations

Although there have been transitional periods characterized by factionalism within the dominant party (1824–1832) and interludes when third parties posed a major threat to the major parties (1892, 1912, 1924), party competition in the United States has been predominantly of the two party variety. Even when one of the major parties had disintegrated, the two party division has reestablished itself. And although one party frequently has been overwhelmingly dominant in the national government, the opposition party has been able to retain the loyalty of a sizable segment of the electorate. Despite the prevalence of this pattern of two party competition, scholars have had difficulty explaining the persistence of dualism. Certainly, there is no one cause of the phenomenon.

The institutional explanation. The standard American arrangement for electing national and state legislators is the single member district system—whoever receives a plurality of the vote is elected. In contrast to proportional representation, which utilizes multimember districts and rewards all serious parties with its proportionate share of the legislative seats, the single member system permits only one party to win in any given district. It is a system that permits only two parties to have a reasonable chance of victory. Third or minor parties are normally condemned to perpetual defeat—not a prescription for longevity—unless they can combine forces with a larger party. The single member system certainly creates incentives for two broadly based parties capable of winning legislative district pluralities. Experience of other nations—the Third Republic of France, Canada, and the United Kingdom—suggests that single member districts by themselves are not a sufficient answer to the question of why America has two parties. The single member district can only encourage this type of competition.

A further institutional nudge toward two party competition is provided by the electoral college system for choosing presidents. Election as president requires an absolute majority of the electoral votes. This requirement makes it unlikely that a third party can ever achieve the presidency without combining with or absorbing another major party. In addition, the states' electoral votes are allocated under a winner-take-all arrangement. All that is required to capture a state's electoral votes is a plurality of the vote in that state. Like the operation of the single member district, this system works to the disadvantage of third parties which have little chance of winning any state's electoral votes, let alone a sufficient number of states to elect a president.

The historical explanation. This explanation emphasizes the impact of the special circumstances of the initial political conflicts in the new nation and the tendency for human institutions to perpetuate themselves and preserve their initial form. The initial confrontation that the country faced was the issue of ratification of the Constitution, an issue of an yes-no character that tended to divide the nation in a dual manner. The small farmers and debtors of the interior were pitted against the mercantile and financial interests of the coastal regions. The initial lines of cleavage were built upon two great complexes of interests—the agricultural interests and the financial/mercantile interests. Such a dual split was possible because the social and economic structure of society was far less complex and specialized than that of today. Partisan conflict thus began in an era when a dualist cleavage existed. The pattern of two party politics persisted, however, even though the society changed. As V.O. Key has observed:

> The great issues changed from time to time but each party managed to renew itself as it found new followers to replace those it lost. The Civil War, thus, brought a realignment in national politics, yet it re-enforced the dual division. . . . As memories of the war faded new alignments gradually took shape within the matrix of the preexisting structure, with each party hierarchy struggling to maintain its position in the system.[20]

The cultural explanation. American society has not been characterized by blocs of people irreconcilably attached to a particular ideology or creed. Racial, religious, and ethnic minorities, though often encountering discrimination, have generally been able to find a niche in society and have not tended toward separatism. Religious tensions have existed, but open conflict has never been common and First Amendment rights have generally enjoyed protection. Nor has class consciousness been as common in the United States as in European nations. Labor parties have had little appeal to American working men and women. In addition, there has been widespread acceptance of the constitutional order and a capitalist economic system.

While diversity abounds within American society, the ingredients for multiparty politics have largely been lacking. No group is seeking to restore the prerogatives of the Church as a state religion; no major group is seriously advocating monarchy, socialism, or communism; a labor party would have a few adherents; serious advocates of giving over the ownership of factories and large farms to the workers are scarce. Should such groups exist in significant numbers, multiparty politics would be possible. But in their absence, two party politics is feasible. It is possible for one party to be slightly to the left of center—liberal—and the other to be slightly right of center—conservative—and still gain widespread electoral support. Thus the Democrats and the Republicans can attract divergent cores of support that have quite different policy viewpoints and still compete for the vote of the vast majority of Americans who consider themselves to be middle-of-the-roaders.

It is difficult to assign weights to the three explanations of two party politics that have been discussed above. Clearly, America's form of competition is the result of a combination of forces that have conspired to produce dualism.

Parties as Coalitions

Throughout their history, American parties have been broadly based coalitions. Both majority and minority parties have attracted to their banners significant support from virtually every element of society, but the core of support for the major parties has consistently differed. The New Deal coalition that so dominated the political scene for thirty years was composed of white southerners, blacks, blue collar workers, urban Catholics, ethnic minorities, and Jews. By contrast, the core of GOP strength was northern white Protestants, business and professional people, small town residents, suburbanites, and midwestern farmers. Party coalitions change over time, however, in response to new crises and issues that test the ability of party leaders to hold the diverse elements within their coalitions. The test for today's Republican leaders, who have been so successful in the presidential elections of the 1980s, involves holding together a diverse three-headed coalition composed of (1) traditional middle- and upper-middle-class economic conservatives, (2) New Right religious fundamentalists, and (3) former Democratic conservatives, primarily white southerners.[21]

The coalition nature of the parties means that intraparty conflicts can be of crucial importance in shaping the direction of governmental policy and the nature of party competition. For example, during the first part of the century, when the GOP was dominant, the struggles between the Stalwart and Progressive Republicans were in reality contests over the direction of national policy and the nature of the governing coalition. The battles between conservative and northern liberal Democrats for that party's soul since 1937 have heavily influenced the scope and nature of governmental actions as well as the character of interparty competition. Similarly in the 1980s and 1990s, the struggles within the GOP between New Right social conservatives and traditional economic conservatives (who tend to be moderate on social issues) have had a major impact upon governmental policy and helped stall federal anti-abortion and school prayer initiatives. While American party history is clearly characterized by competition between two parties, the nature of that competition has varied considerably. Samuel J. Eldersveld has noted there have been three types of party politics since 1800.[22] The first is relatively *balanced two party competition* between the two major parties, such as the period of Republican-Democratic competition that has existed since the end of World War II as the parties have traded control of the presidency. There have been eighty-eight years of such balanced two party competition. See Figure 2–1.

While some Americans tend to think of balanced two party

Figure 2–1: Patterns of Party Politics, 1800–1988

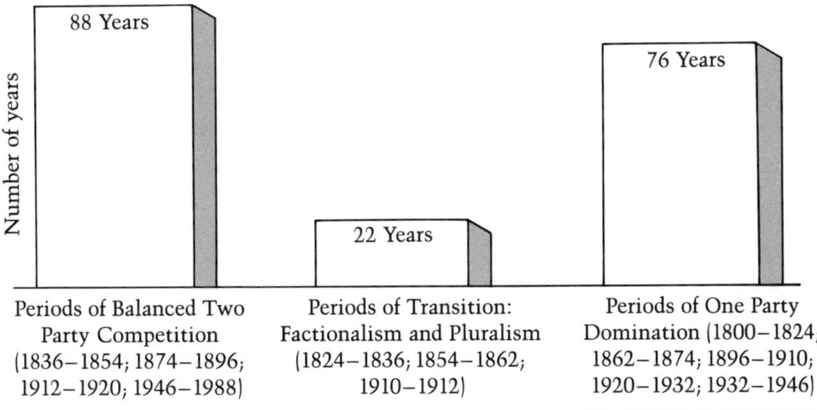

Source: Adapted from Samuel J. Eldersveld, *Political Parties in American Society* (New York: Basic Books, 1982), Table 2.2, p. 36.

competition as the norm, an almost equally prevalent pattern has been *one party dominance.* There have been five periods of sustained one party dominance, the most recent being the Democratic era of 1932–1946. In addition, there have been periods of *transitional pluralism* (factionalism within the dominant party). These periods of pluralist competition within the dominant party have twice preceded the emergence of a new major party. Thus the dominant Jeffersonian coalition engaged in a series of intraparty struggles for the presidency between 1824 and 1832 before the Whig party emerged. Similarly, schisms within the Democratic and Whig parties between 1854 and 1860 occurred as the Republican party was taking its place as a major party. The split between the Progressives and Stalwart Republicans in 1910–1912 resulted in a three way division of the vote in 1912 and permitted the minority Democrats to elect a president.

Eldersveld's analysis makes clear that the history of party competition is not the story of uninterrupted, balanced, two party competition at the national level. Three patterns of competition have existed throughout the nation's history and all three have existed during the twentieth century. Interestingly, the longest time span any pattern of party politics has existed uninterrupted is the period of two party competition that has existed since World War II—an over forty year interval from 1946 to 1988. Despite the turbulence of this postwar era, the party system has shown "a capacity for absorbing and containing threats to the system."[23]

The Stability of Republican-Democratic Conflict since 1860

Since 1860, the Republicans and Democrats have confronted each other as the major combatants of the electoral arena. Each party has sustained dramatic swings of fortune—landslide wins, cliff-hanger victories, and demoralizing defeats. These swings of electoral fortune, which can occur in a short time span, are captured in Figure 2–2, which presents data on the two parties' percentages of the popular vote for president. For example, the Democratic percentage of the two party vote for president went from 61 percent in 1964 to only 38 percent eight years later in 1972. Despite the fluidity of electoral patterns both in the long run and the short term, the contest has been consistently a test of Republican-Democratic strength since 1860. The durability of this partisan division despite the potential for political dislocation caused by two World Wars, depressions, waves of new immigrants, industrialization, urbanization, and changes in life-style deserves probing. Why have not such dislocations caused a changed array of parties? Why have not third party movements emerged to challenge and replace one or both of the major parties the way they have in the United Kingdom, Western Europe, and Canada?

Eldersveld posits three explanations for the persistence of the equilibrium of conflict between Democrats and Republicans.[24] One

Table 2–2 Major Parties Absorb Third Parties

Third Party	Year	Percent of Popular Vote	Electoral Votes	Fate in Next Election
Anti-Masonic	1832	7.8	7	endorsed Whig candidate
Free Soil	1848	10.1	0	received 4.9% of vote
Whig-American	1856	21.5	8	party dissolved
Southern Democrat	1860	18.1	72	party dissolved
Constitutional Union	1860	12.6	39	party dissolved
Populist	1892	8.5	22	endorsed Democratic candidate
Progressive (T. Roosevelt)	1912	27.4	88	returned to Republican party
Socialist	1912	6.0	0	received 3.2% of vote
Progressive (LaFollette)	1924	16.6	13	returned to Republican party
States' Rights Democrat	1948	2.4	39	party dissolved
Progressive (H. Wallace)	1948	2.4	0	received 1.4% of vote
American Independent	1968	13.5	46	received 1.4% of the vote
John B. Anderson	1980	7.1	0	did not run in 1984

Sources: Congressional Quarterly, *Guide to U.S. Elections* (Washington, D.C.: Congressional Quarterly, 1975); *Statistical Abstract of the United States*, 1986.

Figure 2–2: Republican and Democratic Percentages of the Popular Vote for President, 1896–1988

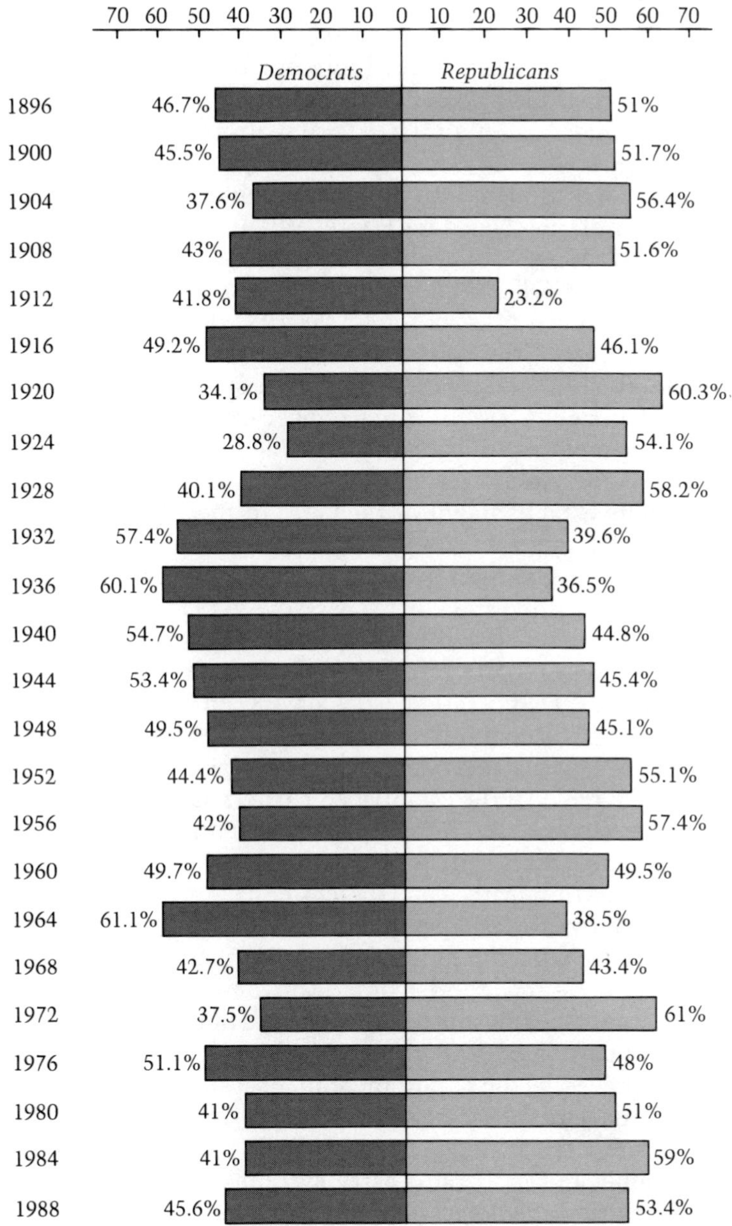

reason is the parties' *capacity for absorption of protest.* Major third party protest movements have periodically arisen since 1860, but none has been able to attract a sufficient core of voters, campaign workers, and funds to sustain themselves. Each has flowered briefly and then withered as it was absorbed into one or both of the major parties. The Populists of 1892 were taken into the Democratic party in 1896 as the Democrats appropriated their platform and nominated William Jennings Bryan. Although Bryan never gained the presidency in three tries, he was brought into the government as Wilson's Secretary of State. Similarly, Theodore Roosevelt's Bull Moose Progressives of 1912 and the Robert LaFollette Progressives of 1924 were absorbed back into the GOP fold four years after their attempts to create third party movements. Most of the Dixiecrats who bolted in 1948 and almost cost Harry Truman the election were back in the Democratic party for the 1952 and 1956 elections against Eisenhower. Party insurgents and dissidents who are often dubbed extremists almost inevitably become members of the party establishment within a short period of time. The Goldwater conservatives, who challenged the eastern moderate establishment of the GOP in the 1960s, are now part of the establishment; as are the New Left liberals of the Democratic party who sought the presidential nomination for Senators Eugene McCarthy (Minn.) and George McGovern (S.D.) in 1968 and 1972.

Professor Leon D. Epstein has argued that one of the reasons that Republican and Democratic parties have been so successful in absorbing protest has been the existence of the direct primary to nominate candidates. This uniquely American institution permits insurgents outside the ranks of the established party leadership to use an intraparty route to power. By winning party nominations through the direct primary, insurgents gain access to the general election ballot without organizing third parties and thereby enhancing their chances of general election victories. Epstein also argues that the direct primary has institutionalized Republican and Democratic party electoral dominance because voters become accustomed to participating in party primaries and choosing between groups of individuals competing for their party's label. Partisan attachments are further encouraged, he believes, by the requirement in most states that primary voters publicly declare their party affiliations or even register as Republicans or Democrats in order to participate in primary elections.[25]

The Republican-Democratic party system has also been sustained by the parties' *ideological eclecticism.* The Democrats have moved from populist radicalism in 1896, to conservatism in 1904, to progressivism in 1912, to Roosevelt's New Deal in the 1930s and

1940s, to New Left foreign and economic policy in 1972, to Jimmy Carter's moderate liberalism in 1976, to Mondale/Dukakis social and economic liberalism in the 1980s. The GOP has been equally eclectic in policy orientation—from Roosevelt's progressivism in 1904, to the conservatism of normalcy in the 1920s, to the modern moderate Republicanism of Eisenhower in the 1950s, to Reagan's economic and social conservatism of the 1980s, to Bush's "kinder and gentler" conservatism of the 1990s. This nondoctrinaire approach to issues and changing conditions has made it possible for the two parties to respond and adapt as circumstances seemed to dictate. This ideological flexibility has enabled the parties to tolerate within their ranks a wide variety of viewpoints. It is possible for hard-core Republican conservatives like Senators Jesse Helms (N.C.) and J. Strom Thurmond (S.C.) to coexist and share power within the Senate with moderate/liberal Republicans such as John Chafee (R.I.), Mark Hatfield (Ore.), and Bob Packwood (Ore.). Just as southern conservatives like Senators Sam Nunn (Ga.) and Howell Heflin (Ala.) coexist as Democrats with such liberals as Howard Metzenbaum (Oh.) and Edward Kennedy (Mass.).

The two parties have also exhibited *coalitional flexibility*. That is, they have demonstrated an ability to attract votes from virtually all elements of society, even from groups which are normally viewed as a part of the opposition. For example, the Republicans in the presidential elections of the 1980s demonstrated a capacity to win over 40 percent of the vote among labor union families, even though this group is normally Democratic. Similarly, Jimmy Carter was able to recapture the South for the Democratic party in 1976, only to lose it to Ronald Reagan and Republicans in 1980. The party coalitions are not static in character. They are in a constant process of "breakup, modification, and reconstruction."[26]

The Realignment Phenomenon

Throughout American party history there have been periodic *realignments* at quite regular intervals. During a realignment, significant changes occur within the electorate: a minority party becomes the majority party (1860, 1932); one party achieves an infusion of strength that enables it to remain dominant (1896); changes in the partisan loyalties of voters develop (1860, 1932). In a penetrating analysis of critical elections in American history, Walter Dean Burnham noted that realignments "recur with rather remarkable regularity approximately one in a generation, or every thirty to thirty-eight years."[27] He noted realignments tend to occur as major crises intrude on the society and economy when "politics as usual" is not adequate to deal with the problems. The racial and sectional tensions of the 1850s and the Depressions of the 1890s and 1930s are examples of crises that could not be accommodated within the existing party structure. The result was highly polarized campaigns, with heightened public interest, that resulted in critical realignments of voters.

Burnham also observed that third party protests were a "protorealignment phenomena," which occurred before each realignment and reflected the inability of the existing major parties to meet the expectations of large segments of society.[28] Thus the Anti-Masonic party in the northeastern states preceded the emergence of the Second Party System; the Free Soil party arose prior to the collapse of the Second Party System and rise of the Republicans; the Populist uprising in 1892 took place before the McKinley-Bryan realigning election of 1896; and the LaFollette Progressive party of 1924 foreshadowed the problems that were to result in the New Deal realignment of 1932.

The periodic nature of realignments approximately every thirty to thirty-eight years following a major third party protest has led to speculation about the likelihood of a post-New Deal realignment. By 1968 the requisite number of years had elapsed for a realignment to occur. In addition, major third party movements had occurred—George Wallace's American party received 13 percent of the vote in 1968 and John Anderson garnered 7 percent in 1980. As the Republicans achieved presidential victories in 1968 and 1972, amid the domestic turmoil that accompanied the Vietnam War and domestic strife, and then again in 1980, 1984, and 1988 with unabashedly conservative candidates, political analysts scoured the election returns and poll data for evidence of an electoral realignment.

There has been ample evidence of change. The percentage of voters declaring themselves to be independents increased in the 1960s and early 1970s. Republican identifiers, who had fallen to a smaller percentage of the electorate than independents during the 1960s and 1970s, increased substantially after the 1984 election. There has been a high level of ticket splitting as voters seemed quite content to elect Republican presidents but then provide them with Democratic watchdogs in Congress. There have also been the previously noted changes in the voting allegiances of various voting blocs, most notably the shift of white southerners to the GOP and the overwhelming support given the Democrats by black voters.

Despite the efforts of analysts to find in these data evidence of a major realignment—especially after the Republican sweep of 1980 which gave them not only the presidency but control of the Senate for the first time in twenty-eight years and thirty-four additional House seats—no consensus has yet emerged concerning the existence of a realignment. Republican presidential victories in five of the last six elections, the rise in the proportion of the voters who consider themselves Republicans, and the shift of white southerners to the GOP are seen by some as signs of realignment. Continued Democratic dominance of the House of Representatives, governorships, and state legislatures, however, is often pointed to as evidence that no major realignment has occurred.[29] And as of 1990, the Republicans had not become the new majority party. Although the issue of whether or not a modern day realignment has occurred remains unresolved, there is widespread agreement that the last twenty-odd years have produced two very different Republican and Democratic parties in terms of their programmatic orientations and their bases of electoral support. The dominant issues of the 1980s—foreign policy, cultural values, and social welfare policy—have caused Americans to engage increasingly in ticket splitting, producing an extended period of divided party control of the national government. The people's preference for a president who espouses a nationalistic foreign policy and traditional cultural values has given the Republicans a decided advantage in recent presidential elections. However, Americans' desire for a continuation of governmental social welfare benefits to which they had become attached has caused voters to return consistent Democratic majorities to the House of Representatives.[30]

Parties in Decline?

A review of American political history reveals the amazing durability and resilience of political parties. Even so, many observers see a bleak future ahead for the parties. But just as the evidence of realignment is contradictory, so too is that concerning the condition of parties. The signs of party decline most frequently cited include the receding impact of partisanship on voter choice; the changed nature of presidential nominating politics that has taken power from party leaders and transferred it to the media, candidate organizations, and amateur activists; the increased role played by PACs in funding campaigns; and the rise of the professional campaign and media consultants. But not all the indicators are negative concerning the state of the parties: the national party organizations have achieved unprecedented legal control over their state party affiliates in delegate selection procedures for national conventions; the national party committees (especially the Republicans) have developed increasingly effective fund raising and professionalized campaign operations; state party organizations show signs of increased organizational strength over their status in the 1960s; and the parties have demonstrated that they can adapt to the growth of PACs by serving as coordinators of PAC activities. Clearly, American parties are in a state of transformation. At the same time, they demonstrate a capacity to persist.[31] The patterns of change and persistence within various phases of party activity will be a focus of ensuing chapters.

Suggestions for Further Reading

Barone, Michael. *Our Country: The Shaping of America from Roosevelt to Reagan.* New York: Free Press, 1990.

Burnham, Walter Dean. *Critical Elections and the Mainsprings of American Politics.* New York: Norton, 1970.

Chambers, William Nesbit, and Burnham, Walter Dean, eds. *The American Party Systems: Stages of Political Development.* New York: Oxford University Press, 1967.

Chambers, William Nesbit. *Political Parties in a New Nation: The American Experience.* New York: Oxford University Press, 1963.

Eldersveld, Samuel J. *Political Parties in American Society.* New York: Basic Books, 1982.

Epstein, Leon D. *Political Parties in the American Mold.* Madison: University of Wisconsin Press, 1986.

Kleppner, Paul; Burnham, Walter Dean; Formisano, Ronald P.; Hays, Samuel P.; Jensen, Richard; and Shade, William G. *The Evolution of the American Electoral System.* Westport, Conn., Greenwood Press, 1981.

Ladd, Everett Carll. *American Political Parties: Social Change and Political Response.* New York: Norton, 1970.

Mayhew, David R. *Placing Parties in American Politics.* Princeton, N.J.: Princeton University Press, 1986.

Sundquist, James L. *Dynamics of the Party System.* Washington, D.C.: Brookings Institution, 1973.

Notes

1. Data on the public's attitudes toward political parties are summarized in William J. Keefe, *Parties, Politics, and Public Policy in America,* 5th ed. (Washington: CQ Press, 1988), p. 11. For a more complete consideration of public support for parties, see Jack Dennis, "Trends in Public Support for the American Party System," *British Journal of Political Science,* vol. 5 (1975), pp. 187–230.
2. Everett Carll Ladd, *American Political Parties: Social Change and Political Response* (New York: W. W. Norton, 1970), pp.80–81.
3. Quoted by V. O. Key, Jr., *Politics, Parties, and Pressure Groups,* 5th ed. (New York: Crowell, 1964), p. 203.

4. Ladd, *American Political Parties,* p. 81.
5. Ibid., p. 87.
6. Ibid., p. 82.
7. Bureau of the Census, U.S. Department of Commerce, *Historical Statistics of the United States: Colonial Times to 1970* (Washington, D.C.: U.S. Government Printing Office, 1975), p. 1072.
8. Richard P. McCormick, "Political Development and the Second Party System," in William Nesbit Chambers and W. D. Burnham, eds., *The American Party Systems: Stages of Political Development* (New York: Oxford University Press, 1967), p. 342.
9. Ladd, *American Political Parties,* p. 99.
10. Ibid., pp. 105–106.
11. V. O. Key, Jr., *Politics, Parties, and Pressure Groups,* 5th ed. (New York: Crowell, 1965), p. 168.
12. For a comprehensive analysis of the development of state and local party organizations, see David R. Mayhew, *Placing Parties in American Politics* (Princeton, N.J.: Princeton University Press, 1986), especially Chapter 8.
13. V. O. Key, Jr., "A Theory of Critical Elections," *Journal of Politics,* 17 (February 1955); p. 11.
14. Key, *Politics, Parties, and Pressure Groups,* p. 186; Samuel Lubell, *The Future of American Politics,* 2nd ed., rev. (Garden City, N.Y.: Doubleday, 1956), Chapter 3.
15. Ladd, *American Political Parties,* pp. 175–176.
16. The impact of the direct primary on American parties is thoroughly analyzed by Leon D. Epstein, *Political Parties in the American Mold* (Madison: University of Wisconsin Press, 1986); see especially chapters 5 and 6.
17. See Mayhew, *Placing Parties in American Politics,* p. 323.
18. See Martin P. Wattenberg, *The Decline of American Political Parties 1952–1984* (Cambridge: Harvard University Press, 1984); and his "From a Partisan to Candidate-centered Electorate," in Anthony King, ed., *The New American Political System,* Second Version (Washington, D.C.: American Enterprise Institute, 1990), pp. 139–174.
19. For the discussion of the changed nature of American electoral politics and possible future developments, see Thomas E. Cavanagh and James L. Sundquist, "The New Two-Party System," in John E. Chubb and Paul E. Peterson, eds., *The New Directions in American Politics* (Washington, D.C.: Brookings Institution, 1985), pp. 33–68; Paul R. Abramson, John H. Aldrich, and David W. Rohde, *Change and Continuity in the 1988 Elections* (Washington, D.C.: CQ Press, 1990), Chapters 5 and 11; and Wattenberg, "From a Partisan to Candidate-centered Electorate."
20. Key, *Politics, Parties, and Pressure Groups,* p. 208.
21. Wattenberg, "From a Partisan to Candidate-centered Electorate," pp. 157–169.
22. Samuel J. Eldersveld, *Political Parties in American Society* (New York: Basic Books, 1982), pp. 35–36.

23. Ibid., p. 36.
24. Ibid., pp. 40–43.
25. Leon D. Epstein, *Political Parties in the American Mold* (Madison: University of Wisconsin Press, 1986), pp. 131–133, 243–245.
26. Eldersveld, *Political Parties*, p. 42.
27. Walter Dean Burnham, *Critical Elections and the Mainsprings of American Politics* (New York, W. W. Norton, 1970), p. 26.
28. Ibid., p. 27.
29. See Paul Allen Beck, "Incomplete Realignment," in Charles O. Jones (ed.), *The Reagan Legacy: Promise and Performance* (Chatham, N.J.: Chatham House, 1988), ch. 5.
30. This argument is developed and debated in Byron E. Shafer ed., *The End of Realignment* (Madison: University of Wisconsin Press, 1991).
31. See Epstein, *Political Parties in the American Mold.*

CHAPTER 3

Characteristics of the American Party System

The United States was the first nation to develop modern political parties which aligned the electorate around national issues and organized at the national, regional, and local levels to nominate candidates, contest elections, and organize governments. The early American parties stood in sharp contrast to the "capital factions" that passed for parties in Great Britain. However, as other nations followed the American example of extending the franchise to nonproperty owners, they too developed political parties capable of structuring the vote and organizing governments. Indeed, wherever elections have been conducted on a continuing basis at the national and regional levels, political parties exist. They have proved essential for organizing and mobilizing a mass electorate. As party conflict has been institutionalized in Western democracies, the party systems of these nations have come to share certain attributes: long established parties, a limited number of parties seriously contesting for office, electoral alignments focused around national issues, and class based patterns of electoral support. While the American party system shares many traits with other Western democracies, its peculiar combination of characteristics makes it distinctive.

Two Party Competition with Variations

The continuous competition between the Republicans and the Democrats for over 130 years has given the American party system a two party character. Only these two parties contest for control of the presidency, Congress, governorships, and state legislatures. This sets the United States apart from most other nations which, while having a limited number of major parties, normally have more than just two. The dominant position of the two major parties is reflected in the operation of the Federal Election Campaign Act, which bestows special benefits upon major parties—defined as those parties receiving 25 percent of the popular vote for president. These benefits include federal matching funds for presidential candidates seeking party nominations, federal grants for holding national conventions, and public funding at the maximum level in general election campaigns for president. Only the Republican and Democratic parties have qualified as major parties eligible for the highest level of governmental support, which gives them a substantial advantage over minor parties.

The phrase the *two party system* masks a great deal of variation in the extent and nature of interparty competition in the United States. Two party competition aptly describes competition for selected offices in some jurisdictions, but there are also offices

Table 3–1 Major Party Dominance of Presidential Voting, 1948–1988

	Candidates for President		Percentage of Popular Vote		
Year	**Republican**	**Democrat**	**Republican**	**Democratic**	**Total**
1948	Dewey	Truman	45.1	49.6	94.7
1952	Eisenhower	Stevenson	55.1	44.4	99.5
1956	Eisenhower	Stevenson	57.4	42.0	99.4
1960	Nixon	Kennedy	49.5	49.7	99.2
1964	Goldwater	Johnson	38.5	61.1	99.6
1968	Nixon	Humphrey	43.4	42.7	86.1
1972	Nixon	McGovern	60.7	37.5	98.2
1976	Ford	Carter	48.0	50.1	98.1
1980	Reagan	Carter	50.7	41.0	91.7
1984	Reagan	Mondale	58.8	40.6	99.4
1988	Bush	Dukakis	53.4	45.6	99.0

Source: Statistical Abstract of the United States, 1990, p. 244.

and regions in which the norm of strong interparty competition is not met.

Party Competition at the National Level

The presidency. Viewed from a national perspective, presidential elections are highly competitive. In the eleven presidential elections since World War II, the parties have alternated control, with the Republicans winning seven times and Democrats four times. The two party character of presidential voting is reflected in Table 3–1, which presents data on the percentages of the popular vote cast for Republican and Democratic candidates in recent elections. Between 1948 and 1988, the Republican–Democratic share of the popular vote has never been lower than 86.1 percent (1968) and has averaged 97.4 percent.

The Congress. The Democrats have controlled the Congress during most of the time since 1946. The GOP held both the House and Senate only after the 1946 and 1952 elections and the Senate alone following the 1980–1984 elections. Despite the lopsidedness of Democratic control of the two chambers, the national popular vote for the House, like the vote for president, shows a high level of competition and two party dominance. The combined Republican-Democratic share of the popular vote for the House of Representatives has exceeded 99 percent in every election since World War II. The minority Republican party share of the popular vote has never dipped below 40.5 percent and it has averaged 46.1 in twenty-one elections.

Party Competition at the State Level

A measure of state level interparty competition can be obtained by combining indicators of party voting strength: (1) percentage of votes won by each party in gubernatorial elections; (2) percentage of seats won by each party in each house of the state legislature; (3) the length of time each party controlled the governorship; and (4) the proportion of the time in which control of the governorship and the legislature has been divided between the parties.[1] When these data are combined into a single index of competitiveness for the period 1981–1988, a clear majority of the states fail the test of competitiveness (see Figure 3–1). Twenty-two states are either one party Democratic or modified one party Democratic, while six states qualify as a modified one party Republican.

Figure 3–1 makes clear the lingering impact of the Civil War on American politics. Every state in the Old Confederacy except Tennessee is either in the one party Democratic or modified one party Democratic category. In addition, the border states of Kentucky, Maryland, Oklahoma, and West Virginia have modified one party Democratic state party systems. The one party character of southern and border states, more than 125 years after the Civil War reflects not only the enduring nature of party loyalties, but the difficulty the minority party has in penetrating the electoral system sufficiently to win state legislative elections. For example, even after the Republican gains in presidential, senatorial, and congressional elections in the South during the 1980s, the Democrats in 1989 controlled at least 77 percent of the state senate seats in the eleven states of the Old Confederacy. Democratic control of the lower houses of state legislatures was also pervasive. In every southern state but Tennessee, they held more than 60 percent of the lower house seats and in six states their majorities were at least 80 percent.

Research comparing social and economic conditions within the states has revealed that socioeconomic diversity contributes to interparty competitiveness. A heterogeneous population permits both parties to build up support among selected groups in society because of the inevitable conflicts, tensions, and differences that socioeconomic diversity breeds. Such indicators of socioeconomic diversity as population size, educational attainment, and home ownership are each correlated to interparty competition. In addition, the strength of the party organizations also affects partisan competition. Strong party organizations capable of mobilizing the vote tend to encourage competitive politics.[2]

Variations in Levels of Competition for Different Offices

The index of competitiveness described in the preceding section is based exclusively upon the outcome of *state* elections and gives more weight to control of state legislatures than it does to winning the governorship. As a result, this index can obscure the extent to which interparty competition exists in contests for various offices.

Statewide elections. There is substantial evidence of a high level of interparty competition in most statewide elections. In the ten presidential elections between 1952 and 1988, 23 of the states have

Figure 3–1: Levels of Interparty Competition in the States, 1981–1988

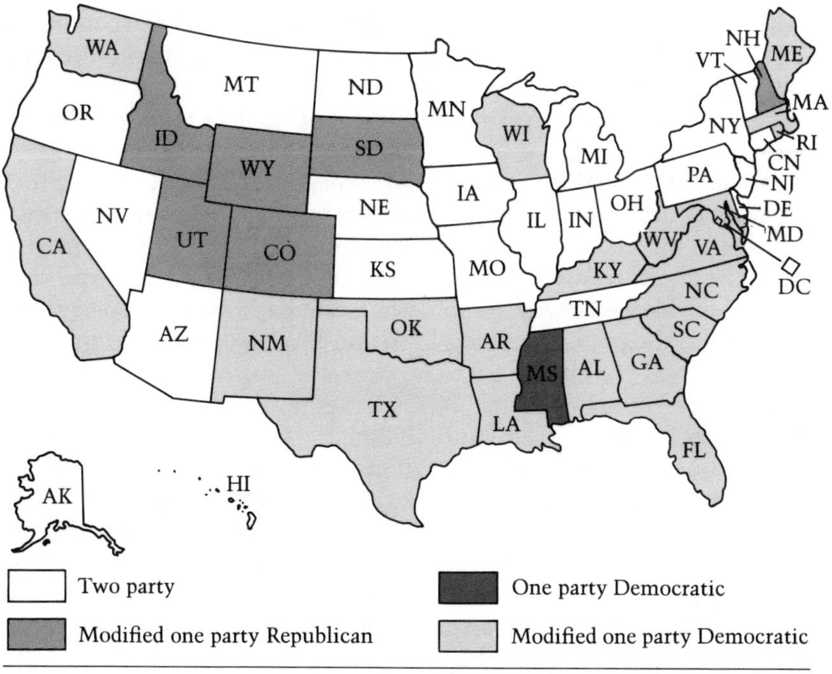

Two party
One party Democratic
Modified one party Republican
Modified one party Democratic

Source: John F. Bibby, Cornelius P. Cotter, James L. Gibson, and Robert J. Huckshorn, "Parties in State Politics," in *Politics in the American States: A Comparative Analysis*, 5th ed., ed. V. Gray, H. Jacob, and R. Albritton (Glenview, Ill.: Scott, Foresman/Little, Brown 1990), p. 92.

been carried by the Democratic and Republican parties at least three times. Every state of the Old Confederacy has been won by the Republican presidential nominee at least four times since Eisenhower's penetration of the South in 1952. In 1988, George Bush (Republican) carried sixteen of twenty-two Democratic one party and modified one party states shown in Figure 3–1.

A more complete picture of the level of interparty competition at the state level in presidential elections can be seen in Table 3–2, which shows the percentage of the popular vote garnered by the party which won the state's electoral votes. In four of the ten elections between 1952 and 1988, two-thirds of the states were won by margins of less than 54 percent of the vote; and only in the national landslides of 1964, 1972, and 1984 were a majority of the states carried by margins of 60 percent or more.

Further evidence of increasing interparty competition in statewide elections can be found in senatorial contests. This was particularly apparent in 1980 when twenty-five (76 percent) of thirty-three Senate elections were won by less than 60 percent of the vote. In elections between 1980 and 1990, 33 percent of the 203 senators elected had margins of less than 55 percent, and 82 percent had margins below 60 percent. The heightened level of competition for senatorial seats is also revealed by the fact that from 1980 to 1990 only three (Arkansas, Louisiana, and Tennessee) of the once solidly Democratic states of the old Confederacy failed to elect at least one Republican senator.

Gubernatorial elections have also become competitive. Table 3-3 presents data on the extent of partisan change in control of governorships since 1950. During the 1950s, only 23.6 percent of gubernatorial elections resulted in a change in party control of state executive mansions. In that decade, no southern state had a switch in party control, but in the period between 1980 and 1989, 43 percent of the elections resulted in a change in party control of southern governorships. It is not just the states of the Old Confederacy that are now characterized by frequent partisan shifts. Democrats have elected governors and alternated control since the 1950s in such traditional bastions of Republicanism as Maine, Vermont, North and South Dakota, Kansas, and Nebraska. In 1990, fourteen (38.9%) of the thirty-six gubernatorial contests resulted in a change in party control.

Congressional elections. While interparty competition is increasingly the norm in statewide elections, it has become relatively rare in elections to the House of Representatives. On average, almost three-fourths of the members of Congress elected between 1980 and 1988 won with an excess of 60 percent of the vote (see Figure 3–2).

Table 3–2 Winning Percentage of the State Popular Vote in Presidential Elections, 1952–1988

Winning Party's Percent of State	Number of States									
popular vote	1988	1984	1980	1976	1972	1968	1964	1960	1956	1952
Less than 55%	19(38%)	7(14%)	33(66%)	34(68%)	6(12%)	41(82%)	8(16%)	35(70%)	11(23%)	15(31%)
55–59%	22(44%)	11(22%)	7(14%)	12(24%)	12(24%)	7(14)%	15(30%)	11(22%)	31(44%)	16(33%)
60–64%	9(18%)	20(40%)	6(12%)	1(2%)	16(32%)	2(4%)	14(28%)	4(8)%	10(21%)	8(17%)
65–69%	0(0%)	8(16%)	3(6%)	2(4%)	9(18%)	0(0%)	9(18%)	0(0%)	4(8%)	7(15%)
70 + %	0(0%)	4(8%)	1(2%)	0(0%)	7(14%)	0(0%)	4(8%)	0(0%)	2(4%)	2(4%)
Total	50	50	50	50	50	50	50	50	48	48

Sources: Congressional Quarterly, *Presidential Elections since 1789* (Washington, D.C.: Congressional Quarterly, 1983), pp. 112–119; *Statistical Abstract of the United States*, 1990, p. 246.

Table 3–3 Party Change in Control of Governorships, 1950–1989

Decade	No. of Gubernatorial Elections	Percent of Elections with a Party Change[a]
1950–1959	174	23.6(41)
1960–1969	156	35.3(55)
1970–1979	144	38.9(56)
1980–1989	122	35.2(43)

a. An election with a party change is defined as any election in which control of the governorship shifts from one party to another.

Sources: Adapted from Larry Sabato, Goodbye to Goodtime Charlie 2nd ed. (Washington, D.C.: CQ Press, 1983), pp. 120–121; the 1980–1989 data is derived from appropriate volumes of the *Statistical Abstract of the United States.*

The lack of competitiveness in these districts is reflected in the inability of most challengers to raise enough funds for meaningful campaigns against incumbents. In 1988, Democratic challengers to Republican incumbents who won by 60 percent or more, averaged only $85,414 in expenditures compared to the Republican incumbents' $352,394 in average spending. Republican challengers to Democrats with 60 percent plus winning margins were almost as severely disadvantaged. Their average expenditure was $71,285 compared to average Democratic incumbent expenditures of $326,931.[3] Such resource advantages on the side of incumbents means that in most districts the challenger's party is normally confronted with the task of recruiting a "willing loser" to run against the incumbent.

Incumbency has become a powerful advantage. Indeed, it is so strong that in any given congressional election, over 90 percent of the incumbents seeking reelection will win. As a result, the extent of party change in control of House seats is extremely low. In the six elections between 1980 and 1990, on average, only twenty-four (5.5 percent) seats changed party control and only once did 10 percent or more of the seats switch party control.

Not only has the incumbency factor reduced partisan turnover in the House, it has also resulted in higher levels of electoral security. Incumbents are not only winning, they are winning by comfortable margins. Even freshman representatives elected initially by narrow margins are able to win comfortably in their first reelection contest. This phenomenon of the "sophomore surge" (Table 3-4) will customarily remove many members from the ranks of those who are considered vulnerable and who are likely to attract strong opposition candidates and campaign efforts.

Figure 3–2: Party Competition for House Seats, 1970–1988

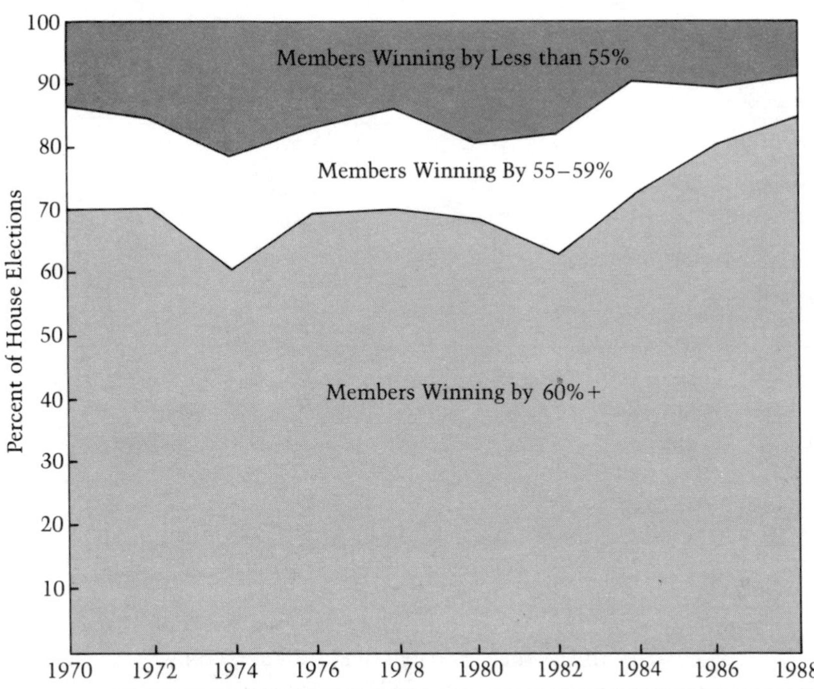

Source: Statistical Abstract of the United States; National Journal, Nov. 10, 1985, pp. 2143–2145.

State legislative elections. The frequent absence of meaningful two party competition found in congressional elections is also present in elections to the state legislatures.[4] One party domination of legislative contests is commonplace in many of the states. The Democratic party has maintained almost total domination of state legislative elections in five southern states (Alabama, Arkansas, Georgia, Louisiana, and Mississippi) where the party held on average over 80 percent of the upper and lower house seats between 1953 and 1990. Other states characterized in the 1980s by one-party control of state legislatures include Maryland, Massachusetts, Rhode Island, and West Virginia for the Democrats; and Arizona, Colorado, Idaho, Kansas, South Dakota, and Wyoming for the Republicans.

As is true of the U.S. House of Representatives, incumbent re-election rates are extremely high in many state legislatures. In California between 1978 and 1986, for example, incumbent state senators

Table 3–4 The Sophomore Surge, 1974–1990: A Comparison of Representatives' First and Second Elections

Year of the First Election	Percentage of Popular Vote		
	First Election	Second Election	Increase
Class of 1974	55.9	63.4	+7.5
Class of 1976	60.9	70.1	+9.2
Class of 1978	58.6	67.7	+9.1
Class of 1980	56.0	62.4	+6.4
Class of 1982	59.1	68.5	+9.7
Class of 1984	55.9	66.5	+10.6
Class of 1986	58.9	70.9	+12.0
Class of 1988	58.3	67.7	+8.6

Sources: Alan Ehrenhalt (ed.) *Politics in America,* 1986, 1988, 1990 (Washington, D.C.: Congressional Quarterly); *Congressional Quarterly Weekly Report,* Jan. 9, 1982 and Feb. 23, 1991; Michael Barone and Grant Ujifusa (eds.), *The Almanac of American Politics, 1990* (Washington, D.C., 1989).

had a 93 percent reelection rate and lower house incumbents won reelection 98 percent of the time. Reelection rates of at least 90 percent also existed in Rhode Island, New York, Pennsylvania, Michigan, Wisconsin, Missouri, and Kentucky.[5]

It is clear from this brief survey of statewide, congressional, and state legislative elections that there is tremendous variability in the extent of interparty competition depending upon which type of election is being considered. The phrase "American two party system" accurately captures the totality of party competition, but it fails to capture the continuum of party competition found in the United States.

Decentralized Power Structures

It is hard to overstate the extent to which American political parties are characterized by decentralized power structures. Except for a few isolated urban machines, there is almost a total absence of hierarchical relationships within American parties. Within the party in government, presidents cannot assume that representatives and senators of their party will necessarily follow their leadership on public policy issues. Within the party organization, the national institutions of the party have a narrow range of authority over state party delegate selection procedures for national conventions, but they rarely meddle in nominations and organizational affairs of state parties. Few constraints operate upon the party in the electorate. Even incumbent presidents have found that they could not depend upon the party's voters to give them support either in bids for renomination or reelection. Power in the American parties is fragmented and scattered among many institutions, organizations, and individuals at the national, state, and local levels.

The Impact of the Constitution

Separation of powers. The Founding Fathers purposely sought to make it difficult for any individual or faction to gain control over the national government by creating a national government composed of three branches. As a result, representatives and senators are elected separately from the president and for terms of varying length. Each has a different constituency.

The looseness of the American parties is, in part, a response to the constitutional separation of powers. Because separation of powers permits divided control of the government, political parties are free to concentrate their efforts towards winning the presidency, Congress, or just one house of Congress. The minority Republicans, for example, have frequently focused their campaign drives on the White House (e.g., 1972, 1984, and 1988) and in 1986 and 1990 targeted Senate races for special emphasis. With presidents, senators, and representatives each elected from separate constituencies for staggered terms, it is small wonder that these elected officials of the same party have only a minimal sense of interdependence. The highest prize of American politics—the presidency—can be gained without simultaneously having a partisan majority in Congress. Presidents, therefore, can operate with a significant degree of independence from their party colleagues in Congress. Representatives and senators, each elected from their own particular constituency, need not be supportive of their party's president for electoral survival. Indeed, it is often prudent for the national legislators to put some distance between themselves and their president.

The incentives toward party unity and discipline are substantially stronger in countries with parliamentary regimes. In such systems, control of the legislature is the prerequisite for achieving the prime ministership or cabinet office. Control of the executive goes to the party or coalition of parties that has a legislative majority. And when that majority is lost through electoral setbacks, the cabinet must resign and make way for the opposition. Loss of the legislative majority through defections by dissident partisans or coalition members can force a cabinet either to resign or call new elections. Neither option is a pleasant one because they threaten legislators' tenure or their chances to serve in the cabinet—the most prestigious and powerful positions in public life. The parliamentary system thus creates powerful incentives toward party unity and conforming to wishes of the party leadership. But in the United States the institutional incentive to support party leadership and the president is lacking and instead independent minded behavior is encouraged.

Because the separation of powers principle is embedded not just in the national Constitution, but also in state constitutions, its party fragmenting consequences are also felt at the state level. State legislators frequently operate quite independently of their party's governor and party leadership.

Federalism. Federalism—the constitutional division of governmental power between the national government and the states—has made it difficult for political parties to develop as other than decentralized institutions. American parties did not antedate the writing of the Constitution and they, therefore, had to organize themselves to contest state elections as well as presidential races. When the American parties were developing in the nineteenth century, there were powerful incentives to organize strong state parties because "national and state political stakes were more nearly equal than they are now."[6] Although the states are less important relative to the national government in the 1990s than they were in the nineteenth century, the states continue to be potent political entities worthy of major investments by the parties to secure control. Parties organized around state as well as national elections tend to become decentralized and confederative in character. This pattern of decentralization has been strengthened by each state imposing upon its parties a unique set of statutory regulations under which the parties must operate.

Fifty semiautonomous state governments, each having a multitude of local governmental units, have created thousands of partisan elected officials, party leaders, and organizations with their own constituencies and cadres of supporters. Such localized bases of support mean that these elected officials are in a position to assert their independence from national party leaders. Often the interests of state and national party leaders and elected officials are not the same. State party leaders and candidates are likely to place a higher priority upon electing governors and state legislators than in winning control of the White House or Congress. For example, Stanley M. Friedman, the Democratic leader of the Bronx, made the following comment when asked during the 1984 presidential primary about whether he worried about presidential politics.

> It doesn't affect our life one bit. National politics—President and such—are too far removed from the bread and butter things that matter to local leaders and mayors and governor. The local leader cares about a senior citizen center, a local concern.[7]

State and national party leaders frequently come into conflict on organizational matters. Sensing the advantage of having the first presidential nominating event in the nation, Iowa Democrats, for example, defied the Democratic National Committee concerning the date of the precinct caucuses used to select 1984 national convention delegates. The distinct interests, constituencies, and bases of support which federalism creates for national, state, and local party leaders and elected officials means that party unity is always under stress. The decentralizing forces inherent in the separation of powers system are given an encouraging boost by federalism.

The Impact of Nomination and Campaign Practices

Nominations and general election campaigns are not party dominated processes in the United States. Elected officials gain nomination and election primarily through reliance on highly personalized campaign organizations, which may be supplemented by party resources. This means that parties do not control access to elective office. As a result, party leaders are not in a position to impose discipline on elected officials, who know that the party cannot assure either their electoral survival or ascent up the political ladder.

Nominations in the states. Nominations to congressional, state, and local office, with few exceptions, are made via the direct primary. This open and participatory process makes it extremely difficult for any but the most disciplined style party organization (e.g., the old Daley machine in Chicago) to control nominations and access to the general election ballot. The direct primary encourages candidates to build highly personal campaign organizations. Once a candidate is nominated in a primary, the local or national party leadership is obliged to accept that individual as a bona fide nominee of the party, whether the person was its preferred candidate or not.

The direct primary means that neither national, state, nor local party organizations are in a position to control nominations to Congress. This is in vivid contrast to most Western democracies in which parliamentary nominations are internal party decisions made by the organizational leadership. In such systems, the party organization is in a position to impose discipline on legislators because it determines which candidates will bear the party label in elections.[8] Lacking such control over nominations, American parties are not in a position to impose discipline on representatives and senators.

Presidential nominations. Presidential nominating politics of the post-1968 era is characterized by presidential primaries that determine the candidate preferences of a majority of the delegates, open and participatory state party caucuses, and intense media coverage. Unlike the pre-1968 period, party leaders no longer exercise decisive influence over the selection of presidential nominees. Influence has shifted to candidate organizations, campaign consultants, candidate or issue oriented activists, and the mass media—especially television. As Jimmy Carter demonstrated in 1976, it is possible for a party outsider—a person largely unknown to a party's national and state leadership and inexperienced in national government—to gain a major party nomination. Even incumbent presidents are not immune from strong renomination challenges as Presidents Gerald Ford in 1976 and Jimmy Carter in 1980 discovered. Since party organizations cannot even guarantee incumbent presidents renomination, presidents, like senators and representatives, take office with an ambiguous relationship to their party. Their sense of party obligation is often limited.

General election campaigns. The decentralizing forces unleashed by nomination processes are reinforced by the manner in which general election campaigns are conducted. National trends in public opinion, national media, and campaigns do influence the outcomes of congressional, state, and local elections. Candidates, however, are aware that to a significant degree elections are determined by local factors and their ability to achieve a favorable balance of campaign resources over their opponents. With such a favorable balance of resources, the skillful campaigner can overcome adverse national swings of voter sentiment and gain election.

Congressional campaigns in particular reflect this highly individualized campaign environment. Most candidates maintain highly personalized campaign organizations and raise funds from nonparty sources, such as political action committees (PACs) which contributed $108.6 million to House candidates in 1989–90. The resourceful congressional incumbent normally uses the prerequisites of office to project an image of electoral invincibility and will raise a substantial campaign war chest. These activities often scare off serious challengers. National or state parties customarily provide only a small percentage of the money needed to mount a reelection drive. As a result, congressional candidates are, in Gary Jacobson's words, "largely on their own when it comes to financing the campaign directly."[9] Electoral survival requires cultivating trust among one's constituents and maintenance of a personal organization. Since the party cannot ensure continued congressional tenure, it is not surprising that parties have difficulty gaining high levels of party unity on congressional roll calls. With no party to protect them, representatives and senators have created a congressional system that bestows on each member substantial resources for year around campaigning and a committee system that enables them to build support among constituencies essential for reelection.[10]

Presidential campaigns are also organized to a significant degree outside the party structure. This type of candidate oriented campaign organization is encouraged by the Federal Election Campaign Act. Candidates who agree to accept public funding of their campaigns are required under the Act to forego fund raising activities, and the Republican and Democratic National Committees are restricted to modest levels ($8.3 million in 1988) of expenditure on behalf of their presidential and vice presidential nominees. Presidential candidates accepting public funding are also required to set up a committee to receive and expend the public funds. The law, therefore, creates an incentive for major party presidential nominees to follow their natural preference for campaign organizations which are devoted exclusively to their own candidacies and which function at some distance from their national party committees.

The tie between party organizations and candidates at all levels has also been weakened by changes in the techniques of campaigning and the resulting escalation in campaign costs. The modern campaign for major office today requires media experts, pollsters, computer specialists, direct mail consultants, accountants, lawyers, research specialists, and campaign consultants to perform get-out-the-vote activities and public relations functions that were once the province of party organizations. As candidates have relied increasingly upon these non-party sources for essential services, the influence of the party over elected officials has diminished.

Candidates of the 1990s running for major office tend to set up shop on their own and operate as relatively independent political entrepreneurs with personalized organizations, campaign war chests, media advertising, and, once elected, a sizable staff to assist in electioneering. It is small wonder that such American politicians feel quite independent of their parties. By contrast, the British members of Parliament are heavily dependent upon their parties. The party organization controls nominations; television time is allocated to parties not individual candidates; the parties sharply limit the amount that candidates can spend on their own campaigns; and once elected the average M.P. has few of the staff resources and other prerequisites available to members of Congress. The British M.P.'s are, therefore, much more dependent upon their parties and much more likely to submit to party discipline.

Some Counter Trends: Nationalizing Influences

Decentralization of power pervades American parties. This attribute, however, can be overemphasized. Parties have both their national and confederative aspects. Federalism fragments the parties, but national forces have always played a significant role. Leon Epstein has observed:

> However much party organizations . . . have come to establish largely independent state and local bases, their electoral support originated in national and specifically presidential alignments. In other words, the party labels under which organizations could win (or lose) state and local offices derived electoral value from their national association.[11].

The nationalizing tendencies within American parties can be seen in (1) the impact of national forces on state voting patterns; (2) the expanded role played by national party organizations; and (3) the growth of national "presidential parties."

The impact of national trends on state voting patterns. State politics does not function in isolation from national political forces. Partisan loyalties are forged in the heat of presidential campaigns, and voters tend to support the same parties in both national and state elections. These national influences on voting make it difficult for third party movements to survive at the state level. For example, two of the strongest third parties of the pre-World War II era were the Progressives of Wisconsin and the Farmer-Labor Party in Minnesota. Each was forced to merge into one of the major parties by the 1950s because the pull of national partisan alignments within the state electorates was so strong that the parties faced inevitable defeat.

Even without the complications caused by third party movements, it has become increasingly difficult for a state to maintain a party alignment of voters that is significantly different from the way they align themselves in presidential elections. The strong nationalizing influences in American life make it burdensome for a state party and its candidates to adopt policy positions significantly at odds with the national image of the party. A case in point is the Democratic party of the South. The southern wing of the party has since the New Deal sought to project a more conservative image than the national Democratic party. However the disparity between the southern Democrats and the national party has been declining since the 1960s, as fewer and fewer Democrats elected to Congress from the South can be classified as conservatives ("Boll Weevils") and Democratic governors espouse the policies of the national party. The public's tendency to perceive a link between national Democratic policy and southern Democrats, plus the changing demography and economy of the region, made possible the Republican electoral advances in the presidential elections of 1952, 1956, and 1964. These electoral beachheads were followed by Republican victories in congressional, senatorial, and gubernatorial elections. By 1990, every state of the Old Confederacy had at least one Republican congressman (including a majority in the large Florida delegation); seven of twenty-two senators were Republican; and every state but Georgia and Mississippi had elected a Republican governor between 1966 and 1990. Clearly, the electoral alignments of the South were becoming increasingly similar to those of the rest of the country. The Democratic "solid South" no longer exists for presidential, senatorial, gubernatorial, and many congressional elections.

The impact of national electoral forces is particularly noticeable in midterm elections. Reformers have sought to insulate state elections from national tides of opinion by scheduling these elections for the midterm when the president is not on the ballot. Such timing of state elections, however, has not had the anticipated effect. In midterm elections, the consistent pattern of the president's party losing House seats carries over to gubernatorial elections. In all but two midterm elections between 1950 and 1990, the president's party has suffered a loss of governorships. The exceptions were 1962 when there was no net change; and 1986 when the Democrats were defending twenty-seven seats, an unusually large number, and the GOP was defending only nine. The average loss was five seats. Proportionally, gubernatorial elections appear more susceptible to national trends, which normally work against the president's party, than do elections for national offices such as senator and representative. (See Chapter 8 for a more detailed discussion of state elections at midterm.)

Expanded role of the national party. Both the Republican and Democratic national party organizations have achieved increased influence since the 1960s, but in distinctly different ways. Following the divisive Democratic Convention of 1968, the national Democratic party embarked upon major reforms of its delegate selection procedures. This reform effort took the form of an elaborate series of rules governing delegate selection procedures that the state parties were required to follow. Authority to enforce these rules was vested in the Democratic National Committee (DNC). Operating through its enforcement arm, the Compliance Review Commission, the DNC has forced state parties to comply with national party rules in delegate selection matters. Faced with this authority vested in the national party, the state parties engaged in a massive restructuring of their internal procedures to bring them into conformity with national party policy. The United States Supreme Court further strengthened the position of the national party vis-à-vis its state affiliates when it upheld the principle that national party rules take precedence over state statutes and party rules in matters pertaining to delegate selection.[12]

One of the most celebrated instances of the national party demonstrating its supremacy over state parties came in Wisconsin. National Democratic party rules banned presidential primaries in which persons other than those publicly professing a preference for the Democratic party participated (i.e., the DNC banned open primaries). Wisconsin has had an open presidential primary law since 1905, when it became the first state to enact a presidential primary statute. The open primary tradition of the state is a strong one, consistent with the state's independent and Progressive history. Despite the clear preference of the Wisconsin Democratic party and the Democratic controlled state legislature for maintaining the open primary tradition, the state was forced to abandon the open presidential primary and select 1984 delegates to the Democratic convention via a caucus system. The DNC has continued to assert its legal authority to enforce national party rules upon state parties even though it has now relented and permitted Wisconsin to operate an open presidential primary. Austin Ranney believes that the power conferred upon the Democratic national party organization by these rules and court decisions are so sweeping that the national party's legal authority is "at its highest peak since the 1820s."[13]

The national Republican party also gained increased influence, but in a vastly different manner than by enforcement of nationally mandated rules. By contrast, the Republicans sought to maintain the confederate character of their party by giving state parties wide latitude in matters of delegate selection and internal operation. National party power, however, has been extended through an extensive multi-million dollar program to provide financial and technical assistance to state and local party organizations and candidates. Through these activities, the Republican National Committee (RNC) has achieved an expanded role in the political system and created a relationship of interdependence between the national party and its state and local affiliates.[14] The DNC has followed the RNC example of expanding its services to its state affiliates so that it too is an increasingly significant participant in state elections.[15] Its more limited resources, however, have meant that it is not in a position to provide the same level of assistance as the RNC.

The national party role has also become increasingly more important in senatorial and congressional races. The senatorial and congressional campaign committees of both national parties have also become increasingly aggressive in recruiting candidates, helping to fund those candidates, and providing them with staff and technical assistance.[16]

The growth of the "presidential party." Prior to the 1970s, presidential nominations were dominated by the leaders of state and local party organizations—state and county party chairmen, governors, senators, and mayors. They exercised their influence through the caucus system of delegate selection—the process by which two thirds of the delegates were chosen. Few states used presidential primaries and it was possible to win presidential nominations without even entering a single primary. The reform era of the 1970s changed all this. As presidential nominations became dominated by presidential primaries, presidential aspirants sought the nomination through direct appeals to the primary electorate. Party leaders became less important and the personal organizations of the candidates and the media took on greater importance.

While most political scientists believe that these changes have weakened political parties, the development of candidate centered presidential politics has included one positive party development. A new "presidential party"—the national following of activists gathered about a candidate—has emerged.[17] These organizations are more ad hoc in character than the regular party structures, but they do have substantial continuity. For example, the core of support for the Reagan presidential nomination campaigns of 1976 and 1980 came from the Goldwater movement of 1964. Similarly, the liberals of the Stevenson era remained in place to work for Eugene McCarthy and three successive Kennedy candidacies. These networks of issue oriented activists can have an impact above and beyond presidential elections. They can also be used to mobilize support for the programs of presidents. President Reagan, for example, used the Reagan network of supporters to mobilize grassroots lobbying support for his legislative program in Congress with considerable success.

Broadly Based Electoral Support

In some countries, electoral alignments closely reflect social and economic cleavages—Catholics versus Protestants, rich versus poor, city versus the countryside, unions versus business, recent immigrants versus old line nativist stock. In such societies, parties have little meaning aside from the social groups they represent. When party allegiances closely reflect social and economic cleavages, political conflict is more likely be bitter and unrestrained, as the tragic histories of Northern Ireland and Lebanon demonstrate. American parties, however, are quite different. Partisan loyalties cut across social and economic divisions. The result is parties that are broadly based coalitions of diverse and even conflicting elements. Such parties, because of the diversity of their followings, have great difficulty maintaining unity among their elected officials and in enunciating clear statements of party policy. But coalition type parties do provide a means of reconciling and compromising conflicts within society.

Evidence of the coalition nature of American political parties is revealed in the voting behavior of various socioeconomic groups in recent elections (see Table 8–7, Chapter 8). Clearly, the core elements of electoral support for the two parties are quite different and reflect the New Deal realignment discussed in Chapter 2. Persons from labor union households, blacks, manual laborers, Catholics, and Jews are more likely to support the Democrats than the Republicans; while Protestants, professional and business people, and the college educated tend to be Republican voters. These differences in the core constituencies of the two parties should not obscure the fact that both parties draw significant levels of support from virtually every major socioeconomic group in American life. The only exception to this generalization is the black voters who have become overwhelmingly Democratic since 1964.

The extent to which electoral support for American parties cuts across various socioeconomic divisions can be seen by examining the voting patterns of groups commonly thought of as safely in the camp of one party or the other. Persons from labor union households are usually considered to be overwhelmingly pro-Democratic. However, the Republicans can normally expect to receive the votes of at least one third of these people, and in years such as 1984, when there was a national trend toward the GOP, the Republican percentage of the union vote can reach as high as 46 percent. Similarly, in 1980, 1984, and

1988, Republican presidential nominees carried the Catholic vote. Predominantly Republican groups also give substantial support to the Democrats. Between 1980 and 1988 the Democratic share of the professional and managerial vote averaged 36 percent.

Nonprogrammatic Parties

All parties have an interest in policy. Among the parties of Western nations, however, there is great diversity in the extent to which the parties are programmatic and the prime policy makers of the system. According to Leon D. Epstein, programmatic parties have policy positions that "are part of a settled long-range program to which the party is dedicated in definite enough terms to mark it off from rival parties."[18] The labor and socialist parties of Western Europe are examples of programmatic parties committed to policies that will maintain public ownership of some major economic enterprises. The British Conservative party, though less doctrinal than Labour, is also programmatic in the sense that it is committed to preserving capitalism against major opposition. Its pursuit of this goal was particularly aggressive under the leadership of Prime Minister Margaret Thatcher (1979–1990). American parties are quite different. Their policy positions tend to be ad hoc in character and adopted to meet immediate problems or electoral circumstances and not based upon long range programs to which the parties are committed. Neither the Democrats nor the Republicans have a clear image of the type of society they wish to foster. Neither party is committed to socialism or unfettered capitalism. Both have modified their positions frequently on such issues as government regulation of business, foreign policy, and the extent of government support for social welfare programs. It is even common for prominent leaders of seemingly divergent viewpoints to combine forces in the Congress. Thus liberal Democratic Senator Tom Harkin (Iowa) and conservative Republican Orin Hatch (Utah) were key advocates of the Americans with Disabilities Act of 1990, which prohibited discrimination against persons with disabilities; and liberal Edward Kennedy (D–Mass.) worked with conservative Dan Quayle (R–Ind.) to pass job training legislation.

The broad coalition nature of the parties' electoral support makes it extremely difficult for them to make ideological, consistent, and coherent policy appeals to the voters representing such a wide spectrum of interests and viewpoints. Even if the parties were inclined toward programmatic politics, their decentralized character would make enforcing party unity next to impossible.

The substantial policy diversity that exists *within* each party is

Table 3–5 Ideological Diversity within the Republican and Democratic Parties in the U.S. Senate, 100th Congress, 1st Session, 1990

Democratic Liberalism Scores

The senators' liberalism scores shown below are stated as percentiles and are based on their average scores on economic, social, and foreign policy issues. For example, a score of 90 on the liberalism scale means that the senator was more liberal than 90 percent of the total Senate membership.

Liberal Democrats	*Percentile*
Leahy (Vt.)	93.5
Metzenbaum (Ohio)	92.8
Sarbanes (Md.)	92.7
Adams (Wash.)	92.3
Simon (Ill.)	91.3
Mikulski (Md.)	91.3
Burdick (N. Dak.)	88.3
Riegle (Mich.)	87.7
Matsunaga (Hawaii)	87.2
Moynihan (N.Y.)	86.8
Middle of the Road Democrats	
Reid (Nev.)	65.8
Leiberman (Conn.)	63.8
Fowler (Ga.)	62.8
Graham (Fla.)	61.7
Dixon (Ill.)	55.0
Moderate to Conservative Democrats	
Johnson (La.)	51.7
Nunn (Ga.)	50.8
Ford (Ky.)	49.7
Bensten (Tex.)	48.8
Boren (Okla.)	48.2
Breaux (La.)	47.7
Exon (Nebr.)	43.0
Hollings (S.C.)	42.8
Shelby (Ala.)	33.0
Heflin (Ala.)	31.1

Republican Conservatism Scores

The senators' conservatism scores shown below are stated as percentiles and are based on averages of their scores on economic, social, and foreign policy issues. For example, a score of 90 on the conservatism scale means that the senator was more conservative than 90 percent of the total Senate membership.

Conservative Republicans	*Percentile*
Symms (Idaho)	94.8
Wallop (Wyo.)	94.8
Nickles (Okla.)	93.7
Armstrong (Colo.)	93.0
Garn (Utah)	92.2
McClure (Idaho)	92.2

Table 3–5 *(continued)*

Conservative Republicans	*Percentile*
Lott (Miss.)	89.8
Thurmond (S.C.)	89.5
Mack (Fla.)	88.8
McConnell (Ky.)	88.7
Gramm (Tex.)	88.7
Middle of the Road Republicans	
Kassebaum (Kans.)	67.8
Gorton (Wash.)	67.5
Danforth (Mo.)	66.3
Rudman (N.H.)	64.7
Stevens (Alaska)	61.3
D'Amato (N.Y.)	60.3
Moderate to Liberal Republicans	
Durenberger (Minn.)	56.7
Packwood (Oreg.)	55.0
Specter (Pa.)	53.3
Heinz (Pa.)	52.3
Cohen (Maine)	49.2
Chafee (R.I.)	47.8
Jeffords (Vt.)	45.8
Hatfield (Oreg.)	38.5

Source: Adapted from *National Journal*, Jan. 27, 1990, pp. 196–211.

shown in Table 3–5, which portrays the extent of liberalism among Democratic senators and the extent of conservatism among Republicans on scales developed by the *National Journal*.[19] The basic policy orientation of the two parties is divergent, with the most conservative senators found within the GOP and the most liberal senators residing in the Democratic party. Within that basic pattern, however, the two parties are far from monolithic in their approach to public policy issues. Liberals, moderates, and conservatives cohabit within both parties. Given this lack of internal policy agreement, the parties are rather weak instruments of governmental policy making. The various constituencies of party officeholders pull them in different directions. The problem of relying upon party loyalty to implement government policies is shown in Table 3–6, which presents data on congressional support for the president's legislative program. Presidents are not able to count upon the loyalty of their party's members in the Congress. The levels of defection can be significant. Even as effective a party leader as Ronald Reagan was able to achieve only a 68 percent average support score from House Republicans during his two terms in office.

Table 3–6 Support for President's Position on Roll Call Votes by Members of the President's Party in Congress, 1954–1990

			Average Percent of Members of President's Party Supporting his Position	
Years	**President**	**Party**	**Representatives**	**Senators**
1989–1990	Bush	Republican	66	76
1981–1988	Reagan	Republican	68	79
1977–1980	Carter	Democrat	69	69
1974–1976	Ford	Republican	72	65
1969–1974	Nixon	Republican	73	63
1964–1968	Johnson	Democrat	71	81
1961–1963	Kennedy	Democrat	75	83
1954–1960	Eisenhower	Republican	80	68

Sources: Norman J. Ornstein, Thomas E. Mann, and Michael J. Malbin. *Vital Statistics on Congress, 1989–1990* (Washington, D.C.: Congressional Quarterly, 1990), pp. 196–197; *Congressional Quarterly Weekly Report,* Dec. 22, 1990, p. 4208.

The internal unity problems of the congressional parties are further illustrated by Table 3–7, which lists Republican senators who voted in opposition to President Bush's position at least 30 percent of the time in 1990. This high level of opposition to the position taken by a fellow Republican in the White House occurred among both moderates like Mark Hatfield (Oreg.) and such arch conservatives as Jesse Helms (N.C.).

Given the lack of party unity that often exists in Congress, it is frequently necessary to form cross-party alliances to pass legislation. President Reagan, for example, relied upon Republicans and conservative/moderate (mainly southern) Democratic House members to pass major budget and tax policy changes in 1981. This alliance of Republican and southern Democrats has been dubbed the Conservative Coalition. It has been an important force in congressional deliberations. In congressional roll calls between 1965 and 1988, this coalition of a majority of the Republicans and a majority of the southern Democrats existed on average in 20 percent of the House and Senate roll calls. When this Conservative Coalition appeared in congressional voting, it gained legislative victory on 74 percent of the roll call votes.[20]

While it is clear that American parties are quite nonprogrammatic and contain substantial policy differences within their ranks, this line of argument must not be carried too far. It should not be inferred that there are no significant differences in the policy orientations of the Republican and Democratic parties. As noted in chapter

1, shifts in party control of the national government—as during the Reagan and Johnson administrations—have resulted in major changes in public policy. It does make a difference whether Republicans or Democrats are in control of Congress and the presidency. Table 3–5, while demonstrating the policy diversity within the parties, also points up the differences in policy orientation *between* the two parties. The Democratic members of Congress are substantially more liberal, on the whole, than are the Republicans.

Though much maligned by cynical reporters, party platforms also show substantial differences between the parties. Analyses of recent party platforms reveal significant differences between the two parties and consistent efforts by the officeholders of the two parties to implement those platforms. In 1988, there were sharp differences between the Democratic and Republican platforms on such issues as taxes, balanced budget amendments, abortion, defense, and foreign policy. The platform is important, Gerald Pomper has observed, because

> it summarizes, crystallizes, and presents to the voters the characteristics of the party coalition. . . . The stands taken in the platform clarify the parties' positions on . . . controversies and reveal the nature of their support and appeal.[21]

Not only are the policy positions of the parties' platforms and their elected officials different, but so are their rank and file voters and activist participants. Although both Republican and Democratic

Table 3–7 Republican Senators Voting Most Frequently in Opposition to the President's Position on Senate Roll Calls in 1990

Senator	Percent of Votes Opposed to President's Position
Cohen (Maine)	56
Hatfield (Ore.)	51
Jeffords (Vt.)	46
Heinz (Pa.)	43
Specter (Pa.)	42
Chafee (R.I.)	42
Packwood (Ore.)	41
Pressler (S.D.)	39
Durenberger (Minn.)	35
Helms (N.C.)	32
D'Amato (N.Y.)	31

Source: Congressional Quarterly Weekly Report, 48 (Dec. 22, 1990), p. 4209.

rank and file voters tend to be moderate in ideology, Democrats are more liberal than Republicans. The ideological orientations of party activists (national convention delegates) show even greater differences between the parties. Party activists in both parties tend to be much more extreme in ideological positions, with Republican activists considering themselves much more conservative than GOP rank and file voters, and Democratic activists ranked more liberal than Democratic voters. For example, in a *New York Times*/ CBS poll of 1988 national convention delegates and rank and file party voters, 39 percent of Democratic delegates considered themselves liberal, while only 25 percent of Democratic voters thought of themselves as liberals; among Republicans, 60 percent of the delegates said they were conservatives compared to 43 percent of the GOP voters.[22]

Party activists, who are highly influential in nomination contests and in providing campaign support, are an important force that pulls the two parties apart on policy. Candidates must have the support of these party workers. The fact that in the Republican party they are more conservative and in the Democratic party more liberal than the parties' rank and file voters means that there are strong pressures within the system maintaining differences in policy between the parties. But even with these differences, American parties remain relatively nonprogrammatic and pragmatic in their approach to issues.

Quasi-Public Institutions with Ambiguous Membership

In most democracies other than the United States, political parties are considered private organizations like the Elks, American Legion, Rotary, or American Bar Association. They make and enforce their own rules concerning qualifications for membership, organizational structure, and activities. There are few laws governing their internal decision making processes. Membership normally involves a process of application and approval. Members are then expected to assume obligations such as paying annual dues. In return, party members are permitted to take part in party activities such as the selection of candidates.

By contrast, American parties are quasi-public institutions that are heavily regulated by statute, especially state laws. The very existence of American parties is almost mandated by state statutes that legally define parties, prescribe their organizational structure, membership criteria, leadership selection methods, and the procedures for nominating candidates. By controlling who may vote in party primaries, for example, state statutes set the qualifications for membership in American parties. In closed primary states, voters are required to state publicly their party preference before being allowed to participate in the preferred party's primary. Party membership in these circumstances is essentially a matter of self-designation. In open primary states, it is possible to vote without ever publicly professing a preference for one party over another. The voters decide in the secrecy of the voting booth in which party's primary they will vote. Austin Ranney has observed that such statutory regulation of party membership has made the Republican and Democratic parties

> unique among the world's parties in that neither has effective control of its own legal membership and there is no formal distinction between member and supporter.[23]

In some jurisdictions, including Wisconsin and Minnesota, the party organizations do have modest sized dues-paying memberships. But these formal members have few privileges that are not extended to non-dues-paying supporters of the party. Both are entitled to participate in primary elections to select the party's nominees. Party membership in the United States is, therefore, an ambiguous phenomenon and largely a matter of self designation.

The extensive regulation of parties by state statutes in such matters as membership, organization, leadership selection, nominations, and campaign finance has meant that parties are not free to run their own internal affairs as they see fit. Not unlike public utilities that provide public services in a manner prescribed by law, parties also perform essential public functions under government regulations.[24] They are, therefore, quasi-public institutions with relatively open membership qualifications.

Weak Parties, But Substantial Partisan Influence

While sharing many features in common with the parties of other Western democracies, American political parties have a distinguishing set of characteristics—two partyism, decentralized power structures, broadly based electoral coalitions, moderate policy orientations, and quasi-public status. Taken as a whole, these are features which make for only moderate party influence on governmental policy-making. At the same time, party influences pervade the political system—in electoral politics and in organizing governmental institutions. This seeming contradiction of parties being relatively weak, decentralized, and lacking in unity, while at the same time being an important—but not necessarily dominant—influence on electoral and governmental politics is one of the distinguishing aspects of the American political system.

Suggestions for Further Reading

Eldersveld, Samuel J. *Political Parties in American Society*. New York: Basic Books, 1982.

Epstein, Leon D. *Political Parties in the American Mold*. Madison: University of Wisconsin Press, 1986.

_______. *Political Parties in Western Democracies*. New York, Praeger, 1967.

Herrnson, Paul S. *Party Campaigning in the 1980s*. Cambridge, Mass.: Harvard University Press, 1988.

Keefe, William J. *Parties, Politics, and Public Policy in America*. 5th ed. (Washington, D.C.: CQ Press, 1988).

Rosenstone, Steven J., Behr, Roy L., and Lazarus, Edward H. *Third Parties in America: Citizen Responses to Major Party Failure*. Princeton, N.J.: Princeton University Press, 1984.

Sorauf, Frank J., and Paul Allen Beck, *Party Politics in America*, 6th ed. Glenview, Ill.: Scott, Foresman/Little, Brown, 1988.

Notes

1. The index of competitiveness was developed by Austin Ranney, "Parties in State Politics," in Herbert Jacob and Kenneth Vines, eds., *Politics in the American States*, 3rd ed. (Boston: Little, Brown, 1976), pp. 59–61.
2. Samuel C. Patterson and Gregory A. Caldeira, "The Etiology of Partisan Competition," *American Political Science Review* 78 (September 1984): 691–707. See also John F. Bibby, Cornelius P. Cotter, James L. Gibson, and Robert J. Huckshorn, "Parties in State Politics," in Virginia Gray, Herbert Jacob, and Robert B. Albritton, eds., *Politics in the American States: A Comparative Analysis*, Fifth Edition (Glenview, Ill., Scott, Foresman/Little, Brown, 1990), pp. 92–93.
3. Norman Ornstein, Thomas E. Mann, and Michael J. Malbin, *Vital Statistics on Congress, 1989–1990* Washington, D.C.: CQ Press, 1990), p. 78.
4. David Ray and John Havick, "A Longitudinal Analysis of Party Competition in State Legislative Elections," *American Journal of Political Science* 25 (February 1981): 122–123.
5. Malcolm E. Jewell and David Breaux, "The Effect of Incumbency on State Legislative Elections," *Legislative Studies Quarterly*, 13 (November 1988), p. 501.
6. Leon D. Epstein, *Political Parties in Western Democracies* (New York: Praeger, 1967), p. 33.
7. Maurice Carroll, "For Once, a Primary Unites a Party," *The New York Times*, March 25, 1984, p. 6E.

8. For a fascinating account of how British parties can control parliamentary nominations to enforce party discipline, see Leon D. Epstein, "British M.P.s and Their Local Parties: The Suez Cases," *American Political Science Review* 54 (June 1960), pp. 627–639.
9. Gary Jacobson, *The Politics of Congressional Elections* (Boston: Little, Brown, 1983), p. 55.
10. David Mayhew, *Congress: The Electoral Connection* (New Haven: Yale University Press, 1974).
11. Leon D. Epstein, "Party Confederations and Political Nationalization," *Publius* 12 (Fall, 1982), p. 71.
12. *Democratic Party of the United States of America v. Bronson C. LaFollette*, 449 U.S. 897 (1981).
13. Austin Ranney, "The Political Parties: Reform and Decline," in Anthony King, ed., *The New American Political System* (Washington, D.C.: American Enterprise Institute, 1978), p. 230.
14. John F. Bibby, "Party Renewal in the National Republican Party," in Gerald Pomper, ed., *Party Renewal in America* (New York: Praeger, 1981), pp. 102–115.
15. Paul Taylor, "Chairman Took on Formidable Task," *Washington Post*, July 17, 1988, pp. A25, A30; Dom Bonafede, "Kirk at the DNC Helm," *National Journal*, March 22, 1986, pp. 703–707.
16. On the expanding role of the national parties, see Paul S. Herrnson, *Party Campaigning in the 1980s* (Cambridge; Harvard University Press, 1988).
17. John Kessel, *Presidential Campaign Practices* (Homewood, Ill.: Dorsey Press, 1980), Chapter 3; Leon D. Epstein, "Party Confederations and Political Nationalization," pp. 77–79.
18. Epstein, *Political Parties in Western Democracies*, p. 262.
19. Richard E. Cohen and William Schneider, "The More Things Change . . .," *National Journal*, Jan. 27, 1990, pp. 195–221.
20. *Congressional Quarterly, Weekly Report*, December 30, 1989, p. 3553.
21. Gerald M. Pomper and Susan S. Lederman, *Elections in America* (New York: Longman, 1980), p. 173.
22. *New York Times*, Aug. 14, 1988, p. 14Y.
23. Austin Ranney, *The Governing of Men*, 4th ed. (Hinsdale, Ill.: Dryden Press, 1975), p. 199.
24. Leon D. Epstein, *Political Parties in the American Mold* (Madison: University of Wisconsin Press, 1986), ch. 6.

CHAPTER 4

Party Organizations

Party organization in the United States conjures up a variety of strikingly different images, depending upon one's perspective.

> To a ward committeeman in Chicago, the party organization is a hierarchically run machine that dispenses jobs, social services, and help with the governmental bureaucracy in return for electoral support.
>
> To a Minnesota Democrat, the party organization is a group of issue oriented liberals who take party platforms seriously, seek to control primary election outcomes through party endorsements of candidates, and work as campaign volunteers.
>
> To a rural southern Democrat, the party organization is a group of courthouse politicians who perfunctorily fill formal positions, but whose activity is limited.
>
> To many state legislators, the party organization that really matters is the state legislative campaign committee chaired by the party leader in the legislature, which provides money and technical assistance to candidates.
>
> To the staff member of the Republican National Committee, the party organization is a large bureaucracy consisting of hundreds of paid professionals using the most sophisticated techniques and operating with a nonelection year budget in excess of $30 million.

As these illustrations suggest, party organization in the United States exists in an almost infinite variety of forms. The type of organization operating in any political jurisdiction depends upon a variety of factors: the level of government involved (e.g., local, state, or national), the type of governmental regulations under which it must operate, the extent of interparty competition that exists, the clientele or bases of party support, regional and local traditions, and the nature of the electorate. Generally, however, American political party organizations are *cadre* type rather than *mass membership* parties. Cadre parties are characterized by a small number of leaders and activists who maintain the organization, recruit candidates, seek to influence nominations, and campaign for the party's nominees. The party organization is active mainly during the election season and the party in the electorate has little impact on the organization or control over its elected officials. By contrast, a mass membership party is characterized by a large dues-paying membership that plays an active role in selecting party leadership and in developing policy positions. The mass membership party tends to be active the year around and exerts substantial influence over the party's governmental officeholders.

The American cadre type of party structure is based upon a complex set of interlocking national party rules, state and federal statutes, and state and local party rules. It is organized to carry out its primary task—the winning of elections. Party organization, therefore, is built around geographic election districts, starting with the basic unit of election administration, the precinct. Above that in ascending order are city/village/town committees, county or township committees, legislative district committees, congressional district committees, state central committees, and at the national level the national committee (see Figure 4–1). Although the party organization builds from the local precinct to the national committee, this structure should not be viewed as a hierarchy. As V. O. Key, Jr., observed, party organization "may be more accurately described as a system of layers of organization."[1] Each separate layer focuses its efforts on the elections within its particular jurisdiction. Thus county parties are concerned first with control of the courthouse offices, state committees with the governorship, and the national committees with control of the presidency. At the same time, each level of party organization normally needs to obtain the collaboration of other layers of organization to achieve their objectives. But as Key has noted, "that collaboration comes about, to the extent that it does come about, through a sense of common cause rather than by the exercise of command."[2]

This layered organizational structure which characterizes American parties is called *stratarchy*; "an organization with layers, or strata, of control rather than centralized leadership from the top down."[3] Each stratum has its own organization and functions to perform and each is quite autonomous within its own sphere, while maintaining contact with party units above and below. Samuel Eldersveld has noted that a special component of stratarchy is *reciprocal deference*. That is, between the layers of organization "there is a tolerance of autonomy, of each layer's status and its right to initiative, as well as tolerance of inertia."[4] This tolerance stems from the lack of effective sanctions which higher levels of the party may exercise over lower level units and the fact that each strata needs the assistance of the other for such activities as fund raising and mobilizing the vote. The spirit of tolerance for autonomy was captured by a midwestern state party chairman who commented about his relationship with the county party organizations in his state.

> At best we are a loose confederation. I have no jurisdiction over county chairmen. I'd have resented a state chairman telling me what to do when I was county chairman.

Supplementing and at times dominating the loosely structured system of formal party organization are thousands of organizations formed by individual candidates seeking both their party's nomina-

Figure 4–1: Layers of Party Organization in the United States

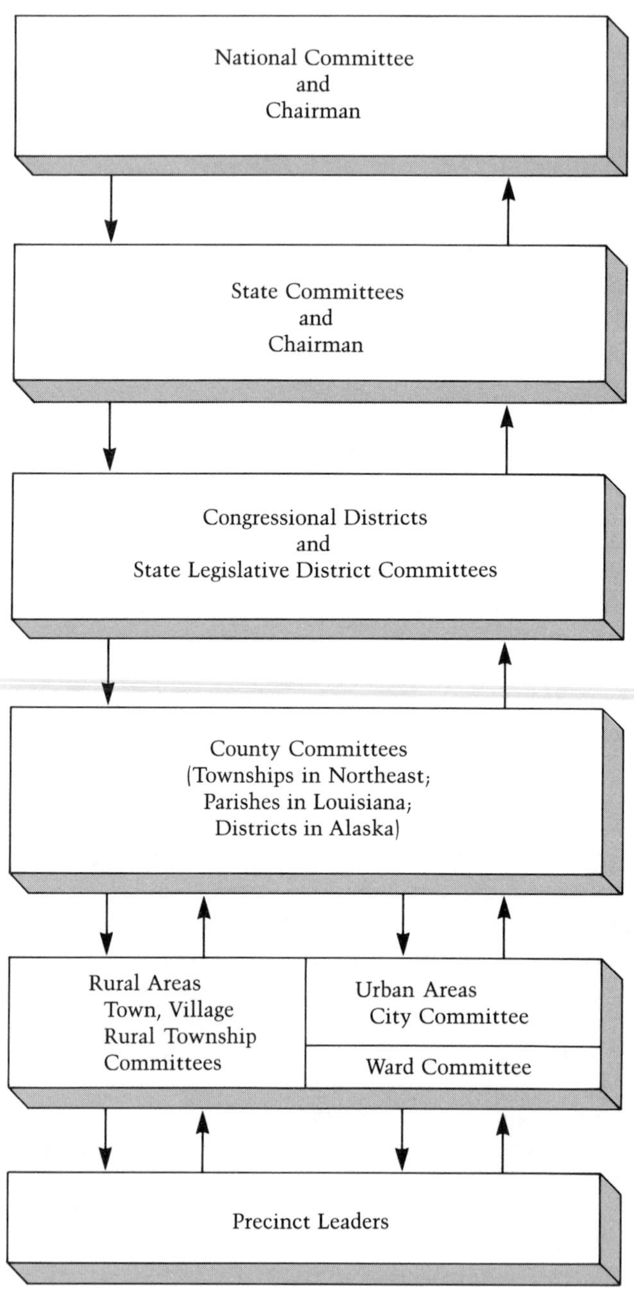

tion and general election victory. These personal candidate organizations are focused upon winning elections for a single individual for one office. Often, especially in the case of the organization presidential candidates, they command greater financial resources, professional staff, and volunteer workers than regular party organizations. They are, however, less permanent and less encompassing in their electioneering activities.[5]

The National Parties

The National Committees

Traditionally the national party committees have been cited as classic examples of the decentralized character of American parties. These bodies composed of delegates from the respective state parties were created in the mid-1800s to serve as the interim agents of the party conventions. Since their principal function during the post-Civil War era was managing the presidential campaign, the committees were active for only a few months during a four year period. It was not until the chairmanship of Will Hayes (1918–1921) that the Republican National Committee (RNC) established a year round headquarters with full time paid staff; and the Democratic National Committee (DNC) did not do so until 1928. The ad hoc character of national committee staffing extended well into this century, with the campaigns of 1928 and 1932 conducted largely by congressmen, senators, governors, and other party notables with the assistance of borrowed professionals.

Gradually the national committees became more institutionalized with expanded full time staff, elaborate division of labor, heightened professionalism, and larger budgets.[6] Thus since 1950, the size of the DNC staff has never dipped below forty persons, and the RNC has exceeded eighty. These personnel perform fund raising, public relations, voter mobilization, national convention management, campaign management and training, research, and policy development functions. Although the budgets and staff increased and the functions of the committees have been extended from an exclusive concern with presidential elections, the committees traditionally exercised little power. The leading study of the RNC and DNC published in 1964 characterized national committee politics as "politics without power."[7] While this was something of an exaggeration, the phrase did aptly capture the inability of the national committees to exert significant influence upon the behavior of state and local party leaders and elected officials. National committees are the most inclusive organization within the parties. Only the national committee represents the party organizations of the 50 states plus ex officio representation for important elected officials and organized interests. Active and aggressive leadership of the national committee is capable of generating publicity for the party, raising campaign funds, and initiating new activities at the national, state, and local levels. The national committee can be an effective catalyst for stimulating the party organization, even though its formal powers are limited. This has been especially true for the party which does not hold the White House. For the out-party, the national committee is normally a major arena of party activity and struggles for power.

National committee membership. For most of their history, the RNC and the DNC had roughly comparable bases for committee membership. Each state party organization selected a national committeeman and woman to serve on the committee. State party chairmen were made members of the RNC in the 1960s and the Democrats adopted this policy in the 1970s. The committees' membership reflected the confederate nature of the national parties with each state having equal representation and its national committee members serving essentially as party ambassadors from their states.

As a part of a series of major party reforms, the Democrats significantly changed the basis for representation on the DNC in 1974. These changes involved a major expansion of the size of the committee, representation for elected officials and various party auxiliaries, and equal representation of the sexes. The principle of state equality was abandoned in favor of a formula which took into account the population of the state and its record of support for Democratic candidates. The Republicans have not moved to change their representational scheme and maintain the principle of state equality and a confederate party structure. The composition of the DNC and RNC is described in Figure 4–2. The large number of people serving on the national committees, especially the DNC, has meant that deliberative action is almost impossible at national committee meetings. Instead, the locus for decision making is with the national chairman and the executive committees, which meet prior to national committee meetings. The full national committees normally ratify the recommendations of the chairman and executive committee.

The observer of DNC and RNC meetings is immediately struck by the fact that the differences between the two committees go well beyond their respective sizes. Differences in style of operation and party constituencies are apparent.[8] Republican National Committee meetings are extremely well organized and professionally staffed.

Figure 4–2: Composition of the Republican and Democratic National Committees

Republican National Committee	Number	Democratic National Committee	Number
1 national committeeman for each state, D.C., Guam, Puerto Rico, American Samoa, and Virgin Islands	55	National committee members—apportioned among the states on the same basis as national convention delegates (at least 2 per state)	224
1 national committee-woman for each state, D.C., and territory	55		
State chairman from each state, D.C., and territory	55	State party chair and next highest official of the opposite sex from each state, D.C., Puerto Rico, American Samoa, Guam, Virgin Islands, and Democrats abroad	112
(Republican rules provide ex officio membership on the RNC executive committee for representatives of the following: Republican Finance Committee, National Federation of Republican Women, Republican State Chairmen's Advisory Committee, Young Republican National Federation, College Republican National Committee, National Republican Heritage Groups Council, National Black Republican Council, Republican National Hispanic Assembly, National Conference of Republican Mayors, Republican Leadership of the House and Senate, National Conference of Republican County Officials, and the National Republican Legislators Association.)		Chair of Democratic Governors Association, plus 2 additional governors	3
		Two Democratic leaders from the House and Senate	4
		Chair of Democratic Mayors Conference, plus 2 additional mayors	3
		Chair of Democratic County Officials Conference, plus 2 additional officials	3
		Chair of Democratic State Legislative Leaders Associations, plus 2 legislators	3
		Chair of National Democratic Municipal Officials Conference, plus 2 officials	3
		President of Young Democrats and 2 members	3
		President of National Federation of Democratic Women, plus 2 members	3
		DNC officers	9
		Not more than 45 additional members	45
Total	165		415

There is an air of formality and relative order about the conduct of the meetings. DNC meetings are less well organized, informal, and have a rather ad hoc character. Orderliness prevails in RNC sessions, while confusion is common at DNC meetings. The major subunits of RNC gatherings are meetings of the state chairmen and regional associations. There are also informal meetings of various ideological and candidate factions. The DNC has all of these types of subunits and factions, but in addition has active caucuses for blacks, Hispanics, and women which have played a major role in DNC meetings. Through the efforts of Chairman Paul Kirk (1985–89), these caucuses lost official recognition in 1985. Kirk believed that the prominence of the caucuses was conveying an image of the party as a collection of special interests. The caucuses continue to exist on an informal basis, however, and the black, women's and Hispanic caucuses retained ex officio representation on the DNC Executive Committee.[9] There is no comparable specialized representational structure—formal or informal—within the RNC. This no doubt reflects the important role which organized groups have traditionally played within the Democratic coalition. By contrast, the Republicans, with their more homogeneous constituency and middle class orientation, have had a less extensive and explicit relationship with organized groups.

The national chairman. Because the national committees are unwieldy in size and meet but twice a year, the national chairman plays a key role in determining how the committee will operate. The chairman, in turn, relies upon the staff to implement his policies. Republican and Democratic rules now require that the chairman serve on a full time basis. This prevents elected officials like United States senators and representatives from becoming national chairmen. It has been traditional at national conventions for presidential nominees to designate a national chairman for the upcoming campaign. This designation is then ratified by the national committee. Similarly, incumbent presidents are accorded the power to designate who will serve as their party's chairman. Presidents and presidential nominees have frequently found themselves severely constrained in making chairmanship selections, especially when seeking to replace an incumbent chairman. National chairmen often develop powerful supporters and loyal constituencies within their parties. These forces can effectively resist even presidential nominee pressure to oust a chairman. This was apparent at the 1984 Democratic Convention when the nominee, Walter Mondale, found it necessary in the interest of party harmony to withdraw his plan to dump DNC Chairman Charles Manatt and replace him with former Carter Administration Budget Director, Bert Lance. Concerns for party unity also led the Reagan organization to keep Bill Brock (1977–81) on as RNC chairman for the 1980 campaign.

For the party which does not control the presidency—the out-party control of the national chairmanship is an important element in the struggle for intraparty ascendancy. Losing presidential campaigns inevitably breed struggles for control of the national committee. Often this takes the form of attempts to depose the national chairman. For example, Senator Barry Goldwater's choice for chairman, Dean Burch (1964–65), was forced to resign after the disastrous 1964 Republican campaign; and Jean Westwood (1972), Senator George McGovern's pick for DNC chair in 1972, found it necessary to relinquish her post after the Nixon landslide.

Traditionally there have been two basic styles of national committee leadership. One was the speaking chairman, who saw the role as one of acting as spokesperson on behalf of the party, generating publicity and criticizing the opposition. Senator Robert Dole (Kan.) during his tenure (1971–73) as RNC chairman played this role, using his often caustic wit to defend the Nixon Administration and attack the Democrats. Similarly, President Bush in 1990 selected Secretary of Agriculture Clayton Yeutter, a man with little campaign or day-to-day party management experience, to be RNC chairman because he wanted a spokesman for broad party themes.

The growing institutionalization of the national committees, with their enlarged staffs and budgets, and the rules requirement that chairmen serve on a full time basis, has meant that increasingly national chairmen have tended to emphasize not their role as party spokespersons, but their role as organizational leaders. The classic example of a chairman who emphasized building an effective party organization (a "nuts and bolts" chairman) was Ray C. Bliss (1965–69), who headed the RNC after the 1964 electoral disaster. Bliss seldom spoke in public and devoted his energies toward rebuilding the GOP organizations—especially in metropolitan areas.[10] Lee Atwater, President Bush's first RNC chairman (1989–90), built his reputation as a hard-nosed campaign strategist and organizer. Recent Democratic chairmen have also had party organizational backgrounds. Charles Manatt (1981–85), DNC chairman after the 1980 defeat of President Jimmy Carter, had been chairman of the party's finance committee; Paul Kirk (1985–89) had been party treasurer and a Kennedy campaign aide; and Ron Brown, who was elected chairman in 1989 (the first black to lead a national committee), previously served as chief counsel and deputy chairman of the DNC. Each of these Democratic chairmen has emphasized building a national organization that could compete with the more fully developed RNC organization.[11]

Frequently, a major responsibility of the national chairman is maintaining or restoring a sense of party unity. The national chairman, therefore, must give recognition to the various factions (congressional, gubernatorial, candidate, racial, ideological, and regional), mediate disputes, and negotiate compromises on party rules and policy positions. One of the most skilled mediators of intraparty squabbles was DNC chairman Robert Straus (1972–1977), who guided the party after the internal divisiveness of the McGovern nomination and defeat. Similarly, RNC Chairman Bill Brock successfully reunited the GOP after President Gerald Ford's loss in 1976 by getting various elements of the party to work together on organization-building initiatives.

The national chairmen who have been considered the most effective have generally been those leading the out-party. Out-party chairmen have considerable flexibility and can exert an independent influence on their party because they normally have personally campaigned for the post and developed a core of supporters among party leaders. DNC Chairman Ron Brown, for example, has even publicly challenged congressional Democrats to take a stand against President Bush's capital gains tax proposals and urged support for a controversial plan put forth by Senator Patrick Moynihan (N.Y.) to cut Social Security taxes. By contrast, the chairman of the party which controls the White House—the in-party—has little flexibility or independence. Such a chairman serves at the pleasure of the president and tends to be dominated by the political operatives at the White House. President Reagan's first RNC chairman, Richard Richards, spoke candidly about this phenomenon when he noted:

> It is a tough, tough job to be National Chairman when you have the White House . . . every clerk and secretary in the White House thinks that they can do your job better than you can, and they don't even know what you do.[12]

Some presidents have even sought to quite literally dismantle the national committee as a source of party leadership and have concentrated party leadership in the hands of White House staffers. The Nixon Administration tended to downplay the role of the RNC as a campaign mechanism to help all GOP candidates and instead emphasized the chairman's role as a publicist for the president. Another notable example of White House neglect of the national party machinery occurred during the Carter Administration, when the president and his staff through inattention to the party organization left the DNC unprepared for the 1978 midterm elections.[13] Then, as the 1980 elections approached, the Carter White House used the meager financial resources of the DNC to fund presidential polls by the president's pollster, Pat Caddell. The DNC and its chairman scarcely maintained any semblance of neutrality in the Carter-Kennedy battle for the nomination and because of their involvement in that campaign were not in a position to work with state parties to prepare them for the general election.[14]

Recent Republican presidents Reagan and Bush have been more supportive of their party's national committee. Reagan's political office in the White House worked closely with the RNC, especially in the area of fund raising; and President Bush, who served as RNC chairman (1973–1974), has actively campaigned for Republican candidates, enthusiastically engaged in party fund raising, and personally contacted Democratic officeholders who have switched to the GOP. More than any of his recent predecessors, he has downgraded the White House political office and relied upon the RNC to handle party related aspects of his administration. Even with the White House staff playing a less prominent role in RNC affairs, however, it has been clear that the RNC acts in accordance with presidential priorities, and White House Chief of Staff John Sununu acts as the enforcer.[15]

Committee activities. The actual work of the national committees is done by their professional staffs. While the titles of the administrative divisions of the RNC and DNC vary slightly, both have staff specialists for fund-raising, political operations (assistance to candidates and party organizations), public relations, voter mobilization, liaison with voter groups, convention and meeting arrangements, and administration. The in-party also has an office that handles liaison with the White House and the administration. There are, however, significant differences between the two national committees in terms of their financial resources, level of staffing, and activities. Because of its highly successful direct mail and large contributor programs, the RNC has a superior financial base. For example, in the 1987–1988 election cycle the RNC had net receipts of $91 million based upon 1.2 million contributions (average size $61.25). By contrast, the DNC had net receipts of $52 million. Since 1980, when it ended the campaign with a $1 million debt, the DNC has made substantial progress in narrowing its fund-raising gap with the GOP.

The RNC's financial resources have enabled it to engage in a wide range of activities designed to assist GOP candidates from presidential to city hall levels and to strengthen state and local party units. Among the RNC programs are the following[16]:

Finance: contributions to candidates in 1987–1988 ($326,480 to House candidates and $2 million to targeted state legislative races); and expenditures on behalf of candidates ($8.2 million for the Bush-Quayle campaign)

Voter list development: a national voter list with 100 million names in 1988 to assist in get-out-the-vote efforts

Voter contact programs: a $40 million dollar Victory '88 vote contact program operated in conjunction with state and local parties—generated 50 million pieces of mail and 30 million phone calls to potential voters

Technical services: candidate seminars, polls for candidates, precinct targeting data, assistance with election law compliance, preparation of print and electronic media advertising, redistricting, computer based programs

Institutional advertising: In 1988, $11.5 million was spent on advertising for the Republican party

Local elections: financial and technical assistance to candidates for state and local offices

Communications: specialized publications for state leaders, county leaders, and party rank and file; opposition research on Democratic opponents

Speakers bureau: prominent GOP leaders provided to 270 state and local party events in 1988

State and local party development: regional directors to assist state parties in developing stronger organizations; financial grants to state and county parties

Respected political observers believe that the RNC development of a well funded, sophisticated, and professional campaign operation has had a major impact on election outcomes. Larry Sabato, for example, noted that in 1982, despite adverse economic conditions, "the Republicans were able to buy a hedge against normal midterm losses by attracting strong candidates early, and by using their financial and technical tools . . . [in] marginal races where an additional technology-generated 2 percent of the vote could tip the election."[17]

Burdened by debts for most of the period between 1968 and the early 1980s, lacking the RNC's direct-mail fund-raising capability, and traditionally dependent upon organized labor for many electioneering activities, the DNC was not a major factor in Democratic campaigns. However, following its defeat in 1980, the national Democratic party began strengthening its organizational capacity by quite consciously following the example of the RNC.[18] As a result of these efforts, Republican party organizational advantages in campaigns have been reduced, and the DNC has become an increasingly important participant in campaigns. In the 1989 gubernatorial campaigns, for example, the DNC sent $100,000 and a dozen field organizers into New Jersey and $300,000 and thirty staffers to Virginia to assist the successful campaign of Douglas Wilder. In addition, the DNC developed a program of "coordinated campaigns" for the 1990 elections in which the DNC shared the costs of voter identification and get-out-the-vote efforts with state parties and candidates' organizations. This included a $2–3 million program in California, a key partisan battleground.[19]

Revitalization and party centralization. Until the 1970s, national committees had been viewed as so weak and lacking in political clout that a landmark study in 1964 characterized them as "political without power."[20] They were largely the creatures of and financed by state party organizations. Today, no informed observer would describe the national committees with a phrase like "politics without power." Indeed, the entire relationship between the national committees and their state affiliates has been transformed. The traditional emphasis on the decentralized character of American parties is still quite appropriate, but power and influence have increasingly been flowing toward the national party organizations. This process of power centralization has occurred through national party rules enforcement and providing funds and services to state parties.

The DNC has achieved increased power within the Democratic party through its role as the initiator and enforcer of national party rules governing delegate selection to the national convention. This power was gained through a series of party reform commissions starting with the McGovern-Fraser Commission appointed after the divisive 1968 convention. This commission and its successor commissions recommended to the DNC a detailed and codified set of party rules governing delegate selection.

The DNC has used this newfound legal authority to compel state Democratic parties to bring their delegate selection procedures into compliance with national party rules. Failure to comply can result in a state's national convention delegation not being seated at the convention. Faced with this type of national party sanction, the state parties embarked upon a massive restructuring of their internal procedures. This impressive display of national party legal authority over party organizations culminated in a series of United States Supreme Court decisions upholding the principle that national party rules take precedence over state party rules and state statutes in matters of delegate selection.[21]

Although these Supreme Court decisions confer similar authority upon the national Republican party, it has not followed the Democratic route of imposing restrictions on state parties. Indeed, it has followed a conscious policy of refraining from exercising this authority and has sought to maintain the confederate character of the party organization. This GOP reluctance to extend its rule enforcement authority should not be interpreted as indicative of an absence of centralizing tendencies within the party. Within the Republican party, centralization has moved forward since the 1960s through a series of RNC programs designed to strengthen state and local organizations and to assist federal, state, and local candidates. Through its extensive programs of assistance to party organizations and candidates, the RNC has significantly increased its influence over state parties because most are anxious to participate in RNC initiated programs and share in their benefits. As one midwestern Republican state chairman commented, "I figure that I should go along with the National Committee as much as possible because I want as much of their money as I can get." By using their ample financial resources to aid state parties and candidates, the RNC has achieved an enlarged role in the political process and increased the functional interdependence of the national and state Republican parties.[22]

As the DNC has followed the Republican example of extending significant amounts of aid to its state affiliates, it, too, has achieved enhanced influence. For example, in 1986 the DNC initiated a $1.2 million program of providing professional staff to sixteen target states. In exchange for this infusion of DNC resources, state Democratic parties were required to sign an agreement committing them to continue the DNC sponsored party-building programs and to cooperate with the DNC in presidential nominating procedures and national campaigns.[23] Like the RNC, the DNC operated multimillion dollar programs to elect state legislators in 1990.

Because of programs of support for state parties and candidates that were initiated on a large scale first by the RNC and recently on a more limited scale by the DNC, the direction in the flow of intraparty funds has been reversed. Since the 1980s, the flow in both parties has been from the national party to the state party organizations instead of in the more traditional state to national party direction. The national committees are, therefore, no longer dependent upon their state organizations and have achieved substantial autonomy as well as enhanced leverage over their state party organizations because of their superior financial and technical resources. A byproduct of this revolution in intraparty patterns of influence has been an unprecedented level of party integration.[24]

Party integration in federal election campaigns. Large-scale transfers of party funds from the national committees to state parties are encouraged by provisions of the Federal Election Campaign Act (FECA). The act imposes strict limits on the amount of money national parties can contribute or expend on behalf of candidates for the presidency and Congress. The FECA does, however, permit state and local parties to spend without limit on "party building" activities such as voter registration and get-out-the-vote drives. As a result, both national parties collect large sums of money (estimated in 1988 at $30–50 million) and then transfer them to state and local party organizations for support of "party building" activities that assist candidates for the presidency and Congress. In 1988, both the RNC and the DNC, while operating through state party organizations, directed major get-out-the-vote operations in key states. These programs resulted in the state parties playing a major role in the national campaigns and in their operating with unusually large campaign staffs. In California, for example, the Democratic Campaign '88 operation had a paid staff of 500 working out of twelve field offices; and in Ohio, the GOP state organization sent out 4 million pieces of mail and made 1.5 million telephone contacts with voters.[25]

Because the FECA encourages the national committees to channel money into the state parties in an effort to affect the outcome of federal elections, the national and state parties are becoming increasingly well integrated under national party leadership.

The Hill Committees

Increasingly important elements of the national party are the congressional and senatorial campaign committees. These organizations—whose official names are Democratic Congressional Campaign Committee (DCCC), National Republican Congressional Committee (NRCC), Democratic Senatorial Campaign Committee (DSCC), and the National Republican Senatorial Committee (NRSC)—are organizationally autonomous from the national committees and operate quite independently. The members of these Capitol Hill committees are members of the House and Senate. These committees concentrate their efforts on holding their parties' marginal seats and on assisting challengers with a reasonable chance of success against opposition party incumbents.

The Federal Election Campaign Act (FECA) imposes severe restrictions on the amount of money party committees can contribute to congressional and senatorial candidates ($5,000 per election to House candidates or $10,000 for the primary and general election combined, and $17,500 for senatorial candidates). Such restrictions mean that national party committees can have only minimal impact on congressional and senatorial campaigns through direct contributions to candidates. For example, in 1988 direct party contributions were only 4 percent of total House candidate receipts and 9 percent of total Senate candidate receipts.[26]

In addition to being authorized to make limited contributions directly to candidates, the party organizations are also permitted by the FECA to make expenditures in support of their parties' candidates. These monies are called *coordinated expenditures* and are normally used for polls, producing campaign advertising, and buying media time—major expenses that involve technical expertise. The limits on coordinated expenditures, unlike the direct contribution limits, are adjusted at each election for inflation. In 1990, the coordinated expenditure limit for party committees was $25,140 for each House race. The congressional campaign committees also engage in candidate recruitment and training. Because of its significantly superior financial resources, the NRCC has been a much more important source of campaign support for its candidates than has the DCCC, though in 1982–1990 the Democratic committee became substantially more active.

The senatorial campaign committees are in a position to play a substantially more prominent role than the congressional committees. The FECA permits coordinated expenditures on behalf of senatorial candidates at a level of two cents times the voting age population of the state, with the amount adjusted for inflation since 1974. Under this formula, the amount of money that a party committee may spend can in populous states be significant. For example, the coordinated expenditures limit in 1990 for a Senate race in Texas was $605,270. This limit can be doubled by a device first developed by the Republicans and approved by the courts. Through a technique called an agency agreement, the NRSC has assumed the spending quota of state party committees and thus been able to double the national party spending limit in selected states. As a result of this device, both the Republican and Democratic senatorial campaign committees have been able to pump large sums into key races. For example, in the 1988 California contest between Republican Senator Pete Wilson and Democrat Leo McCarthy, Wilson was supported by $1.88 million in coordinated expenditures, while $1.87 was spent to support his opponent.[27] In most states, the NRSC's greater financial resources enabled it to engage in a higher level of coordinated expenditures than was possible for the DSCC.

Representatives and senators receive the bulk of their campaign support from nonparty sources and remain intensely independent in their policy positions. However, the increasingly important role played by national party committees in recruiting, training, and financing candidates has caused some observers to speculate on the possibility of increased party unity in roll call voting in Congress as a result of the prominent role played in campaigns by the national party organization.

Unofficial Party Groups

Because American parties are coalitions of diverse and competing interests, elected officials, and factions, there is constant maneuvering for advantage within the parties. To achieve their heightened influence over presidential nominations and party policy, organizations periodically are formed by like-minded elected officials and party activists. Within the Democratic party, this tendency was exemplified by the creation in 1985 of the Democratic Leadership Conference (DLC). The DLC was formed by moderate and conservative Democrats, led by Senators Sam Nunn (Ga.) and Charles Robb (Va.) and Governor Bill Clinton (Ark.), who were concerned that domination of the party by liberals would doom its prospects for taking over the White House. To project a moderate policy image of the party, the DLC has created a Washington "think tank," the Progressive Policy Institute, issued policy proposals, and in 1991 held a national convention. The convention passed policy resolutions, provided a public forum for prominent moderate Democrats, and generated considerable controversy when it declined to give Jesse Jackson an invitation to address the convention. The DLC has also sought to develop a grassroots base of support by creating chapters in approximately half of the states. Because it is seeking to influence the future direction of the Democratic party, the DLC inevitably finds itself in competition with the DNC, and relations between them are tense. There is also competition within the party from an alternative unofficial Democratic organization—the liberal-oriented Coalition for Democratic Values.

Because they have won three successive presidential elections (1980, 1984, and 1988), the Republicans in recent years have spawned fewer unofficial party groups. However, the generally conservative tenor of Republican platforms and presidential nominees has resulted in the creation of the Republican Mainstream Committee, a network of moderate and pro-choice Republicans led by Representative Jim Leach (Iowa) and former RNC Chairperson Mary Louise Smith.

State Parties

State Parties and the Law

As noted in Chapter 3, there is a tendency in the United States for extensive statutory regulation of parties by the states. These regulations take an almost infinite variety of forms. Some states engage in only a minimal amount of regulation, while others have extensive party regulatory statutes. Most states regulate party membership (which voters may participate in primary elections), organizational structure, access to the general election ballot, methods of nomination, and campaign finance. There is, however, a great deal of variation among the states in the extent and manner of regulation.

Data collected by the Advisory Commission on Intergovernmental Relations demonstrates both the pervasiveness and the variety of state regulation: thirty-six states regulate the procedures used to select state committee members; thirty-two states stipulate the composition of state committees; twenty-two states specify when these committees must meet; twenty-seven states regulate their internal rules and procedures. Only five states (Alaska, Delaware, Hawaii, Kentucky, and North Carolina) do not specify some aspect of the parties' organizational structure, procedures and composition.[28]

A major factor in proliferation of party regulatory statutes in the United States was the spread of the direct primary as the principal nominating device for state and congressional office. Requiring parties to nominate candidates via the primary meant that the states had to enact laws which defined parties, fixed eligibility to vote in party primaries, regulated the conduct of primary elections, and assured general election ballot access to primary winners. Regulations such as these almost mandate the existence of political parties and have made state parties quasipublic agencies. Their legal position has much in common with that of public utilities. Both the party and the utilities perform essential public functions under the protection of the law.[29] Both, however, must submit to extensive statutory regulation.

While most state parties have a status similar to that of public utilities, the legal position of the parties is in the process of modification as a result of a series of recent Supreme Court decisions holding that political parties have First and Fourteenth Amendment rights of free political association. In the case of *Tashjian* v. *Connecticut* (1986), the Court ruled that Connecticut could not constitutionally ban voters who registered as independents from voting in the Republican primary after the state GOP had authorized both registered Republicans and independents to vote in a Republican primary.[30] The Court also struck down (*Eu, Secretary of State of California* v. *San*

Francisco County Democratic Central Committee, (1989) a series of unusually restrictive provisions in the California statutes that had banned party endorsements in primary elections, limited state chairmen's terms to two years, and required the state chairmanship to be rotated between residents of northern and southern regions of the state.[31] The *Eu* and *Tashjian* decisions caused some to speculate about the possibility of state parties being "privatized" and freed from being treated as quasi-state agencies. However, such an outcome is highly unlikely, as it would require the abandonment by the states of primary elections as the principal means of nominating partisan candidates for public office. Since the states are not likely to take such an unpopular step and the Supreme Court is not apt to require it, continued extensive state regulation of parties will probably continue into the foreseeable future. The *Tashjian* and *Eu* decisions make clear, however, that there are limits to the amount of party regulation the Court will tolerate.

The State Committees

In each of the states there is a Republican and Democratic state committee. The actual title varies, but a common title is Republican or Democratic State Central Committee. State statutes and party by-laws determine the basis for membership on the state committee. Committee members may be elected to represent counties, congressional districts, legislative districts, major municipalities, or party auxiliary groups like the Federation of Republican Women, Young Republicans, and Young Democrats. The size of these bodies varies from about 20 persons in Iowa to over 1000 in California. Because the size of state committees is frequently unwieldy and their meetings infrequent, many state parties rely heavily upon an executive committee to carry out state committee functions between meetings. The responsibilities of the state committees include overseeing the work of the state chairman and the headquarters staff, calling of state conventions, adoption of party policies, supervision of platform drafting, fund raising, and assisting candidates and local organizations.

The State Chairman

With state committees composed of part-time volunteers, the person responsible for directing the activities of the state party is the state chairman. Most state chairmen are elected by the state committee (73 percent) and 27 percent are chosen by state party conventions.

Approximately three quarters of the state chairmen are elected to two year terms with the balance chosen for four years. The turnover, however, is high, with tenure averaging less than three years. State parties, therefore, are plagued with lack of continuity in their leadership. Each chairman faces a unique set of circumstances, but the main duties of the chairman include supervising the headquarters staff, fund raising, candidate recruitment, serving as a party spokesperson, liaison with elected officials, and strengthening local organizations. In addition, state chairmen serve as members of their parties' national committees.

The Role of the Governor

The role of the state chairman is substantially influenced by whether the party holds the governorship or is the out-party. The most obvious means of exerting gubernatorial influence is through involvement in the selection of a party chairman. Most are involved in this process to some degree either through dissuading unwanted candidates or through actually designating the chairman. A survey of state chairmen in 1979–1980 revealed that approximately 50 percent of the Democratic chairmen attributed a determinative role in their selection to the governor, while 31 percent of the Republican chairmen said that the governor determined the selection of the chairman (see Table 4–1).[32]

As a result of such gubernatorial involvement in party affairs, the state chairman is frequently not an independent political leader within the party. Governor Mario Cuomo of New York, for example, has tight control over the state Democratic party, as do the governors in Maryland and New Jersey. Indeed, some governors view the state chairman as their surrogate within the party organizations and feel free to use the position to further their objectives. Thus, former Governor Brendon Byrne of New Jersey—where a governor has extensive patronage powers that are managed through the party machinery—chose as his first chairman a county chairman whose support was critical for his initial election. He next selected a potential opponent for the gubernatorial nomination as state chairman in an effort to coopt his rival.[33] It is an unusual governor who seeks actively to direct the state party and its headquarters operation. A majority of state chairmen do find it necessary, however, to consult the governor on key decisions. In selected instances the relationship between the state chairman and governor can create a strong government-party link. Some governors include their party chairman in cabinet and legislative leadership meetings and use the chairman as a legislative lob-

Table 4–1 Governor's Role in State Party Organization[a]

Governor's Involvement	Democrats	Republicans	Total %
Selection of State Chairman			
little or no role	17.6%	53.8%	33.3
acquiescence	29.4	15.4	23.3
instrumental role	52.9	30.8	43.3
Necessary to Have Governor's Support before Acting			
generally not	52.9	38.5	46.7
on some issues	47.1	61.5	53.3
General Characteristics of Governor's Relationship to Party			
none	5.9	15.4	10.0
advisory	94.1	46.2	73.3
responsive	0.0	38.5	16.7
Candidate Recruitment			
little or no involvement	47.1	0.0	26.7
advisory	35.3	84.6	56.7
responsive	17.6	15.4	16.7
Fund Raising			
little or none	29.4	0.0	16.7
responds to requests	58.8	61.5	60.0
active fund raiser	11.8	38.5	23.3

a. 27 sample states, 1979–80

Source: Cornelius P. Cotter, James L. Gibson, John F. Bibby, and Robert J. Huckshorn, *Party Organizations in American Politics* (New York, Praeger, 1984), p. 112. Copyright © 1984 by Praeger Publishers. Reprinted by permission of Greenwood Publishing Group, Inc.

byist. The following comment by a New England state chairman illustrates a close gubernatorial-state chairman tie:

> I'm the Governor's agent. My job is to work with him. If I look good—he looks good because I'm his man. I don't bother him with messy stuff. He expects me to handle it my way. I meet with the leaders on his behalf. I'm the liaison to the city and town leaders.

There are also governors who view the state party organization as a potential rival center of power and consciously seek to limit its role in state politics much like the way presidents have dismantled their national committees and concentrated political resources in their own offices and campaign committees. Wisconsin's Governor Patrick Lucey (1971–1977) followed this pattern in spite of his having been an unusually effective state party chairman prior to being elected governor. In a few instances, there has been open hostility between the governor and the state organization, as was the case during the tenures of Governor Jerry Brown in California, Edward King in Massachusetts, and Rudy Perpich in Minnesota.

The more common pattern is one in which the governor is consulted on key issues and assists the state party, when requested to do so, on such matters as fund raising and candidate recruitment. A midwestern Republican chairman in a state with a long tradition of professionalized leadership summarized such a cooperative relationship as follows:

> I don't go to his office and he doesn't come over here. . . . A lot of people think he isn't interested in the party. But that's just not true. He cares and he helps me. His attitude is "What can I do to help?"

The governor corroborated his chairman's comments by saying:

> [name of state chairman] doesn't want to be governor and I don't want to be party chairman.

State Party Organizational Strength

It has been commonplace to assert that state parties are organizationally weak or "virtually dead.[34] Recent scholarship, however, has revealed that state parties are organizationally stronger than they were in the 1960s.[35] Evidence of the increasingly institutionalized character of state parties with a capacity to provide services to both candidates and local organizations is reflected in the following indicators.

Permanent headquarters. By the 1980s most state parties maintained a permanent state headquarters in the state capital. However, in the 1950s and 1960s, it was not unusual to have the state organization being run out of the home or business office of the chairman. For example, seventeen of forty-one former state chairmen responding to a survey reported that during 1960–64 they operated without a headquarters. Today such practices have virtually been abandoned and a party headquarters is an institutionalized aspect of state parties. Increasingly, state headquarters house the computer-based technology of modern fund raising and campaigning. One of the most sophisticated is the Florida GOP, which operates a high-tech headquarters packed with computer hardware, telephone banks, and printing facilities, with a $6 million budget in 1988.[36]

Figure 4–3: Staffing Patterns of State Party Organizations

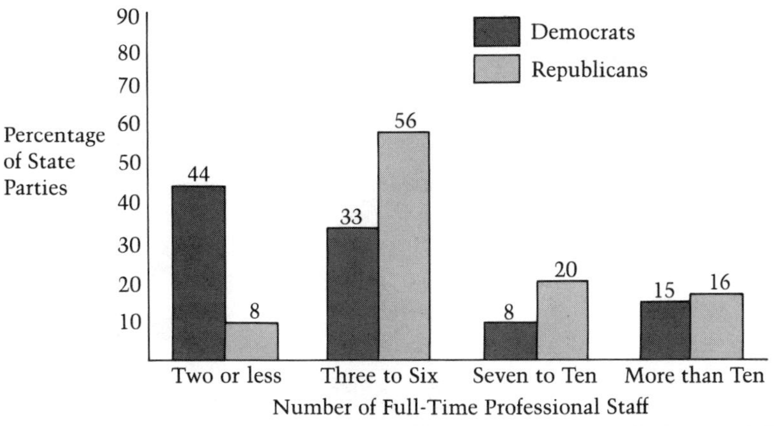

Source: ACIR survey of state party chairs

Professional leadership and staffing. The requirement of directing the work of a headquarters staff and utilizing the increasingly sophisticated methods used in fund raising, public relations, research, data analysis, voter contact, and campaigning have provided an impetus for professional leadership. Ad hoc and volunteer staffing arrangements that may have sufficed in an earlier era are no longer viable. Approximately 30 percent of state chairmen work on a full-time basis and practically all state parties have either a full-time chairman or an executive director. Headquarters staffs have also grown in size, and there is increased specialization among the staff personnel. In addition to the chairman, executive director, and clerical staff, a moderate-sized headquarters will usually include the following personnel: a political director (campaign and organizational-building specialist), finance director, comptroller, communications director, and field operations supervisor. (For data on state party staffing, see Figure 4–3.)

Budgets. In a classic study of political money, Alexander Heard found in the 1950s that two thirds of the Republican state committees had a centralized fund-raising structure, but that only fifteen employed full time finance personnel. He also discovered that most Democratic state organizations had failed to develop regularized fund-raising systems and instead relied upon ad hoc techniques for raising funds.[37] The average annual state party budget during 1960–1964 was approximately $188,000. By the 1980s, supporting a profes-

Figure 4–4: Annual Budgets of State Political Parties

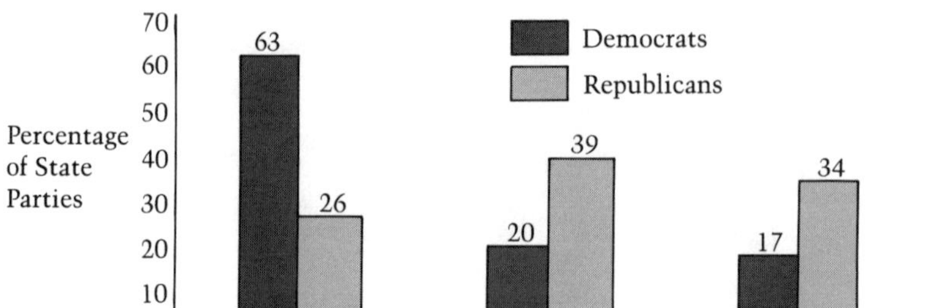

Source: ACIR survey of state party chairs.

sionalized headquarters staff that utilized the latest campaign techniques required larger budgets, a regular flow of revenues, and systematic fund raising. A 1984 survey of state parties by the Advisory Committee on Intergovernmental Relations (ACIR) revealed that the average state party budget was $558,000 (Republican average: $795,000; Democratic average: $260,000), and that 38 percent have annual budgets in excess of $500,000. (See Figure 4–4.) As these figures suggest, the Republicans are much more likely than the Democrats to have regularized their fund-raising methods and to employ full time finance directors. Most have also developed direct mail and telephone solicitation programs (sustaining memberships) for small and medium-sized givers to complement large-giver programs. Though they still lag behind the Republicans, the Democrats have made progress in direct mail and regularized large-giver programs.[38] The Democrats, however, tend to rely more heavily on dinners, a small number of large givers, the Dollars for Democrats program of the Association of Democratic State Chairs, and such techniques as bingo games.

Since the ACIR survey in the mid-1980s, there have been substantial increases in many state party budgets as a result of national party committees transferring to them large sums of money. These funds were used for so-called "party-building" programs designed to strengthen the campaigns of candidates for the presidency and Congress. For example, the Illinois Democratic party had only $350,000 to help its candidates in 1986. However, in 1988, it received over $2 million from the DNC which enabled it to run its first voter registration drive in 25 years and crank up a large scale direct-mail program.[39]

Party programs. The development of permanent headquarters, professional staff, and financial resources makes it possible for state parties to implement programs directed toward assisting candidates and building stronger statewide organizations. The assistance given to candidates includes financial contributions, which are most likely to go to gubernatorial and state legislative candidates rather than to people running for the U.S. House and Senate. Although both Republican and Democratic state parties are active in support of candidates, the greater resources of the GOP parties have enabled them, on average, to provide a broader and more sophisticated array of services than their Democratic counterparts. Virtually all state parties now conduct campaign seminars for their candidates and campaign managers and it has become routine to provide assistance with advertising, polling, research, election law compliance, and voter mobilization. State parties also engage in candidate recruitment. As statewide elections for governor and U.S. senator have become more competitive between the parties, it has become less necessary for the parties to seek out candidates for these offices. As a result, there is increased emphasis within state parties on recruiting candidates for state legislative posts.

A trend toward organizationally stronger parties. When Cotter, Gibson, Bibby, and Huckshorn combined the above indicators of party strength into an index of state party organizational strength, they found that both Republican and Democratic state parties were organizationally stronger than they had been in the early 1960s (Table 4–2).[40] This strengthening of state party organizations was partic-

Table 4–2 Trends in State Party Organizational Strength

Organizational Strength Score	1960–1964	1965–1969	1970–1974	1975–1980
Democrats				
Mean score[a]	−.87	.00	−.06	−.48
N	15	21	24	60
Republicans				
Mean Score[a]	−.47	.19	.33	.41
N	17	30	44	77

Party organizational strength scores for state parties are based on a theoretical scale of −3.00 (weakest) to +3.00 (strongest).

a. Range −2.6–+2.0. Overall mean: 0; standard deviation 0.996.

Source: Adapted from James L. Gibson, Cornelius P. Cotter, John F. Bibby, and Robert J. Huckshorn, "Assessing Party Organizational Strength," *American Journal of Political Science* 27 (May 1983): 211.

Table 4–3 Organization Strength of Republican and Democratic State Parties, 1975–1980

Level of Party Organizational Strength	Number of State Parties					
	Republican		Democratic		Total	
	N	Percent	N	Percent	N	Percent
Strong	8	18	2	4	10	11
Moderately strong	27	60	11	24	38	42
Moderately weak	9	20	26	58	35	39
Weak	1	2	6	13	7	8
Total	45	100	45	99[b]	90[a]	100

a. Data available for 90 of 100 state parties.

b. Total does not sum to 100% due to rounding.

Source: From *Politics in the American States: A Comparative Analysis*, 4th ed., edited by Virginia Gray et al. Copyright © 1983 by Virginia Gray, Herbert Jacob, and Kenneth Vines. Reprinted by permission of Harper Collins Publishers.

ularly noteworthy because it occurred during a period when many observers believed that parties were in a state of general decline as fewer voters were guided by partisanship in making their election day choices, as PACs became more involved in campaign finance, candidates became more independent of their parties, and campaign/media consultants took on larger responsibilities for campaigns. The organizational strength of state parties and their role in election campaigns is likely to grow, because the national party organizations are channeling huge sums of money and technical resources into their state affiliates and working through them to assist candidates for federal office. The emergence of state parties with enhanced levels of organizational strength is testimony to the remarkable durability and adaptability of these institutions in the face of major changes in the electoral system, including challengers for political influence.

Party differences—Stronger Republican organizations. Although state parties are organizationally stronger than they were in the early 1960s, there are important interparty differences. As is true at the national level, Republican state organizations tend to be stronger than those of the Democrats. Table 4–3 shows these party differences in organizational strength: 73 percent of the parties in 1975–1980 in the strong or moderately strong category are Republican, while 76 percent of the weak to moderately weak parties are Democratic. This Republican advantage exists in all regions, even the traditionally Democratic South.

The existence of stronger Republican party organizations at the national and state levels reveals one of the differences between Republican and Democratic politics. For the Republicans, the party organization tends to be an important resource in the electoral process. There are indications that beginning in the late 1980s Democratic state parties became increasingly significant sources of campaign resources for candidates.[41] Even so, Democratic state party organizations are generally a much less significant campaign resource than their Republican counterparts. The difference in the organizational strength between the two parties probably is tied to their relationship to nonparty organizations which seek to influence elections.

Table 4–4—reporting the results of a survey of state party chairmen that sought to determine the relationship of state parties to nonparty groups—shows striking differences between the parties. Democratic chairmen were significantly more likely to report that they received support from nonparty organizations than were the Republicans. None of the Democratic leaders claimed that they received no nonparty support for the party, while one third of the Republicans made this assertion. These data suggest that the Republicans need strong party structures because of the low levels of nonparty support which is available to them. By contrast, the Democrats have less need for strong organizations, since they can at least partially compensate for their relative organizational weakness with the assistance that they receive from nonparty organizations.

As expected, there are sharp differences in the types of groups from whom the state chairmen reported receiving assistance. Almost 90 percent of the Democratic leaders said that they obtained support

Table 4–4 Nonparty Group Support for State Parties, 1979–1980

	Percent of State Chairmen Mentioning Group Support to Party	
Type of Organization	**Democrats**	**Republicans**
Business, Farm or Professional	11%	48%
Social Action (black, Hispanic, feminist)	37	7
Labor Union	89	4
Teachers	41	4
Party Auxiliary Organization	0	15
No Nonparty Organization Mentioned	0	33

Data are based upon interviews with 27 Republican and 26 Democratic state chairmen from 27 sample states in 1979–80.

Source: Cornelius P. Cotter, James L. Gibson, John F. Bibby, and Robert J. Huckshorn, *Party Organizations in American Politics* (New York: Praeger, 1984), p. 138.

from labor unions and 41 percent reported help from teachers' groups. Labor and teacher support was noticeably lacking in the lists of groups supportive of Republicans. Business groups were the most common source of GOP support, but the prevalence of business help for the Republicans was not as great as that of union sustenance for the Democrats. Nearly 50 percent of the Republican chairmen listed business groups as sources of support, while 11 percent of the Democratic leaders did so. The social action groups (blacks, Hispanics, feminists) were also more likely to support the Democrats. In terms of the types of support received, financial assistance is the most common type of aid. Again, however, there are significant party differences. Democrats are much more likely to receive assistance in getting out the vote and in the provision of volunteer workers than are the Republicans. When the GOP receives nonparty group assistance, it is normally with fund raising (see Table 4–5).

State Legislative Campaign Committees

Increasingly important elements of the state party organizational structure are the legislative campaign committees. These organizations are fashioned after the congressional and senatorial campaign committees at the national level. They are composed of incumbent legislators who raise funds and hire staff to assist their parties' legislative candidates. In some states these committees have become substantially more important than the regular state party as a source of support for legislative candidates. In Ohio, for example,

Table 4–5 Assistance to State Parties by Nonparty Groups: Instances of State Chairmen Mentioning Receipt of Support

	Democrats		Republicans	
Type of Activity	**N**	**Percent**	**N**	**Percent**
Fund-raising	40	31	26	51
Get-out-the-vote	37	28	5	10
Research	13	10	7	14
Volunteers	39	30	12	24
Endorsements	1	1	1	1
Total	130	100	51	100

Multiple responses counted. N = 27 sample state Republican chairs; 26 sample state Democratic chairs, 1979–1980.

Source: Cornelius P. Cotter, James L. Gibson, John F. Bibby, and Robert J. Huckshorn, *Party Organizations in American Politics* (New York: Praeger, 1984), p. 141.

the GOP state senate campaign organization, which in 1988 spent $3.6 million, is credited with orchestrating Republican control of the chamber.[42]

In addition to the legislative campaign committees, legislative leaders in some states have developed personal fund-raising mechanisms that they use to channel funds to their party's legislative nominees. The most notable example of a legislative leader assuming a major responsibility for legislative campaigns has been the speaker of the California Assembly, Willie Brown. In 1987–1988 he spent $2.7 million.[43] Such activities of legislative leaders, of course, strengthen their support among party colleagues in the legislature and make their reelection to leadership posts more likely.[44]

County and Local Parties

The most frequently cited type of local party organization is the big city machine best exemplified by the Cook County Democratic organization during the era of Mayor Richard J. Daley.[45] This organization was run as a hierarchy by the mayor who worked through his ward leaders and their precinct captains. The organization was sustained by patronage. Ten thousand city jobs were distributed on the basis of patronage. A single ward leader could have as many as 500 jobs to distribute to his followers. The organization's ward and precinct leaders also served as ombudsmen, assisting residents with their problems in dealing with governmental agencies. Loyalty to the organization and its candidates was achieved through the material or tangible rewards that the organization provided.[46]

This style of politics is not unique to Chicago or the Democratic party. Traditional organizations still function in such places as Philadelphia and Albany. One of the most professional and effective party organizations is the Republican party of Nassau County (Long Island), New York. Most members of the party executive committee hold patronage positions in county government; the county chairman is a full-time salaried leader; the party raises more money than the GOP state committee, owns a three story headquarters building, operates its own printing plant and artist's studio, and makes extensive use of pollsters.[47] Indeed, this organization has emerged as the strongest force in New York state Republican politics.

There are also well funded and professionalized local parties based upon volunteers rather than patronage. One of the most effective is the GOP of Santa Clara County, California. It has a paid executive director, a headquarters, complete with computerized volunteer and voter lists, and a sophisticated targeting system for reaching voters.[48]

Such organizations, however, are not the norm of American local politics. Most county parties are not bureaucratic or hierarchically run organizations. Their leaders and workers are part-time volunteers; there is no permanent headquarters or paid staff; activity is not a year round phenomenon, but rather cyclical, and concentrated around campaign season. Although it has been commonplace to assert that parties are in a state of decline and may even be dying, case studies of local parties and national surveys reveal substantial party activity at the county level. For example, in Middlesex County, New Jersey, two thirds of the district leaders reported that they worked in excess of six hours a week for the party during campaigns and over 40 percent indicated that they often engaged in voter registration, telephone canvassing, and door-to-door canvassing.[49]

Table 4–6 reports the findings of a nationwide survey of county leaders. It demonstrates that the lack of a bureaucratic structure does not necessarily imply a low level of party activity. It should also be noted that there are virtually no important party differences in the level of campaign activity engaged in by Republican and Democratic county parties. While Republican organizations are stronger at the national and state levels, they do not appear to be more active at the county level. Comparisons between the results of surveys of county party activity in the mid-1960s and 1980s do not support the thesis that parties are in decline. Rather, the direction of change is toward more active county parties.[50] Such national level studies, however, tend to obscure the tremendous diversity that exists among county and precinct party organizations. The range runs from counties

Table 4–6 Campaign Activities of County Level Party Organizations, 1984

	Percentage of Parties Reporting Activity	
Activity	**Democrats**	**Republicans**
Coordinated county level campaigns	65	70
Sent mailings to voters	66	75
Conducted registration drives	79	78
Organized telephone campaigns	76	78
Newspaper advertising	61	66
Distributed posters or lawn signs	81	83
Door-to-door canvassing	67	69
Utilized public opinion surveys	22	26
Purchased billboard space	10	10

Source: James L. Gibson, John P. Frendreis, and Laura Vertz, "Party Dynamics in the 1980s: Change in County Party Organizational Strength, 1980–1984," *American Journal of Political Science* 33 (Feb. 1989): 75.

which literally have no party organization to those with paid staff, permanent headquarters, and computer facilities. Even parties with full organizational structures, however, may be characterized by organizational slack. For example, Eldersveld's study of Wayne County (Detroit) led him to conclude there is a "tendency for local activists to perform at a minimal level of efficiency, without too much system, in a rather hit-and-miss mode of operation."[51] He found, for example, that canvassing of voters and election day work frequently went undone. Although Eldersveld's studies do not support the proposition that parties are becoming weaker, they do point up the tremendous diversity among local party organizations and the difficulty these organizations have in realizing their full potential.

A force that may cause county parties to become more effective is the increased interest in local parties being demonstrated by the national party committees. As their fund-raising capacity has increased, the Republicans, in particular, have been providing financial and technical assistance to county parties.

Does Party Organization Make a Difference?

A key question concerning party organizations is whether or not they can make a difference in determining election outcomes. Journalistic reports and scholarly case studies provide evidence that the party organization can have a critical impact. For example, the California Republican party allocated $350,000 to fund a special absentee voter project in 1982. Absentee ballot packets were sent to 2.6 million voters by the party. When voters returned their absentee ballot applications, the party organization helped insure their delivery to state election officials. This effort helped the Republican gubernatorial nominee, George Deukmejian, overcome a 19,886 vote deficit in election day ballots. He received 302,343 absentee votes—113,231 more than his opponent.[52] Informed observers also believe that the extensive efforts of national-level Republican committees in 1982, a time of severe economic recession, prevented the party from losing in excess of fifty House seats and enabled it to retain control of the Senate.[53] Despite such indications of the impact of party organization, it has been difficult to generalize about the consequences of party organizational strength because of the isolated and local character of most studies. Recently, however, political scientists have begun to conduct national (cross-sectional) analyses of the impact of party organizational strength. These studies have demonstrated that party organizations do influence election outcomes. Cotter and his associates, in a study of thirty-two nonsouthern states during the last half of the 1970s, found that there was a strong correlation (+.46) between the ability of parties to increase their share of the vote and their holding an organizational strength advantage over the opposition party.[54] Similarly, it has been demonstrated that party organizational strength at the county level encourages interparty competition,[55] recruiting a full slate of local candidates (which contributes to higher vote totals for candidates at higher levels),[56] and increased voter turnout.[57]

The relationship between electoral success and party organizational strength is exceedingly complex. In some states, organizational strength is essential to maintain electoral ascendency against an organized opposition party, as has been true for the Michigan Democrats, Minnesota Democrats, and the Indiana Republicans. But in other states where a party has had a long history of electoral dominance—such as the Massachusetts Democrats or Mississippi Democrats—there is often little incentive to build an effective organization. By contrast, the minority party does have an incentive to build an effective organization in order to achieve a competitive status. This latter strategy has certainly characterized the modern day Republican state parties in the South, where the GOP is substantially better organized than the Democratic party. After a long period of organization building in the South, the Republicans achieved significant electoral victories, especially in presidential, senatorial, and congressional elections during the 1970s and 1980s. The case of the Republicans in the South indicates that the impact of party organizational strength may not be its effect on the elections in any given year. Rather, its role may be in providing the infrastructure for candidates and activists to continue to compete in the face of short term defeats until conditions are favorable for the minority party. This pattern is illustrated by the Florida Republicans, which had long been the state's minority party in spite of increasing organizational strength. In 1986, however, it was able to take advantage of favorable circumstances and win the governorship. It followed up that victory by electing a U.S. senator, gaining a majority in the state's House delegation, and winning additional state legislative seats in 1988. The implications of state and local party organizational strength extend beyond state elections. Presidential elections can also be affected.

The Party Activists

Party organizations require officers, workers, and volunteers—political activists willing to give their time, talents, and treasure for the success of the party and its candidates. There are a variety of incentives that cause people to become actively involved in political activity.

Incentives to Participate

Patronage and preferments. Some become involved in politics because of direct material rewards. Patronage, awarding government jobs to the supporters of the winning candidate, has a long tradition in American politics dating at least to the era of Jacksonian democracy. Andrew Jackson believed that "to the victor belongs the spoils" and that the average citizen was qualified to hold appointive governmental office. Patronage appointees traditionally have been a major source of party workers. Civil service laws (appointment on the basis of merit, using competitive examinations), reform movements, and court decisions have reduced the number of patronage positions available for the parties to fill. Patronage, however, remains a significant basis for recruiting political workers. In Chicago, it is estimated that 10,000 of the city's 41,000 jobs are at the disposal of the mayor, ward committeemen, aldermen, and the heads of such governmental bodies as the Park District and Sanitary District.[58] Patronage can also be extensive in state government. The governor of New Jersey, for example, in addition to appointing major department heads to the governor's cabinet, also appoints, with the consent of the state Senate, all state judges, state and county prosecutors, tax officials, and many salaried and nonsalaried commission, board, and authority members. Until 1986 in Indiana, the party winning the governorship provided lucrative employment to trusted party leaders by awarding them auto license franchises. Under this system, the commissioner of motor vehicles, who was appointed by the governor, awarded auto license franchises to 184 branch managers, most of whom were party county chairmen. Franchise holders were authorized to sell auto and drivers licenses to Indiana residents. The state supplied these franchise holders with drivers and auto license forms and determined the fee for each. The franchise holders could also charge a fee for the services they provided. The manager retained all the profits after deducting expenses, including salaries for himself and his staff. The license franchise system provided an estimated 1,300 jobs for the party faithful. Of course, franchise holders were expected to make contributions to the state and county party organization. Approximately $500,000 (some estimates run in excess of $1 million) of the $2.3 million 1984 budget of the Indiana Republican party was raised in this manner.[59] Despite the size of the federal bureaucracy, the patronage available to the president is quite limited—about 5000 jobs of which approximately 2000 are in policy-making positions.

Not all patronage is dispensed by governmental executives. Members of Congress, state legislators, and city council members normally hire their staffs on the basis of political loyalty. These officials may also exert heavy influence on the appointments made by the executive branch. Some executive appointments are actually controlled by legislators, as in the case of senatorial influence over the appointment of federal judges, marshals, and attorneys. In spite of its organization building potential, patronage poses problems for party leaders. The number of positions available for distribution on the basis of patronage has been declining, due to the spread of the civil service system. In addition, the federal courts have limited the ability of elected officials to dismiss government employees who fail tests of party loyalty, such as the requirement that they work for candidates. A further problem for the parties in making patronage appointments is that governmental jobs may carry with them qualifications that deserving party workers cannot meet—such as legal training or skill in operating sophisticated equipment. In addition, most available patronage positions have little appeal to the educated, middle class persons that the parties are seeking to enlist in their ranks. Traditionally, patronage has been most appealing to the disadvantaged. A final problem for party leaders is the fact that elected officials may seek to use their appointing power to build a personal following rather than to strengthen the more inclusive party organization.[60]

Patronage jobs are not the only material incentive available to political leaders. Governmental officials can give preferential treatment to persons they are seeking to recruit into party service or reward for past service. Preference in the awarding of government contracts has been a traditional way of rewarding business leaders who supported the winning candidate. The importance of government contracts to the construction industry has been a major reason for the industry's involvement in campaign finance. Preference can also be extended through administrative decisions and leniency in the enforcement of governmental regulations. Heavily regulated businesses (e.g., liquor, transportation) are normally involved in politics in a major way.

Elected office. Holding major elected office carries with it prestige and power not found in most patronage positions. Party involvement can provide a stepping-stone to elective office. There are today few party organizations that are so strong that they can guarantee a party nomination to a preferred candidate. At the same time, party involvement and the support derived from party workers can be an essential ingredient in securing the nomination to a key office. The allure of elected office appears to be quite strong among state party chairmen. Huckshorn discovered that between 1964–1980, twelve former state party chairmen were elected to governorships and that another twenty lost either in the primary or general elections. Seven former state chairmen were elected to the U.S. Senate and twenty-five ran but were defeated.[61]

Because parties play a significant role in nominations and have control over important campaign resources, incumbent officeholders frequently play an active part in party affairs. This involvement helps them hold their existing positions secure and provides a basis for moving up the ladder of elected positions.

Social benefits. Not all the benefits of political participation are based upon material rewards. There are also solidarity or social benefits. The friendships and camaraderie of the organization can be a strong force that binds individuals to the party. Similarly, the sense of recognition that an individual feels when a prominent elected official calls one by name in a crowd, personally acknowledges letters or phone calls, or extends an invitation to a social gathering can cause individuals to engage in political work on a continuing basis.

The studies of Detroit and Los Angeles area party activists by Eldersveld found that such benefits as "personal friendship with candidate," "desire for social contacts and friendships," "fun and excitement of politics," "feeling of recognition in the community," and "being close to influential people" are important reasons for participation in party politics. The longer people participate in party work, the more important such personal motivations become. Although many first engaged in political activity out of concern for issues or ideology, the longer they participated the less important these concerns became as group solidarity incentives took a greater prominence.[62]

Issues and ideology. Politics ultimately involves the direction which governmental policy will take. It is not, therefore, surprising that an important motivational force for participation is concern for issues and ideology. Concern for public policy is especially important in creating a stimulus for entry into party work. Persons anxious about nuclear war, school busing, abortion, civil rights, women's rights, the environment, and the scope of government activity can be stimulated to take part in politics. Issue oriented concerns are, however, difficult to sustain as a basis for continuing participation because of their transitory nature and the frustrations they frequently cause. Social or solidarity motivations for participation are easier to maintain in most communities.

A variety of studies focusing upon party activists operating in different settings—local party organizations to national conventions—indicate that issue oriented incentives have become more common in

American politics. Classic examples of activists concerned about ideological purity are the Goldwater delegates to the 1964 Convention in San Francisco.[63] Many of these delegates viewed compromise as immoral and were quite prepared to cast aside whole groups of voters and lose the election for the satisfaction of being right on the issues. This ideological fervor of the right found parallel expression on the political left among McCarthy delegates at the explosive Democratic convention in Chicago in 1968 and with many McGovern supporters in 1972. Concern for ideology has continued to be important to convention delegates in the 1980s.[64]

The Distinctiveness of Activists

Most Americans' political involvement seldom extends beyond the minimal act of periodically voting. Political activists are, therefore, set apart from the average citizen by their high levels of political participation. They also have other distinctive characteristics. First, activists tend to come from families that are active and interested in politics. Second, party activists are generally of relatively high socioeconomic status. Politics takes time, knowledge, and financial resources. These commodities tend to be concentrated among the middle and upper middle classes. The party leadership corps are not, therefore, necessarily representative demographically of their party's voters. Analysis of the social backgrounds of state party chairmen demonstrates this tendency of political leaders to come from upper middle-class backgrounds. Over 70 percent of the state chairmen serving between 1975 and 1980 were from either professional, business, or managerial occupations.[65] Similarly, 69 percent of Republican and 55 percent of Democratic delegates to the 1988 conventions had incomes in excess of $50,000.

Party activists are also distinguishable from ordinary voters in terms of ideological orientation. Activists are much more likely to view the world from an ideological perspective and adopt a liberal or conservative position on issues. As would be expected, Democratic and Republican activists tend to see politics from differing ideological vantage points, with Democrats being significantly more liberal than Republicans. Studies of national convention delegates have consistently documented the substantial ideological differences between Republicans and Democrats. As can be seen in Figure 4–5, Democratic and Republican delegates are further apart ideologically than are rank and file voters of the two parties. There is also an ideology gap between each party's activists and its party voters. Figure 4–5 also illustrates this pattern by comparing the ideology of national convention delegates and party voters. Republican activists are much more conservative than GOP voters,

Figure 4–5: Ideological Self-Identification of National Convention Delegates and Party Rank and File Voters, 1984 (Mean Scores of Delegates and Rank and File Voters)

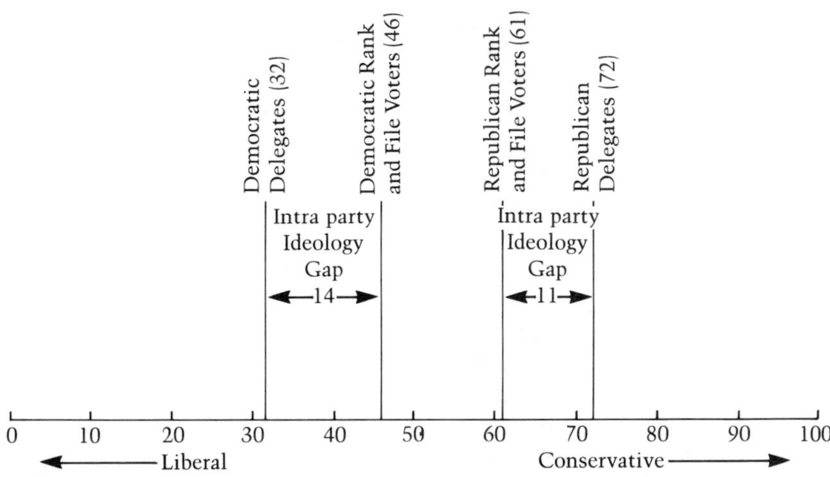

Source: Adapted from Warren E. Miller, *Without Consent: Mass-Elite Linkages in Presidential Politics* (Lexington: University of Kentucky Press, 1988), p. 35. Copyright © 1988 by the University of Kentucky Press.

while Democratic leaders are significantly more liberal than their party's voters. A similar pattern emerges from analyses of the ideological orientation of state party activists. Democratic activists are consistently more liberal than state opinion and Republican activists are consistently more conservative than state opinion.[66]

The ideological orientations of party activists have profound implications for the functioning of the American political system because these are the individuals who have influence over nominations, party policy positions, and campaign strategy. While there is an overall tendency for Republican activists to be conservative and Democratic leaders to be liberal, neither party's activists constitute a solid bloc. As a result, there is constant tension within each party between the true believers who want party policy to reflect their policy views and those party activists of a more moderate persuasion who are willing to compromise on ideology in order to attract a wider spectrum of voters. Nowhere is this tension more apparent than at national party conventions where ideologically oriented delegates struggle with pragmatic party leaders over positioning the party on the issues. For example, President Gerald Ford was forced to accept a more conservative platform than he and his advisers wished because in 1976 a majority of Republican delegates were strongly conservative. Similarly, President Jimmy Carter acquiesced to a series of amendments to the 1980 Democratic platform because the delegates were substantially more liberal than his publicly stated positions. Although the convention strategists of both Democrat Michael Dukakis and Republican George Bush were somewhat more successful in controlling the content of their parties' platforms in 1988, these documents still reflected the ideological orientations of the party activists. The ideology gap between the activists of the two parties, therefore, pushes the two major parties apart and helps to give them their distinctive policy orientations.

The parties are also pushed apart because candidates are normally recruited from the ranks of the activists. In addition, activists are an important constituency of candidates. Candidates need campaign workers and financial contributors, and they need them *before* they make their appeals to the mass electorate in the general election. Winning elections first requires putting together a campaign organization, adequate financing, and securing a party nomination. In these endeavors party activists are especially important. But these middle-class activists are not apt to be attracted by material rewards like patronage. It is, therefore, necessary to motivate them through intangible rewards—such as participation in a just cause. Because of the need to appeal to an activist constituency that is more liberal in the Democratic party and more conservative in the Republican party than rank and file party voters, it is often difficult for centrist candidates to secure their parties' presidential nomination. A candidate for the Republican presidential nomination needs strong conservative credentials to appeal to the activist constituency that plays a dominant role in nominations. For this reason otherwise attractive candidates such as Governor Nelson Rockefeller (N.Y.) in 1960, 1964, and 1968, or Senator Howard Baker (Tenn.) in 1980 found it difficult to make a strong bid for the nomination. In similar fashion, moderate Democrats, without strong liberal credentials, such as Senator John Glenn (Oh.) in 1984 or Senator Henry Jackson (Wash.) in 1976 were forced to drop out early in the primary season.

Amateur and Professional Role Orientations

The apparent increase in party participation based upon issue oriented concerns has caused political scientists to distinguish between the *amateur* and *professional* role orientations of activists. Amateurs are concerned primarily with ideas and issues. They want candidates and party platforms that are correct and unequivocal on the issues. Amateurs are seldom attracted by material rewards like patronage and are motivated out of ideological concerns. They want to win elections, but they are reluctant to compromise with principle in order to secure an electoral majority. Professionals tend to give priority to winning elections and maintenance of the party organization. They are less concerned with clear statements of party principles and policies and more likely to be motivated by material and solidarity type rewards.

Since James Q. Wilson, in his influential book *The Amateur Democrat,*[67] first identified the amateur style of participation among urban Democratic clubs, evidence of increased amateur role orientation among activists has been identified in other elements of the parties, especially among national convention delegates.[68] Because maintaining the party organization has not been a high priority for amateurs and their seemingly doctrinaire issue stands have at times prevented them from vigorously supporting party nominees, there has been concern among political observers that amateurism would seriously weaken the parties.[69]

One of the reasons it is difficult to determine whether amateurs are weakening the parties is that there are few pure amateurs or professionals. Both the amateur and professional styles are more tendencies than they are actual pure types. Surveys reveal that a substantial proportion of activists exhibit characteristics of both amateurs and professionals. David Price has observed that recent conventions give evidence of professionals acting in a manner that would be expected of amateurs. For example, many of the Republican regulars of 1964, who opposed the nomination of Senator Barry Goldwater (Ariz.), declined to unite behind the ticket, as was true of some Democratic professionals of 1972, who supported Henry Jackson and Hubert Humphrey against the Democratic nominee, Senator George McGovern (S.D.).[70] At the local level, Wilson found as amateurs made a personal investment in party politics they "acquired the habits and motives of the professional."[71]

Research on county and state party organizations indicates that amateurism has not had the harmful consequences that some had predicted. A survey of state party organizations demonstrated that party organizational strength was not influenced by the role orientations of the state chairmen. When state chairmen assume office—whether they are amateurs or professionals—they are forced to assume responsibility for an institutionalized party with a bureaucratized headquarters operation. An organizational imperative, therefore, operates to cause even amateur activists to engage in activities that recognize the common organizational needs of the state party.[72] Amateurs and professional chairmen also have been found to operate their county parties in comparable ways.[73] It would appear, therefore, that the impact of amateurism on state and local party organizations is less pronounced and detrimental to parties than was initially assumed when the amateur style was identified among substantial numbers of national convention delegates.

Party Organizations: Adaptable and Durable

As voters during the 1960s and 1970s were shown to be less influenced by partisan considerations and as competing types of organizations like PACs, campaign/media consulting firms, and candidate organizations gained heightened prominence, there were dire predictions about the future of party organizations. One prominent journalist, who espoused the thesis of party decline, even wrote *The Party's Over.*[74] This chapter's survey of party organizations in America demonstrates that parties have shown qualities of adaptiveness and durability in a changing and frequently hostile political environment. There is even evidence of increased organizational strength, especially among national party organizations. It has also been shown that party organizations can have an impact on a party's capacity to win elections. American parties, however, are characterized by a diffusion of power and stratarchial power relationships. They function under unusually restrictive statutory regulations and they exist in a wide variety of forms with differing levels of effectiveness.

Suggestions for Further Reading

Cotter, Cornelius P.; Gibson, James L.; Bibby, John F.; and Huckshorn, Robert J. *Party Organizations in American Politics.* New York: Praeger, 1984.

Eldersveld, Samuel J. *Political Parties in American Society.* New York: Basic Books, 1982, Part II.

Epstein, Leon D. *Political Parties in the American Mold.* Madison: University of Wisconsin Press, 1986. Chapters 5, 6, 7.

Gray, Virginia; Jacob, Herbert; and Albritton, Robert B.; eds., *Politics in the American States,* Fifth Edition. Glenview, Ill.: Scott, Foresman/Little Brown, 1990. Chapter 3.

Herrnson, Paul S. *Party Campaigning in the 1980s.* Cambridge: Harvard University Press, 1988.

Huckshorn, Robert J. *Party Leadership in the States.* Amherst: University of Massachusetts Press, 1976.

Kayden, Xandra, and Mahe, Eddie, Jr., *The Party Goes On: The Persistence of the Two-Party System in the United States.* New York: Basic Books, 1985.

Mayhew, David R., *Placing Parties in American Politics.* Princeton, N.J.: Princeton University Press, 1986.

Schwartz, Mildred A. *The Party Network: The Robust Organization of Illinois Republicans.* Madison: University of Wisconsin Press, 1990.

Notes

1. V. O. Key, Jr., *Politics, Parties, and Pressure Groups,* 5th ed. (New York: Crowell, 1964), p. 316.
2. Ibid.
3. Samuel J. Eldersveld, *Political Parties in American Society* (New York: Basic Books, 1982), p. 99.
4. Ibid.
5. Joseph S. Schlesinger argues that these candidate organizations are basic units of the party. See his "The New American Political Party," *American Political Science Review* 79 (Dec. 1985): 1152–1169.
6. The development of the national committees into institutionalized bureaucracies is described in Cornelius P. Cotter and John F. Bibby, "Institutional Development of Parties and the Thesis of Party Decline," *Political Science Quarterly* 95 (Spring 1980): 1–27.
7. Cornelius P. Cotter and Bernard C. Hennessy, *Politics without Power: The National Party Committees* (New York: Atherton, 1964).
8. For an insightful analysis of the differing political cultures of the Republican and Democratic parties, see Jo Freeman, "The Political Culture of the Democrats and Republicans," *Political Science Quarterly* 101, no.3 (1986), pp. 327–356.
9. James R. Dickenson, "DNC Withdraws Recognition of 7 Caucuses," *Washington Post,* May 18, 1985, p.A7; Peter Bragdon, "DNC Approves Kirk's Plan To Alter Democrats' Image," *Congressional Quarterly Weekly Report* (June 29, 1985), p. 1287.
10. John F. Bibby and Robert J. Huckshorn, "Out-Party Strategy: Republican National Committee Rebuilding Politics, 1964–66," in Bernard Cosman and Robert J. Huckshorn, eds., *Republican Politics: The 1964 Campaign and Its Aftermath for the Party* (New York: Praeger, 1968), pp. 205–233.
11. James A. Barnes, "Ron Brown's Fast Start," *National Journal,* May 6, 1989, pp. 1103–1107; Paul Taylor, "DNC Chairman Finds His Party in Robust Health, Predicts Fall Gains," *Washington Post,* June 30, 1990, p. A6.
12. Committee for Party Renewal, *Party Line* (February 1983), p. 7.
13. David S. Broder, "A Neglected Democratic Party," *Washington Post,* June 14, 1978; David S. Broder, "A.K.A. Difficult Circumstances," *Washington Post,* March 4, 1981.
14. David Adamany, "Political Parties in the 1980s," in Michael J. Malbin, ed., *Money and Politics in the United States* (Chatham, N.J.: Chatham House 1984), p. 86.
15. See Burt Solomon, "Bush's Zeal for Partisan Duties Tempered by His Bipartisan Style," *National Journal,* October 28, 1989, pp. 2650–2651; and

James A. Barnes, "Reinventing the RNC," *National Journal,* Jan. 14, 1989, pp. 67–71.

16. *A Legacy of Leadership: 1988 Chairman's Report* (Washington, D.C.: Republican National Committee, 1989).
17. Larry Sabato, "Parties, PAC's and Independent Groups," in Thomas E. Mann and Norman I. Ornstein, eds., *The American Elections of 1982* (Washington, D.C.: American Enterprise Institute, 1983), p.81; *see also* Gary C. Jacobson, "Party Organization and Campaign Resources in 1982," *Political Science Quarterly,* 100 (Winter 1985–86): 603–626.
18. Rhodes Cook, "Democrats Develop Tactics: Laying Groundwork for 1984," *Congressional Quarterly Weekly Report* (July 3, 1982), pp. 1591–1595.
19. Paul Taylor, "DNC Chairman Finds His Party In Robust Health, Predicts Fall Gains," *Washington Post,* June 30, 1990, p. A6.
20. Cornelius P. Cotter and Bernard Hennessy, *Politics without Power* (New York: Atherton, 1964).
21. *Democratic Party of the United States of America v. Bronson C. LaFollette;* 449 U.S. 897 (L981) and *Cousins v. Wigoda,* 419 U.S. 477 (1875).
22. The contrasting patterns of party centralization are discussed more fully in John F. Bibby, "Party Renewal in the National Republican Party," in Gerald Pomper, ed., *Party Renewal in America: Theory and Practice* (New York: Praeger, 1981), pp. 102–115.
23. David Broder, "The Force," *Washington Post,* April 2, 1986, p. A23.
24. See John F. Bibby, Cornelius P. Cotter, James L. Gibson, and Robert J. Huckshorn, "Parties in State Politics," in Virginia Gray, Herbert Jacob, and Robert B. Albritton, *Politics in the American States: A Comparative Analysis* (Glenview, Ill.: Scott, Foresman/Little, Brown, 1990), pp. 108–111.
25. Ronald Brownstein, "Precinct Power," *National Journal,* Nov. 5, 1988, pp. 2777–2781; Paul Taylor, "GOP Strategist 'Carpet-Bombs' Buckeye State," *Washington Post,* Nov.4, 1988, p. A21; and Richard L. Berke, "In Election Spending: Watch the Ceiling, Use the Loophole," *New York Times,* Oct. 3, 1988, pp. 1,13Y.
26. David B. Magleby and Candice J. Nelson, *The Money Chase: Congress Campaign Finance Reform* (Washington, D.C.: Brookings Institution, 1990), p. 102.
27. Federal Election Committee press release, March 27, 1989.
28. For a detailed analysis of state regulation of parties, see *The Transformation of American Politics: Implications for Federalism* (Washington, D.C.: Advisory Commission in Intergovernmental Relations, 1986), pp. 123–160.
29. For an insightful consideration of political parties as public utilities, see Leon D. Epstein, *Political Parties in the American Mold* (Madison: University of Wisconsin Press, 1986), ch. 6.
30. *Tashjian v. Republican Party of Connecticut* (1986). For an informed commentary on the impact of *Tashjian,* see Leon D. Epstein, "Will

American Political Parties be Privatized?" *Journal of Law and Politics* 5 (Winter 1989): 239–274.
31. *March Fong Eu, Secretary of State of State of California, et al.* v. *San Francisco County Democratic Committee, et al.*, (1989).
32. Cornelius P. Cotter, James L. Gibson, John F. Bibby, and Robert J. Huckshorn, *Party Organizations in American Politics* (New York: Praeger, 1984), p. 111.
33. Joseph P. Sullivan, "In New Jersey, the Party Is the Second Part," *New York Times*, June 8, 1981, p. E6.
34. V. O. Key, Jr., *American State Politics, An Introduction* (New York: Knopf, 1956), p. 287.
35. See Cotter, Gibson, Bibby, and Huckshorn, *Party Organizations in American Politics*; Robert J. Huckshorn, *Party Leadership in the States* (Amherst: University of Masschusetts Press, 1976).
36. James Barnes, "Reinventing the RNC," *National Journal*, Jan. 14, 1989, p. 70; and Larry Sabato, *The Party's Just Begun: Shaping Political Parties for America's Future* (Glenview, Ill.: Scott, Foresman, 1988), p. 91.
37. Alexander Heard, *The Costs of Democracy* (New York: Anchor Books, 1962). pp. 264–267.
38. *Transformation in American Politics*, pp. 112–113.
39. Carol Matlack, "Joining the Big Boys," *National Journal*, March 17, 1990, p. 646.
40. James L. Gibson, Cornelius P. Cotter, John F. Bibby, and Robert J. Huckshorn, "Assessing Party Organizational Strength," *American Journal of Political Science* 27 (May 1983): 193–222.
41. Matlack, "Joining the Big Boys," pp. 646–647.
42. "Guru in Ohio," *Congressional Quarterly Weekly Report*, November 4, 1989, pp. 29–79. For detailed analyses of legislative campaign committees in New York, see Jeffrey M. Stonecash's articles, "Working at the Margins: Campaign Finance and Party Strategy in New York Assembly Elections," *Legislative Studies Quarterly* 13 (Nov. 1988): 477–494; and "Campaign Finance in New York Senate Elections," *Legislative Studies Quarterly* 15 (May 1990): 247–262.
43. "Changing Money's Role Is No Easy Task," *Congressional Quarterly Weekly Report*, Nov. 4, 1989, p. 2987. In California, cash transfers between legislators' campaign treasuries are now banned.
44. Rob Gurwitt, "How to Succeed at Running a Legislature: Pack a Mighty Wallet," *Governing*, May 1990, pp. 26–31.
45. For a complete survey of traditional party organizations, see David R. Mayhew, *Placing Parties in American Politics* (Princeton, N.J.: Princeton University Press, 1986).
46. An analysis of the current status of the Cook County organizations is found in William Crotty, ed., *Political Parties in Local Areas* (Knoxville: University of Tennessee Press, 1986), Chapter 6.
47. Frank Lynn, "At Last, a Last Hurrah for Margiotta?" *The New York Times*, May 8, 1983, p. 6E; Tom Watson, "All Powerful Machine of Yore

Endures in New York's Nassau," *Congressional Quarterly Weekly Report* (Aug. 17, 1985), pp. 1623–1625.

48. David S. Broder, "Ground War Heating Up in California," *Washington Post*, Sept. 18, 1988, p. A16.
49. Kay Lawson, Gerald Pomper, and Maureen Moakley, "Party Linkage at the Base: Middlesex County, New Jersey," paper prepared for the annual meeting of the American Political Science Association, Sept. 1–4, 1983, Chicago.
50. James L. Gibson, Cornelius P. Cotter, John F. Bibby, and Robert J. Huckshorn, "Whither the Local Parties?: A Cross-Sectional and Longitudinal Analysis of the Strength of Party Organizations," *American Journal of Political Science* 29 (Feb. 1985):139–159; James L. Gibson, John P. Frendreis, and Laura Vertz, "Party Dynamics in the 1980s: Change in Party Organizational Strength 1980–1984," *American Journal of Politic Science* 33 (Feb. 1989): 139–160.
51. Eldersveld, *Political Parties in American Society*, p. 145.
52. Jay Mathews, "Absentee Ballots GOP Opposed Swung the Vote for Deukmejian," *Washington Post*, Feb. 27, 1983, p. A9.
53. Larry Sabato, "Parties, PACs, and Independent Groups," in Thomas E. Mann and Norman J. Ornstein, eds., *The American Elections of 1982* (Washington, D.C.: American Enterprise Institute, 1983), ch.3.
54. Cotter, Gibson, Bibby, and Huckshorn, *Party Organizations in American Politics*, Chapter 5.
55. Samuel C. Patterson and Gregory A. Caldeira, "The Etiology of Partisan Competition," *American Political Science Review* 78 (Sept. 1984): 691–707.
56. John P. Frendries, James L. Gibson, and Laura Vertz, "The Relevance of Local Party Organizations," *American Political Science Review* 84 (March 1990): 225–235.
57. Gregg W. Smith, "Party Organizations and Voter Turnout: The 1988 Elections," a paper prepared for the Annual Meeting of the American Political Science Association, San Francisco, 1990. For further evidence on the impact of county party organizations on the vote, see William J. Crotty, "Party Effort and Its Impact on the Vote," *American Political Science Review* 65 (June 1971): 439–450.
58. Nathaniel Sheppard, Jr., "The Spoils of Chicago's Political War: Money and Power Go to the Winners," *New York Times*, May 14, 1983, p. 7.
59. E. R. Shipp, "Political Use of Auto Fees Is Challenged in Indiana," *New York Times*, May 29, 1984, p. 9; David S. Broder, "Indiana's Fading License Dream," *Washington Post*, Oct. 24, 1985, p. A3.
60. Frank J. Sorauf, *Party Politics in America*, 5th ed. (Boston, Mass.: Little, Brown, 1984), pp. 89–91.
61. Robert J. Huckshorn, "The Social Background and Career Patterns of State Party Chairpersons—1930–1980" (unpublished manuscript, 1982).
62. Eldersveld, *Political Parties in American Society*, p. 178; and Samuel J. Eldersveld, "The Party Activist in Los Angeles: A Longitudinal View,

1956–1980," in William Crotty, ed., *Political Parties in Local Arenas,* pp. 103–107.

63. Aaron Wildavsky, "The Goldwater Phenomenon: Purists, Politicians, and the Two Party System," *Review of Politics* 27 (July 1965): 386–413.
64. On the ideology of convention delegates, see Herbert McCloskey, Paul J. Hoffman, and Rosemary O'Hara, "Issue Conflict and Consensus among Party Leaders and Followers," *American Political Science Review* 54 (June 1960): 406–427; Jeane J. Kirkpatrick, *The New Presidential Elite* (New York: Russell Sage, 1976); and Warren E. Miller, *Without Consent. Mass–Elite Linkages in Presidential Politics* (Lexington: University of Kentucky Press, 1988).
65. Huckshorn, "The Social Background and Career Patterns of State Party Chairpersons—1930–1980."
66. Robert S. Erikson, Gerald C. Wright, Jr., and John P. McIver, "Political Parties, Public Opinion, and State Policy in the United States," *American Political Science Review* 83 (Sept. 1989): 736–738.
67. James Q. Wilson, *The Amateur Democrat: Club Politics in Three Cities,* (Chicago, Ill.: University of Chicago Press, 1962).
68. Kirkpatrick, *New Presidential Elite;* Thomas H. Robeck, "Amateurs and Professionals: Delegates to the 1972 Republican National Convention," *Journal of Politics* 37 (May 1975): 436–468.
69. Kirkpatrick, *New Presidential Elite,* p. 350.
70. David E. Price, *Bringing Back the Parties* (Washington, D.C.: CQ Press, 1984), p. 31.
71. Wilson, *Amateur Democrat,* p. 5.
72. Cotter, Gibson, Bibby, and Huckshorn, *Party Organizations in American Politics,* pp. 141–149.
73. Michael A. Maggiotto and Ronald E. Weber, "Amateurs and Professionals; The Case of the County Party Chairperson," (paper prepared for the Conference on Political Parties in Modern Societies, Northwestern University, Sept. 21–22, 1978.
74. David S. Broder, *The Party's Over: The Failure of Politics in America* (New York: Harper and Row, 1971); for a scholarly discussion of the possibility of partyless politics, see Walter Dean Burnham, *Critical Elections and the Mainsprings of American Politics* (New York, Norton, 1970).

CHAPTER 5

Nominations for State and Congressional Offices

Although Americans pride themselves on having operated with free elections for almost two hundred years, the voter's choice in general elections is severely limited. In most elections, citizens are faced with choosing between Republican and Democratic nominees, or "wasting" their vote on a third party candidate who has only the remotest chance of winning. The functioning of American democracy, therefore, is affected in critical ways by the decisions the two major parties make in selecting persons to bear their labels in the general election. For the party, the nomination process is a crucial part of its activities. It is this activity more than any other which distinguishes the political party from other political organizations such as the AFL-CIO, Americans for Democratic Action, Common Cause, Chamber of Commerce, or Farm Bureau. Only political parties nominate candidates on their own labels and present them to the voters as their official representatives. The nomination is also critical for the parties because selecting the "right" candidate can determine whether a party will win or lose the general election. A candidate lacking in appeal to the party's traditional voters and independents, or one who divides rather than unites the party's electorate and workers, is not likely to gain public office. Finally, the nomination process is important to the party because control of the party is at stake. Influence over the selection of party nominees goes a long way toward determining which party factions will gain ascendency in terms of the policy direction of the party and the rewards which elected officials bestow upon their supporters.[1] The critical character of the nomination process for the parties was aptly summarized by the late E.E. Schattschneider.

> Unless the party makes authoritative and effective nominations, it cannot stay in business. . . . The nature of the nomination procedure determines the nature of the party; he who can make nominations is the owner of the party . . . .[2]

In most Western democracies, the selection of candidates rests in the hands of the party organization—the party officers and activists. Operating largely without government regulation, these leaders designate the party's candidates and there is no appeal to the party-in-the-electorate of their decisions. The average voter participates only in the general election—a contest between the parties—and not in the intra-party contest to select nominees. Nominating processes in the United States, by contrast, not only involve party activists, but also permit extensive participation by rank and file voters. Indeed, a persistent trend in the evolution of nominating practices in the United States has been toward increasing the opportunities for popular participation and weakening the capacity of party organizational hierarchies to control candidate selection for local, state, and national offices. The American nomination process is not only unique for the amount of popular participation that it permits, but also for the wide variety and high level of statutory regulation that governs it.

The Evolution of the Direct Primary

From Legislative Caucus to Party Convention

After the American Revolution, the legislative caucus evolved as the principal means of making nominations for state offices. The legislative caucus was a meeting of all the party's elected members of the state senate and house of representatives. A similar method of nomination—the congressional caucus—was used to select presidential candidates. The legislative caucus was not a particularly representative institution, because it left unrepresented those districts which had elected opposition party legislators. To correct this problem, some of the states used a "mixed caucus" system, which permitted special delegates, representing districts held by the opposition party, to participate in the caucus to nominate candidates.

Andrew Jackson's failure to gain the presidential nomination from the oligarchs of the congressional caucus in 1824 and the subsequent defeat of the caucus nominee, William H. Crawford, contributed in a significant way to the demise of the caucus system. Jackson was a popular figure—the hero of the Battle of New Orleans and a symbol of democracy and egalitarianism. His backers sought to discredit the caucus system. It was replaced by a convention system of nomination.

The convention process normally started with local or precinct caucuses that selected delegates to attend county conventions. The county conventions then selected delegates to a state party convention. The state conventions nominated the party's candidate for statewide office such as governor, attorney general, and secretary of state. Courthouse candidates were nominated by the county conventions and there were also congressional district conventions to select candidates for the United States House. Its supporters considered the convention system to be a democratic reform designed to permit greater popular participation and improved representation for party rank and file voters. Like the legislative caucus, the convention nominating process fell into disrepute. The convention process was susceptible to manipulation and domination by party leaders and "bosses," who were often under the influence of well financed interests anxious to gain favorable concessions from state governments. It was charged that conventions too often selected candidates who were not the popular choice of party voters. There was a further problem of convention nominations being tantamount to election in one party areas so that, in effect, the actual choice of public officials was being made at party conventions and not by the voters at the general election.

The Direct Primary: "Escape from One-Partyism"

Early in the twentieth century, the convention system was replaced in most states by the direct primary—nomination of party candidates by the voters directly. The primary permitted direct expression of voter preferences and struck down "the intermediate links between rank and file of the party and would-be candidates."[3]

While there was a great deal of oratory during the time when the direct primary was being adopted about democracy, citizen participation, corrupt party machines, and special interests, V. O. Key has concluded that the primary was "at bottom an escape from one-partyism."[4] The Civil War and Reconstruction made the South a one party Democratic area. The direct primary, therefore, evolved in the South as a means to permit popular government where interparty competition of a meaningful nature had ceased. The importance of a lack of interparty competition as an impetus to adoption of the direct primary is illustrated in Virginia and North Carolina, the southern states that held out the longest against instituting primaries. These were also the southern states with the highest level of interparty competition during the 1880s and 1890s, the decades preceding widespread adoption of the primary.[5]

The electoral realignments of the 1890s solidified Democratic one party dominance of the South, but also created one party Republican areas in the Northeast, Midwest, and West. The primary, therefore, spread through these states as interparty competition diminished and GOP state convention nominations became tantamount to election. In 1903, Wisconsin was the first state to enact a comprehensive direct primary law. In states with more established party systems and real two party competition, such as New York, Delaware, Connecticut, and Rhode Island, the primary was adopted more slowly.

Although one of the reasons for instituting the direct primary was to deal with the problems created by one-partyism, there is evidence that the introduction of the direct primary frustrated and delayed the development of two party competition. The primary weakened the minority party because it focused public attention upon contests within the dominant party. Voters were channelled into the primary of the dominant party because that was where the election was actually being decided. Persons with political ambitions also gravitated into the majority party because they saw little future in the minority party. These patterns of behavior caused V. O. Key to conclude that "primary competition tended to be substituted for general election competition; competition within parties for competition between parties."[6] He believed that without the direct primary interparty competition would have come sooner to one party areas of the North and South.

The Direct Primary and Progressivism

The direct primary embodied an essential element of faith of the reformist progressive movement of the early twentieth century. The progressives believed intermediaries between the people and their government should be removed and that the voters should be able to choose nominees for office without encroachments on their sovereignty by party leaders. Robert M. La Follette, Sr., the leader of the Wisconsin Progressives, stated the case for the direct primary.

> Under our form of government the entire structure rests upon the nomination of candidates for office. This is the foundation of representative government. If bad men control nominations we cannot have good government. . . .
>
> [We] must abolish the caucus and convention by law, place nominations in the hands of the people, and make all nominations by direct vote at a primary election.
>
> With nominations of all candidates absolutely in the control of the people . . . the public official who desires re-nomination will not dare to seek it, if he has served the machine and the lobby and betrayed the public trust.[7]

The Progressives fought for the direct primary not only because it was consistent with their democratic faith, but because it provided a means of challenging the power of established party leaders, achieving political power, and fulfilling personal ambition. La Follette in Wisconsin, Hiram Johnson in California, and other Progressive leaders used the primary to strengthen their faction's influence within the dominant Republican party of their states.

The Direct Primary in the South

While the direct primary in the North was designed to provide a forum for electoral competition and advance the fortunes of the progressive faction of the GOP, in the South the movement supporting the direct primary had a different mix of motives. The direct primary was designed to unify the Democratic party under conservative leadership, weaken the Republican opposition, and prevent black voters from having electoral influence. Use of the primary to select Democratic candidates, it was thought, would give greater legitimacy to the nominee than would selection by party conventions, and the party might thereby be unified. It was hoped that settling intraparty differences in the primary and presenting a united front in the general election would reduce the influence of the opposition parties and their voters—mainly blacks, who up until the Depression of the 1930s were overwhelmingly Republican. Southern Democratic parties also adopted rules barring blacks from voting in party primaries, in order to prevent any candidate or faction from making appeals to black voters in order to gain a party nomination.[8]

The advocates of the primary in the South were largely successful in achieving their goals. The Democratic primary became the only significant election; only in states with concentrations of Republicans in mountain areas was the GOP a force of modest significance (e.g., Tennessee, Kentucky, Virginia, North Carolina); and the white primary effectively excluded blacks from the electoral process.

Post-World War II Trends

During the years after the war, the primary was instituted in those states which had been holdouts. In 1976, Indiana adopted the primary for nominating statewide candidates and became the last of the holdout states to accept the primary. Other states which became primary states were Rhode Island (1947), Connecticut (1955), and New York (statewide offices, 1967). In enacting the primary laws, Rhode Island, Connecticut, and New York also made provision for preprimary endorsement of candidates by the party organizations.[9]

The nature of southern primaries has also changed with the demise of the whites only primary, the enfranchisement of blacks, and the emergence of strong Republican parties. Blacks are now an increasingly larger proportion of the southern Democratic party's supporters and active participants in the primaries as both voters and candidates. While it was only a minor force in southern state politics, the Republican party frequently opted to take advantage of a provision in state law which permitted nominations via conventions. As the party has gained electoral strength in the region, it has increasingly used the primary to nominate its candidates.[10]

State Regulation of the Direct Primary

There is tremendous diversity among the states in the operation of the direct primary. The constitutional principle of federalism permits the states wide latitude in tailoring their election laws to fit state traditions, political conditions, and the preferences of state leaders and voters.

Nomination by Convention

Although the direct primary is the predominant method of nominating candidates, thirteen states either permit or require conventions. In Connecticut, for example, the winner of the party's endorsement at the state convention automatically becomes the nominee unless challenged in the primary by a candidate who received at least 20 percent of the convention votes. Several of the southern states (Alabama, Georgia, South Carolina, and Virginia) permit the parties to nominate either by primary or convention. In recent years, both parties in Virginia have picked their statewide candidates at state party conventions. However, after losing two consecutive gubernatorial elections, the GOP in 1989 opted to use the primary in an effort to build popular interest in the party. The primary winner, former attorney general Marshall Coleman, however, was defeated by Democratic Lt. Gov. Douglas Wilder, the nation's first black to be elected governor. The convention method of nomination, of course, enhances the influence which party leaders have over the nominating process because candidates cannot appeal effectively over the heads of party leaders to rank and file voters, as in a primary.

Party Affiliation Requirements for Voting

There is wide variation among the states in terms of the party affiliation requirements imposed in order for a voter to participate in primaries. The states array themselves along a continuum regarding the severity of their party affiliation requirements from those which restrict participation to registered partisans to others with no restrictions (see Table 5–1).

Closed primaries. Twenty-six states have closed primaries. In these states, voters must register as party affiliates in order to vote in a party primary. Participation is thus restricted to those who are willing to register publicly as partisans; those who register as independents are barred from voting. Among the closed primary states, New York is particularly restrictive, because voters wishing to change

Table 5–1 Party Affiliation Requirements for Voting in Direct Primaries

Closed: Party Registration Required; changes permitted in fixed time period before primary	**Semiclosed: Voters may register or change party registration on election day**	**Semiopen: Voters required to publicly request party ballot**	**Open: Voter decides in which primary to vote in privacy of voting booth**	**Blanket**	**"Nonpartisan"**
Arizona	Colorado[4]	Alabama	Hawaii	Alaska	Louisiana
California	Iowa	Arkansas	Idaho	Washington	
Connecticut[1]	Kansas[4]	Georgia	Michigan		
Delaware	Maine[4]	Illinois	Minnesota		
Florida	Massachusetts[4]	Indiana	Montana		
Kentucky	New Hampshire[4]	Mississippi	North Dakota		
Maryland	New Jersey[5]	Missouri	South Carolina		
Nebraska[2]	Ohio	Tennessee	Utah		
Nevada	Rhode Island[4]	Texas	Vermont		
New Mexico	Wyoming	Virginia	Wisconsin		
New York					
North Carolina[3]					
Oklahoma					
Oregon[3]					
Pennsylvania					
South Dakota					
West Virginia[3]					

1. Unaffiliated voters may vote in some Republican primaries but not in Democratic primaries.
2. Unaffiliated voters may vote in either party's primary for U.S. Senator or Representative.
3. Unaffiliated voters may vote in Republican primaries.
4. Unaffiliated voters may declare a party at the polls.
5. New voters may declare a party at the polls.

Sources: The Book of the States, 1990–91; Leon D. Epstein, "Will American Political Parties Be Privatized?" *Journal of Law and Politics*, 5 (Winter 1989): 239–274; and Malcolm E. Jewell and David M. Olson, *Political Parties and Elections in American States* (Chicago, Ill.: Dorsey Press, 1988), pp. 89–92.

their party registration and participate in a primary must have made that change one year before the primary. Wyoming and Iowa, however, have used their registration laws to make their states' primaries less closed. Voters are permitted in these states to change their party registration on election day. A slightly different registration procedure, designed specifically to accommodate the large segment of voters who consider themselves to be independents, exists in Massachusetts and New Hampshire. There persons not registered with any party are permitted to shift their registration to Republican or Democrat on primary election day.

There are also several state Republican parties that permit unaffiliated voters (voters not designating party affiliations at the time of registration) to vote in their primaries. As a result of the *Tashjian* decision, (see chapter 4) in which the Supreme Court held that a state could not prevent a party from opening its primary elections to unaffiliated voters, the Republican parties of Connecticut, North Carolina, Oregon, and West Virginia have opened their parties to unaffiliated voters. In each of these states, Republicans constituted a minority of the registered voters. The GOP state organizations therefore sought to take advantage of the *Tashjian* decision in an effort to encourage greater public interest in their party's affairs. In addition, Nebraska permits unaffiliated voters to vote in either party's primary for United States senator or representative (but not for governor).[11]

The justification for the closed primary is that since primaries are the process through which *party* nominees are chosen, only party affiliates with a reasonably stable commitment to the party should be permitted to vote. It is argued that the selection of a nominee is one of the most important decisions that a party makes and it should not be turned over to nonparty members or made vulnerable to "raiding" from outsiders, who lack a long-term commitment to the party. Party organization leaders have traditionally preferred the closed primary system because it prevents "cross-overs" by voters from the opposition party, creates a known constituency to whom appeals for support can be made, and makes control of the nomination process somewhat easier to achieve.

Public statement of party preference required. In ten states (mainly in the South) voters are not required to register as party affiliates, but they are required to acknowledge publicly in which party's primary they wish to participate. No official record is kept of the voters' publicly stated preference, and voters are free to change their party preference at each primary. Some states require voters to submit their preference in writing and a few states require a voter to swear that they support the party, if their participation in a primary is challenged. None of these requirements, however, constitutes a serious barrier to voter participation in the primaries of their choice.

Open primary. Ten states provide for the open primary in which no requirements concerning party affiliations are imposed upon persons voting in the primary. In open primary states, the voters decide in the privacy of the voting booth in which party's primary they wish to vote. As in the previously described types of primaries, voters in open primary states are restricted to voting in only one party's primary. Particularly open primaries occur in states such as Wisconsin and Minnesota which combine open primary laws with election day registration at the polls. In these states, a voter need not be registered prior to the primary in order to vote, since registration is permitted at the polls on primary election day.

The basic rationale for the open primary is that all voters should be permitted to participate in the crucial decisional process of selecting nominees for public office and that such participation should not be restricted to those who publicly acknowledge a partisan preference. In addition, the advocates of the open primary stress that it protects the privacy of party preference and electoral choice.

Blanket primary. Washington and Alaska operate under the most "open" primary procedures. The blanket primary permits the voter to take part in more than one party's primary by switching back and forth between parties from office to office. It is, therefore, possible for an elector to vote in the Republican primary for governor, the Democratic primary for United States senator, the Republican primary for United States representative, and Democratic state legislative primaries.

"Nonpartisan" primary. An unusual variation on the open primary was instituted in Louisiana in 1975 through the persistent efforts of Democratic Governor Edwin W. Edwards. Under this system all candidates, irrespective of party affiliation, are listed alphabetically within office blocks on the ballot. If a candidate receives a majority of the votes cast in the open primary, then that candidate is elected and no general election is held for that office. If, however, no candidate receives a majority of the votes cast in the open primary, then the two candidates with the highest number of votes, irrespective of party, will face each other in the general election.

Although this system has been in operation only a short period, it appears to have aided incumbent legislators in gaining reelection and discouraged legislative candidacies among the minority Republicans.[12] In some instances, it has also eliminated the general election as a contest between the parties. For example, in 1983 Edwin Edwards received 62 percent of the vote, defeating the incumbent Republican governor, David Treen, and several minor candidates in the primary, and was declared elected. In 1987, the GOP candidate for governor, Robert Livingston, finished a distant third (19 percent of the vote) in the primary behind Democrats Buddy Roemer and Edwin Edwards, who received 33 and 28 percent of the vote respectively. Edwards, who had been tried but not convicted on bribery charges, then conceded the general election to Roemer.

Regulation of Candidacies and Cross-Filing

In addition to regulating which persons may vote in a party primary, states decide the qualifications a candidate must meet in order to run. Most of the states permit a person to run in only one party's primary and only the most minimal tests of party membership are required. However, three states (Connecticut, New York, and Vermont) permit candidates to seek simultaneously the nomination of more than one party. Up until 1959, California was the most notable example of this practice, which is called cross-filing. Under California's cross-filing system, a candidate could run in both the Republican and Democratic primaries and if this candidate won both parties' primaries, then the individual's name would go on the general election ballot as both the Democratic and Republican nominee. This was a system that tended to favor the long dominant Republican party, whose candidates were apt to be better known. They, therefore, benefited from the generally lower turnout and lower levels of voter knowledge of candidates that exists in primaries. In a number of instances, prominent Republicans won both parties' nominations for state constitutional offices and the United States Senate. One consequence of cross-filing in California was to delay a build up in strength by the minority Democratic party, because the majority party could bore from within by capturing the nominations of the weaker party. V. O. Key has observed that "The rule limiting entry to candidacy in the party primary is . . . a rule of critical importance in maintenance of party competition."[13]

An interesting variation of cross-filing exists in New York, where it operates to encourage minor parties and facilitate coalitions of the Democratic party with the Liberal party and the Republicans with the Conservative party. New York permits parties that nominate candidates by convention—the Liberals and Conservatives—to nominate the same candidate as the major parties. It is, therefore, common for Democratic nominees to appear on the general election ballot in both the Democratic and Liberal party columns. Since both the Liberal and Conservative parties have a substantial electoral following, their nomination of one of the major party candidates can provide a significant infusion of votes to the major party nominees. At the same time, the possibility of these parties refusing to nominate their coalition partner's candidate and instead running their own candidate, or even nominating the other major party's nominee, can pose a serious threat to their coalition partner's electoral prospects. The Liberal and Conservative parties are, therefore, in a position to exert leverage on the major parties to nominate candidates acceptable to the third parties. For example, in 1982 Edward V. Regan, the Republican state comptroller, withdrew from the race for the gubernatorial nomination when it became clear that state party leaders would not endorse him because the Conservative party had indicated that it did not favor his candidacy and instead preferred Lewis Lehrman, an outspoken conservative. New York's cross-filing process and multiparty system create a unique process of intrigue and bargaining for party nominations. The results of these maneuverings frequently have a major impact on the outcome of general elections.[14] For example, the 1980 Senate race was a three-way contest because the Liberal party declined to nominate the Democratic nominee, Elizabeth Holtzman, and instead ran the incumbent Jacob Javits, who had lost the Republican primary to Alfonse D'Amato. Running as the Republican-Conservative nominee, D'Amato eked out a narrow win while receiving 45 percent of the vote compared to 44 percent for Holtzman and 11 percent for Javits. Clearly, the split Democratic-Liberal vote contributed to D'Amato's victory, as did the contribution to his vote total made by voters who cast their ballots for him as the Conservative party nominee.

Regulation of the Proportion of the Vote Required for Nomination: The Run-Off Primary

The normal practice in the states is for the nomination to go to the candidate who receives the most votes (a plurality) in the primary, even if that individual receives less than a majority of the votes cast. In nine southern and border states, a majority of the vote in the primary is required for nomination, and in North Carolina 40 percent of the primary vote is required for nomination. If no candidate receives a majority, then a second or run-off primary is held between the top two finishers in the first primary. This system was instituted in the South during an era when the Democratic party was dominant and its nomination was tantamount to election. To assure that the person nominated in the Democratic primary, and therefore "elected," had the support of a majority of Democratic voters, the run-off primary was instituted.

The potential for a second primary diminishes the internal party pressures for preprimary coalition formation, and, therefore, tends to increase the number of candidates in the initial primary. The run-off can also result in a different candidate winning the nomination than led in the first primary. Among the prominent members of Congress whose initial election to Congress occurred after finishing second in the first primary and then winning the run-off are Senators Sam Nunn (D–Ga.) and Phil Gramm (R–Tex.) (Gramm was first elected to the House as a Democrat), House Judiciary Committee Chairman Jack Brooks (D–Tex.), and former Democratic Congressional Campaign Committee Chairman Beryl Anthony (D–Ark.).[15]

The rise of the Republican party in the South has dramatically altered the importance of the Democratic primaries. Democratic nominees are no longer assured of general election victory. Larry Sabato has noted that with increased Republican strength in general elections, voter participation in Democratic primaries has waned as voters have delayed their balloting participation until the general election, "when it really matters."[16] For example, in Texas, turnout in the Democratic party dropped from 1.8 million in 1978 to 1.4 million in the hotly contested 1990 gubernatorial primary.

Even though general elections have become increasingly important in the South, the second primary system has emerged as a major point of contention within the Democratic party. The enfranchisement of black voters in the South and their overwhelming allegiance to the Democratic party have meant that blacks are now a major factor in Democratic nominating politics, both as voters and as candidates. Their impact has been enhanced by the growing support which Republicans are gaining from the white urban and suburban middle class and young voters. As a result of this combination of factors, black candidates periodically gain a plurality of the vote in the initial primary. Some have then failed to win a majority in the run-off as the white vote coalesced around a white candidate. In his 1984 presidential campaign, Jesse Jackson lobbied to put an anti-runoff plank in the Democratic party platform on the grounds that it disadvantaged black candidates. Democratic leaders resisted Jackson's plea because they were fearful that such a course would cause further erosion of support among white voters should the Democrats nominate a black to face a white Republican in the general election.

In 1990, the Bush administration through the Department of Justice entered the controversy. It filed suit against the run-off system in Georgia, charging that it discriminated against minority voters. If the courts sustain the Justice Department's challenge to the run-off system, political analysts believe that the net effect will be to help Republican candidates in the South. It is thought elimination of the run-off system would make it easier for black candidates to win Democratic party nominations. However, since such candidates might not have broadly based support within the Democratic party, which has seen a massive erosion of support among southern whites, Republican candidates' electoral prospects could be enhanced. As a result, southern Democratic leaders have accused the Bush administration of fostering an unholy alliance between the GOP and black groups and of filing the suit for partisan reasons rather than to combat discrimination.[17]

Regulation of Access to the General Election Ballot: "Sore Loser" Laws

The importance of a party nomination is enhanced if a candidate who loses a primary is not permitted to run in the general election as an independent. In twenty-seven of the states, the legislatures have enacted "sore loser" statutes that prevent independent candidacies by persons who lost a primary nomination (Table 5–2). Such statutes limit the extent to which intraparty factional struggles can be carried over into the general election. Critics charge, however, that these laws unduly limit candidacy. This was the claim of John B. Anderson as he sought to gain access to the presidential ballot in 1980 after his abortive campaign for the Republican nomination. The Supreme Court, however, has upheld the constitutionality of "sore loser" statutes.[18]

Preprimary Endorsements

Clearly the intent of the progressive reformers and one of the consequences of the direct primary has been to reduce party organization control over nominations. Party organizational influence has not, however, been totally removed from the process and this is especially true in those states which utilize preprimary endorsements by the party organizational leadership. Endorsements can be statutory mandates, informal practices of the party organization, or a practice of party affiliated organizations.

Table 5–2 State "Sore Loser" Laws

States with "Sore Loser" Laws	States without "Sore Loser" Laws
Arizona	Alabama
Arkansas	Alaska
California	Connecticut
Colorado	Florida
Delaware	Georgia
Idaho	Hawaii
Illinois	Indiana
Kentucky	Iowa
Maine	Kansas
Maryland	Louisiana
Massachusetts	Mississippi
Michigan	Montana
Minnesota	Nevada
Missouri	New Hampshire
Nebraska	New Jersey
New Mexico	New York
North Carolina	Oklahoma
North Dakota	Rhode Island
Ohio	South Dakota
Oregon	Texas
Pennsylvania	Vermont
South Carolina	Virginia
Tennessee	West Virginia
Utah	Wisconsin
Washington	
Wyoming	

Sources: David E. Price, *Bringing Back The Parties* (Washington, D.C.: CQ Press, 1984), 128, 129; *Washington Post*, July 10, 1986, p. A3.

State Statutory Requirements for Endorsement

In eight states, there are statutory provisions mandating preprimary endorsement by the party organization meeting in state convention (see Table 5–3). The existence of these statutory requirements for endorsing conventions reflects the ability of the party organizations in these states to retain a significant role in the nomination process even while the state legislatures were succumbing to the pressures for the direct primary. Endorsement frequently carries with it the right to have one's name placed on the primary ballot or to be listed first on the ballot. In Delaware and Rhode Island, for example, endorsed candidates have an automatic right to a place on the primary ballot, but other candidates must qualify by circulating petitions. Access to the ballot may also be restricted by requiring that a

Table 5–3 Preprimary Endorsements

Statutory Requirements for Endorsement	Extralegal Endorsement
Colorado	By Official Party
Connecticut	Organization
Delaware	Illinois (Dem.)
New York	Louisiana (Dem. & Rep.)
New Mexico	Massachusetts (Dem. & Rep.)
North Dakota	Michigan (Dem.)
Rhode Island	Minnesota (Dem. & Rep.)
Utah	Ohio
	Pennsylvania
	Virginia
	Wisconsin (Rep.)[a]
	By Party Affiliated Groups
	California Rep. Assembly;
	California Dem. Council

a. Endorsement is optional and has not been used for statewide office since 1978.

Sources: Malcolm E. Jewell, *Parties and Primaries: Nominating State Governors* (New York: Praeger, 1984), pp. 35, 38; Charles P. Hadley, "Louisiana Endorsements," *Comparative State Politics Newsletter* 4 (Oct. 1983): 3–4; Advisory Commission on Intergovernmental Relations, *The Transformation in American Politics* (Washington, D.C., 1986), p. 14.

candidate receive a fixed percentage of the convention delegate votes in order to enter the primary. In Connecticut, the minimum convention vote required is 20 percent. This requirement prevented former U.S. Representative Toby Moffett from challenging Governor William A. O'Neill in the 1986 Democratic primary.

Extralegal Endorsements

Eighteen of the state parties engage in preprimary endorsements through nonstatutory or extralegal procedures. For example, both parties in Massachusetts and Minnesota regularly endorse candidates at state party conventions and the Wisconsin Republicans have an optional endorsement procedure, which has not been used for statewide candidates since 1978. Since the 1930s the Illinois Democratic State Central Committee has engaged in preprimary endorsements through the practice of slate-making. The State Central Committee, which has been dominated by the Cook County Democratic organization, informally draws up a slate of approved candidates for the party's nomination to state office. There are also unofficial party endorsements by party affiliated groups in California. These unofficial party affiliates, including the Republican Assembly and the California Democratic Council, seek to influence nominations through their group endorsements. In addition, it is not unusual for party organizations to make quietly unofficial endorsements and also attempt to discourage candidates from entering the primary. Malcolm E. Jewell reports, for example, that Illinois Republicans sometimes endorse candidates through their state central committee or county chairmen's association, and party leaders in Ohio and Pennsylvania also frequently endorse candidates.[19]

Extralegal endorsement practices often reflect a desire on the part of party activists to select candidates committed to a particular political faith or faction. Wisconsin's conservative Republicans, the Stalwarts, initiated the party's endorsement procedures during the 1920s in an effort to wrest control of the GOP primary from the La Follette Progressives, and in 1934 La Follette's followers finally split from the GOP and formed a separate party that lasted until 1946.[20] Protecting a liberal political ideology has played a major role in the Minnesota Democratic-Farmer-Labor (DFL) party's utilization of endorsement. Not all endorsement activities are motivated, however, solely out of ideological concerns. An interest in maintaining political control, not ideology, has been a major motivation of the Illinois Democratic State Central Committee in its slate-making. Other party interests that can be advanced through endorsement are selecting the strongest candidate and avoiding a divisive primary that could split the party for the general election.

Consequences of Preprimary Endorsements

Reduced primary competition. Preprimary endorsement reduces the amount of competition in primaries. Candidates who fail to gain endorsements often withdraw from the race and do not enter the primary. An example of this occurred in the contest for the Republican nomination to the United States Senate in Connecticut in 1982. George Bush's brother, Prescott Bush, mounted a formidable challenge against maverick Republican Senator Lowell Weicker. Weicker had frequently been at odds with the state GOP organization and the Reagan White House. Despite past differences, state party leaders rallied around Weicker on the grounds that he would be the strongest candidate against the Democrats and secured the party endorsement for the senator. Mr. Bush then dropped out of the race. Jewell's data show that between 1946 and 1982, 77.5 percent of northern state primaries were contested. However, in states where statutory endorsements were in effect, there were contested primaries in 42.3 percent of the cases, and in 66.7 percent of the cases in states with extralegal endorsements.[21] While these data suggest that statutory endorsement procedures are more effective in restricting competition than informal procedures, it should be noted that several of the states with statutory endorsement have traditionally been strong organization states, while the states using extralegal techniques frequently have weak party structures in the Progressive tradition. Strong organizations can more effectively discourage candidates from entering primaries if they fail to gain endorsement. Preprimary endorsements have their greatest impact in reducing primary competition through the elimination of minor candidates. Major challengers, however, can normally mount effective primary campaigns even without endorsements, as former Governor Rudy Perpich demonstrated in 1982 when he did not even seek endorsement and then handily defeated the Minnesota DFL endorsed candidate for governor.

Endorsed candidates tend to win. There is also evidence that endorsements influence the outcomes of primary elections. Jewell found that between 1946 and 1982, the endorsed candidate won 77 percent of the time.[22] The Minnesota DFL has been one of the most successful parties in using endorsement to gain nominations for its candidates. Through 1982, only two DFL endorsed candidates for a gubernatorial nomination had been upset and it was not until 1978 that a senatorial endorsee, Congressman Donald Fraser, was defeated in the primary.[23] The Minnesota and Wisconsin Republicans up until the late 1970s also had strong records of controlling nominations through endorsement. Endorsement is particularly effective if the party organization making the endorsement is in a position to deliver significant campaign resources—money, staff, volunteers—to the favored candidate. In evaluating Jewell's impressive numbers concerning endorsement success rates, it is well to keep in mind that endorsement often goes to incumbents and other strong candidates, who could probably win primary elections with or without party endorsement.

There are, of course, disadvantages that may attach themselves to endorsement. An endorsed candidate may be labeled the tool of the party "bosses" or "kingmakers"—an especially damaging label in states with political cultures that value political independence and are suspicious of parties. United States Representative Robert Kasten found endorsement was not an asset in the 1978 Wisconsin GOP primary for governor. The state GOP provided him with only modest support in his primary campaign against a charismatic university chancellor, Lee Dreyfus. This left him with the onus of being perceived as the "organization" candidate, while receiving no significant tangible benefits from the party. Dreyfus exploited Kasten's status as an endorsed candidate and stressed his own independence from party ties and won the primary.

The impact of endorsements reaches beyond which candidate wins the primary to affect the conduct of campaigns. The research of Sarah Morehouse demonstrated that party endorsement in gubernatorial primaries tends to affect the amount of money spent on primary campaigns and the impact that campaign spending has upon primary election outcomes. In states without preprimary endorsement systems, more money is spent on primary elections, and campaign spending is highly related to the outcome of the primary contests. By contrast, in states with preprimary endorsing conventions, less money is spent and that money is not a major explanation for the success of candidates in the primaries.[24]

Increasingly frequent challenges. There are indications that endorsement is having reduced impact even in states with traditions of strong party organizations and records of success in gaining nominations for the endorsee. For example, in Minnesota challenges to the endorsed candidates in both parties have been regular occurrences since 1978; and in New York, Mario Cuomo won his first gubernatorial nomination by defeating the Democratic party's endorsed candidate, New York's colorful and controversial mayor, Ed Koch.

Competition in Primaries

It was the expectation of the reformers that the direct primary would stimulate competition among candidates for party nominations. This hope has not been fulfilled, however. In a substantial percentage of the primaries, nominations either go uncontested or involve only nominal challengers to the front runner. The two key determinants of intraparty competition in the primaries are the extent of the interparty competition and incumbency.

The Impact of Interparty Competition

V.O. Key first demonstrated that competition in primaries is significantly influenced by the pattern of two party competition that exists within a state or district. Competition in primaries is greatest where a party's prospects in the general election are the highest.[25] Recent research by Morehouse has confirmed Key's earlier findings of the relationship between the level of interparty competition in a state and the extent of primary competition. In gubernatorial primaries between 1956 and 1978, she found that Democratic primary competition was most intense in one party Democratic states, followed in order by states that lean Democratic and in two party states. She further found that competition for Republican gubernatorial nominations was most intense where the GOP had its best chance of winning—in two party competitive states (there were no one party Republican states identified in her study).[26]

Impact of general election prospects on primary competition is also evident in congressional nominations. When those prospects are good, especially if no incumbent is running, the primary field is likely to be crowded. For example, when Congressman Henry Reuss retired in 1982, after holding a safe Democratic seat in Milwaukee for twenty-eight years, there were ten candidates for the Democratic nomination to succeed him. The winner, James Moody, received 19 percent of the vote and five other candidates received more than 10 percent. Of course, when the prospects of victory in the general election are dismal, there is little or no competition for party nominations. Indeed, in congressional districts that heavily favor the incumbent's party, it is frequently impossible for the minority party to induce anyone to even enter the primaries. Thus in 1988, there were eighty (18 percent of the total) House districts in which one of the major parties failed to nominate a candidate.

Incumbents Win

Incumbency is a distinct advantage in nominating contests and the presence of an incumbent in a primary is usually enough to discourage serious opposition. Jewell and Olson found that between 1960 and 1986 Democratic gubernatorial primaries were contested 65 percent of the time when incumbents were seeking renomination, but when no incumbent was running 86 percent of the primaries were contested. For the Republicans, the comparable figures were 56 and 74 percent.[27] The tendency of incumbents to discourage primary opposition is also prevalent in state legislatures.

An illustration of the intense competition that can occur when no incumbent is running can be illustrated by recent Democratic gubernatorial primaries in Kentucky, where the state constitution limits governors to one consecutive term. In 1979, nine candidates entered the primary, which was won narrowly by a political outsider, John Y. Brown, the Kentucky Fried Chicken magnate. Brown gained his victory by garnering 29 percent of the vote, while two of his opponents had over 23 percent of the vote. His successor, Martha Layne Collins, also had to face stiff primary opposition in 1983. Four years later another political outsider with a large campaign war chest, Wallace Wilkinson, won the nomination with 34.5 percent of the vote in an eight-candidate field that included two former governors.

Since incumbents tend to scare off competition in the primaries, they, of course, win renomination in overwhelming proportion. Thus between 1977 and 1990, 113 incumbent governors sought renomination and 107 (95 percent) were successful.[28] In those rare instances when incumbent governors have been defeated, it is normally the result of serious intraparty rifts. For example, the fractious Democrats of Massachusetts have twice in succession failed to renominate an incumbent. In 1978 Edward King, a conservative Democrat, bested the liberal incumbent, Michael Dukakis, only to be ousted by Dukakis in the 1982 primary. In 1978, the regular Democratic organization of Illinois, led by Mayor Richard J. Daley of Chicago, was able to defeat the Democratic maverick governor, Daniel Walker, in the primary.

The advantages of incumbency are particularly striking in nominations for the United States House of Representatives. Between 1980 and 1990, the percentage of incumbent representatives renominated never dipped below 97 percent. The incidence of primary victories for incumbent senators was also high—consistently above 90 percent (see Table 5–4). For most members of Congress, the primary is not unlike the common cold; it is a nuisance; but it is seldom fatal.

The Impact of Nominating Procedures

The type of nominating procedures used within a state also affect the extent of primary competition. As noted previously, states which use preprimary endorsement procedures have lower levels of competition because of the ability of party organizations to restrict candidacies in these states. Run-off primaries tend to multiply the number of candidates in the initial primary, as do blanket primaries. Interestingly, studies of competition for nominations for governor and senator in open and closed primary states have found that there is less competition in open primary states than in closed primary states. The closed primary is not therefore a very effective technique for promoting party stability and limiting primary competition, despite the fact that open primaries are generally viewed as particularly damaging to party organizations and an encouragement to crossover voting.[29]

Table 5–4 Renomination Rates of Incumbent United States Representatives and Senators, 1980–1988

	Incumbent Representatives					Incumbent Senators				
	Seeking	Renominated		Defeated		Seeking	Renominated		Defeated	
Year	Renomination	N	Percent	N	Percent	Renomination	N	Percent	N	Percent
1990	406	405	99.8	1	0.2	31	31	100	0	0.0
1988	408	407	99.8	1	0.2	27	27	100	0	0.0
1986	393	391	99.5	2	0.5	28	28	100	0	0.0
1984	395	392	99.2	3	0.8	26	26	100	0	0.0
1982	393	383	97.5	10	2.5	31	30	96.8	1	3.2
1980	398	392	98.5	6	1.5	27	25	92.6	2	7.4
Totals	2392	2369	99.0 (Mean)	23	1.0 (Mean)	170	167	98.2 (Mean)	3	1.8 (Mean)

Sources: Thomas E. Mann, Norman J. Ornstein, and Michael J. Malbin, *Vital Statistics on Congress, 1989–1990* (Washington, D.C.: CQ Press, 1990), pp. 56–57; *Congressional Quarterly Weekly Report,* Oct. 20, 1990, p. 3538.

Voter Turnout in Primaries

Just as the reformers' high hopes for competition in primaries have been largely unfulfilled, so too have their expectations concerning voter participation. An average of only about 30 percent of the voting age population votes in gubernatorial primaries in years when both parties have contested primaries. If only one party has a major primary contest, voter participation is often substantially lower. Turnout tends to be highest in the West, where several of the states also have high turnout rates in general elections. Turnout is also relatively high in southern states, especially within the Democratic party which historically has dominated state and congressional elections in the region.[30] Indeed, because the Democratic primary was the real election in the South until recently, turnout was traditionally higher in southern primaries than general elections. As the Republican party has grown in strength since the 1950s, however, the vote in southern gubernatorial primaries has shrunk as a proportion of the general election vote in all of the southern states. With the frequently low level of turnout that prevails in primary elections, questions naturally arise about the representativeness of primary voters.

Personal Characteristics and Turnout

The same sorts of personal characteristics that are associated with voting in general elections are operative in primaries. Primary voters tend to be better educated and older than nonvoters. They are also more knowledgeable concerning politics, more interested in campaigns, and have a greater sense of civic duty. Primary voters rank even higher in these characteristics that distinguish voters from nonvoters than do voters in general elections. Primary turnout is also strongly affected by the strength of a person's party identification (i.e., one's psychological attachment to a political party). Political scientists have consistently demonstrated that the stronger an individual's party identification (e.g., being a strong Republican versus a weak Republican) the more likely that person is to vote. Jewell's study of primary voting has shown that party identification has an even stronger and more consistent impact on primary turnout than it does in general elections. He also found that party identification was especially important in determining which younger and less interested voters will vote in primaries.[31]

The tendency of party activists to have higher rates of turnout in primaries and also to have stronger ideological orientations than rank and file voters has caused political scientists to consider whether patterns of voter turnout bias the outcomes of primary.[32] That is, do the patterns of primary turnout introduce a bias into the results of primaries, which in the Republican party favors conservative candidates and in the Democratic party helps liberal candidates? Some studies of presidential primaries have indicated that such biases do operate. However, there have been few analyses of state level primaries that have dealt with this issue. Studies of the Wisconsin primary revealed that primary voters are not unrepresentative of their nonvoting fellow partisans in either issue positions or candidate preferences.[33] As Jewell and Olson have pointed out, there is probably little reason to expect that there would be a consistent pattern of unrepresentativeness in turnout across the states.[34] Turnout is likely to be affected by the particular mix of candidates on the ballot in any given state's primary. If a liberal Democratic incumbent is running against token opposition, moderate and conservative partisans may have little incentive to vote, whereas a contest for an open seat between clearly identified liberal and conservative candidates could stimulate these people to vote in larger numbers.

Political/Institutional Influences on Turnout

There are a variety of political/institutional variables that affect turnout. These variables relate to the statutory regulations surrounding the primary, the nature of the party system, and the levels of competition that exist in primary contests.[35]

Majority versus minority party status. Turnout tends to be highest in the primary of the party which has the greatest likelihood of winning the general election, precisely because that party's contest is more likely to determine which person will eventually hold public office.

Competition. Competition for a party's nomination spurs voters to participate in primaries. In the absence of a real contest for a nomination, voter turnout diminishes. A party's share of the primary electorate may vary dramatically depending upon whether or not it has a red hot contest in a given year. For example, in the 1980 Wisconsin primary for United States senator, the Republican share of the total primary vote was 63.7 percent and the Democratic share was 35.9 percent. In that year, there was an intense, three-way fight for the GOP nomination and no contest on the Democratic side where incumbent Gaylord Nelson was seeking renomination. By contrast in 1988, it was the hotly contested four-way race for the Democratic senatorial nomination, which featured record levels of expenditure by businessman Herbert Kohl, that attracted the largest share (59.2 percent) of the voters. The less intense GOP primary drew only 40.8 percent of the vote. The extent of competition is influenced by such factors as *endorsement* and *incumbency*, both of which operate to depress competition and thus indirectly reduce turnout. Traditions of competition in state primaries, as in the one party South, can have the effect of stimulating turnout.

Closed versus open primaries. Because open primaries do not require voters to disclose publicly a partisan preference, open primaries tend to have higher levels of turnout than do closed primaries. Independents can be precluded from participation in closed primary states.

The National Party Organizations and Nominations in the States

The recruitment and nomination processes within the states illustrate the decentralized character of the American party system. Despite the importance of congressional and senatorial nominations for the functioning of the national level parties, the national party organizations have traditionally played only a minor role in candidate recruitment and nomination. Recruitment has largely been a matter of self-selection, with aspiring members of Congress determining on their own when the time was ripe for them to move from careers in statehouses, city halls, courthouses, or the private sector to the Congress. Aspiring representatives and senators put together personal organizations to contest first the primary and then the general election. Party leaders in Congress and occasionally the president sometimes gave informal encouragement to promising candidates, but it was traditional for the national party leadership to stay aloof from state nomination contests.

A classic example of national party weakness in influencing congressional nominations occurred in 1938, when President Franklin D. Roosevelt sought to purge dissident conservatives in the primaries. Despite the fact that Roosevelt was at the zenith of his popularity during this period, his intervention in the primaries against incumbent senators in Oklahoma, Georgia, South Carolina, and Maryland failed. His inability to influence primary election outcomes paralleled the experience of President William Howard Taft and Senate Republican Leader Nelson Aldrich (R.I.), who sought to oust western progressives in the Republican primaries of 1910. Usually, the president and national party leaders have remained silent, even when their loyal supporters have been challenged in the primaries.

The traditional hands-off policy of the national parties toward congressional and senatorial nominations is changing. Starting in 1978 for the Republicans and in 1982 for the Democrats, the national congressional campaign committees began systematic efforts to identify, recruit, and assist potential congressional candidates. Because the Republicans started earlier and have a larger staff and superior financing, their effort has been more extensive than that of the Democrats.[36]

The process, as practiced by Republicans, first involves *targeting* the districts. Voting and demographic data are analyzed to determine which districts offer the greatest potential for GOP victory. After the targeting is completed, the *recruitment* of candidates is initiated. Using data from the targeting procedure, the profile of an "ideal" candidate for the district is identified and an effort is made by the party's field staff to find a potential candidate to match the profile. The field staff seek strong campaigners and, therefore, tend to prefer persons already holding elective office, who also understand working with the media. To entice candidates into running, financial support, technical assistance with the campaign, and training are provided. The parties also seek to serve as liaison persons with the political action committees (PACs) to help the candidates secure the necessary financing. The concern is always to find the strongest candidate.[37] The intensity of the National Republican Congressional Committee involvement in candidate recruitment was underlined by Co-Chairman Edward Rollins, who noted that ten of the thirty House races targeted in 1990 would be "my own races—places where I've gone out and recruited candidates and cleared the way for their nomination."[38]

It is, of course, difficult to determine whether the activities of national party organizations were decisive in the decisions of candidates to seek party nominations in target constituencies. However, as one staffer of the Democratic Congressional Campaign Committee (DCCC) observed,

> A telephone call from one's county or state party chairman may not be quite enough to encourage someone to subject him or herself to the hard work and personal sacrifice associated with running for Congress, but a call from Tony Coehlo [Chairman of the DCCC], promising party assistance in fundraising and campaign advertising . . . and a few calls from some other well-known party leaders might be just enough to get a person to commit him or herself.[39]

The national senatorial campaign committees have also become increasingly aggressive in candidate recruitment and in supporting favored candidates in the primaries. For example, in 1984 the

National Republican Senatorial Committee (NRSC) contributed funds to its preferred candidates in contested Republican primaries in Tennessee, Nebraska, and New Jersey, while the Democratic Senatorial Campaign Committee (DSCC) was given credit for encouraging outgoing Governor William Winter of Mississippi to challenge Senator Thad Cochran and for convincing Representative Paul Simon to undertake a successful challenge against Senator Charles Percy of Illinois. Occasionally, the NRSC has asked the White House to become involved in persuading candidates to run. President Reagan, for example, was pivotal in getting former Vermont governor Richard Snelling to run for the Senate in 1986.[40]

Occasionally, the national parties put their money on the wrong horse and the candidate favored by the national party loses the primary or the general election. Of course, this causes substantial ill feeling and embarrassment to the national party. For example, in 1978 the national Republican party gave support to the primary opponent of Roger Jepsen in the Iowa senatorial primary, but Jepsen went on to win the primary and general election. The NRSC also suffered embarrassment in 1984 for its activist recruitment policy and for assisting favored candidates in primary elections. It actively recruited Elliott Richardson to run for the Senate in Massachusetts, only to see him lose the primary, while the candidates who were supported in the Tennessee and Michigan primaries ran poorly in the general election.

National party involvement in congressional and state level nominating politics frequently extends to *negative recruitment*—discouraging unwanted candidacies. A dramatic example occurred in Ohio in 1990, when Republican National Chairman Lee Atwater, with White House backing, played a crucial role in quashing a Republican primary and assembling the desired state party ticket. After meeting with Atwater, Bob Taft III was persuaded to drop his challenge to former Cleveland mayor George Voinovich in the gubernatorial primary and instead run for secretary of state. Republican strategists hoped this ticket would enable them to win both offices and thereby gain control of the legislative redistricting in 1991.[41]

The action of the national parties in recent years to involve themselves actively in nominating politics within the states is a sharp departure from past practice and holds the potential to change significantly the character of American politics. Continuing recruitment efforts and high levels of candidate support may create a pool of candidates in the states whose primary ties are to the national party. To the extent that these candidates perceive national party support to have been a critical factor in their nomination and election, they may feel a sense of obligation to the leaders who helped them in their hour of need. That sense of obligation is a potential lever of influence for the congressional leaders in seeking to affect the voting of representatives and senators in the halls of Congress. To date, however, the new activism of the congressional and senatorial campaign committees has not been used by party leaders in Congress to enforce discipline and unity. An aggressive future leader, however, could seek to expand influence over colleagues on the basis of campaign support that has been provided. Such a leader might also threaten to withhold it from dissident members.

The Direct Primary and the General Election

The primary, of course, has significant implications for the general election. It narrows the field of candidates and choice available to the voter. The outcome of a primary may also affect a party's general election prospects—enhancing those prospects if a strong candidate wins and diminishing the chances of winning if a weak candidate is nominated. Party leaders are frequently concerned about the potential divisiveness of a contested primary. They fear that a hotly contested primary will leave the party disunited for the general election. Preprimary endorsements are one method of seeking to prevent divisive primaries. Others include channeling financial and campaign support to a preferred candidate in an effort to discourage opposition. There are many frequently cited examples of divisive primaries which have resulted in the party's nominee going down to defeat. Former Vice President Spiro Agnew, for example, first came to national attention when in 1966, as the Republican nominee for governor of Maryland, he defeated a Democratic candidate who had won an extremely bitter primary using an anti-open housing slogan ("your home is your castle") that was widely believed to be racist in character. Similarly in 1986, Guy Hunt was successful in his bid to become the first Republican governor of Alabama since Reconstruction because of a protracted dispute within the Democratic party over which candidate had won a hotly contested run-off primary.

Despite these and other examples of a party going down to defeat after a divisive primary, there is no consistent pattern which demonstrates that contested primaries are necessarily damaging. Of course, one reason that primary contests do not consistently result in general election losses is that primary competition is most frequent within the stronger of a state's two parties.[42] There are also circumstances when a contested primary may help the nominee. Battling for a party nomination normally generates substantial publicity for the candidates and keeps their names before the public. A tough primary fight may even enhance the image of the winning candidate as an attractive personality, skilled campaigner, and person who is knowledgeable about critical issues. The absence of a primary fight can push a candidate off the evening news programs and front pages of the papers in the crucial months of the spring and summer before an election. Such lack of publicity and testing of the candidate in a primary can be a serious liability in the general election.

The Direct Primary and Political Parties

The institutionalization of the direct primary as the principal method of nominating state and congressional candidates in the United States is part of a long-term trend toward shifting power away from party leaders to rank and file voters. In their effort to weaken the capacity of parties to control the selection of candidates for major elective office, the reformers of the progressive era have been largely successful. In only a handful of jurisdictions are party organizations sufficiently strong that they can bestow their endorsement upon a candidate and assure the individual's nomination in a primary. Even the much vaunted Cook County (Illinois) Democratic organization can no longer control congressional nominations in many parts of Chicago and it was unable to nominate its preferred candidate for mayor in the 1979 and 1983 Democratic primaries.

As the impact of preprimary endorsements and the national congressional campaign committees illustrate, however, party support can be helpful to a candidate in gaining a nomination. Party organizational support is not irrelevant in the primary process, but it is seldom sufficient to secure a nomination. Rather, the candidate must build a personal organization and following among the voters if the hurdle of the primary is to be cleared successfully. The direct primary has, therefore, contributed to a candidate centered type of politics in America, in contrast to the more party centered politics of most Western style democracies that do not utilize the primaries for nominations.

Although the direct primary has contributed to a weakening of political parties organizationally, Leon D. Epstein believes that the primary helps to account for the extraordinary and continued *electoral dominance* of the Republican and Democratic parties. He believes that the direct primary institutionalized the Republican and Democratic labels in electoral politics. The primary provides unusual opportunities for insurgents to win major party nominations and thereby forego the normally self-defeating process of running as third party candidates. Challengers to established party organizational leadership are thus encouraged to seek intraparty avenues to power and voters become accustomed to choosing from among individuals and factions that are competing for a party label.

Epstein's argument, of course, is paradoxical. It asserts that while strengthening the parties electorally, the primary has weakened the party organization and the party in the government. The primary has thus by statute institutionalized the electoral looseness of American parties, but in the process also has acted as a party preservative. But as preservatives in food processing change the nature and quality of what is being preserved, the direct primary has left the parties as persistent electoral labels whose importance is frequently questioned after election day.[43]

Suggestions for Further Reading

Epstein, Leon D. *Political Parties in the American Mold*. Madison: University of Wisconsin Press, 1986. Chapters 6 and 8.

Jewell, Malcolm E. *Parties and Primaries: Nominating State Governors*. New York: Praeger, 1984.

Jewell, Malcolm E., and Olson, David M. *American State Political Parties and Elections*, 3rd ed. Chicago, Ill.: Dorsey Press, 1988. Chapter 4.

Key, V.O., Jr. *American State Politics: An Introduction* New York: Knopf, 1956.

Notes

1. Austin Ranney and Willmoore Kendall, *Democracy and the American Party System* (New York: Harcourt, Brace, 1956), pp. 267–269.
2. E.E. Schattschneider, *Party Government* (New York: Farrar and Rinehart, 1942), p. 64.
3. V.O. Key, Jr., *American State Politics: An Introduction* (New York: Knopf, 1956), pp. 87–88.
4. Ibid., p. 88.
5. Ibid., p. 91.
6. Ibid., p. 117.
7. Ellen Torelle, ed., *The Political Philosophy of Robert M. La Follette* (Madison, Wis.: Robert M. La Follette Co., 1920); pp. 29–31.
8. Malcolm E. Jewell, *Parties and Primaries: Nominating State Governors* (New York: Praeger, 1984), pp. 9–11.
9. Ibid., pp. 11–12.
10. Malcolm E. Jewell and David M. Olson, *American State Political Parties and Elections*, rev. ed. (Homewood, Ill.: Dorsey Press, 1982), p. 107.
11. The impact of the *Tashjian* decision is analyzed in Leon D. Epstein,

"Will American Political Parties Be Privatized?" *The Journal of Law and Politics* 4 (Winter 1989): 239–274.

12. Thomas H. Kazee, "The Impact of Electoral Reform: 'Open Election' and the Louisiana Party System," *Publius* 13 (Winter 1983): 135–138.
13. V.O. Key, Jr., *Politics, Parties and Pressure Groups*, 5th ed. (New York: Knopf, 1964), p. 393.
14. For an analysis of the operation of New York's cross-filing system, see Howard A. Scarrow, *Parties, Elections and Representation in the State of New York* (New York: New York University Press, 1983), pp. 55–80.
15. Phil Duncan, "Jackson's Anti-Run-Off Push Divides Southern Democrats," *Congressional Quarterly Weekly Report* (May 5, 1984), p. 1034.
16. Larry Sabato, *Goodbye to Good-Time Charlie: The American Governorship Transformed* (Washington, D.C.: CQ Press, 1983), pp. 119, 124.
17. Holly Idelson, "Justice Issues A Challenge to Southern Runoff Law," *Congressional Quarterly Weekly Report*, Aug. 11, 1990, p. 2605; and Michael Oreskes, "Seeking Congressional Seats, GOP Discovers Ally in Voting Rights Act," *New York Times*, Aug. 20, 1990, p. A10 Y.
18. David E. Price, *Bringing Back the Parties* (Washington, D.C.: CQ Press, 1984), pp. 132–133.
19. Jewell, *Parties and Primaries*, pp. 36–37.
20. Frank J. Sorauf, "Extra-Legal Parties in Wisconsin," *American Political Science Review* 48 (Sept. 1954): 692–704.
21. Jewell, *Parties and Primaries*, pp. 66–67; see also Andrew D. McNitt, "The Effect of Endorsement on Competition for Nominations: An Explanation of Different Nominating Systems," *Journal of Politics* 42 (Feb. 1980): 257–266. See also Tom W. Rice, "Gubernatorial and Senatorial Primary Elections: Determinants and Consequences," *American Politics Quarterly* 13 (Oct. 1985): 434–435.
22. Jewell, *Parties and Primaries*, p. 67.
23. Ibid., pp. 149–195. On the Minnesota Democrats' success in influencing the outcomes of state legislative primaries, see Joseph A. Kunkle III, "Party Endorsement and Incumbency in Minnesota Legislative Nominations," *Legislative Studies Quarterly* 13 (May 1988): 211–224.
24. Sarah M. Morehouse, "Money versus Party Effort: Nominating Governors," *American Journal of Political Science* 34 (Aug. 1990): 706–724.
25. Key *Politics, Parties and Pressure Groups*, pp. 379–380; Key, *American State Politics*, pp. 107–111.
26. Sarah McCally Morehouse, *State Politics, Parties and Policy* (New York: Holt, Rinehart and Winston, 1981), pp. 180–183; Rice, "Gubernatorial and Senatorial Primary Elections," pp. 433–434.
27. Malcolm E. Jewell and David M. Olson, *Political Parties and Elections in American States*, 3d ed. (Chicago, Ill.: Dorsey Press, 1988), p. 105.
28. Thad Beyle, "Governors," in Virginia Gray, Herbert Jacob, and Robert B. Albritton, eds., *Politics in the American States*, 5th ed. (Glenview, Ill.: Scott, Foresman/Little, Brown, 1990), p. 214 (Beyle data updated to include 1990); see also Morehouse, *State Politics, Parties, and Policy*, p. 184.

29. Andrew D. McNitt, "The Impact of State Legislation on Political Campaigns," *State Government* 53 (Summer 1980), p. 137; Rice, "Primary Elections," pp. 435–437.
30. Jewell and Olson, *Political Parties and Elections in American States*, 3d ed., p. 110.
31. Jewell, *Parties and Primaries*, p. 176.
32. V.O. Key considered the consequences of unrepresentative primary electorates in his *American State Politics*, pp. 153–165.
33. Austin Ranney, "The Representativeness of Primary Electorates," *Midwest Journal of Political Science* 12 (May 1968): 224–238; Austin Ranney and Leon D. Epstein, "The Two Electorates: Voters and Non-Voters in a Wisconsin Primary," *Journal of Politics* 28 (Aug. 1966): 598–616.
34. Jewell and Olson, *American State Political Parties and Elections*, p. 136.
35. Jewell, *Parties and Primaries*, pp. 193–195; Patrick J. Kenney, "Explaining Turnout in Gubernatorial Primaries," *American Politics Quarterly* 11 (July 1983): 315–326; Patrick J. Kenney, "Explaining Primary Turnout: The Senatorial Case," *Legislative Studies Quarterly*, 11 (Feb. 1986), pp. 65–73.
36. For a description of national party candidate recruitment activities, see Paul S. Herrnson, *Party Campaigning in the 1980s* (Cambridge, Mass.: Harvard University Press, 1988), pp. 48–54.
37. Bruce W. Robeck and Gary C. Jacobson, "National Party Recruitment of Congressional Candidates," Legislative Studies Section, APSA, Newsletter, (Nov. 1984), pp. 7–10.
38. David S. Broder,"National GOP Abandons Hands-Off Policy in Primaries," *Washington Post*, May 22, 1990, p. A6.
39. Herrnson, *Party Campaigning in the 1980s*, p. 54.
40. Ibid., pp. 52–53.
41. Broder, "National GOP Abandons Hands-Off Policy in Primaries," p. A6.
42. Jewell and Olson, *American State Political Parties*, p. 149; see also James E. Piereson and Terry E. Smith, "Primary Divisiveness and General Election Success in Gubernatorial Elections," *Journal of Politics* 37 (May 1975): 555–562.
43. For a full exposition of Epstein's intriguing argument concerning the electoral impact of the direct primary on parties, see Leon D. Epstein, *Political Parties in the American Mold* (Madison: University of Wisconsin Press, 1986), pp. 244–245.

CHAPTER 6

Presidential Nominating Politics

Vice President Hubert H. Humphrey, while winning the 1968 Democratic presidential nomination, did not open his campaign until March of that year and did not enter a single presidential primary. Instead he depended upon his support among party leaders. By contrast, Governor Michael Dukakis of Massachusetts campaigned for two years and contested 36 primaries on his way to the 1988 Democratic presidential nomination. Humphrey's campaign was funded with contributions from private individuals and organizations; Dukakis's campaign was fueled by a combination of private contributions and funds assigned to him under the national government's policy of providing matching grants to candidates.

The differing paths to presidential nominations taken by Humphrey and Dukakis, both holders of major public office and leaders of the northern liberal wing of their party, reflect the fundamental changes that have occurred in presidential nominating politics since 1968. A process once dominated by party leaders, who heavily influenced the selection of national convention delegates, is now a process which is candidate centered. A process that once relied upon internal party procedures to select delegates through caucuses and conventions now relies primarily upon presidential primaries to determine the allocation of delegates among contenders for a party's nomination. Participation was once restricted to party regulars in the caucus and convention states and to primary voters in a few primary states. Now presidential nominating politics is an open and participatory process characterized by mass citizen involvement in primaries and open access to party caucuses. Now that the presidential primaries and some caucuses receive saturation media coverage, the media has far reaching influence concerning who ultimately wins a nomination. Presidential nominating politics of the 1990s is candidate centered, primary focused, participatory, and media intensive.

Methods of Delegate Selection

The national nominating conventions held in the summer of presidential election years are the culmination of a long season of campaigning to select convention delegates. The delegates, meeting in convention, nominate the party's candidates for president and vice president, adopt a platform, and approve rules that will govern the party. The composition of the convention, of course, determines the nature of the decisions the convention will make on the nominations, platform and rules. The processes of delegate selection, therefore, are critical to the outcomes of the convention.

There are three principal methods of delegate selection: (1) the presidential primary; (2) the party caucus/convention process; and (3) automatic selection by virtue of the party or elected position an individual holds. Both parties use the presidential primary and caucus/convention selection processes, but only the Democrats have automatic delegates (see Figure 6–1). The various states are free to devise their own methods of delegate selection as long as those methods conform to guidelines contained in the rules of the national Republican and Democratic parties. The procedures for selection of delegates are frequently set forth in state statutes, which may be supplemented by state party rules. In the absence of state statutes governing delegate selection, state parties may adopt rules to determine how delegates will be chosen. Because each state legislature and/or state party organization is involved in devising the procedures for delegate selection, there are a wide variety of practices followed within the states.

State Delegate Selection Procedures Must Conform to National Party Rules

Although the states have some latitude in determining how their delegates to national conventions will be chosen, the procedures they devise must be in strict conformity with national party rules. In other words, national party rules take precedence over state statutes and state party rules in matters of delegate selection. A state delegation that is not chosen in conformity with national party rules runs the risk of not having its delegation seated at the national convention—a severe sanction, which the national party can impose.

The most celebrated instance of conflict between a state party and its national organization over the delegate selection procedures took place in Wisconsin. In 1903 Wisconsin was the first state to adopt a presidential primary law, but it was a law which also provided for conducting the presidential primary under open primary procedures. After 1974, national Democratic party rules forbad selecting delegates through open primary procedures and thus Wisconsin's law was out of conformity with national party rules. Wisconsin sought to maintain its open primary, but the United States Supreme Court upheld the right of a national party organization to determine delegate selection procedures.[1] Wisconsin Democrats, therefore, were forced in 1984 to abandon the open presidential primary for selecting their convention delegates and adopt caucus procedures that satisfied the national Democratic party. In an effort to put this often bitter controversy behind it and prepare for the 1988 elections, the Democratic National Committee in 1986 agreed to permit states with open primary traditions (Wisconsin and Montana) to utilize open presidential

Figure 6–1: Delegate Selection to National Convention, 1988

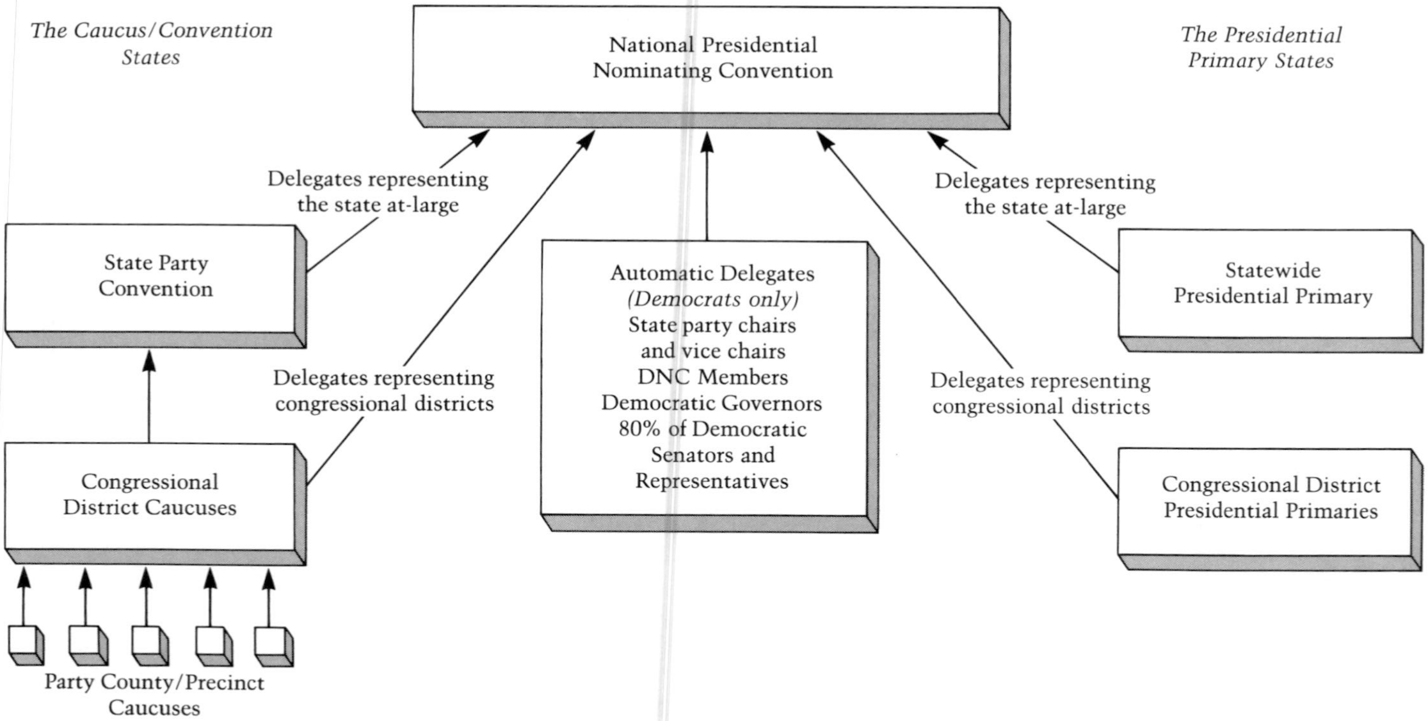

The Caucus/Convention States

The Presidential Primary States

National Presidential Nominating Convention

Delegates representing the state at-large

State Party Convention

Delegates representing congressional districts

Congressional District Caucuses

Party County/Precinct Caucuses

Automatic Delegates
(Democrats only)
State party chairs and vice chairs
DNC Members
Democratic Governors
80% of Democratic Senators and Representatives

Delegates representing the state at-large

Statewide Presidential Primary

Delegates representing congressional districts

Congressional District Presidential Primaries

primaries. While making this accommodation to Wisconsin, the DNC continued to assert its power to regulate delegate selection procedures. Thus Wisconsin conceded the principle of the national party's legal supremacy, but the national party conceded the substance of the open primary issue.

Presidential Primaries

The largest share of convention delegates are chosen through procedures which involve presidential primaries. In 1988, there were thirty-four Democratic and thirty-five Republican presidential primaries that were used to allocate delegates among presidential candidates. These primaries determined the allocation of 66.6 percent of the delegates to the Democratic convention and 76.9 percent of the total GOP delegates. In addition, there were three Democratic and two Republican primaries which were so-called "beauty contests"—they tested the popularity of the candidates, but were not used to allocate delegates to the national conventions.[2] The number of states and territories using the presidential primaries has increased significantly since 1968, when sixteen Republican and seventeen Democratic primaries were used in the selection of slightly over one-third of the delegates (see Figure 6–2).

However, the number of primaries held in any given presidential election year has been subject to considerable variation depending on political conditions. Thus, in 1984, there were only twenty-one primaries used to select Republican delegates due to the fact that Ronald Reagan was unopposed for his party's nomination. The number of Democratic primaries used to select delegates fell from thirty-five in 1980 to twenty-four in 1984 because of Democratic leaders' efforts to reduce the number of primaries which they considered excessive and often divisive.

With the largest share of the delegates selected through procedures that involve presidential primaries, it has become imperative for presidential candidates to enter virtually all of the primaries in order to win sufficient delegates to gain a convention majority. The importance of the primaries, however, goes beyond the number of delegates which are at stake in these contests. The results of primaries constitute an ostensibly objective indicator of a candidate's ability to win the election. Primaries, therefore, are particularly important because of the image of candidate popularity, electibility, and momentum they can convey.

The mechanics of the presidential primaries vary from state to state depending upon applicable state laws and party rules. For exam-

Figure 6–2: The Proliferation of Presidential Primaries, 1968–1988

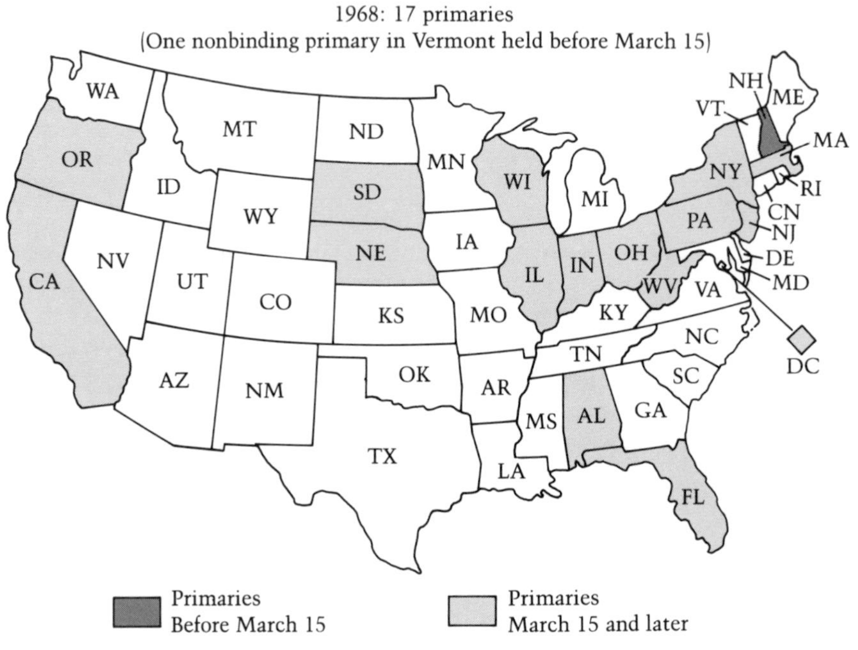

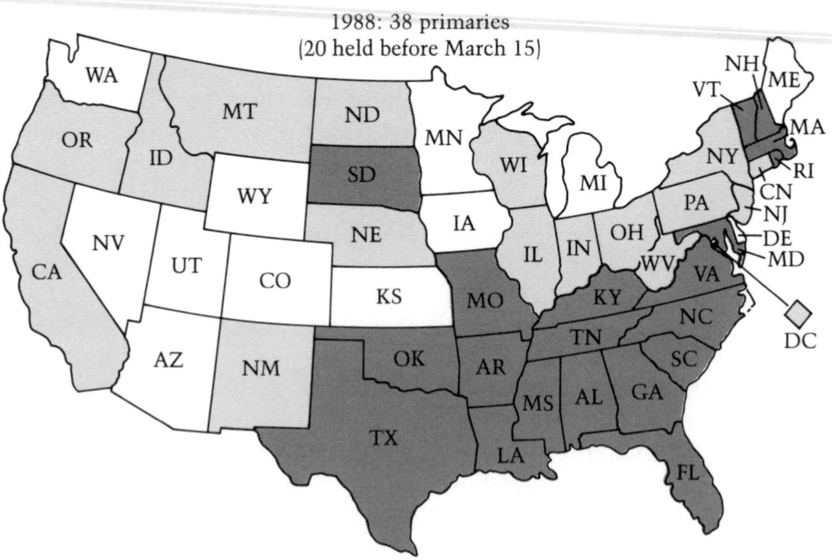

Note: Both maps include "binding" primaries that selected delegates and "nonbinding" primaries that were beauty contests only. Neither Alaska nor Hawaii holds presidential primaries. South Carolina held a primary for Republicans only.

Source: Adapted from Michael Nelson, ed., *The Elections of 1988* (Washington, D.C.: CQ Press, 1989), p. 30.

ple, in some states the names of individuals who are running for delegate positions are on the ballot and voters vote directly for delegates. In other states, the names of the presidential candidates are on the ballot, but the names of persons seeking to be delegates are not. There is normally a contest for delegates in each congressional district and an additional contest to determine how the delegates who will represent the state at large will be allocated among the presidential candidates. A presidential candidate, therefore, can lose the statewide vote and fail to win any at large delegates and still pick up delegates by making a strong showing in the primaries of individual congressional districts within a state.

State Party Caucuses and Conventions

Until the 1972 conventions, a majority of the states used state party caucuses and conventions to select delegates. For example, in 1968 approximately two-thirds of the delegates to national conventions were chosen via party caucuses and conventions. This is a procedure which involves a relatively small proportion of the electorate. It is party members and activists who normally have the interest, motivation, and knowledge to participate in the series of party meetings that culminate in congressional district and state party meetings to choose delegates.

In caucus/convention states, the process of delegate selection involves a progression of party meetings starting at the local level, running through the congressional district, and culminating in a state party convention. The process normally begins with local caucuses at either the precinct or county level. Party members and activists attend these meetings, often after having been mobilized by presidential candidate organizations or interest groups. Local caucus participants register their candidate preferences and also elect representatives to the next level of party organizational meeting in the process—the congressional district caucus. At the congressional district caucus, representatives chosen by the various local caucuses meet to (1) register their preference for the party's presidential nominee; (2) elect delegates to the national convention to represent the congressional district; and (3) elect delegates to the state party convention. The national convention delegates selected to represent the congressional district at the national convention are chosen to reflect the extent of support candidates for the presidency have among the congressional district caucus participants. Delegates from the various congressional districts in a state then meet in a state party convention to elect national convention delegates to represent the state at large.

Because the caucus system is an internal party process, it places a premium on a candidate having dedicated supporters—the type of people who are willing to spend evenings and weekends taking part in lengthy party meetings. It also requires an effective organization to mobilize people to turn out and support the candidate at each stage in the process. It is essential that a presidential candidate's organization have intimate knowledge of the state laws and party rules for delegate selection and of intraparty politics. Whereas presidential primaries are media oriented in order to appeal to a mass electorate, the caucus/convention process is more of an intraparty affair which requires an efficient organization.

Combination Presidential Primary and Convention Systems

Some states use a combination of the presidential primary and party convention to choose their national convention delegates. Illinois, for example, uses a presidential primary to elect national convention delegates to represent the state's congressional districts. However, it uses a state party convention to choose the delegates that will represent the state at large. There are also states in which presidential primaries are purely popularity contests that have no binding effect on delegate selection. After holding their primaries the party organizations in these states (in 1988, Democrats in Idaho, North Dakota, and Vermont; Republicans in Vermont and Virginia) then actually choose their national convention delegates through a caucus/convention process.

Automatic Unpledged Delegates

In an effort to increase convention participation by party leaders and elected officials, the Democrats for their 1984 convention made provision in their rules for granting automatic delegate status to major party leaders and elected officials. These delegates would not be officially pledged to any presidential candidate. Under Democratic rules, national committee members, state party chairs and vice chairs, and Democratic governors are automatically convention delegates as are 80 percent of the Democratic members of the United States House and Senate. Designation of the congressional delegates is made by the House and Senate Democratic caucuses. In 1988 there were 645 so-called "superdelegate" slots (15.5 percent of the total delegates) at the Democratic convention. There are no automatic delegates to Republican national conventions. Republican party leaders and elected officials must go through the regular primary and caucus procedures in order to become delegates.

Phases of the Nomination Process

Achieving a presidential nomination has become a fulltime, often four year endeavor. Indeed, the task is so demanding that individuals holding a major public office frequently conclude that they cannot pursue the presidency and also discharge their public duties. As a result, a substantial share of the major party nominees, excluding incumbent presidents, in recent years have been politicians out of office: Democrats Jimmy Carter (1976) and Walter Mondale (1984); Republican Ronald Reagan (1980). Similarly, major contenders such as Ronald Reagan (1976), George Bush (1980), and Jesse Jackson (1984 and 1988) held no public office during their quests for the presidency, and other strong candidates, like Democratic Senators Edward Kennedy (D-Mass.) in 1980, Gary Hart (D-Colo.) in 1984, and Albert Gore (D-Tenn.) did not hold party leadership positions in the Senate. Indeed, the process of gaining a major party nomination is so demanding that it is widely believed that Senator Howard Baker (R-Tenn) retired from the Senate and his post as majority leader in 1984 because he did not believe that he could pursue the presidency in 1988 while simultaneously serving as his party's leader in the Senate. Similarly, Senator Gary Hart, an early front runner for the 1988 Democratic nomination, decided not to seek reelection to the Senate in 1986 so that he might concentrate on the presidential contest. Exceptions to the tendency of individuals with major governing responsibilities not to seek presidential nominations occurred in 1988, when Massachusetts Governor Michael Dukakis won the Democratic nomination and Senate Minority Leader Bob Dole (Kansas) mounted a major drive for the GOP nomination. The lengthy and often intense schedule of the presidential nominating process can be broken down into a series of phases that culminate with the national convention.[3]

Phase I: Laying the Groundwork and Preliminary Skirmishing

During the period following a presidential election, prospective candidates for a presidential nomination four years hence begin the planning and preparations for their campaigns. This frequently involves recruiting a professional staff experienced in national politics, creating a political action committee (PAC) and tax exempt foundation to fund candidate activities, and developing a campaign plan.

Candidates crisscross the nation making appearances before the state party conventions, civic groups, trade associations, unions, and candidates' fund raisers in an attempt to gain media attention and make contacts with party leaders. Iowa and New Hampshire are inevitable and frequent stops on the campaign itinerary of presidential candidates, because these states hold critical early events in the national convention delegate selection process. For Republican presidential aspirants, Michigan has also become the focus of early campaigning. Precinct caucuses, the first step in the state GOP's delegate selection process, are held two years in advance of the national convention (August 5, 1986 for the 1988 national convention). Trips abroad are also scheduled so that the candidate can be pictured with world leaders and an image of experience in foreign affairs can be conveyed.[4]

The extent of early campaign preparations and maneuvering can be seen in the activities of prospective candidates during 1985—three years in advance of the 1988 presidential election. Political action committees (PACs) or tax exempt foundations, set up to avoid the restrictions of the Federal Election Campaign Act, were already operating on behalf of Republicans George Bush, Jack Kemp, Bob Dole, Howard Baker, Pierre duPont, and television evangelist Pat Robertson, and for Democrats Gary Hart, Richard Gephardt, and Bruce Babbitt. Although the PACs are created ostensibly to contribute money to a variety of candidates for nonpresidential offices and the foundations to sponsor educational and charitable activities, their real purpose is to promote presidential candidates. Bush's PAC, The Fund for America's Future, was used to pay for "an operation that has strong similarities to a skeleton presidential campaign."[5] It helped organize a PAC "steering committee" of prominent Republicans from across the country and a 658 member Michigan "steering committee." The Michigan group was a counter to the Kemp organization having announced the endorsement of their candidate by seven congressional district leaders at the annual Mackinac Island GOP conference, where the various Republican contenders sparred with each other for grass roots support.[6] Gary Hart's foundation, The Center for New Democracy, engaged in research to flesh out his 1984 "new ideas" campaign, while Kemp's foundation has financed travel abroad and staff advance work.

The pace of presidential campaigning intensifies during the year of the midterm elections as the candidates seek to play a prominent role in assisting their parties in congressional, senatorial, and state elections. There are appearances at fund raisers for party candidates from Maine to California. Most of the major contenders have their own personal PACs which fund their campaign forays and provide contributions to state and congressional candidates. The strategy is to create a sense of obligation among officeholders that can be converted later into commitments of support for the presidential nomination.[7]

During the year preceding the presidential election, the pace of campaigning accelerates with frequent visits to key primary states. One of the staples of this phase of the campaign has been appearances at state party conventions, which occasionally conduct straw polls of candidate popularity among the delegates. These tests of popularity among party activists are used by the candidates to demonstrate support for the nomination. Straw polls, however, carry special risks for the early front-runner candidate, who may be upset by a well-organized campaign conducted by a less well-known candidate. Thus in 1987, the Bush campaign found it necessary to send one of its top staff members to Wisconsin in June 1987 to assure a Bush straw poll victory at the GOP state party convention.

It is also essential in the year before the presidential primaries begin for candidates to raise serious money for their nomination campaigns. There are two types of candidates that have special advantages in raising campaign war chests—candidates with national stature and those who can compensate for a lack of national stature through access to well-heeled constituencies. In 1988, Vice President George Bush and Senate Republican Leader Bob Dole (the 1976 vice presidential nominee of the GOP) were candidates of national stature who near the end of 1987 had raised $18.1 million and $13.2 million respectively. Governor Michael Dukakis and the Reverend Pat Robertson, less well known candidates, were also highly successful in the early fund-raising. Robertson, the television host of "The 700 Club," tapped into the fundamentalist Christian community to raise $14.2 million by the end of 1987; Dukakis was able to use his Greek heritage to mine the Greek-American community around the country. He was also successful in raising funds from residents of Massachusetts, their business associates in other states, and persons who did business in the state. As a result of their fund-raising success, these candidates were in a position when the primaries and caucuses began in early 1988 to devote their energies to campaigning while their rivals were still seeking funds. Their more ample financial resources also enabled them to compete in more of the states holding early primaries and caucuses than was possible for their rivals.[8]

It is not just the party regulars and financial contributors that are courted. Candidates also woo interest groups that can provide their campaigns with organizational muscle and grassroots workers. Democratic candidates in recent years have sought the support of the

AFL-CIO, the National Education Association (NEA), the National Organization of Women (NOW), and other liberal organizations. Republican presidential aspirants have tried to line up support among conservative interest groups.

Although organized interests can play critical roles in mobilizing people to turn out and support a favored candidate at primaries and caucuses, too close an identification with interest groups does have its downside. For example, the support of the AFL-CIO, NEA, and NOW was extremely helpful to Walter Mondale's 1984 campaign in the early primaries and caucuses. However, the endorsements of these organizations also left him vulnerable to charges by his opponents that he was the candidate of the "special interests." As a result of the Mondale experience, Democratic candidates were more subtle in 1988. They solicited help from the interest groups, but avoided heavy pressure for endorsements.[9]

The normal pattern of intense organization building, fund raising, and public appearances associated with presidential candidacies in the initial phase of the nomination process was unusually slack between 1989 and 1991. For the Republicans, this was not surprising. With incumbent President George Bush riding a wave of popular approval after the Persian Gulf War of 1991 and his renomination considered a foregone conclusion, it was not necessary for him to engage in extensive preparations for the primaries and caucuses. Even among Democrats there was strikingly little overt activity on the part of prospective candidates for the presidential nomination. As of August 1991, only one person had formally announced his candidacy, former senator Paul Tsongas of Massachusetts (1979–1986). Diminished Democratic hopes of winning the White House in 1992 because of three successive defeats and President Bush's popularity after the Persian Gulf War with Iraq seemed to have caused prominent Democrats to hold off mounting their campaigns or to postpone their presidential quests until 1992. The failure of Democratic candidates to engage in early preparations for the 1992 nominating process, however, meant that the massive organizational and fund raising required to compete would have to be done in a compressed time schedule.

Phase II: Delegate Selection—The Early Contests

The early contests for delegates are important not only because of the number of delegates at stake, but also because of the benefits that attach to doing well in these events. Events of critical importance are the Iowa caucuses, the first major delegate selection event of the season, and New Hampshire's first in the nation primary. Each receives saturation TV coverage. The results of these early contests establish front runners for the nomination and begin the process of narrowing the field of candidates. Those who do well in these events gain publicity, standing in the polls, increased fund raising capacity, and support from influential party leaders. Those who falter in the early contests find that their poll ratings, fund raising, and support from prominent leaders all diminish, and many are forced to drop out of the race.

The early stage of the primary and caucus season has been described as the "media fishbowl" phase of the presidential nominating campaign.[10] It is a time when the electronic and print media have their greatest impact through their allocation of coverage to the candidates and their assessments of who won and who lost delegate selection contests. These assessments help to winnow the field of candidates. What matters most in the early contests is how the results of the primaries and caucuses are interpreted. One need not come in first in the primaries and caucuses to achieve a major publicity victory. Indeed, a candidate can come in first in an early primary and still be considered a loser. For example, in 1972 Senator Edmund Muskie (D-Me.) received 46 percent of the New Hampshire Democratic primary vote in a multicandidate field. Senator George McGovern (D-S.D.) came in second with 37 percent. McGovern, however, was viewed as the winner because he did better than expected, while Muskie did less well than the anticipated 50 percent he was supposed to receive in a state bordering on his native Maine.

The Iowa caucuses and New Hampshire primary, 1988. The importance of the early contests was vividly demonstrated in 1988. George Bush, the front runner for the GOP nomination, sustained a near fatal blow with his third place finish in the Iowa caucuses behind Bob Dole and Pat Robertson, each of whom gained reams of favorable publicity for their strong showings. Dole's campaign in particular gained momentum (dubbed the "Iowa bounce" by journalists) as the battleground for the GOP nomination shifted to the New Hampshire primary. Dole's Iowa bounce, however, was quickly deflated by Bush's come-from-behind 38 to 28 percent victory in New Hampshire, where Robertson finished a weak third with 9 percent of the vote. As a result of the New Hampshire primary, Bush was back in front; the Dole and Robertson campaigns were severely weakened; and the other candidates (Kemp, Haig, and DuPont) were effectively out of the race.

On the Democratic side, the Iowa caucuses and New Hampshire primary established Michael Dukakis as a major contender for the nomination. He gained a third place finish in Iowa, trailing the first and second place finishers from the neighboring states of Missouri and Illinois, Representative Richard Gephardt and Senator Paul Simon. Dukakis then scored an impressive victory (36 percent) over Gephardt (20 percent) and Simon (17 percent) in New Hampshire. As was the case with Dole, failure to capitalize on the "Iowa bounce" severely slowed the campaign momentum of both Gephardt and Simon and left Dukakis the front runner, with Jesse Jackson and Senator Albert Gore (Tennessee) still in the race. Gore's strategy was unusual in that he ignored Iowa and New Hampshire and sought to build his campaign around successes in the next round of primaries and caucuses on Super Tuesday—when every southern state, plus Massachusetts, Rhode Island, and several western states, held their primaries or caucuses.

Super Tuesday, 1988. Super Tuesday was an innovation in presidential nominating politics introduced by southern Democratic leaders seeking greater influence for the South in the selection of Democratic nominees. They believed that if all the southern states held their primaries or caucuses on the same day, the candidates would be forced to campaign heavily in the South and "talk southern"—appeal to moderate and conservative southern Democrats. With southern influence over the selection process enhanced, it was hoped that the eventual nominee would have a better chance of carrying southern states in the November general election.

The large number of primaries and caucuses occurring on Super Tuesday gave an advantage to the candidates who were well organized on a multistate basis and well funded. Among the Republicans George Bush, who was coming off a New Hampshire win, was the only candidate with an organization capable of waging a full-scale campaign in each of the states conducting primaries or caucuses on Super Tuesday. He won a smashing victory over Dole and Robertson on Super Tuesday with a majority of the vote in twelve of sixteen primary states and a plurality in the other four. For all intents and purposes, the contest for the GOP nomination was over after Super Tuesday. Bush had won it.

The outcome of Super Tuesday on the Democratic side was less decisive. The big loser was Gephardt, who won only his home state of Missouri. Simon did not contest Super Tuesday due to a lack of resources but concentrated on the upcoming primary in his home state of Illinois. The fortunes of the two candidates with southern ties, Jackson and Gore, were enhanced through strong showings, while Dukakis's victories in Florida and Texas demonstrated support in the

South. The campaign now moved on to the next round of primaries with Dukakis in the lead.

Super Tuesday did not turn out as its sponsors had hoped. No candidate with special appeal to southerners, particularly moderate and conservative whites, had emerged as the likely Democratic nominee. Indeed, Jackson and Dukakis, candidates with limited appeal to southern whites, had been strengthened. It appears that Super Tuesday was indecisive and disappointing to its southern Democratic sponsors for the following reasons: (1) a substantial share of moderate and conservative white southerners chose to vote in the Republican primaries; (2) most of the Democratic candidates lacked the organization and financial resources to compete effectively in more than a handful of states; and (3) there was no prominent southern Democratic moderate like Senator Sam Nunn of Georgia in the race.

Phase III: Delegate Selection—The Later Primaries and Caucuses

The early primaries and caucuses normally establish which candidates are serious contenders and who is the front runner. In John Kessel's phrase, there is a "mist clearing" that occurs after the initial contests.[11] For example, in the 1984 Democratic nominating race, it had become clear by the time of the Illinois primary (March 20) that the original eight man race was now a three way contest. Walter Mondale and Gary Hart were locked in a close competition and Jesse Jackson had demonstrated that he could sustain his campaign by virtue of his strong support among black Democrats. Similarly, in the 1988 Democratic nominating contest it was clear by the time of the New York primary on April 19 that there was a three-way battle for the Democratic contest among Dukakis, Jackson, and Gore, the candidates who had shown strength on Super Tuesday. New York was the first nonsouthern state in which Gore had mounted a major campaign effort. A weak third place finish with only 10 percent effectively ended his presidential bid. With Dukakis receiving a majority of the vote (51 percent) and Jackson (37 percent), the Democratic nominating contest was down to a two person race, with Dukakis in a dominating position. Jackson continued to compete and even outspent Dukakis in California, but Dukakis won all eleven of the late primary states by large margins.

During the later primaries and caucuses, a candidate must be able to keep up the momentum created in the early contests. This requires a nationwide organization and substantial financial resources. But organizations can crumble and financial resources can dry up unless they are nourished by primary victories and some prospect of winning the nomination. Thus in 1980 as President Carter increased his delegate lead over Edward Kennedy, the Senator's organization became increasingly strapped for funds, which in turn reduced the effectiveness of his campaign. What had started as a "Cadillac" style campaign organization was reduced to operating on a more modest basis.[12]

Theoretically, it is possible for a candidate to make a comeback after Super Tuesday by doing well in delegate-rich California and the populous states of the northeast and the midwest (Michigan, New York, Pennsylvania, Ohio, and New Jersey) that have not yet held their primaries or caucuses. However, no candidate in recent years has been able to mount a successful comeback during the later primary and caucus phase of the nominating season. Thus, in 1988, Bush and Dukakis—the candidates who emerged from Super Tuesday with the greatest momentum and best organized and financed campaigns—were able in the later primaries and caucuses to engage in essentially a mopping up operation that assured a majority of the delegates and ballot nominations at the national conventions.[13]

For the front runner, it is not necessary to win all or even a majority of the later primaries in order to gain the nomination. What is required is gaining a substantial share of the delegates being chosen in each state. For example, in the twenty primaries held after the March 20, 1984, Illinois primary, Walter Mondale won seven, Gary Hart eleven, and Jesse Jackson two. Mondale was still able to win the nomination because delegate allocation rules in the states permitted him to gain a large proportion of the delegates, even though he did not gain a majority or plurality of the popular votes in the primaries. Thus, while Hart narrowly defeated Mondale in the Ohio primary by a margin of 42 to 40 percent in the popular vote, Mondale still won 44 percent (sixty-seven delegates) of the state's delegates compared to 51 percent (seventy-nine delegates) for Hart. Similarly, Jimmy Carter in 1976 lost nine of the last thirteen nonsouthern primaries, but still won the nomination because state delegate allocation rules requiring proportional representation enabled him to win a significant share of the delegates at stake. In addition, his organization was rounding up delegate support in caucus/convention states, where the inevitability of his nomination at the national convention was stressed.

Normally by the end of the caucus and primary season it becomes clear who the eventual nominee will be, because the candidate organizations and news media keep a running count on the candidate preferences of the delegates as they are chosen. George Bush, Ronald Reagan's main competition for the 1980 Republican nomination,

The 1988 Presidential Primaries

Democratic Primaries: Dukakis Shows Electoral Strength Early and Gains Victory after Super Tuesday

	Turnout	Dukakis	Jackson	Gore	Gephardt	Simon	Hart
Total	23,230,525	**42%**	29%	14%	6%	5%	2%
Time Periods							
Pre-Super Tuesday	245,757	**39**	11	6	24	11	4
Super Tuesday	9,706,636	26	**27**	26	13	2	3
Post-Super Tuesday	13,278,132	**54**	31	5	1	7	1
Regions							
East	5,840,912	**58**	29	6	3	2	1
Midwest	5,309,377	**42**	27	6	8	14	1
South	7,885,020	23	28	**30**	10	2	3
West	3,839,038	**61**	34	2	0	1	0
Territories	356,178	23	**29**	14	3	18	8
Racial Composition							
Over 20% black	3,312,000	20	**38**	28	7	1	3
Under 20% black	19,918,525	**46**	28	11	6	5	2
State Size							
Megastates[a]	12,942,452	**49**	31	7	4	6	1
Congressional							
Districts Won	445	271	88	52	14	20	0

Republican Primaries: Bush Delivers a Knockout Blow to Rivals on Super Tuesday

	Turnout	Bush	Dole	Robertson	Kemp
Total	12,169,003	**68%**	19%	9%	3%
Time Periods					
Pre-Super Tuesday	494,154	**39**	31	15	10
Super Tuesday	4,853,434	57	24	13	5
Post-Super Tuesday	6,821,415	**78**	15	6	1
Regions					
East	2,029,040	**72**	17	7	3
Midwest	3,187,297	**67**	23	8	2
South	4,190,456	**58**	21	14	5
West	2,758,237	**81**	13	5	0
Territories	3,973	**97**	3	0	0
Megastates[a]	6,921,307	**74**	16	8	2

a. Megastates: Democratic—California, Florida, Illinois, New Jersey, New York, Ohio, Pennsylvania, and Texas; Republican—California, Florida, Illinois, New Jersey, Ohio, Pennsylvania, and Texas.

Sources: Congressional Quarterly Weekly Report, July 16, 1988, p. 1950, and Aug. 13, 1988, p. 2252.

bowed to the inevitability of Reagan's nomination when he withdrew from the race over a month before the convention. He commented, "I am an optimist. But I also know how to count to 998 [the number of delegates needed for the GOP nomination.]"[14] The winners of the 1984 and 1988 Republican and Democratic nominations were also known in advance of the conventions. Both Dukakis and Bush in 1988 were already engaged in screening potential vice presidential running mates. They did not, however, go so far as Walter Mondale had in 1984 when before the convention he designated Representative Geraldine Ferraro (N.Y.) as his choice for the vice presidential nomination.

Although it usually becomes clear who the presidential nominees will be during the later primaries and caucuses, this stage in the nominating process can have crucial and long term implications for the outcome of the general election. Lengthy, contentious, acrimonious primary campaigns cost the eventual nominee valuable time needed for intraparty fence mending and planning of general election campaign strategy. As veteran political reporter Rhodes Cook of Congressional Quarterly has observed, "The longer the battle for the nomination drags on, the less chance the party has to win."[15]

Phase IV: The Convention—Ratifying the Decision of the Primaries and Kicking Off the General Election Campaign

National conventions are no longer deliberative bodies whose delegates weigh the competing claims of rival candidates for the nomination. Conventions ratify the decisions of the preconvention campaign fought out in presidential primaries and caucuses. The principal significance of the modern day national convention, therefore, is that it is the kickoff of the general election campaign. It is an opportunity for the party and its nominee to set the themes of the campaign and project a favorable candidate image during a period when the party will have a virtual monopoly on television news coverage. *The Washington Post's* respected national politics reporter, David Broder, summarized the significance of conventions as follows.

> Convention week is important, not because it marks the end of the nominating period, but because it is the start of the general election. It is the time when most voters take their first serious look at the candidates and their parties and begin to focus on the choice they will make in November.[16]

The nominations now are made on the first ballot. No convention has gone beyond the first ballot in selecting a nominee since the 1952 Democratic convention, which chose Adlai Stevenson on the third ballot. Even though the actual nomination may have been decided well in advance of the convention, what happens at the convention and how it is presented in the news media can have important implications for the campaign.

During the first two days of a convention, the major items on the agenda are the reports of the convention committees—Credentials, Permanent Organization, Rules, and Resolutions (Platform). The full convention must consider these reports and then adopt or amend them before the convention can proceed to the nomination stage of its schedule. The Credentials Committee makes recommendations to the full convention concerning which delegates from a given state should be seated in those instances where there is a dispute about who are the bona fide and properly chosen delegates. The Committee on Permanent Organization, now largely a pro forma group, nominates persons to serve as the permanent officers (e.g., permanent chairman, secretary, parliamentarian, sergeant at arms). The Rules Committee recommends the procedures under which the convention will operate and the Resolutions Committee drafts the party platform.

The tone of any convention is heavily influenced by the strength of the coalitions supporting the various candidates for the nomination.[17] A convention where the candidates are relatively close in delegate strength is apt to be contentious and potentially divisive (e.g., Republicans in 1976). By contrast, in those instances where one candidate is the overwhelming choice of the delegates (e.g., Republicans in 1980, 1984, and 1988, Democrats in 1976 and 1988) the convention is frequently harmonious and serves to unify the party. A leading candidate with only a narrow majority of the delegates is often confronted with a series of tests on credentials, rules, or platform issues in the early days of the convention. In challenging the front runner of these issues, rival candidates hope to make a strong showing on a test vote, thereby casting doubt in the minds of weakly committed delegates about the ability of the front runner to actually gain a convention majority for the nomination.

The Kennedy forces in 1980, for example, mounted a campaign for what they dubbed an "open convention." This was an effort to change the convention rules to permit delegates to vote for their preferred candidate irrespective of the candidate to whom they were pledged by virtue of the outcome of primaries and caucuses in their home states. The Kennedy campaign hoped to free delegates from their commitments to President Carter so that some of them might switch to Kennedy, who was viewed as being ideologically closer to the delegates than Carter. The Carter organization naturally opposed this move to weaken potentially its base of delegate support. When Carter won this key test of strength by over 500 votes, Kennedy announced that he would not allow his name to be put in nomination. Thus the critical vote in the convention was not the roll call on the nomination, but the test of Carter strength on the rules.

The critical test votes may also come on credentials or platform issues. For example, there was a major credentials dispute at the 1972 Democratic convention, which resulted in the seating of McGovern rather than Humphrey delegates from California and Illinois. The outcome of these credentials fights assured McGovern of the nomination. Sensing the risk inherent in these test votes, the front runner may decline to be drawn into a confrontation. The Reagan organization in 1976 sought a confrontation with President Gerald Ford's forces over the wording of foreign policy planks in the Republican platform. The proposed Reagan amendment to the Resolutions Committee draft was thought to be embarrassing to the Administration and its secretary of state, Henry Kissinger. Ford's strategists understood that Reagan's foreign policy plank had substantial appeal to the generally conservative delegates. Ford's spokesmen, therefore, endorsed the Reagan platform language on foreign policy and avoided any chance of losing a critical test vote. President Carter's strategists made a similar decision at the 1980 Democratic convention when they accepted a series of Kennedy platform amendments rather than risk losing an open Carter-Kennedy fight on the floor of the convention. Carter, like Ford, through this maneuver was able to avoid the appearance of weakness in an early test of convention strength.

A candidate with overwhelming delegate support, such as President Reagan in 1984 or Lyndon Johnson in 1964, does not need to worry about crucial test votes because any opposition is too weak to mount a serious challenge. In these circumstances, the convention takes on something of the atmosphere of a coronation—a celebration of the nominee. With the eventual nominee's organization in full control of every facet of the convention, the emphasis is on presenting the best possible image of the party and candidate for the viewing audience on television. The 1984 and 1988 Republican conventions, which renominated President Reagan and nominated vice president Bush are classic examples of conventions designed for television and in which there were virtually no visible disagreements. The conventions were planned to convey the image of a party united behind a popular and experienced leader.

The convention provides the nominee with an opportunity to unify the party by making overtures to the various factions of the party, especially those which lost the presidential nomination. Concessions are frequently made on the platform or rules. In 1988, for example, it became clear before the Democratic Convention that Michael Dukakis, the prospective presidential nominee, would reach an accommodation with Jesse Jackson. Jackson commanded substantial delegate strength and was pressing to have his issue concerns addressed in the party platform and rules. He also indicated that as the runner-up in the nominating contest, he deserved to be offered the position of Dukakis's vice presidential running mate. In the interest of party harmony, the Dukakis forces made nine platform concessions to Jackson and agreed to two rules changes for the 1992 nomination. These rules changes were (1) a requirement that each state's delegates be allocated in accordance with the proportion of the vote received by the candidates in primaries or caucuses, and (2) a reduction in the number of super or automatic delegates (rescinded by the Democratic National Committee in 1990). The party unifying function of these concessions was marred somewhat when Jackson was not offered the vice presidential nomination and then learned about the selection of Senator Lloyd Bensten (Texas) from a reporter rather than from Dukakis.

The vice presidential nomination is, however, often used to unify the party and broaden the presidential nominee's electoral support. Dukakis's selection of Senator Bensten was an attempt to appeal to moderate and conservative Democrats, especially southerners, who had deserted the party in the Reagan elections. Jimmy Carter, a moderate southerner, also used the vice presidential nomination to unite the party and broaden his electoral base in 1976 by selecting a northern liberal, Sen. Walter Mondale (Minn.), as his running mate. George Bush's choice of Senator Dan Quayle (Ind.) in 1988 was designed to appeal to younger voters and reassure conservatives.

The climax of the convention is the nominee's acceptance speech, a major media event which provides an opportunity to bind up wounds within the party, portray the candidate in a highly favorable manner, and present the themes of the campaign. Most nominees receive a postconvention "bounce" in the polls. The Gallup Poll, for example, reported an 11 percent "bounce" in Dukakis's lead over George Bush following the 1988 Democratic convention. Jimmy Carter got an even more dramatic 15 percentage point postconvention bounce in 1976, as the heretofore little known former Georgia governor was spotlighted before a mass television audience. As the Dukakis example demonstrates, a sizeable postconvention "bounce" and lead in the polls is no assurance of a general election victory in November. Even so, the image of the candidate and party created at the convention can be extremely important. A divisive convention like that of the Republicans in 1964 or the Democrats in 1968 can be highly damaging to a party since between 54 and 78 percent of the voters make up their minds about how they will vote by the end of the conventions.[18]

The Ongoing Process of Party Reform

Political rules are never neutral. They benefit some and are hurtful to others. Nowhere are these truisms more apparent than in the rules governing presidential nomination politics. These rules have, therefore, been and continue to be points of contention among the various party factions struggling to control presidential nominations. The immediate causes of the latest surge of nomination reforms were the divisive Democratic convention of 1968 and the Watergate revelations of the early 1970s. Each brought in its wake a series of changes in the process.

The Democrats' Quadrennial Reform Process

The McGovern-Fraser Commission. There was widespread belief within the Democratic party in 1968 that the convention of that year had been unrepresentative of the sentiments of Democratic voters and that party leaders had used unfair tactics in securing the nomination for Hubert Humphrey. In an effort to placate the dissidents and confident that a mainline Democrat, Senator Edmund Muskie (Maine), would be the nominee in 1972, party regulars readily agreed to the reformers' demand for a commission to overhaul Democratic rules of delegate selection. This commission came to be known as the McGovern-Fraser Commission for the men who served as its chairmen, Senator George McGovern and Representative Donald Fraser (Minn.). The Commission adopted a series of guidelines, subsequently approved by the Democratic National Committee (DNC), that dramatically changed the process of delegate selection in the states. The McGovern-Fraser Commission reforms imposed the following restrictions upon the state parties.[19]

- Required that state parties take affirmative steps to ensure representation of blacks, women, and youth in "reasonable relationship to the group's presence in the population of the state."
- Required that state parties have written rules of delegate selection, give public notice of all meetings, and have uniform statewide times and dates for meetings.

- Required that three-fourths of a state's delegation be chosen at or below the congressional district level.
- Forbade mandatory assessments of delegates and eased the requirements (e.g., number of signatures on a petition) that a state party could impose in order for a person to run for delegate.
- Banned the unit rule under which all of a state's delegate votes would be cast as a unit in accordance with the preferences of a majority of the state delegation.
- Required delegate candidates to specify their candidate preference or state that they were uncommitted.
- Forbade proxy voting in the selection process for delegates.
- Restricted the number of delegates that a party committee could select to 10 percent of the total size of the state delegation.
- Prohibited party officials elected prior to the calendar year of the convention from selecting delegates.

As David Price has pointed out, the "most obvious effect of these rules was to reduce the ability of party leaders to influence or control the delegate selection process."[20] Traditional party dominated systems of delegate selection were abolished. Caucus systems which involved party officeholders coming together to start the process of delegate selection were banned and replaced by participatory conventions in which any professed Democrat could participate. Also prohibited were "delegate primaries." This was a system used in New York and Pennsylvania under which party notables ran for delegate under their own names without indicating on the ballot their preferred presidential candidate. Both the party official caucuses and the "delegate primaries" had assured party leaders of a dominant voice in delegate selection within their states. Byron Shafer, the leading analyst of the McGovern-Fraser reforms, has noted that these changes put party officeholders at "an active disadvantage" and meant that "the guaranteed role of the regular party has been discarded."[21]

Adoption of the McGovern-Fraser reforms by the DNC and its willingness to enforce these rules vigorously required state Democratic parties to change their delegate selection rules to bring them into conformity with national party rules. Since the delegate selection procedures of many of the states were specified in state statutes, it was also necessary for state legislatures to revise their statutes governing delegate selection. Therefore, there was a massive overhauling of delegate selection procedures in the states both by statutory enactment and party rules change. One of the consequences of these changes was a proliferation of presidential primaries. Rather than risk using caucus/convention procedures that might run afoul of the new Democratic rules and result in a state's delegation to the national convention not being seated, some states adopted the presidential primary as a safe alternative. The presidential primary also had widespread appeal during this reform era because of its participatory nature and seemingly representative character. Between 1968 and 1972 the number of Democratic presidential primaries jumped from seventeen to twenty-three and to thirty in 1976. While the immediate impetus for changes in delegate selection procedures occurred within the Democratic party, the Democratic reforms had a spillover effect on the GOP. State legislatures in revising their statutes to make them conform to the McGovern-Fraser rules frequently adopted the same or similar rules for both Democrats and Republicans. The number of Republican primaries, therefore, also increased dramatically between 1968 and 1976 (from sixteen to twenty-eight).

The Mikulski Commission. McGovern's devastating defeat in the 1972 presidential election prompted calls for a review of the Democratic rules, especially by elements of the party, including state party chairmen and organized labor, who believed that they had lost their rightful place in conventions due to the new rules. A new reform commission was, therefore, appointed—the Mikulski Commission (chaired by Representative Barbara Mikulski of Maryland). This commission was controlled by reform advocates who were not inclined to undo the work of the McGovern-Fraser Commission. It did, however, move the party away from strict quotas in state delegations for blacks, women, youth, and minorities. Instead, it required that each state party have an affirmative action plan for insuring adequate representation of minorities and women. These plans had to be approved by the DNC.

The Mikulski Commission also adopted a proportional representation requirement in the composition of state delegations. Any candidate who received at least 10 percent of the vote in a primary or caucus was to be entitled to a proportionate share of the delegates being chosen. The commission took action against open presidential primaries by requiring state parties to "take all possible steps to restrict participation in the delegate selection process to Democratic voters only." This provision was aimed at states like Michigan and Wisconsin which permitted crossover voting in their primaries and which many Democratic leaders believed had resulted in an embarrassingly high vote total for George Wallace in 1964, 1968, and 1972. The reforms of the McGovern-Fraser Commission and the Mikulski Commission were incorporated into the Democratic Charter which was adopted by the party's mid-term convention in 1974.

The Winograd Commission. The process of quadrennial revision of the Democratic rules continued after the 1976 convention and election with the work of a commission chaired by the State Democratic chairman of Michigan, Morley Winograd. This commission strengthened the prohibition on open presidential primaries. It also sought to reduce the length of time (the "window") during which delegate selection events could occur. In an effort to encourage state parties to select more elected officials and party officers as delegates, additional at-large delegates were allocated to each state equal to 10 percent of the state's base allocation of delegates.

The Hunt Commission. Unhappiness with the Carter Administration and his overwhelming defeat in 1980 provided the backdrop for another reform commission chaired by Governor James Hunt of North Carolina. This commission had four principal factions—supporters of either Walter Mondale or Edward Kennedy, organized labor, and state party chairmen. Labor and state chairmen wanted to restore some of the influence they believed they had lost as a result of previous reforms, while the Mondale and Kennedy supporters were seeking to protect their candidates' interests. It is not surprising, therefore, that the Hunt Commission recommendations tended to benefit well-known candidates and strengthen the role of party and elected officials.

The key recommendations of the Hunt Commission included the following.[22]

- *Retention of strong affirmative action requirements in the selection of state delegations.* State parties were required to set specific goals for affirmative action, and the requirement of equal division of state delegations between men and women was retained.
- *Provision for unpledged delegate status for party and elected officials.* Each state chair and vice chair would be delegates as would two-thirds of the Democratic senators and representatives. Democratic governors, and mayors of cities with a population of over 250,000 would be given preference in selecting a state's unpledged delegates.
- *Dilution of the proportional representation requirements.* In an attempt to gain an early consensus on the nominee and not drag out the divisiveness of the nomination struggle, the "threshold" (the minimum vote) that a candidate had to receive in order to qualify for delegates was raised to 20 percent. Winner-take-all ("loophole") primaries were permitted at the congressional district level. Bonus systems were also authorized under which a candidate could receive a bonus delegate if he won a primary.

- *Shortening the delegate selection season*. Because of the length of the delegate selection season and the disproportionate influence of the early contests, especially the Iowa caucuses and the New Hampshire primary, an attempt was made to shorten the time during which delegate selection events could be held.

The changes in Democratic procedures occasioned by the work of the Hunt Commission had significant implications for the 1984 nominating contest. The dilution of the proportional representation requirements in the allocation of a state's delegates was particularly helpful to the Mondale candidacy. Mondale was the best known candidate in the race after having served as vice president and having twice been the party's nominee for that office. He also had a superior organization and more extensive financial resources, which permitted him to campaign effectively in all the states. These organizational resources enabled him to run major campaigns in the states with "loophole" primaries and bonus systems. As a result, Mondale's primary victories netted him a higher percentage of delegates than Hart and Jackson gained for their share of the vote. His 39 percent of the vote in the primaries won him 49 percent of the delegates, compared to Hart's 36 percent of the vote gaining him 36 percent of the delegates. Jackson received 18 percent of the vote for 10 percent of the delegates.[23]

Mondale also benefited significantly from the addition of unpledged party and elected officials to the delegate lists. A CBS survey done just prior to the convention showed Mondale with more than a 300 vote margin over Hart and Jackson among the unpledged party and elected official delegates.[24] Not surprisingly, Hart and Jackson demanded that the Fairness Commission, which recommended changes in Democratic rules for the 1988 convention, reduce the number of unpledged party and elected official delegates and strengthen the proportional representation system that was weakened by the Hunt Commission.

The Fairness Commission. In response to the complaints of Gary Hart and Jesse Jackson that the 1984 rules had worked to their disadvantage, the Democratic party created another reform commission to formulate rules changes for the 1988 nomination. Under the influence of DNC Chairman Paul Kirk and Fairness Commission Chairman Don Fowler, the proposed changes for 1988 were relatively minor and reflected a desire on the part of national committee leadership to provide greater continuity to Democratic nominating procedures than had been present in the past. Among the key recommendations of the Commission were the following:

- Lowering the thresholds of votes required to win delegates in caucus and primary states from 20 to 15 percent. This recommendation partially met the complaints of Jesse Jackson that the 20 percent threshold operative in 1984 had prevented him from gaining his fair share of the delegates.
- Expanding the number of automatic delegates from 60 to 80 percent of Democratic senators and representatives, and making all Democratic governors automatic delegates.
- Authorizing all members of the DNC to be automatic, unpledged delegates.
- Permitting Wisconsin and Montana to return to an open primary to select their delegates.
- Granting exemptions for the New Hampshire primary and Iowa caucuses to be held in advance of the "window" of early March to June for primaries and caucuses.

Rules issues for the 1992 convention. In 1988, delegate selection rules continued to be a focus of controversy, and compromises relating to the rules for the 1992 nomination were again used as a basis for securing a harmonious convention. The winning candidate, Michael Dukakis, made two important concessions on the rules for the 1992 convention to his principal rival for the nomination, Jesse Jackson: (1) the allocation of delegates among candidates was to reflect more closely each candidate's share of the primary or caucus vote; and (2) a sharp reduction (approximately 250) in the number of automatic (super delegates) was to occur by eliminating most Democratic National Committee (DNC) members as automatic delegates.

Both of these changes were considered beneficial to a potential Jackson candidacy in 1992. Jackson claimed that because several states did not use a proportional representation system to allocate delegates to candidates, he did not get his rightful share of the delegates. Hence he sought a rule of proportional representation in all the states. Jackson's effort to reduce the number of automatic delegates reflected the fact that the 1988 automatic delegates overwhelmingly supported Dukakis and helped provide him with a convention majority.

After the convention, however, the DNC restored all of its members to their status as automatic delegates. The DNC did, however, approve proportional representation as the basis for allocating delegates among the candidates. It also voted to permit the delegate selection process to start one week earlier in March. This latter change was an invitation to California to move up the date of its primary to March 3 in an effort to have the delegate-rich California primary play an early and more decisive role in selecting the Democratic nominee. If the California and other state primaries were held at the beginning of the primary season, it was thought that the nomination would be decided earlier, thereby reducing the length of the divisive nomination process.

The Unreformed Republicans

Reform of party rules has become a regular quadrennial activity and source of intense controversy within the Democratic party as contending interests, factions, and candidates seek to shape the rules for the next nominating contest to their advantage. The Republicans have followed a quite different strategy and have sought to maintain the basic party structure and rules which evolved prior to the era of the McGovern-Fraser Commission.[25] Party rules of delegate selection have not been a major source of controversy within the GOP the way they have been for the Democrats. The element of the Democratic party that supported Senators Eugene McCarthy (Minn.) and Robert Kennedy (N.Y.) in 1968 and which thought that the rules had prevented their side from winning the nomination demanded reform. By contrast, the intense ideological element of the more homogeneous Republican party has not found the rules a barrier to party influence and ascendancy. As far back as 1964, the conservative wing of the party demonstrated the permeability of the party structure and succeeded in nominating its candidate, Senator Barry Goldwater (Ariz.). In 1976, it almost upset an incumbent president when Ronald Reagan nearly gained the nomination over President Gerald Ford. The conservatives succeeded in nominating Reagan in 1980 and 1984 and were generally satisfied with George Bush in 1988. From the Republican perspective, its nominating procedures have worked quite well. It has produced nominees capable of garnering broad electoral support, including four electoral college victories and one near miss since 1972.

Republican rules are harder to change.[26] It is not possible under Republican rules for the Republican National Committee (RNC) to promulgate rules changes affecting an upcoming national convention in the way the DNC can. The normal method of rules change in the GOP is for the RNC Rules Committee to recommend changes to the full national committee, which in turn makes recommendations to the national convention rules committee. The committee then makes a report to the convention which must give final approval to a proposed rules change. This lengthy procedure imposes major obstacles to any major revisions of GOP rules and prevents tampering with the rules between conventions. There are also significant substantive differences between the rules of the two parties.

Delegate apportionment. The GOP uses a significantly different formula to apportion delegates among the states. The Republican formula is weighted to reflect the electoral votes and the extent of Republican voting strength in the state. It does not reflect population to the extent that the Democratic formula does. Republican conventions are also somewhat smaller in terms of total delegates than Democratic conventions. In 1988 there were 4161 Democratic delegates and 2277 Republican delegates.

Maintaining the confederate character of the party. The Democratic rules changes that culminated with the adoption of the party charter in 1974 significantly strengthened the national party organization at the expense of the state parties in matters of delegate selection. The national Democratic party has an elaborate set of rules governing these matters which it vigorously enforces upon the state parties. By contrast, the Republican rules give the state parties wide latitude in matters of delegate selection and the RNC has adopted a permissive attitude toward its state parties. Republican rules contain no mandates banning open primaries, setting narrow time limits for delegate selection, requiring affirmative action programs or equal division of the sexes in state delegations, setting threshold requirements or provisions for proportional representation, or stipulating the percentage of state delegations that must be selected at the congressional district level. Further evidence of the party's commitment to maintenance of its confederate character is the requirement of equal state representation on all convention committees. One man and one woman delegate from each state, regardless of state size, is required for each convention committee. The Democrats, by contrast, allocate committee seats in accordance with a more complicated formula that takes into account state population and support for the Democratic ticket.

No automatic delegates. The Democrats have sought to increase the participation in their conventions by party and elected officials by granting them automatic delegate status, but the Republicans have consistently resisted such proposals. The provision for automatic delegates by the Democrats was believed to be necessary because the reforms caused the number of party and elected official delegates to fall off dramatically. The highly structured Democratic rules frequently required such officials to run against their own constituents, if they wished to become delegates. This was an undertaking in which few wished to engage. The less restrictive GOP rules governing delegate selection by state parties have meant that it has been easier within the Republican party to designate party leaders as delegates. As a result, there is no strong pressure in the GOP for giving party leaders automatic delegate status.

These differences between the parties are sufficiently important that some scholars believe that a partial explanation for the Democrats' recent difficulties in presidential politics lies in their continuing process of rules reform.[27] The differences between the largely unreformed GOP and the reformed Democratic party, however, should not obscure the basic similarities in the nomination process as it operates within both parties. In both parties the bulk of the delegates are selected through presidential primaries and it is the early primaries for both Republicans and Democrats that have disproportionate influence upon the choice of a nominee. The process is highly participatory, even in caucus/convention states because party rules and state laws permit participation by even the most nominal of partisans. The media plays a major role in screening the candidates and in interpreting the results of caucuses and primaries. Party organizations and leaders are no longer the dominant players. Their place has been taken by the organizations of the candidates and the media.

Campaign Finance: The Federal Election Campaign Act

The Watergate revelations of campaign finance irregularities in 1972 led the Congress to enact campaign finance reforms, the Federal Election Campaign Act (FECA) Amendments of 1974. The key provision of the act, as it pertains to presidential nomination campaigns, is that relating to public funding. Candidates for major party nominations are eligible to receive federal matching funds for their campaigns, provided they comply with the following conditions.

- Raise at least $5,000 in individual contributions of $250 or less in each of 20 states. Only individual contributions of up to $1,000 can be accepted and only the first $250 counts toward the federal match.
- Abide by an overall expenditure limit which is adjusted prior to each election to account for inflation. In 1988 the overall expenditure limit was $23.05 million, plus an additional 20 percent to cover fund-raising costs.
- Abide by individual state expenditure limits based upon a formula of 16 cents per voter, plus an inflation adjustment.
- Disclose all contributions and expenditures of $200 or more.

Candidates for presidential nominations are not required to accept federal matching funds for their campaigns, and candidates who decline public funding need not abide by FECA expenditures limits. Since the law went into effect, however, only one serious candidate, former Governor John Connally of Texas in 1980, has declined federal funding. The reasons for candidate reluctance to forego federal matching funds include: (1) candidates who rely exclusively on private contributions or their own personal bank accounts are likely to be put on the defensive and be accused of seeking to buy the presidency; (2) matching funds provide an efficient way of supplementing private contributions to fund a campaign; and (3) it is extremely difficult to raise adequate amounts of money without federal matching funds because contribution limits ($1,000 for individuals and $5,000 for PACs) apply even to candidates not accepting matching funds. Connally's reason for not taking matching money was that he believed that FECA state spending limits put him at a disadvantage against the front runner, Ronald Reagan. Connally, therefore, sought to concentrate his campaign in a few key states and spent heavily in those states (i.e., he spent at higher levels than the FECA state expenditure limits would have permitted if he had accepted matching funds). His heavy spending in early southern primaries, however, proved ineffective. He won only one delegate with an expenditure of $13 million and he was forced to withdraw from the race.

The FECA has not made money less important than it was prior to 1974. The FECA changed the rules of the game but the role of campaign funding remained crucial. As Nelson Polsby and Aaron Wildavsky have pointed out, the provision in the law for matching funds can have the effect of magnifying the disparity of funds which various candidates have available. The following example demonstrates how matching funds can accentuate financial disparities among candidates.[28]

Candidate	Amount Raised from Private Sources	+	Federal Matching Funds	=	Total
A	$200,000	+	$200,000	=	$400,000
B	300,000	+	300,000	=	600,000
C	400,000	+	400,000	=	800,000

Federal matching funds in this example have actually doubled the difference among the candidates in financial resources.

Longer campaigns. With the severe limits that the FECA imposes on the amount of money an individual or group can contribute and the stipulation that only individual contributions of $250 or less count toward the federal match, it is necessary to start campaigns for the presidency early. Fund raising is now more difficult and it takes longer to set up a viable fund-raising organization, since much of the money must be obtained through direct mail solicitation.

Centralization of campaigns. Because the FECA contains both a national expenditure limit and individual state expenditure limits for candidates accepting federal matching funds, it is necessary for each candidate's organization to impose stringent expenditure controls in order to prevent violations of the law. Therefore, presidential contenders must plan their campaigns carefully when allocating expenditures among the states. As a consequence, there has been some discouragement of local organizational activity on behalf of candidates. Richard Cheney, who served as President Ford's chief of staff, noted the impact of the law on campaign organizations.

> The experience of the Ford campaign in 1976 showed conclusively that it was easier to discourage grass-roots activity than it was to control it and report it. In previous campaigns, it was possible to tell a local campaign or party official to go right ahead with a project as long as he could go out and raise the money himself and finance it. But now federal law places a premium on actively discouraging such activity because of the danger that it could well lead to a violation of contribution or spending limits in the primary.[29]

Spending limits dictate strategy. Candidate organizations have always had to make strategic decisions concerning which primaries and caucuses to contest and the extent to which campaign resources will be committed to a particular state. With the enactment of the FECA, the task became more complicated because it involved more than weighing of political factors. It also became necessary to consider national and state spending limits. State spending limits make no distinction between caucus/convention states and primary states or between early and late primaries. The state spending limits are based on the voting age population of the state, not the state's political significance. Thus the 1988 spending limits for New Hampshire, a key early primary, and for the convention in Guam were the same—$461,000. The state expenditure limits mean that candidates can no longer spend in a state in accordance with their perceptions of the state's importance in their campaigns. Candidates have, of course, sought ways to skirt the low FECA expenditure limits for strategically important states. Among the devices used to evade the spending limits in the crucial 1988 New Hampshire primary were renting autos in neighboring states for use in New Hampshire, allocating 80 percent of television time purchased on Boston stations (the main media outlets for New Hampshire) to the Massachusetts spending limit, having candidates and staff stay in motels in neighboring states, and adding a request for funds to television ads and then allocating half of the ad cost to fund raising rather than the New Hampshire campaign.[30]

The extreme difficulty of making allocations of funds to specific state campaigns is made even more difficult because the overall national expenditure limits for campaigns accepting matching funds is lower than the total of the state expenditure limits. In 1988 the overall expenditure limit was $23.05 million, while the total of individual state expenditure limits was $70 million, three times the overall spending limit. As a result, candidates and their staffs must control spending carefully in key primary and caucus states, and spend little or no money in other states.

Participation in Presidential Nominating Politics

The extent of participation in candidate selection has been a continuing concern of those who have shaped the rules governing presidential nominating politics. A basic tenet of the progressives, who developed the presidential primary early in this century, was a belief that the citizenry should make presidential nominating decisions, not party leaders. The presidential primary was, therefore, an element in the progressive reform agenda. Latter day reformers, who pushed for the McGovern-Fraser Commission reforms and for greater use of the presidential primary, were also committed to participatory democracy. These reformers believed that more participation in the process would result in more representative conventions, nominees who would have a higher level of legitimacy with the public, and more public support for the political system.[31] In practice, however, participation rates in presidential nominating politics are quite low.

Voter Turnout in Presidential Primaries

Voter turnout in primaries has consistently lagged substantially below that in general elections. The research of Austin Ranney has shown that between 1948 and 1968, presidential primary turnout averaged 27 percent of the voting age population (VAP), compared to 62 percent in the general elections.[32] He noted, however, that many of these primaries were uncontested, i.e., no serious national candidate was competing or only one candidate was on the ballot. In the eleven instances between 1948 and 1968 when a state did have contested elections in both parties' primaries, the turnout averaged 39 percent. In spite of the contests for the GOP and Democratic nominations in 1988, voter turnout was low—an average of 24.4 percent of the VAP.[33] Turnout rates were lowest in Rhode Island, where Republican turnout was 5 percent and Democratic turnout was 11 percent, and highest among Wisconsin Democrats (55 percent).

The proliferation of primaries since 1968 has meant that in absolute terms the number of people voting in presidential primaries has increased significantly. In 1968 there were sixteen Republican and seventeen Democratic primaries in which twelve million voters participated. With thirty-eight Republican and thirty-seven Democratic primaries in 1988, total turnout was at an all-time high of 35.3 million people.[34] The number of persons voting in presidential primaries, however, is subject to wide variation from one election year to another, because the number of states holding primaries is constantly changing. Thus in 1984 with Ronald Reagan uncontested for the GOP nomination, there were only 24 Republican primaries, while the Democrats held 30.[35]

A major point of contention among proponents and opponents of presidential primaries relates to the representativeness of the primary voters. That is, do they distort the choice of nominees because they are not representative of party rank and file voters? All studies of primary turnout demonstrate that the actual voting electorate in presidential primaries tends to be weighted in favor of those who are older, better educated, and more well-to-do. For example, Crotty and Jackson found that 55 percent of the college graduates voted in the 1980 presidential primaries, but only 31 percent of high school graduates did so.[36] Similarly, in 1984, a *New York Times*/CBS survey of Democratic primary voters revealed that while persons with incomes of less than $25,000 constituted 61 percent of all Democrats, persons of this income level were 54 percent of Democratic presidential primary voters nationwide. By contrast, persons with incomes in excess of $25,000 cast 46 percent of the presidential primary votes, even though they constituted 39 percent of all Democrats.[37] These findings respecting the demographic unrepresentativeness of presidential primary voters are similar to those for general elections and gubernatorial and congressional primaries.

There are significant demographic differences in the composition of the Republican and Democratic parties' presidential primary electorates. The Democratic presidential primary voters are much more heterogeneous. Thus on Super Tuesday in 1988, 17 percent of Democratic voters were black; 3 percent were Hispanic; and 14 percent were union members. By contrast, there were negligible numbers of blacks and hispanics among the Republican Super Tuesday voters and union members constituted only 8 percent of the total.[38]

Those who do participate in presidential primaries tend to be more partisan (i.e., have a strong commitment to their party) than nonvoters, irrespective of their party preferences.[39] Regarding the ideological representativeness of presidential primary voters, political scientists have produced conflicting conclusions depending upon the methodology employed. When primary voters are compared with all eligible nonvoters, persons at the more extreme ideological positions—the "extremely liberal," "liberal," "conservative," and "extremely conservative" voters—are more likely to vote than those whose ideologies are more centrist and moderate.[40] However, when presidential primary voters are compared with general election voters who do not vote in primaries, the primary electorate reflects a high level of representativeness.[41] However, the partisan and ideological orientations of presidential primary voters (tending toward liberalism among Democrats and conservatism among Republicans) do have an impact on the strategies of presidential candidates. Republican candidates find it necessary to project a conservative image while seeking their party's presidential nomination, while Democratic aspirants seek to establish their liberal credentials. Indeed, all successful Republican nominees since 1956 have sought to demonstrate that they had strong conservative credentials and no candidate who has campaigned openly as a moderate or liberal has been successful. The Democratic picture is almost a mirror image of the Republicans. Successful Democrats in the modern era have consistently sought to present a liberal image.

Participation in the Caucuses/Conventions

Participation in caucus states is substantially lower than in presidential primary states. Ranney's analysis estimated participation levels in caucus states during the 1976 nominating campaigns were at approximately 1.9 percent of states' voting age population.[42] Some perspective on caucus turnout can be gained by comparing caucus turnout with the vote received by the parties' presidential candidates in 1988. In the Democratic and Republican caucuses held between February and April, when a full field of candidates was still in the race in both parties, Democratic turnout in nineteen states averaged 6.5 percent of Dukakis's general election vote, while Republican turnout in nine states averaged 4.8 percent of Bush's general election vote.[43] The Iowa caucuses, however, do attract participation rates that approach turnout levels in some primaries. It is estimated that between 1976 and 1988, caucus turnout has been between 14 and 20 percent of the registered voters.[44]

Like primary voters, caucus participants tend to be middle and upper-middle class, strongly partisan, with often intense ideological commitments. Candidates who appeal to such individuals are apt to do well in the caucuses. Ronald Reagan is a case in point. Throughout his career in presidential politics, he has had a strong following among Republican activists, many of whom have deeply felt conservative views. In 1980, he won 83 percent of the delegates chosen through caucuses, while George Bush got only 8 percent of the caucus delegates.[45] In the 1984 Democratic nominating contest, it was the party insider, Walter Mondale, who did best in the caucus states because he had strong party organization and labor union support that was capable of turning out their followers on the day of the caucuses. The importance of a strong organization and committed supporters was again evident in 1988. George Bush had far and away the strongest organization to mobilize caucus attendance in the Republican contest, though he did suffer setbacks at the hands of Pat Robertson, who commanded a loyal following of fundamentalist Christians. In the Democratic race, Jesse Jackson's committed followers enabled him to finish first in the important Michigan caucuses and make strong showings in Delaware, Vermont, South Carolina, Texas, and Alaska.[46]

National Convention Delegates

National convention delegates are not a representative cross-section of either their parties' rank and file voters or the adult population. Status as a convention delegate is a reward that is given to only the most intensely involved supporters of the candidates and party workers. As Table 6–1 demonstrates, convention delegates are not a representative cross section of the adult population. Reflecting the general American patterns of participation in party politics, national convention delegates are drawn primarily from generally well educated, middle- and upper-middle-class strata of society. It is these people who have the time, leisure, money, and interest to participate actively in politics. There are, however, differences in the composition of Republican and Democratic conventions, with the Democrats having higher proportions of women, blacks, Hispanics, Catholics, and union officials.

Table 6–1 1988 Republican and Democratic Convention Delegates Compared (Percents)

	Republican	Democrat
Liberal	1%	39%
Moderate	36	50
Conservative	60	5
Men	63	48
Women	37	52
White	96	70
Black	3	21
Hispanic	3	8
Hold party office	60	43
Hold elected office	28	26
18–29 years	4	4
30–39	13	22
40–49	28	33
50–59	30	25
60 and over	25	16
Protestant	70	51
Catholic	24	30
Jewish	2	6
Family Income		
Under $25,000	2	6
$25,000–49,999	21	33
$50,000–99,999	39	40
$100,000 or more	27	16
High School Education or less	10	9
Some college	21	18
College graduate	26	21
Beyond college	42	52
Lawyer	14	14
Executive	21	11
Other profession	12	17
Union official	0	6
Public official	16	16
Government employee	2	9
White collar	2	3
Blue collar	2	3
Homemaker/volunteer	7	3
Retired	8	5

Source: New York Times, Aug. 14, 1988, p. 147. Copyright © 1988 by The New York Times Company. Reprinted by permission.

The most striking differences between Republican and Democratic delegates are not in their socioeconomic characteristics, but in their political philosophies and positions on public policy issues (see Tables 6–1 and 6–2). Republican delegates are strongly conservative in their orientation, while the Democrats tend toward a liberal position. It is also clear that the delegates from both parties are unrepresentative ideologically of both their own party's rank and file voters and the total adult population. Democratic delegates are substantially more liberal than their party rank and file and the general public, while Republican delegates are more conservative than their party's voters and the general public. These are the inevitable consequences of the tendency of party activists to be drawn from the most politically committed elements of society and the processes through which delegates are chosen. Participation is skewed toward the extreme ends of each party's dominant ideological tendency and the convention delegates reflect this bias. The generally liberal character of Democratic delegates and conservative orientation of Republican delegates have implications for the conduct of the conventions and the image that these conventions convey to the public through the news media. Candidates for Democratic nominations operate within a convention context which requires them to adopt positions consistent with a liberal ideology. President Jimmy Carter's 1980 acquiescence to a series of liberal platform planks proposed by his rival, Senator Edward Kennedy, reflected Carter's recognition that the predominantly liberal delegates favored Kennedy's position on platform issues. Likewise, President Ford's reluctant acceptance of a foreign policy plank put forward by supporters of his opponent, Ronald Reagan, at the 1976 GOP convention is evidence that Ford understood that the convention was more conservative than his administration.

Appeals to the hard-core followers of a party at the convention and the publicity which these people naturally gain at conventions have their effect on the image of the party and its candidate conveyed via the media to the public. The prominent role of Jesse Jackson, and other members of the liberal wing of the party at the Democratic convention in 1984 and 1988 certainly projected to voters a generally liberal image of the party nominees, Walter Mondale and Michael Dukakis. Similarly, press attention to Senator Jesse Helms (N.C.), Moral Majority leader Jerry Falwell, and the activist conservatives on the platform committee resulted in a distinctly conservative image for the 1984 GOP convention in Dallas.[47] These images, of course, have implications for the general election because the conventions are the beginning of the general election campaigns.

Table 6–2 Comparison of 1988 National Convention Delegates with Rank and File Party Voters and the General Public (Percents)

	Dem. Delegates	Dem. Voters	Total Adults	Rep. Voters	Rep. Delegates
Political Philosophy					
Conservative	5%	22%	30%	43%	60%
Liberal	39	25	20	12	1
Size of Government					
Prefer smaller government providing fewer services	16	33	43	59	87
Prefer bigger government providing more services	58	56	44	30	3
Domestic Policy					
Favor increased federal spending for education	90	76	71	67	41
Say abortion should be legal	72	43	40	39	29
Government paying too much attention to the needs of blacks	68	45	34	19	14
Foreign Military Policy					
Favor keeping defense spending at least at current levels	32	59	66	73	84
More worried about communist takeover in Central America than U.S. involvement in war there	12	25	37	55	80

Source: New York Times, Aug. 14, 1988, p. 14Y. Copyright © 1988 by The New York Times Company. Reprinted by permission.

Media Politics in Presidential Nominations

The media have always played a significant role in presidential nominating politics because reporters and commentators are inevitably forced to make decisions about which candidates deserve extensive coverage, which candidates did well or poorly in the primaries and caucuses, which candidates are the front runners, and which candidates are surging or fading. The decisions that the media make on such issues have significant effects on the nominating campaign and can influence how the field of candidates is narrowed to a small number of serious contenders. With the opening up of the caucuses and the proliferation of the primaries, the role of party leaders as the arbitrators of presidential nominations has declined, while the role of the media has been expanded.

The impact of the media on presidential nominating politics is illustrated by TV coverage of the Democratic race during the early contests of 1984.[48] Based upon polls which showed Walter Mondale and Senator John Glenn as the leading candidates, the networks accorded the largest share of their coverage to these two candidates during the days prior to the Iowa caucuses. Such an allocation of coverage worked to the advantage of Mondale and Glenn and to the disadvantage of the other candidates—Gary Hart, Ernest Hollings, Reuben Askew, George McGovern, Alan Cranston, and Jesse Jackson. Mondale did well in the Iowa caucuses, as was expected, and, therefore, continued to get substantial media coverage. Hart unexpectedly won second place and immediately was on a media roll. His surprising finish catapulted him into national prominence with a wave of essentially favorable news stories about his against-the-odds rise to serious contender status. Hart was accorded this status on the basis of receiving just 15 percent (15,000) of the votes (Mondale received 45 percent). Interestingly, Hart did only slightly better than McGovern's third place finish (10,700 votes for 13 percent). It was Hart, however, who was accorded serious contender status, while McGovern with virtually the same level of support was largely ignored in terms of press coverage.

During the period between the Iowa caucuses and the New Hampshire primary, Hart received approximately equal television coverage to the front runner, Walter Mondale. This gave Hart's campaign a tremendous boost. Media decisions about whom to cover and who had done well in Iowa, therefore, helped to determine the future course of the nomination contest. Instead of an eight person race, it was essentially a two person race after Iowa.

It was not just the decisions the media made on whom to cover that were important. Equally critical were the decisions that were made concerning the tone of the coverage. In the period between the Iowa and New Hampshire contests, coverage of Hart was essentially positive. Tough investigative reporting on the candidate was postponed—to Hart's great advantage. The extensive and favorable publicity given the Hart campaign as it moved on to New Hampshire gave him significant aid in staging a defeat of the front running Walter Mondale in the snows of New Hampshire. But in the three weeks between New Hampshire's primary and "Super Tuesday" (when on March 13 five states held primaries), the tenor of coverage for Hart changed from soft background pieces about the young candidate with "new ideas" to tough investigative reporting. Questions were raised constantly by the media about such things as whether Hart had been forthright in disclosing information about his name change and age. There was also a questioning in the media about whether or not he was really a candidate with new ideas and whether he had the requisite experience to be president. After this barrage of less than favorable coverage, Hart's fortunes began to fade. On "Super Tuesday" he won two New England primaries and one in Florida, but lost to Mondale in Georgia and Alabama.

Interestingly, those voters who made up their minds about how to vote between New Hampshire and "Super Tuesday" were much less likely to favor Hart than those who made up their minds before New Hampshire, when the Hart coverage was essentially favorable. Clearly, media coverage had an impact on the outcome of the Democratic nomination in 1984. It was not the only important factor, but the early phases of the Hart-Mondale contest demonstrate that presidential nominating politics is media centered and that the media personnel are major participants in the process. The media plays a crucial role in narrowing the field of candidates and in influencing public perceptions of the candidates.

A Lengthy, Candidate Centered, Primary Focused, Participatory, and Media Oriented Process

The American system for nominating presidents is primary focused, open and participatory, candidate centered, and media oriented. It is a process that confounds most European observers who are accustomed to a leadership selection process which is dominated by party leaders. The leaders of political parties in most Western style democracies, except the United States, are chosen by their parties' members in the lower house of the national legislature. British political scientist Anthony King in 1980 noted the contrasting patterns of

American and British leadership selection processes when he made the following observations. He characterized the British system in this way.[49]

1. Party leaders entered politics at an early age and served a considerable number of years in Parliament before being elected leader.
2. Party leaders had served in a number of different national offices prior to their selection.
3. The leaders were assessed and voted upon exclusively by their fellow politicians.
4. The campaigns for the leadership were short, with little wear and tear on the candidates.
5. The cost of the leadership campaigns was low.
6. The process of selecting the leaders was entirely a party process.

By contrast, King noted the American selection process in 1980 had these characteristics.[50]

1. The nominees [Reagan and Carter] entered politics in middle age and neither had much experience in government.
2. Neither nominee had ever served in any capacity within the national government. And neither at the time of first nomination held any public office.
3. The candidates were voted upon and assessed mainly by voters in primaries.
4. The nominating campaigns were exceedingly long and involved enormous wear and tear on the candidates.
5. The cost of the campaigns was high.
6. The process was by no means an exclusively party process.

The post-1968 reforms of the nominating process have served to widen the difference between American and British leadership selection processes. Prior to 1968, the American nomination process involved a more extensive role for party leaders than the current system. The party leader dominated process has been praised because the candidates were assessed by politicians who had worked closely with them and knew their abilities and liabilities. This system, however, was criticized by reformers for its alleged exclusiveness which restricted participation. As controversy rages every four years over the nominating process, note that no selection process is foolproof. The party dominated process that produced Franklin Roosevelt and Dwight Eisenhower as presidential nominees also produced John W.

Davis and Warren G. Harding. Granting that no set of procedures guarantees success, it is important that the presidential nominating process continue to be critically evaluated because structure and procedure do have an impact.

Suggestions for Further Reading

Abramson, Paul R.; Aldrich, John H.; and Rohde, David W. *Change and Continuity in the 1988 Elections.* Washington, D.C.: CQ Press, 1990. Chapter 1.

Crotty, William. *Party Reform.* New York: Longman, 1983.

________, and Jackson, John S., III *Presidential Primaries and Nominations.* Washington, D.C.: CQ Press, 1984.

Grassmuck, George, ed. *Before Nomination: Our Primary Problem.* Washington, D.C.: American Enterprise Institute, 1985.

Kessel, John H. *Presidential Parties.* Homewood, Ill.: Dorsey Press, 1984.

Lichter, S. Robert; Amundson, Daniel; and Noyes, Richard. *The Video Campaign: Network Coverage of the 1988 Primaries.* Washington, D.C.: American Enterprise Institute, 1988.

Polsby, Nelson W. *The Consequences of Party Reform.* New York: Oxford University Press, 1983.

Shafer, Byron E., *Bifurcated Politics: Evolution and Reform in the National Party Convention.* Cambridge, Mass.: Harvard University Press.

Shafer, Byron E. *Quiet Revolution: The Struggle for the Democratic Party and the Shaping of Post-Reform Politics.* New York: Russell Sage Foundation, 1983.

Squire, Peverill, ed., *The Iowa Caucuses and the Presidential Nominating Process.* Boulder, Colo.: Westview Press, 1989.

Notes

1. *Democratic Party of the United States of America v. Bronson C. LaFollette,* 449 U.S. 897 (1981). For a detailed account of the efforts of the national Democratic party to close the Wisconsin primary, see Gary D. Wekkin, *Democrat versus Democrat* (Columbia: University of Missouri Press, 1984).
2. Nonbinding presidential primaries for the Democrats were held in Vermont, Idaho, and North Dakota and for the Republicans in Vermont and Virginia.
3. For a detailed analysis of the phases of presidential nominating politics, see John H. Kessel, *Presidential Parties* (Homewood, Ill.: Dorsey Press, 1984), pp. 249–306.
4. For a detailed account of how Jimmy Carter planned his campaign for the 1976 Democratic nomination, see Jules Witcover, *Marathon: The Pur-*

suit of the Presidency, 1972–1976 (New York: Signet, 1978), pp. 113–126, 141–146.

5. Thomas B. Edsall, " '88 Candidates' New Tricks Stretch Federal Election Law," *Washington Post,* Oct. 20, 1985, p. A1.
6. Paul Taylor, " '88 Presidential Contest Already Astir for GOP," *Washington Post,* pp. A1, A9.
7. For an account of how the PACs of Walter Mondale and Edward Kennedy contributed to Democratic candidates in the 1982 midterm elections, see Rhodes Cook, "Prudent Investing: Presidential Hopefuls Funnel Contributions to Safe Races," *Congressional Quarterly Weekly Report* (Aug. 21, 1982), pp. 2074–2075.
8. Rhodes Cook, "The Nomination Process," in Michael Nelson, ed., *The Elections of 1988* (Washington, D.C.: CQ Press, 1989), p. 32.
9. Ibid., p. 33.
10. Ibid., p. 34. For a detailed account of media coverage of the 1988 presidential primaries, see S. Robert Lichter, Daniel Amundson, and Richard Noyes, *The Video Campaign: Network Coverage of the 1988 Primaries* (Washington, D.C.: American Enterprise Institute, 1988).
11. Kessel, *Presidential Parties,* pp. 254–256.
12. Nelson W. Polsby, "The Democratic Nomination," in Austin Ranney, ed., *The American Elections of 1980* (Washington, D.C.: American Enterprise Institute, 1982), p. 51.
13. Cook, "The Nomination Process," p. 37.
14. Douglas E. Kneeland, "Bush Says He'll Quit Active Campaigning," *New York Times,* May 27, 1980, p. A-1.
15. Cook, "The Nomination Process," p. 38.
16. David Broder, "A Chance to Be 'Presidential,' " *Washington Post,* July 15, 1984, p. 8.
17. Kessel, *Presidential Parties,* p. 257.
18. Herbert B. Asher, *Presidential Elections and American Politics,* 3d ed., (Homewood, Ill.: Dorsey Press, 1984), p. 257.
19. David E. Price, *Bringing Back the Parties* (Washington, D.C.: CQ Press, 1984), pp. 148–149.
20. Price, *Bringing Back the Parties,* p. 149.
21. Byron E. Shafer, *Quiet Revolution: The Struggle for the Democratic Party and the Shaping of Post-Reform Politics* (New York: Russell Sage Foundation, 1983), p. 526.
22. A thorough description and analysis of the Hunt Commission is contained in David E. Price, *Bringing Back the Parties,* pp. 159–183.
23. "Presidential Primary Recap," *Congressional Quarterly, Weekly Report,* June 16, 1984, p. 1442; and Thomas E. Mann, "Elected Officials and the Politics of Presidential Selection," in Austin Ranney, ed., *The American Elections of 1984* (Washington, D.C.: American Enterprise Institute, 1985), p. 106.

24. Mann, Elected Officials and the Politics of Presidential Selection," p. 105.
25. The differing approaches of the Republican and Democratic parties to party reform are described in John F. Bibby, "Party Renewal in the National Republican Party," in Gerald Pomper, ed., *Party Renewal in America: Theory and Practice* (New York: Praeger, 1980), pp. 102–115.
26. The differences between Republican and Democratic party rules are described in more detail in Robert J. Huckshorn and John F. Bibby, "National Party Rules and Delegate Selection in the Republican Party," PS 16 (Fall 1983): 656–666. See also Paul R. Abramson, John H. Aldrich, and David W. Rohde, *Change and Continuity in the 1988 Elections,* (Washington, D.C.: CQ Press, 1990), pp. 18–19.
27. For a critical evaluation of the Democratic reforms, see Nelson W. Polsby, *Consequences of Party Reform* (New York: Oxford University Press, 1983). A sympathetic consideration of the Democratic reforms is found in William Crotty, *Party Reform* (New York: Longman, 1983).
28. Nelson W. Polsby and Aaron Wildavsky, *Presidential Elections: Strategies of American Electoral Politics,* 7th ed. (New York: Scribners, 1988), p. 55.
29. Richard B. Cheney, "The Law's Impact on Presidential and Congressional Election Campaigns, in Michael Malbin, ed., *Parties, Interest Groups, and Campaign Finance Laws* (Washington, D.C.: American Enterprise Institute, 1980), p. 240.
30. Herbert E. Alexander, "The Price We Pay for Our Presidents," *Public Opinion* (March/April, 1989), pp. 46–47.
31. Austin Ranney, *Participation in American Presidential Nominations* (Washington, D.C.: American Enterprise Institute, 1977), p. 14.
32. Ibid., pp. 24–25.
33. Barbara Norrander, "Turnout in Super Tuesday Primaries: The Composition of the Electorate," a paper prepared for the Annual Meeting of the American Political Science Association, Aug. 31–Sept. 3, 1989.
34. "Primary Recap: The Aggregate Vote," *Congressional Quarterly Weekly Report,* July 9, 1988, p. 1892.
35. For an analysis of the factors affecting voter turnout in presidential primaries, see Barbara Norrander and Greg Smith, "Type of Contest, Candidate Strategy, and Turnout in Presidential Primaries," *American Politics Quarterly* 13 (Jan. 1985): 28–50; and Barbara Norrander, "Selective Participation: Presidential Primary Voters as a Subset of General Election Voter," *American Politics Quarterly* 14 (Jan. 1986): 35–53.
36. William Crotty and John S. Jackson III, *Presidential Primaries and Nominations* (Washington, D.C.: CQ Press, 1984), p. 90.
37. "Who Voted in the Democratic Primaries," *New York Times,* June 17, 1984, p. 4E.
38. Norrander, "Turnout in Super Tuesday Primaries."

39. Crotty and Jackson, *Presidential Primaries and Nominations*, pp. 91–92.
40. Ibid., p. 93.
41. See Barbara Norrander, "Ideological Representativeness of Presidential Primary Voters, *American Journal of Political Science* 33 (August 1989): 570–587; see also John G. Geer, "Assessing the Representativeness of Electorates in Presidential Primaries," *American Journal of Political Science* 32 (Nov. 1988): 929–945.
42. Ranney, *Participation in American Presidential Nominations*, 1976, p. 15.
43. Data on caucus turnout was derived from Rhodes Cook, "In 1988, Caucuses Have Been a Place of Political Passion," *Congressional Quarterly Weekly Report*, June 4, 1988, pp. 1524, 1526.
44. Walter J. Stone, Alan I. Abramowitz, and Ronald B. Rapoport, "How Representative Are the Iowa Caucuses," in Peverill Squire, ed., *The Iowa Caucuses and the Presidential Nominating Process* (Boulder, Colo.; Westview Press, 1989), pp. 11–12.
45. Crotty and Jackson, *Presidential Primaries and Nominations*, p. 97.
46. Cook, "In 1988 Caucuses Have Been the Place for Passion," p. 1523.
47. This discussion of media impact on presidential nominating politics relies heavily upon William C. Adams, "Media Coverage of Campaign '84: A Preliminary Report," *Public Opinion* 6 (April/May 1984): 9–13.
48. For an analysis of network coverage of the 1984 conventions, see William C. Adams, "Convention Coverage," *Public Opinion* 7 (Dec./Jan. 1985): 43–48. The most complete consideration of the impact of television coverage upon national conventions and public perceptions of the parties is found in Byron E. Shafer, *Bifurcated Politics: Evolution and Reform in the National Party Convention* (Cambridge, Mass.: Harvard University Press, 1988), especially chapters 7 and 8.
49. Anthony King, "How Not to Select Presidential Candidates: A View from Europe," in Austin Ranney, ed., *American Elections of 1980*, pp. 310–313.
50. Ibid., pp. 315–320.

CHAPTER 7

The General Election: Regulation and Campaign Strategy

Once the field of candidates has been narrowed through the nomination process, the scene of the party battle shifts to the general election. Nominations are intraparty struggles, while the general election is an interparty struggle which operates in a different type of political environment. In the general election competition, there is normally a higher level of citizen interest, an expanded electorate, larger campaign expenditures, and greater media exposure. The nomination is an interim stage in the process of selection of government officials. In the general election, all decisions are final.

A critical factor in influencing the nature of campaigns and the outcome of elections is the set of rules under which the election is conducted. In the American federal system, the rules of the election game are a combination of federal and state regulations. As originally written, the Constitution contained few provisions regulating elections. Article II provided for the election of the president by an electoral college, with the state legislatures free to determine the manner in which their states' electors would be chosen. Article I mandated that senators should be elected by state legislatures and that the House should be chosen by "the people of several states" and that the voters "in each state shall have the qualifications requisite for electors of the most numerous branch of the state legislature." Congress was also empowered to make laws and alter regulations of the states regarding the "Times, Places, and Manner of holding Elections for Senators and Representatives."

As a result of the dearth of constitutional provisions relating to elections, most regulation of elections was left to the states. With each state making its own election rules, there was naturally substantial diversity in state regulations of federal elections. Some states elected members of the House from districts, while other states used at-large electoral systems; some states held elections in even numbered years and others did so in odd numbered years; and some states required only a plurality for election while others required a majority. The diversity of election practices and state prerogatives in these matters has been gradually reduced through federal statutes and constitutional amendments. For example, starting in 1842, federal law required the states to elect representatives from districts in even numbered years on the Tuesday following the first Monday in November. Among the most significant changes in the law regulating elections have been those actions by the federal government to extend the suffrage to blacks, women, and eighteen year olds and to make the Senate a popularly elected body.

Extending the Suffrage

When the Constitution was ratified, exercise of the franchise was commonly limited to those males who could meet property owning or tax-paying qualifications. As a result, it is estimated that one-half to three-quarters of adult males could not vote.[1] By the Jacksonian era, however, the states had removed most of these economic restrictions on voting so that virtually all adult white males could vote.

Voting Rights for Blacks

The first major step toward enfranchising black citizens was ratification of the Civil War amendments, the Fourteenth Amendment guaranteeing all persons the equal protection of the laws, and the Fifteenth Amendment banning denials of voting rights on the basis of "race, color or previous condition of servitude." However, the southern states, where the black population was concentrated, circumvented these amendments through such devices as the poll tax, literacy tests, and white primaries. Requiring payment of a poll tax prior to election day and administering literacy tests in a discriminatory manner meant that blacks had great difficulty having their names entered on the official voting rolls. The white primary further disenfranchised black citizens by excluding them from participation in Democratic primary elections, the real elections in most of the South until well into the 1960s. Physical force and intimidation were also all too frequent techniques used to prevent southern blacks from voting.

Through judicial decisions (e.g., the Supreme Court banned the white primary in 1944)[2] and the federal Civil Rights Acts of 1957, 1960, 1964, and 1965, racial barriers to voting have been largely removed. Particularly important was the Voting Rights Act of 1965, which was renewed by Congress in 1982. It suspended literacy tests in all states and counties in which less than 50 percent of the voting age population was registered to vote in 1964. It also provided for federal registrars to register votes and supervise the electoral process in these areas. The act further required officials in these states to submit to the federal Justice Department any changes in election law so that the Attorney General could review the change and veto those which he deemed discriminatory. As a result of this legislation, black registration has increased dramatically in the South so that it approximates that of whites (see Table 7–1). While blacks were not an important voting bloc prior to the 1960s, they are now a major electoral force overwhelmingly supportive of Democratic candidates in all of

Table 7–1 Voter Registration in Eleven Southern States, 1960–1986[a]

	1960	1970	1980	1986
Whites				
Number[a]	12,276	16,985	24,981	27,028
Percent of Voting Age Population	61.1	69.2	71.9	69.9
Blacks				
Number[a]	1,463	3,357	4,254	5,450
Percent of Voting Age Population	29.1	62.0	55.8	60.8

a. Reported in thousands

Sources: Statistical Abstract of the United States, 1990, p. 264; *Statistical Abstract of the United States, 1972*, p. 374.

the southern states. The number of black elected officials in the region is also on the rise. As of 1988, there were over 4,200 black elected officials in the South.

Women's Suffrage

The movement for women's suffrage began at approximately the same time as that for blacks, but its progress was much more rapid. Although eleven states had given women the right to vote by 1918, it was not until the ratification of the Nineteenth Amendment in 1920 that women generally were permitted to vote. This amendment almost doubled the voting age population in a single stroke. It did not, however, result in any significant changes in the conduct of elections, which party won, or the direction of national policy. Women's voting patterns have tended to be quite similar to those of men. However, in the 1980s, noticeable differences in the way men and women cast their ballots developed and the phrase "gender gap" entered the vocabulary of election analysts (see Chapter 8).

Eighteen-Year-Old Voting

Until 1971, every state but Alaska, Georgia, and Kentucky required that individuals be twenty-one years of age in order to vote. The Twenty-Sixth Amendment lowered that requirement to eighteen and thereby expanded the electorate by some 25 million voters. The young voters' impact, however, has not been great because of their low rates of turnout in elections. Nor have young people tended to line up in overwhelming support of any particular candidate or party. During the 1972 election, the first election when eighteen year olds were eligible to vote, Democratic nominee George McGovern and some analysts anticipated that young voters would support McGovern overwhelmingly. McGovern, however, was disappointed in the vote he received from this age group, which did not behave in a monolithic pattern. In the 1984 and 1988 presidential elections, younger voters tended to favor the Republicans in approximately the same proportions as middle-aged voters.

Nationalization of Voting Rights and State Administration of Elections

Eligibility to vote is now governed largely by the Constitution and federal law, so that voting is a right of national citizenship. Within the strictures of federal law, however, the states continue to play a major role in the electoral process. They set the residency (maximum of thirty days) and registration requirements for voting. These regulations are designed to insure that only the residents of a state participate in its elections and to preserve the integrity of elections by preventing people from voting more than once and in various locations. State statutes governing residency and registration vary widely (see Chapter 8) and can operate in a manner that facilitates or hinders citizen participation in elections. In addition, states may restrict voting by convicted felons and resident aliens. State and local governments are also largely responsible for the administration of elections—printing ballots, providing polling places and poll workers, fixing the hours that the polls are open, counting the ballots, certifying outcomes, and regulating campaign practices on election day (e.g., the extent and nature of campaigning permitted near polling places).

Direct Election of the Senate

Senators were originally selected by the state legislatures in conformity with the Constitution. Senators elected under these circumstances were often considered as ambassadors from their states to the national government and some state legislatures carried the ambassadorial aspects of a senator's duties so far as to instruct senators on how to vote. Occasionally, senators resigned their offices rather than submit to the instructions of their legislatures. More severe problems, however, were caused by the frequent deadlocks that occurred within state legislatures when they sought to elect senators. When such deadlocks happened, Senate seats were left vacant until the impasse could be resolved. A notable example of deadlock took place in

Delaware when an intraparty feud between Republican factions in the legislature left the state without any senatorial representation between 1901 and 1903. In addition to the problems of legislative deadlock, there were charges of corruption in the legislative maneuvering to elect senators and the belief that legislative elections distorted and even blocked the will of the people from being expressed in the Senate. A movement, therefore, developed for direct election of senators by the people, and six states followed Oregon's example of holding nonbinding popular elections for the Senate. The state legislature was then expected to officially confirm the voters' choice. In 1913, the Seventeenth Amendment was adopted requiring the states to select their senators through popular election.

Party Column versus Office Bloc Ballot Forms

The type of ballot that voters use can have an influence on how they vote. There are two common ballot forms in use in the United States. The *party column ballot* is used in twenty-one states.[3] It is arranged so that all the candidates of one party are listed in one column (or row on a voting machine). By marking or punching a single box or pulling a party lever, voters can cast a straight party vote for all the candidates of their preferred party. Thus, the party column ballot encourages straight ticket voting. The other major ballot form is the *office bloc ballot*, which organizes the names of the candidates according to the office they are seeking. This type of ballot, which is used in twenty-nine states, does not permit a voter to cast a straight party vote by making a single mark or pulling a party lever on a voting machine. Therefore, the office bloc ballot tends to discourage party line voting and encourages candidates to attract attention to themselves and only incidentally to their party.[4] The increased use of the office bloc ballot is consistent with a trend in campaign practices and voting behavior which emphasizes voting for individual candidates rather than for a political party.

Financing Elections

Without substantial funds, it is rarely possible to run a credible campaign. Money is not the only critical campaign resource—name identification, charisma, incumbency, volunteers, party organizational support, interest group backing, and a favorable balance within the constituency of party voters are also important. But without money, the basics of a campaign are impossible to obtain. Money purchases a headquarters, staff, polls, media advertising, and travel. As the technology of campaigning has become more advanced and the electronic media has become an indispensable part of major campaigns, campaign costs have escalated dramatically. Professional campaign consultants to advise on the use of the modern campaign technology have become a standard feature of most campaigns for major office. These experts frequently demand large fees for their services. For example, a top campaign consulting firm can collect fees of approximately $100,000 for consulting on senatorial and gubernatorial races, plus $250,000 to $450,000 in media placement fees.[5]

The escalating cost of winning a seat in the House of Representatives or Senate is presented in Figure 7–1, which shows the average expenditure of winning candidates between 1976 and 1988. Whether computed as current costs or current costs adjusted for inflation (constant dollars), expenses for securing a seat in the Congress have shown a sharp increase and required serious candidates to intensify their fund-raising efforts. The costs of other campaigns have also increased dramatically. For example, in 1956 large state gubernatorial campaigns cost on average $300,000 ($1.3 million in 1987 dollars), while the average cost of the thirty-six gubernatorial elections in 1986 was $7.4 million (1987 dollars), and for the three elections held in 1987, $12.4 million.[6] Even state legislative races can be extremely expensive, with some candidates spending approximately half a million dollars in states where a switch in party control of a few seats could result in the change of party control of a legislative chamber.

The level of campaign spending is related to the candidates' chances of winning and the closeness of the contest. For example, in House elections, incumbents and open seat (where no incumbent is running) candidates have the best chance of victory and they normally spend at higher than average levels (see Table 7–2). Closely fought races also cause high spending by both incumbents and challengers.

Analyses of campaign spending and election outcomes have shown that the level of expenditure by a candidate can affect the result, but the individual who spends the most does not necessarily win. Sufficient funds to run an adequate campaign are absolutely essential and large disparities in financial resources can be hurtful to the disadvantaged candidate. Research on House elections demonstrates that campaign spending is particularly important for candidates challenging incumbents. The more challengers spend, the better known they become to the voters and the better able voters are to make an evaluation of them. Gary Jacobson estimated that in 1978 the average House challenger would have to spend $320,000 just to become as familiar to the voters as the average incumbent. Clearly, adequate financing is ab-

Figure 7–1: The Rising Cost of Winning a Seat in the U.S. House and Senate, 1976–1988 (Average Cost of Winning Campaigns for House and Senate)

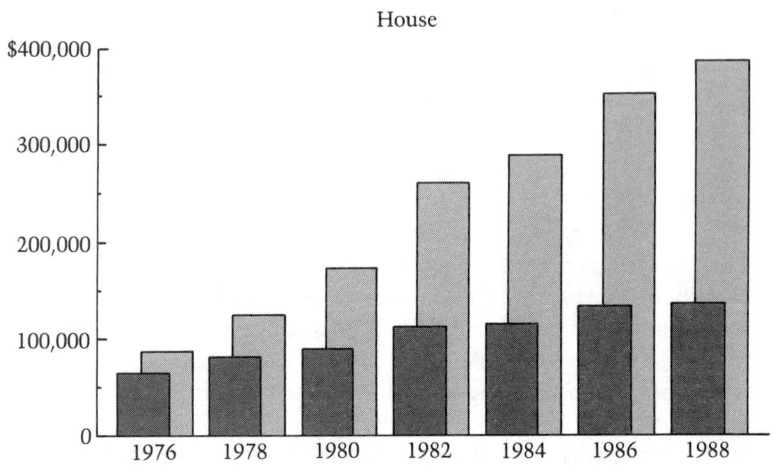

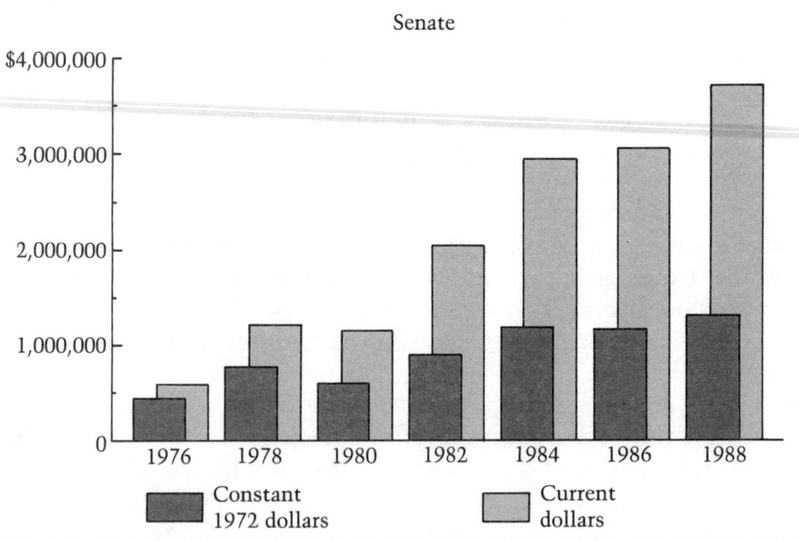

Source: Congressional Research Service.

Table 7–2 Mean Expenditures in U.S. House of Representatives Elections, 1988

	Number	Amount	Difference from Mean
All Candidates	809	$273,811	—
All Incumbents	412	378,316	+ $104,505
All Challengers	346	118,877	− 154,934
Open Seat Candidates	51	480,685	+ 200,874
Republican Incumbents Who Won by Less than 60%	21	711,464	+ 437,653
Democratic Incumbents Who Won by Less than 60%	23	840,145	+ 366,334
Defeated Republican Incumbents	3	469,806	+ 695,996
Defeated Democratic Incumbents	2	935,494	+ 661,683
Republican Challengers Who Defeated Democratic Incumbents	2	349,409	+ 75,599
Democratic Challengers Who Defeated Republican Incumbents	3	809,908	+ 536,097

Source: Norman Ornstein, Thomas E. Mann, and Michael J. Malbin, *Vital Statistics on Congress, 1989–1990* (Washington, D.C.: Congressional Quarterly, 1990) pp. 71–72, 78–79.

solutely critical for challengers. Because incumbents are better known to the voters, high levels of incumbent campaign spending have less effect on their races than is true for nonincumbents.[7] Of course, most challengers have less money to spend on their races than incumbents and this compounds their disadvantage.

Because of the escalating cost of campaigns, the inevitable differences among candidates in their financial resources, and the recurring charges of improprieties, there have been periodic demands for regulation of campaign finance. The resulting statutes at the national and state levels have used the following methods to regulate campaign finance: (1) public disclosure of contributions and expenditures; (2) contribution and expenditure limits; and (3) public funding of campaigns.

Public Disclosure

The Federal Election Campaign Act (FECA) requires that all contributions of $200 or more must be identified and all expenditures of $200 or more must be reported. Candidate committees and parties must also file periodic preelection reports and a final postelection report with the Federal Election Commission (FEC). All of the states also have disclosure laws, which vary widely in their provisions.

MAJOR PROVISIONS OF THE FEDERAL ELECTION CAMPAIGN ACT

Public Disclosure: All contributions of $200 or more must be identified and all expenditures of $200 or more must be reported.

Contribution Limits: In any election (primary or general election) the following limits apply.

Individuals: $1000 per election (primary and general election are considered separate elections)
$20,000 to a national party committee per calendar year
$5000 to other political committees per calendar year
Total not to exceed $25,000 per year

Candidates: not limited in the amounts they can contribute to their *own* campaigns. However, if a presidential candidate accepts public funding, the following limits apply: $50,000 in the prenomination stage; $50,000 in the general election

Multicandidate Committees (e.g. PACs): $5000 per election; $15,000 per calendar year to national party committees

Party Committees: $5000 per election to U.S. House candidates
Republican and Democratic senatorial campaign committees, or RNC and DNC, or combination of both may give $17,500 to U.S. Senate candidates.

Coordinated Expenditures in House and Senate Contests

Party committees (national and state) can spend $25,140 (1990) to support House candidates.

Party committees (national and state) can spend 2¢ per voter (adjusted for inflation) to support Senate candidates.

Matching Funds for Candidates for Presidential Nominations

Major party presidential nomination candidates are eligible for federal matching funds.

To receive federal matching funds, a candidate must:

1. Raise at least $5000 in individual contributions of $250 or less in each of 20 states. Individual contributions of up to $1000 can be accepted, but only the first $250 counts toward the federal match.
2. Abide by an overall expenditure limit ($23.05 million in 1988), plus fund-raising expenses. (Overall expenditure limit is adjusted for inflation for each presidential election year.)
3. Abide by state expenditure limits based upon a formula of 16¢ per voter, plus an inflation adjustment.

Public Funding of the General Election Campaign for President

Major party candidates may elect to receive public funding for their general election campaigns ($46.1 million in 1988). Such funding is conditional upon the candidate's agreeing not to accept or spend other funds in the campaign.

Candidates who do not accept public funds are not limited in the amount they can spend.

(There is no public funding of congressional and senatorial campaigns.)

State and Local Party Spending in Presidential Elections

State and local party organizations are authorized to engage in get out the vote campaigns (signs, handbills, posters, bumper stickers, yard signs, registration drives, etc.) and there are no limits on the amounts they may spend.

National Party Committees

National party committees are authorized to spend $8.3 million in support of their parties' presidential tickets. (1988)

Contribution and Expenditure Limits

In federal elections individuals may contribute no more than $1000 to any one candidate per campaign (primaries and general elections are considered separate) up to a total of $25,000 in an election year. Nonparty political action committees may give no more than $5000 to any one candidate per campaign. In House elections, party committees are restricted to direct contributions of $5000 per candidate per election. This means that party committees can contribute up to a total of $10,000 to House candidates ($5000 for the nomination campaign and $5000 for the general election). Both the national committees and the congressional campaign committees are permitted to make contributions at this level. As a result, national level party committee contributions to House candidates may total $20,000. State party organizations may also contribute directly to congressional candidates. In addition to direct contributions, *party* committees are also authorized to make *coordinated expenditures* on behalf of the party and its candidates. Coordinated expenditures involve spending by the parties to support candidates (e.g., for polls, media production, campaign consultants) which benefits specific candidates, but does not entail direct financial contributions to a candidate's campaign committee. In 1990, the amount of coordinated expenditures authorized by law to assist a particular House candidate was $25,140.

National party committees are permitted to spend more extensively in Senate races. Direct party contributions to senatorial candidates are restricted to $17,500. Party coordinated expenditures are based upon a formula of two cents per eligible voter in the state (adjusted for inflation since 1974). The two cents per voter formula when applied to large states like California or Florida means that party committees are in a position to be of major assistance to their party's nominee for the Senate ($605,271 in the case of Texas and $436,330 for Illinois in 1990). State party committees are also permitted to spend two cents per voter in coordinated expenditures to support senatorial candidates. However, most state parties are not in a position financially to take full advantage of this provision in the law. To compensate for the inability of most state parties to spend to the legal limit in support of senatorial candidates, the Republicans pioneered the development of the "agency agreement" technique. Under this procedure, state parties assign their quota of coordinated expenditures to the national party to act as their agent. As a result of this procedure, the Republican and Democratic senatorial campaign committees have been able to double the level of their coordinated expenditures in key races.

Republican party committees play a more significant role in funding congressional and senatorial campaigns than do Democratic party organizations (see Figure 7–2). For example, in 1988, 7 percent of the $103.1 million raised by Democratic House candidates or expended on their behalf by party committees was derived from Democratic party organizations, while Republican party committees contributed and spent 11 percent of the $96.4 million raised for GOP candidates.[8] It should be noted, however, that the Democratic party made significant strides toward reducing the Republican advantage in party support for congressional and senatorial candidates. In addition to direct contributions to candidates and coordinated party expenditures on their behalf, the Democratic Congressional Campaign Committee has been unusually effective in channeling PAC contributions to candidates involved in close races. However, the continuing gap in fund-raising capacities of the two national party organizations has resulted in their adopting quite different attitudes toward campaign finance reform. With a larger number of incumbents, the superior access to PAC funds that incumbency provides, and a national party structure less capable of raising campaign dollars, the Democrats in Congress have sought changes in the FECA that would impose spending limits on candidates who voluntarily accept public funding, maintain limits on party expenditures, and impose modest limits on PAC contributions. By contrast, Republicans have advocated removing or raising contribution and expenditure limits on parties, opposed expenditure limits on candidates, and sought more severe limits on PAC contributions.[9]

Although political parties are restricted in terms of how much they may spend to support congressional and senatorial candidates, there are no overall limits on the amount the candidates' organizations may spend. The outer range of expenditures in races for positions on Capitol Hill, therefore, can be extremely high. For example, in 1988, Representative Joseph P. Kennedy (D–Mass.) collected $1.4 million for his reelection bid and Senator Pete Wilson (R–Cal.) had total receipts of $11.3 million.

Nor are there limits on how much of their own money candidates may spend in pursuit of public office. The Supreme Court has ruled that the limit on candidate contributions to their own campaigns which was contained in the Federal Election Campaign Act of 1974 was unconstitutional. As a result, some wealthy candidates have lavishly funded their own campaigns. In 1988, for example, Democrat Herbert Kohl, a Milwaukee businessman, spent $6.9 million of his own money while winning an open Senate seat in Wisconsin.

Independent Expenditures

The Supreme Court also struck down as a violation of the First Amendment rights to freedom of speech and association a provision in the FECA which restricted to $1000 the amount that groups could spend to support candidates. This FECA provision limited so-called "independent expenditures" by political action committees and individuals in support of candidates. These are expenditures made by organized groups or individuals without consultation or coordination with the candidate's organization. In senatorial and presidential elections, the magnitude of these expenditures can be great. In 1984 a wealthy Californian, Michael R. Goland, spent over $1 million of his own money to defeat Senator Charles Percy (R.–Ill.), whose Middle East policy he found objectionable. The Federal Election Commission reported that in the 1987–1988 election cycle, $23.4 million was spent through independent expenditures. In the presidential contest, independent spending heavily favored the Republicans ($9.7 million

Figure 7–2: Republican and Democratic Party Support, 1987–1988

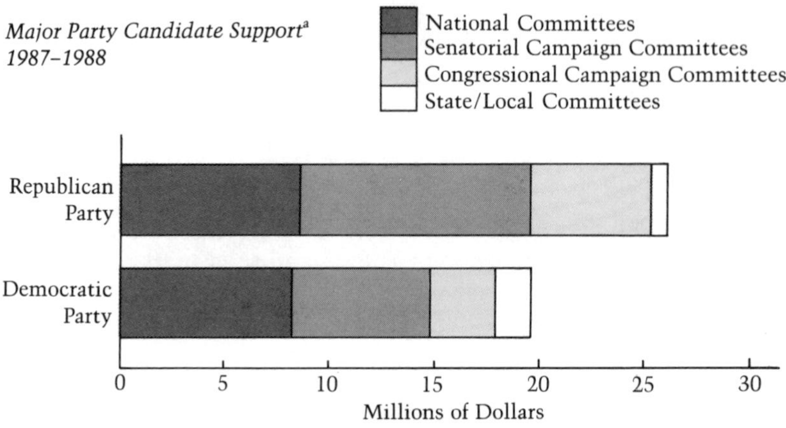

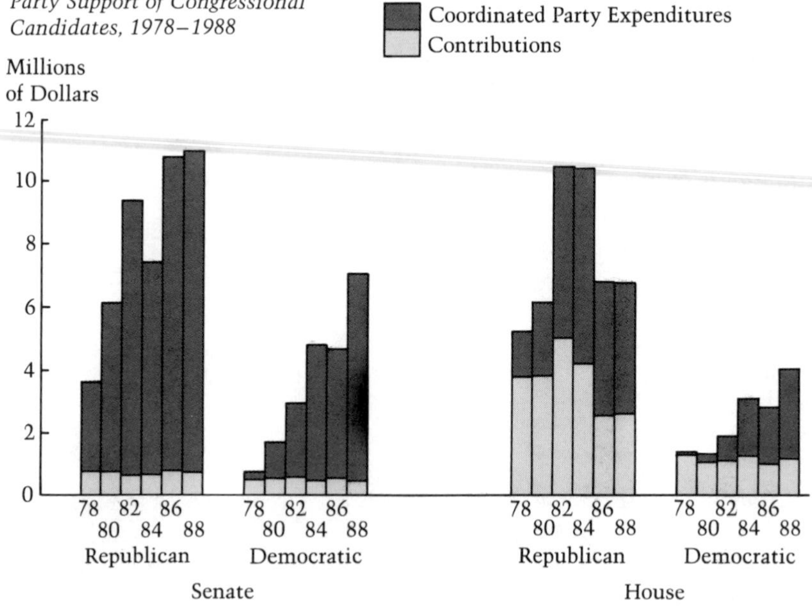

a. Support includes both contributions to and coordinated party expenditures (§441a(d)) on behalf of federal candidates.

Source: Federal Election Commission.

supporting George Bush and $.5 million supporting Michael Dukakis; $3 million in negative spending against Dukakis and $75,000 against Bush). In congressional elections, the picture was more mixed. Independent spending favored House Democrats ($1.6 million to $1.2 million), and Senate Republicans ($3.4 million to $1 million).[10] Only large, well financed interest groups are in a position to engage in significant independent expenditures. A major media campaign effort requires substantial resources. Among the most active is the National Association of Realtors which in 1988 spent $1.4 million, mainly on radio and television advertising, to assist seven candidates.[11]

Another type of campaign expenditure that is constitutionally protected by the First Amendment is money spent by a group while communicating with its membership. Labor unions make major expenditures to educate their members and get them to the polls on election day through newsletters, paid staff members, transportation services, and large scale telephone banks in major cities. The full extent of such expenditures is not known because internal communication and voter mobilization costs are not required to be reported under the law. Informed observers, however, estimate these expenditures in the millions. For example, it is estimated that labor unions spent at least $45 million over and above their direct contributions to candidates in the 1988 presidential primaries and general election, $30 million of it in the general election and all but $5 million on activities that favored Democrats.[12]

"Soft Money"

The FECA contains major "soft money" loopholes which enable individuals, PACs, unions, and corporations to evade federal contribution limits or prohibitions and permit parties to exceed their spending limits in support of federal candidates. "Soft money" involves contributions, sometimes in denominations as large as $100,000, that go to state parties or auxiliary committees set up by the national Republican and Democratic parties. It is ostensibly used for "party building"—activities such as voter registration drives, get-out-the-vote campaigns, and generic advertising that urges voter support for a party's full slate of candidates rather than for specific candidates. This money, however, is actually channelled by the national party committees into states that are critical in a presidential election or have key House and Senate races. In 1988, it is estimated that between $40–45 million of "soft money" was raised, with $28.5 million spent in eight states with large blocks of electoral votes.[13]

Public Financing of Elections

The Federal Elections Campaign Act authorizes public funding of presidential election campaigns for those candidates who qualify and wish to accept the federal subsidy. Major party candidates (defined by the law as the nominees of parties receiving at least 25 percent of the popular vote in the last election) automatically qualify for public funding of their campaigns. Although public funding is not mandatory, a candidate who accepts it must agree to restrict expenditures to the amount of the federal grant and forego all private fund raising. The amount of public funding stipulated by the FECA of 1974 is $20 million, adjusted for inflation ($46.1 million in 1988). Minor parties' presidential candidates also are eligible for a proportionate share of public funding, provided their party received at least 5 percent of the popular vote for president in the previous election. Since the public funding features of the FECA first took effect in 1976, every major party candidate has chosen to accept public funding of his campaign. Acceptance of the federal funds removes from candidates the burden of private fund raising. Another reason why candidates elect to accept public funds is that they are fearful that failure to do so would alienate some voters and put them on the defensive by being charged with being beholden to special interests. Because presidential candidates receive saturation coverage by the news media, the spending limits which the public funding provisions of the FECA impose on candidates are not thought to create any major advantages for either party or for incumbents or challengers. Clearly, however, the use of public funding in presidential elections has tended to equalize the resources available to the Republican and Democratic parties.

The expenditure limits of the Act do affect the management and organization of campaigns. The presidential nominees' personal campaign committees, which are the recipients of public funding, must be organized in a highly centralized manner so that tight expenditure controls can be maintained in order to prevent a violation of the law through overspending. In addition, the nominees' campaign committees direct and coordinate party activities designed to assist the presidential ticket. As was noted above, the FECA permits unlimited "party building" expenditures and thereby encourages voter mobilization activities by state and local parties and by auxiliary party committees created by the national committees. The presidential nominees' campaign committees, therefore, actively engage in coordinating the activities of state, local, and auxiliary party committees in their efforts to mobilize voters.

In addition to public funding of presidential campaigns, twenty-two states have public funding statutes for state elections. These statutes vary from state to state in terms of how the money for public financing of elections is raised, whether the funds are controlled by the candidates or the parties, and which races are eligible to be subsidized. Most plans involve taxpayer checkoffs of one or two dollars per income tax form, although six states use an add-on procedure in which taxpayers indicate on their tax forms a willingness to add a small contribution to the campaign fund. Check-off plans tend to produce higher response rates from taxpayers than do add-on procedures. In most states, the contribution goes into a general campaign fund. However, in several states (including Idaho, Iowa, Minnesota, Oregon, and Utah) the citizens designate on the tax form which party is to receive their contribution. When taxpayers indicate to which party they wish their check-off contribution to go, the Democrats are normally advantaged. Only in Utah does the Republican party receive more in taxpayer contributions than Democrats, although the allocations are relatively equal in Iowa and Idaho.[14]

Public funding of campaigns may be accomplished indirectly by channeling funds through the state and county party organizations (e.g., in Idaho, Kentucky, North Carolina, and Rhode Island). However, the more common practice among the states is for the funds to go directly to candidates. In Oklahoma, a combination of these allocation procedures is used. When the money goes through the party organization, the major consequence of public funding is to permit the party to engage more actively in a broad range of electoral activities. When the public subsidy goes to the candidates, Ruth Jones has found that the public funding is more important to legislative candidates than statewide candidates, to state house of representatives candidates than state senate candidates, to Democratic candidates than Republicans, and to challengers than incumbents.[15]

Three states permit funding of both primary and general election campaigns, but the most common pattern is to restrict public funding to general election campaigns only. State law may also restrict the offices which are eligible for the subsidy. Michigan and New Jersey, for example, restrict public funding to gubernatorial races, while Wisconsin and Minnesota authorize funding of legislative and state constitutional office contests. The experience of Michigan and New Jersey suggests that the availability of the subsidy in primaries can encourage a large field of candidates (e.g., eleven gubernatorial candidates in Michigan in 1982 and sixteen in New Jersey in 1981).[16]

Political Parties and the Federal Election Campaign Act

A key issue in congressional deliberations on regulating of campaign finance through public financing has been whether the national party organizations or the presidential candidates should receive the federal subsidy. Initially in 1966, Congress opted for party control of the funds. Senator Robert Kennedy (D–N.Y.) argued against this approach on the grounds that it would tend to concentrate power in the national party chairmen and diminish the role of state and local parties. Kennedy even envisioned the national chairmen becoming kingmakers under this system since he believed that they could control nominations and discipline state parties through their control of public funds allocated to the parties.[17] Such arguments apparently had an impact because in 1967 Congress suspended its earlier action and in the FECA of 1974 provided public funding to presidential candidates. By giving money to candidates, not parties, the FECA reinforces the decentralized qualities of the American party system and confirms the conception of the party as a candidate dominated structure. Candidates are given discretion to accept or reject federal campaign subsidies, and candidate organizations control the federal funds. Each candidate is required to set up a single central campaign committee which accepts all contributions or federal subsidies and makes expenditures. Under this system it is unlikely that a presidential campaign will ever be run through the national committees of the two parties. As David Price has noted, the FECA gives a modest role ($8.3 million in 1988) to the national committees in terms of campaign spending in presidential elections, but "it builds in the law the assumption that these committees are separate from and ancillary to the candidate's campaign organizations.[18]

Federal law also contains provisions that tend to depress state and local party participation in congressional, senatorial, and presidential campaigns. In presidential elections, strict expenditure limits on the campaign can cause presidential campaign managers to discourage state and local party involvement because such activity, unless it falls within the specially exempted category of voluntary, is counted against the candidate's spending limit. Such rules can cause candidate organizations to constrain state and local parties and to devote greater emphasis to television advertising.[19] State and local party activity in congressional and senatorial elections can also be depressed by the FECA's expenditure limits on parties. Expenditure limits apply to state parties and all their subunits (e.g., county and city organizations) collectively. Therefore, any advertising done by a local party unit to support congressional and senatorial candidates must be counted against the state party's expenditure limits. David Price, a political scientist and former state chairman of the Democratic party in North Carolina, has concluded that "such complexity [in the law] invites evasion, but it also has an unmistakably chilling effect on party participation in federal campaigns."[20]

The FECA further weakened the parties' role in campaigns by enhancing the position of a rival type of organization—the PAC. The FECA permits corporations and unions to communicate with their stockholders, employees, and members on political matters, conduct voter registration and get out the vote drives among these groups, and set up political action committees. As a result of statutory changes which began in 1971, there has been an explosion in the number of PACs and in the amount of money they spend on campaigns, as well as their relative share of campaign expenditures. In the case of House elections, FECA treats parties as almost the equivalent of PACs by limiting party committee direct contributions to candidates to $5000 per election, the same limits which are required of PACs.

The FECA, however, does contain provisions which are quite solicitous of parties. As noted previously, national party committees are permitted to make coordinated expenditures to support House and Senate candidates. In the case of the Senate, these expenditures can be substantial and have a major impact on the races. There are also special provisions pertaining to the national committees of major parties. These provisions include: (1) public funding for national party conventions; (2) authorizing the major party national committees to raise and spend $8.3 million (in 1988) over and above the public subsidy to support presidential candidates; and (3) permitting individuals to contribute up to $20,000 per year to the national committees, while limiting contributions to other multicandidate committees (PACs) to $5000. State parties benefit from the FECA "party building" provisions that encourage the national parties to transfer funds or channel "soft money" contributions their way. This routing of resources to state parties enables these organizations to play a more significant role in campaigns.

Even the public funding provisions of FECA have some positive implications for the Republican and Democratic parties. The law defines a major party as one receiving 25 percent of the vote in the last presidential election and makes such parties' candidates eligible for the full quota of public funding. Given the remoteness of either major party's popular vote for president falling below 25 percent, it would appear that both the Republican and Democratic parties have an assured future with a federal subsidy for their presidential campaigns. Indeed, the FECA almost guarantees through its special treatment of major parties and the incentives it creates for them that these organizations will exist into the future to the virtual exclusion of all others.

The Rise of PACs

Political action committees are major competitors with the parties for influence over the campaign process. As previously noted, the FECA of 1971 and amendments of 1974 significantly expanded the role of PACs, especially corporate PACs. PACs are a type of "political committee" which the statutes grant the right to solicit and accumulate funds for distribution to candidates. The law provides an exemption for corporate PACs from the general rule against federal cam-

Figure 7–3: The Growth of Political Action Committees, 1975–1989

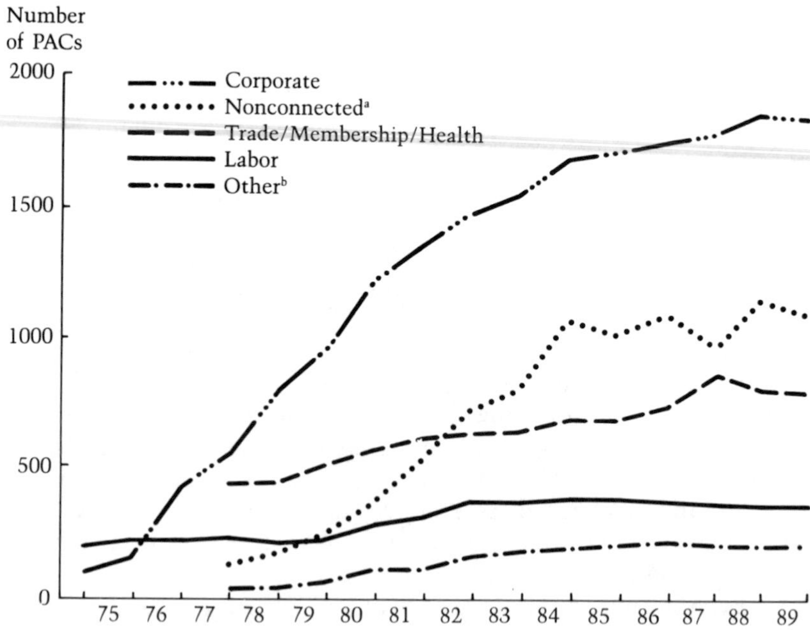

a. For the years 1974 through 1976, numbers are not available for Nonconnected PACs, Trade/Membership/Health PACs and PACs in the "Other" category.

b. "Other" category includes PACs formed by corporations without capital stock and PACs formed by incorporated cooperatives.

Source: Federal Election Commission.

Table 7–3 Funding Sources for House and Senate Candidates in General Elections, 1976–1988

Year	Amount Raised by Candidates and Party Expenditures on Behalf of Candidates ($ Millions)	PACs	Percentage Distribution: Party Contributions and Expenditures	Percentage Distribution: Individuals and Other Sources
House				
1976	$ 66.1	22%	8%	70%
1978	93.6	24	7	69
1980	127.1	28	6	66
1982	189.8	31	6	63
1984	204.0	36	6	58
1986	235.1	36	4	60
1988	248.9	40	4	56
Senate				
1976	39.2	15	4	81
1978	68.9	13	6	81
1980	83.5	19	9	72
1982	127.0	17	10	73
1984	158.0	18	7	75
1986	208.7	21	9	70
1988	199.5	22	9	69

Source: Norman J. Ornstein, Thomas E. Mann, and Michael J. Malbin, *Vital Statistics on Congress, 1989–1990* (Washington, D.C.: Congressional Quarterly, 1990), pp. 85–87.

paign contributions by corporations and federally insured institutions. These institutions may now use corporate funds to offset the costs of setting up a PAC and soliciting contributions to them from stockholders, administrative personnel, and their families. Labor union and trade association PACs are also given legal recognition by the law and given the right to solicit funds from their members. There are also independent PACs, organized by like-minded persons interested in promoting a particular ideology or policy position. All PACs must meet minimum statutory standards concerning the number of contributors and candidate recipients of PAC contributions.

Prior to the 1960s, PACs were largely a labor union phenomenon, patterned after the example of the AFL-CIO's Committee on Political Education (COPE), though the National Association of Manufacturers and the American Medical Association also maintained PACs. The statutory changes of the 1970s, however, spurred a literal explosion in the number of PACs which is revealed in Figure 7–3. Not only has the number of PACs proliferated, but so has their role in campaigns. Their share of the escalating cost of campaigns jumped from 22 percent of

House campaign expenditures in 1976 to 40 percent in 1988. PACs have also dramatically increased their involvement in Senate elections, where their share of campaign expenditures has gone from 15 percent in 1976 to 22 percent in 1988 (see Table 7–3).

One of the most striking characteristics of PAC contribution patterns to House and Senate campaigns is their preference for incumbents. Thus in 1988, 74 percent of all PAC contributions went to incumbents, while 12 percent went to challengers, and 11 percent to open seat candidates. Since the Democrats have by far the largest share of incumbents in the House, they receive the largest share of PAC contributions to House candidates, while in the Senate the parties' share of the PAC monies in any given election year depends heavily upon the number of Republican and Democratic incumbents seeking reelection (see Table 7–4).

The full impact of PACs on political parties has not yet been determined. The conventional wisdom is that PAC growth has weakened the parties. However, there is evidence that both the Democratic and Republican parties have adapted to the PAC phenomenon. The parties solicit funds from PACs and encourage them to contribute directly to needy candidates. In an effort to channel PAC money into targeted races, the parties' national level committees have revealed the results of party commissioned polls to PAC directors, held special candidate receptions for PAC personnel, and set up candidate interviews with PAC represent-

Table 7–4 PAC Contributions to House and Senate Candidates, 1980–1988

Year	Amount ($ Millions)	Percentage Distribution				
		Incumbents	Challengers	Open Seats	Republicans	Democrats
House						
1980	$36.0	69%	20%	11%	46%	54%
1982	57.9	69	18	14	43	57
1984	72.9	78	14	7	39	61
1986	85.2	77	11	13	37	63
1988	99.2	83	9	8	34	66
Senate						
1980	15.9	50	37	13	54	46
1982	21.8	65	22	13	50	50
1984	27.9	64	22	15	53	47
1986	44.6	53	22	26	55	45
1988	44.4	64	17	18	48	52

Source: Norman J. Ornstein, Thomas E. Mann, and Michael J. Malbin, *Vital Statistics on Congress, 1989–1990* (Washington, D.C.: Congressional Quarterly, 1990), pp. 102–109.

atives. Some PACs form close alliances with parties and become a dependable source of support for party candidates, e.g., organized labor's relationship with the Democratic party.

The Electoral College

When voters within a state go to the polls and mark their ballots for the presidential candidate of their choice, they are in fact voting for a slate of presidential electors who will cast that state's electoral votes for president. The election of an American president is not a direct popular vote, but rather an indirect election process in which the voters select electors who in turn make the actual choice of a president. In designing this system, the Founding Fathers envisioned that the presidential electors would be a council of wise men from each state who would render an independent judgment on the best person to hold the nation's highest office. They also expected that the electoral college would, in effect, "nominate" presidential candidates in those instances when no candidate received an electoral college majority, because the House of Representatives would then choose a president from among the top three electoral college vote getters. The Founders also envisioned a nonpartisan selection process. Only the first two elections of George Washington came close to fulfilling the Constitution writers' expectations. Washington was indeed chosen by the electoral college on a nonpartisan basis. But in the ensuing elections, the contests for the president became highly partisan. Competing parties ran slates of candidates for the position of presidential elector within the states and these elector candidates were pledged to support their party's nominee for president and vice president.

Allocation of Electoral Votes among the States

Each state's allocation of electoral votes is determined by its representation in the Congress. An electoral vote is assigned to each state based upon its number of senators and representatives (e.g., California with two senators and fifty-two representatives has fifty-four electoral votes; Vermont with two senators and one representative has three electoral votes). The District of Columbia in accordance with the Twenty-third Amendment is entitled to three electoral votes.

Allocating a State's Electoral Votes: Winner-Take-All

In every state but Maine and Nebraska, the allocation of a state's electoral votes among the presidential candidates is on the basis of a winner-take-all system. The candidate who receives a *plurality* of the state popular vote for president receives *all* of that state's electoral votes, no matter how narrow the candidate's margin of victory. In Maine and Nebraska, the state's electoral votes are allocated on the basis of two electoral votes for the candidate gaining a plurality in the state-wide vote, and one electoral vote for the winner in each congressional district. Although an exception to the winner-take-all rule, Maine has consistently cast all its electoral votes for one presidential candidate. Nebraska initiated the district system for the 1992 presidential election.

Majority in the Electoral College Required for Election

To be elected president, a candidate must receive an absolute majority of the votes in the electoral college (i.e., 270 of the total 538 electoral votes). If no candidate for president receives an electoral college majority, the election is then thrown into the newly elected House of Representatives, which chooses from the three candidates who received the largest number of electoral votes. In making its selection, the House votes by state delegation, with each state having one vote and with a majority of the states required for election. When no vice presidential candidate has a majority of the electoral votes, the Senate chooses the vice president from between the two candidates with the largest number of electoral votes.

The House of Representatives has been required to choose the president only twice. The first time was after the election of 1800, when Thomas Jefferson and his vice presidential running mate, Aaron Burr, both received the same number of electoral votes. This tie vote occurred because electors could not differentiate in casting their two votes between which candidate they preferred for president and vice president under the Constitution as originally written. Rather, the candidate with the largest number of votes was elected president and the candidate in second place became vice president. This system of balloting, which was not well adapted to the emerging party system in which candidates for president and vice president ran as a ticket, resulted in the tie vote between Jefferson and Burr. The House ultimately resolved the tie in Jefferson's favor. In consequence of this bitter controversy, the Twelfth Amendment was added to the Constitution. It provided for electors to vote separately for the offices of president and vice president. The other instance of the House having to decide the election occurred in the election of 1824 when four persons received electoral votes: Andrew Jackson (99 votes), John Quincy Adams (84), William Crawford (41), and Henry Clay (37). With the support of Henry Clay, Adams was selected as president by a majority of one vote.

Electoral College Tendency to Exaggerate the Popular Vote Margin of the Winning Candidate

In three instances, the presidential candidate who was the winner of the popular vote failed to gain a majority in the electoral college. In 1824, Andrew Jackson received a plurality of the popular vote in the 18 states which chose their electors by popular vote (there were twenty-four states in the Union and in six the state legislatures chose the electors). The other cases of the popular vote winner not gaining an electoral vote majority took place in the 1876 contest between Samuel J. Tilden (Democrat) and Republican Rutherford B. Hayes, when Hayes was awarded disputed electoral votes of Oregon plus four southern states, and in 1888 when Grover Cleveland (Democrat) with a 95,096 popular vote plurality lost in the electoral college to Benjamin Harrison (Republican) by a 168 to 233 margin.

Most public discussion of the electoral college focuses upon the possibility of a recurrence of the 1888 outcome when the winner of the popular vote was not able to muster an electoral vote majority. In actual practice, however, the electoral college normally operates in such a way as to exaggerate the popular vote winner's margin of victory. For example, Richard Nixon's 43.4 percent of the popular vote was less than one percent greater than Hubert Humphrey's 42.7 percent. In the electoral college, however, Nixon's margin was a more comfortable 55.9 percent. A more striking example of the extent to which the winner of the popular vote can have his margin of victory exaggerated by the operation of the electoral college occurred in 1980 when Ronald Reagan received 50.7 percent of the popular vote and 90.9 percent of the electoral vote. This consistent pattern of the winning candidate's proportion of the electoral vote being greater than his popular vote percentage is shown in Figure 7–4. Because the popular vote winner and the electoral vote winner have been the same since 1888, there has been little interest within the Congress in changing the electoral college system. It has been argued that the tendency of the electoral college to exaggerate the winning presidential candidate's margin of victory gives the president an opportunity to claim an electoral mandate to govern and implement the policies that were advocated in the campaign.

Encouraging Two Party Politics

The electoral college system works to the advantage of the two major parties and the detriment of minor parties. The combination of a winner-take-all system to determine the allocation of the states' electoral votes and the requirement of a majority in the electoral college to be elected makes it almost impossible for third parties to win a presidential election. To win any electoral votes and have any impact on the electoral vote, a third party candidate must have voter support that is geographically concentrated the way George Wallace's was in the southern states in 1968 or Strom Thurmond's was in 1948. When a third party candidate's support is more evenly spread across the country, as in the case of John Anderson in 1980, the candidate has virtually no hope of winning any electoral votes.

If the electoral college tends to be stacked against third parties

Figure 7–4: Electoral College Exaggerates the Winning Candidate's Margin of Victory

Percent of the Popular Vote and Electoral Vote Received by the Winning Presidential Candidate.

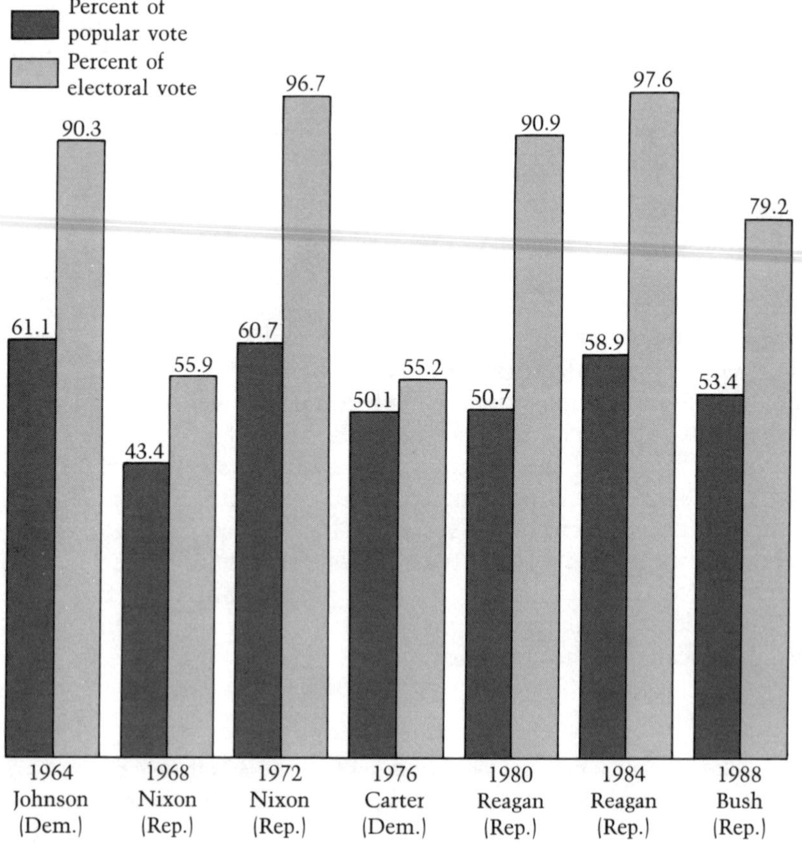

Source: Statistical Abstract of the United States, 1990, pp. 244–245.

winning elections, this does not mean that third parties are without influence. By taking votes that might otherwise have gone to one of the major party candidates, third parties can affect the outcome of the vote. Theodore Roosevelt's Progressive party in 1912 split the normally Republican majority in the country and enabled the minority Democratic candidate, Woodrow Wilson, to be elected. In recent elections, third parties have affected the distribution of electoral votes within particular states, but they have not affected the outcome of the election. For example, in 1980 John Anderson's candidacy and relatively strong showing in the eastern states of Massachusetts, Delaware, New York, and Vermont in all likelihood took votes away from Jimmy Carter and helped Ronald Reagan carry these states with their total of sixty-one electoral votes.

Big versus Small State Advantages

Small states are mathematically overrepresented in the electoral college. This is because their overrepresentation in the House (every state is guaranteed one representative irrespective of population) and the Senate (each state has two senators irrespective of population) guarantees them overrepresentation in the electoral college. Nelson Polsby and Aaron Wildavsky have noted that after the 1980 census the six states with three electoral votes each had 280,000 or fewer citizens per electoral vote, while all the states with thirteen or more electoral votes had 440,000 or more citizens per electoral vote.[21]

It is, however, the large, populous states, because of the winner-take-all system, that mainly benefit from the electoral college. California with fifty-four electoral votes has more electoral votes than the thirteen smallest states combined (six states with three electoral votes and seven states with four electoral votes). This means that narrow victories in large states yield a much higher return in terms of electoral votes than do large pluralities in small states. A vote in California holds the potential of influencing fifty-four electoral votes, while a vote in South Dakota can influence only three.

The critical nature of the big states to a presidential nominee can be seen by the data contained in Table 7–5. The ten largest states have a combined total of 257 electoral votes (48 percent of the total), just 13 short of the 270 needed for election. Without carrying at least some of these large states, it is almost impossible for a candidate to be elected president. It is, therefore, small wonder that presidential candidates tend to concentrate their campaign efforts in those large states where they believe they have a chance of victory. Since these states are normally quite competitive between the two major parties,

Table 7–5 The Impact of the Big States and the Small States on the Electoral College[a]

Smallest States (13)			Largest States (10)		
State	Electoral Votes	Percent of Total Electoral College	State	Electoral Votes	Percent of Total Electoral College
Vermont	3	.0056	California	54	10.00
Delaware	3	.0056	New York	33	6.10
Montana	3	.0056	Texas	32	5.44
South Dakota	3	.0056	Florida	25	4.65
North Dakota	3	.0056	Pennsylvania	23	4.28
Wyoming	3	.0056	Illinois	22	4.09
Alaska	3	.0056	Ohio	21	3.90
Maine	4	.0074	Michigan	18	3.34
New Hampshire	4	.0074	New Jersey	15	2.79
Rhode Island	4	.0074	North Carolina	14	2.60
Nevada	4	.0074			
Idaho	4	.0074			
Hawaii	4	.0074			
Total	45	8.36	Total	257	47.77

a. Based on 1990 census figures.

they are major battlegrounds in presidential elections. Because the electoral college makes large competitive states so important in presidential elections, it also benefits those groups that are geographically concentrated in these states.

Partisan Implications

The pattern of voting in the last five presidential elections has raised questions about whether or not the electoral college now operates to the advantage of the GOP. There is evidence to support the assertion that it does. Since 1968, the Republican presidential candidate has consistently won sixteen of the twenty-one states west of the Mississippi and never less than 84 percent of these states' 166 electoral votes. (On average the GOP has won 89 percent of the region's electoral votes between 1968 and 1988.) Only Minnesota (three times), Hawaii (four), Washington (twice) and Iowa and Missouri (once each) have voted Democratic for president since 1968. With the obvious exception of California, the states of the West are not densely populated and hence somewhat overrepresented in the electoral college. The appeal of Republican presidential candidates in this region has given the GOP a major beachhead in the electoral vote competition, since the 141 electoral votes that the party has won on average in each of the last six presidential elections constitutes 52 percent of the electoral votes needed (270) to elect a president.

A similar pattern has emerged in the South. In only one election since 1968 has the Democratic party gained a majority of electoral votes in the states of the Old Confederacy. That was in 1976 when a fellow southerner, Jimmy Carter, carried all the southern states but Virginia. When a substantial bloc of southern states that are likely to vote Republican in presidential elections is added to Republican-

Table 7–6 A Republican Beachhead in the Electoral College?: Voting Patterns in the West, South, and Key Larger States, 1968–1988

	West[a]	South[b]
Number of states	21	11
Average number of states carried by Republican presidential candidates	19	8[c]
Total electoral votes (1988)	166	138
Average number of electoral votes won by Republican candidates	141 (89%)	101 (74%)

Key Larger States

		Voted Republican for President	
State	**Electoral Votes (1988)**	**Number of Elections**	**Percent**
California	47	6	100%
Illinois	24	6	100
New Jersey	16	6	100
Virginia	12	6	100
Indiana	12	6	100
Ohio	23	5	83
Florida	21	5	83
Michigan	20	5	83
North Carolina	13	5	83
Total	188		

a. West region includes all states West of the Mississippi River except Arkansas, Louisiana, and Texas.

b. South region includes the 11 states of the Old Confederacy (Virginia, North Carolina, South Carolina, Georgia, Florida, Tennessee, Alabama, Mississippi, Arkansas, Louisiana, and Texas).

c. Republican averages are reduced because George Wallace carried five southern states in 1968.

Source: Statistical Abstract of the United States, 1990, pp. 244–245.

leaning states of the West, the Republican presidential candidate for president is in an extremely strong position. This GOP advantage could be enhanced as the Sun Belt states gain additional electoral votes due to continuous population growth reflected in the 1990 census.

In addition, there are a number of key larger states which have demonstrated a tendency in the last six elections to vote Republican. California, Illinois, New Jersey, Indiana, and Virginia have voted Republican in each of the last six presidential elections; and four states, Florida, Michigan, North Carolina, and Ohio have been in the GOP column in five of the last six presidential contests.

The combined effect of Republican voting patterns in the West (including California with fifty-four electoral votes), South, and key states of the Midwest appears to give the GOP a potential advantage in the electoral college (see Table 7–6). One factor, however, which can offset this advantage is the tendency of the whole country, including the West and South, to respond in a similar manner to national economic trends and foreign policy crises. A strong Democratic candidate running in a year when issues favor the Democrats could be expected to make a strong showing in the West and South.

Reform? Direct Popular Vote versus the Electoral College

Most of the criticism of the electoral college has been concentrated upon the possibility that the winner of the popular vote might not win the electoral vote and the "undemocratic" character of the winner-take-all system of allocating electoral votes. Therefore, the great appeal of direct popular vote proposals is that such a system would assure victory to the popular vote winner, be more democratic, and be less complicated.

Interestingly, little attention is paid in popular debates about the electoral college to the advantages the system holds for large states. However, one effect of switching to a direct popular vote system of election would be to reduce the current special importance of the large states. Under a direct vote system, the vote in Delaware or Wyoming would be equivalent to the vote in California, since no electoral votes would be at stake.

However, there is a serious issue concerning the implications of a direct vote system for the nature of the American party system. One of the first questions that would have to be decided concerning a direct vote system would be the issue of how large a plurality of the popular vote would constitute victory. If a simple plurality is all that is required for election, then third party candidates would have little chance of winning and would remain a relatively minor force in American politics. However, the possibility of a candidate's being elected president with less than 40 percent of the votes (a distinct possibility in a simple plurality system—Nixon won with just 43.4 percent in 1968) has troubled many reformers. They have, therefore, tended to support the plan of the American Bar Association which would require a presidential candidate to receive at least 40 percent of the vote in order to be elected. Under this plan, if no candidate received the required 40 percent, there would be a runoff election between the top two presidential vote getters. Such a plan would greatly increase the potential influence of third parties and splinter groups. The possibility of a runoff election creates an incentive for any sizeable organized interest to contest the first election in order to demonstrate its public appeal and thereby put itself in a strong position to bargain with the major party candidates for support in the second election. It is easy to envision the emergence under this system of peace, right to life, women's, black, Hispanic, segregationist, farmers, and other parties. The result could be a splintering of the party system. Under the current electoral college system, such interests are forced to compromise with the major parties before the general election. As a result, the major parties tend to be centrist and moderate in orientation. Those interests that stay outside the fold during the general election are severely penalized because they have no hope of winning. The direct vote system with provisions for a runoff election would dramatically change the incentive structure of American politics and encourage minor parties and a splintering of the existing parties.[22]

Some have advocated a different type of reform—a proportional allocation of a state's electoral votes in accordance with each party's share of the popular vote. For example, if California voted 50 percent Republican, 45 percent Democratic, and 5 percent for a third party candidate, the state's fifty-four electoral votes would be allocated proportionally so that the Republicans would receive twenty-seven electoral votes; the Democrats would get twenty-four; and the third party would win three. Such a system would substantially reduce the current advantage given to the large states by the winner-take-all allocation process. The proportional plan would also increase the likelihood of elections being thrown into the House of Representatives because no candidate gained a majority in the electoral college. For example, both the 1960 and the 1968 elections would have to have been decided by the House because neither major party candidate would have received an electoral vote majority.

Although reform plans abound, there appears little likelihood that the electoral college will be changed in the foreseeable future. The principal reason is that there is little interest in change so long as the electoral college operates (as it has since 1888) to produce a winner who has also won the popular vote. In addition, there are significant interests anxious to protect their advantages under the existing process. Small state senators are determined to retain their state's mathematical advantage under the electoral college and succeeded in getting the Senate to block a direct vote plan passed by the House in 1970. Organized interests concentrated in the large states have also opposed the direct vote reforms because they believe such changes would reduce their potential influence with presidents.[23]

The General Election Campaign

Each campaign is unique. They differ depending upon who the contending candidates are, the nature of the office being sought (executive, legislative, or judicial), the level of government (national, state, or local), the applicable campaign finance and election regulatory statutes, the campaign resources of the candidates, type of nominating campaigns that were conducted, the nature of the constituency, and the tenor of the times (e.g., which issues are salient to the voters). For the incumbent, the campaign is usually a matter of protecting one's inherent advantages of name familiarity and a favorable image while maintaining a favorable balance of campaign resources. For the challenger, who is often underfinanced, the campaign is frequently a time of frantic scrambling to accumulate adequate campaign resources and seeking to find the point of vulnerability in the incumbent's record. In every election cycle, elections are won and lost because of campaign decisions. For example, in 1984, Senator Walter Huddleston (D–Ky.) was forty-six points ahead in the polls and appeared headed for relatively easy reelection to a third term until the campaign of his opponent was ignited and the voters' interest captured by a series of imaginative campaign ads. These ads sought to portray the incumbent senator as a man who shirked his senatorial duties and obligations to his constituents by taking junkets to plush vacation spots at government expense. His challenger's television ads showed bloodhounds on the seemingly illusive senator's trail first at the Capitol, where he was nowhere to be found, and then at a posh Caribbean resort, where his trace was discovered. By the end of the campaign, Senator Huddleston had seen his comfortable lead disappear and on election night Kentucky had a new senator, Republican Mitch McConnell. Further evidence of the importance of campaigns and the timing of campaign efforts is demonstrated by the 1968 presi-

Table 7–7 Time of Decision for Voters in Presidential Elections, 1960–1988

	1960	1964	1968	1972	1976	1980	1984	1988
Before Convention	31%	47%	35%	44%	33%	40%	47%	27%
At Convention	31	25	24	18	21	18	19	31
After Convention	38	34	40	35	46	40	34	42

Source: Center for Political Studies, University of Michigan.

dential race between Republican Richard Nixon and Democrat Hubert Humphrey. After Labor Day, Nixon had a large lead in the polls and seemed assured of a sweeping victory. However, as the campaign wore on, defecting Democrats started to return to the fold and by election day the contest was rated a dead heat. Nixon narrowly won 43.4 to 42.7 percent. Most election analysts believe that had the campaign lasted slightly longer, Humphrey might well have been elected because the momentum of the campaign had switched in his direction. Clearly, campaigns make a difference.[24]

When the Voter Decides

Most voters (normally around 60 percent) in presidential elections make up their minds about the candidate for whom they will vote before or during the nominating conventions (see Table 7–7). A substantial proportion of the electorate, however, does make its decision after the conventions and during the general election campaign. Therefore, the impact of the campaign can be significant, particularly in close races. In presidential elections, many key states are normally won by margins of less than 5 percent of the vote. Ronald Reagan's sweeping electoral college victory in 1980, for example, has tended to mask the fact that he won twelve states by a margin of less than 5 percent of the popular vote. The importance of the campaign can also be seen in the results of a 1980 *New York Times* survey of voters who switched preferences or decided not to vote during the last four days of the campaign. As a result of these last minute decisions concerning whether to vote and candidate preference, Reagan registered a net gain of 1 percent, Carter a net loss of 6 percent, and Anderson a 2 percent loss.[25]

A favorable trend among late deciders frequently is not enough to overcome a substantial lead built up by one's opponent. As Figure 7–5 shows, Michael Dukakis did well among voters who decided during the last days of the 1988 presidential campaign. Bush, however,

Figure 7–5: Time of Decision: The 1988 Presidential Campaign[a]

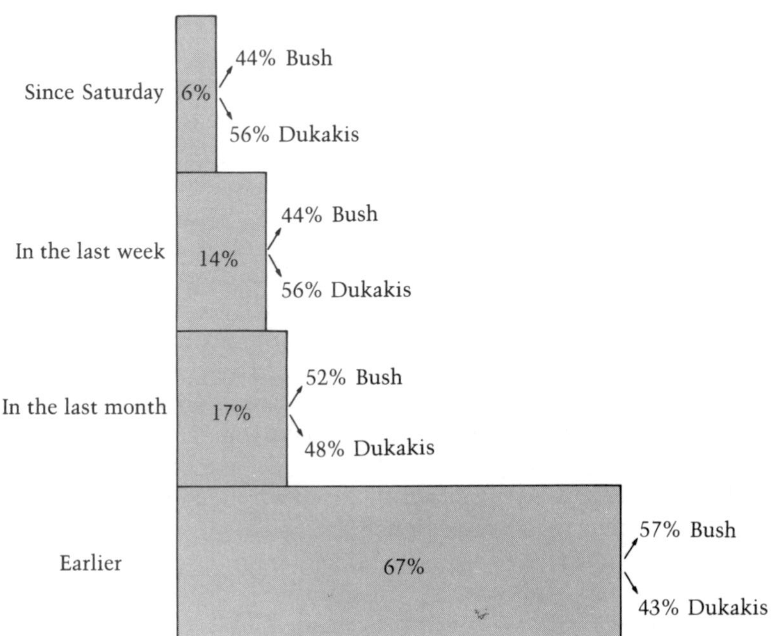

a. Question: When did you know for sure which presidential candidate you would vote for?

Source: 11,645 voters as they left voting booths: CBS/New York Times, Nov. 8, 1988, reprinted in *Public Opinion*, Jan./Feb. 1989, p. 27.

had by that time built up a large lead among those who made their vote choice early in the campaign.

Candidate Centered Campaigns in an Era of Technological Change

In the modern campaign, the candidate tends to be the focus of campaigns, not the party. Most candidates build a personal organization devoted almost exclusively to their own election rather than the election of the party ticket. These organizations recruit volunteers and raise funds independently of the party. Indeed, any campaign for a major office run by a party organization is now a rarity in American politics. The candidate organizations tend to utilize professionals for the various phases of the campaign. These campaign technicians—pollsters, media consultants, direct mail specialists, computer experts, targeting experts, and management specialists—operate as private entrepreneurs outside the regular party organization. Campaign consultants tend to work, however, only for the candidates of one party. There has grown up, therefore, two sets of consultants—one group works almost exclusively for Democratic candidates and another for Republicans. Candidates and consultants have found that it is extremely difficult to develop a relationship of trust and confidence unless it is understood from the beginning that both are on the same side politically. The partisan orientation of consulting firms is reinforced by the fact that the national party organizations, such as the national committees and the congressional campaign committees of both parties, each maintain approved lists of consultants whom they recommend to their parties' candidates.

Although the party organizations are seldom involved in the day-to-day management of campaigns, they can provide essential and timely financial support and in-kind contributions of services such as polls, computer analyses of voting patterns, and phone banks to contact voters. Indeed, the role of national party organizations in campaigns for the House and Senate has been growing rather than declining, especially in the case of the Republican party. Among state parties, however, it is not unusual for them to make no financial contribution even to gubernatorial campaigns. A survey of state parties for the years 1975–1980 revealed that 42 percent of the state party organizations did not contribute to gubernatorial campaigns and that 41 percent failed to support their legislative candidates financially.[26] Since 1960, state parties have shown a pattern of declining assistance to gubernatorial candidates and increased incidence of support for state legislative candidacies. But whatever the level of state party support given to candidates, it is usually but a small proportion of the funds required and it is the personal organization of the candidate that is in charge of the campaign.

The transfer of campaign emphasis from the political party to the candidate's organization has been made possible by a revolution in campaign techniques. The new techniques and technology of campaigning have unalterably changed how people run for public office. Instead of relying upon a hierarchical party organization and precinct committeemen to keep the pulse of public opinion and get out the vote on election day, the modern candidate utilizes an array of sophisticated and expensive techniques that require professionals for their implementation. Public sentiments are measured by public opinion polls. Polling normally begins with a *benchmark poll* taken well in advance of the election and designed to provide a preliminary reading of voter opinion and a baseline from which to measure shifts in public opinion. The benchmark poll is normally followed by a series of polls taken at periodic intervals. In well funded campaigns for major offices, there are also *tracking polls* taken during the final days of the campaign. Tracking polls involve calling approximately 100–150 voters on a daily basis and using a rolling three day average to gauge last minute shifts of opinion. Some candidate organizations involved in close races have credited tracking with giving them the information they needed to make the important last minute adjustments in their campaigns and advertising that gave them their margin of victory.

Survey research is now combined with demographic targeting techniques to sharpen the impact of campaign activities. For example, if polls reveal that a particular set of voters, such as blue collar workers of eastern and southern European heritage, are undecided about for whom to vote, it is important to be able to find these voters within the constituency. Computer analyses of census data can aid in the identification of where these voters reside. With these targeting data in hand, the campaign organization can develop an appropriate plan for directing the campaign's direct mail, phone banks, door-to-door canvassing, and media purchases. The close link between survey research and demographic targeting was summarized by Samuel Kernell, who observed:

> Just as benchmark surveys tell candidates who to appeal to and how, survey-driven targeting identifies where these receptive voters are to be found. Answering these "who," and "how," and "where" questions is indispensable for becoming a serious candidate.[27]

For the actual contacting of voters there are also new techniques. Direct mail specialists can enable candidates to rifle shot their appeals to selected voter groups with a message that is apt to strike a responsive chord with the group being courted. Television has supplanted the political party for national, statewide, and some congressional or local campaigns as the principal conduit between the candidate and the voters. Politicians have adapted to the television revolution by seeking to exploit its capacity to contact individual voters. Media consultants are hired in virtually all major campaigns to develop media advertising. Campaigns also have as one of their objectives the gaining of as much free exposure on newscasts and interview shows as possible. Publicity on hard news programs is particularly valuable because viewers are naturally more wary of candidate advertisements than of candidate images conveyed on regular news programs. Campaigns, therefore, are designed with the help of media consultants to capture as much news publicity as possible. As Austin Ranney has noted:

> One of the most valued tricks of the consultants' trade is knowing how to invent and stage campaign events that will serve *both* the broadcasters' need for good visuals and newsworthiness *and* the candidate's need for free and favorable exposure.[28]

During the 1984 presidential campaign, the Reagan campaign team was widely acknowledged to be particularly skillful in arranging visuals of the president which the networks felt compelled to broadcast and which presented him in a highly favorable manner—e.g., whistle stopping through small towns in Ohio on the route followed by Harry Truman in 1948, meeting with voters dressed in colorful ethnic costumes. Similarly, the Bush organization's media strategy in 1988 emphasized integrating the candidate's campaign appearances and speeches (including the sound bites that were used on evening news programs) with paid media advertising to send a consistent message to the voters.

Among the gimmicks used by candidates to attract news coverage is the "walking" campaign. It was pioneered by Lawton Chiles who walked the length of the Florida peninsula to win a Senate seat in 1970, and by Dan Walker to become Illinois' governor in 1972. Bob Graham, with the help of media consultant Robert Squier, moved from being an obscure state senator to the Florida governor's residence by working one day each at 100 mainly blue collar jobs. The press gave him substantial publicity and Squier filmed Graham at his various jobs and made advertisements from the clips for later use in the campaign.[29]

Free media coverage can also be achieved through unusual policy pronouncements. Thus in Kentucky's 1987 Democratic primary for governor, Wallace Wilkerson was languishing in fourth place at 8 percent in the polls until he called a press conference to denounce the arrival in his state of a new Toyota plant that would employ 2,000 workers. He claimed that each new job would cost the state $136,000 in tax concessions. This novel approach to state economic development was hardly the winning issue for Wilkerson, but it did achieve its objective. As his media consultant observed, "it made people begin to take notice of Wallace by presenting something different." With heightened media coverage as a result of this policy statement, and intensified paid media advertising, Wilkerson went on to win the primary and general election.[30]

In the 1980s and 1990s, a large share of candidates' budgets in statewide races was devoted to television advertisements. Indeed, in big states like California campaigns have become largely television advertising campaigns, as the opposing candidates "debate" each other and seek to influence voters via 30-second television spots designed by media consultants. Often these media campaigns emphasize attack ads, featuring harsh criticism of an opponent's record and character. Criticism of an opponent, particularly one's record in public office, has always been a standard and legitimate part of American electoral politics. However, in recent elections television attack ads have, in the view of many close observers, crossed over the line between legitimate criticism of an individual's record and outright distortion. Increasingly, candidates' organizations have followed a strategy of responding quickly to such attacks either by seeking to correct a gross distortion or by launching an attack ad campaign of their own. As the *Washington Post*'s Paul Taylor has commented:

> When the cross-fire of these kinds of ads begins two rules of engagement stand out: Rebuttals rarely catch up with accusations, and issues rarely compete with character.[31]

In this kind of atmosphere, candidates' media consultants, except for the candidates themselves, become the most prominent and often controversial participants in the electoral process.

The use of media, pollsters, direct mail specialists, computer analysis, and other modern techniques of campaigning requires a campaign plan, a high level of financial support, cash flow management, and skilled management. As a result, most major campaigns involve professional campaign managers and planners. The need for such services has increased the cost of campaigns. It also has encouraged candidate centered campaigning because no party organization is currently in a position to provide candidates with all the sophisticated services they need to run an effective campaign. In their striving to compete, candidates have gone out and personally raised the funds necessary to have access to needed campaign technology and professionals. In the process, the party organization has been largely bypassed and the dominant campaign organization has become the personal organization of the candidate. At the same time, a major new industry has developed—the campaign consultant industry. The parties themselves have even encouraged these trends by insisting that candidates whom they support financially hire professionals and use modern techniques as a condition for receiving national party contributions.

Incumbency

Incumbency normally carries with it advantages. The resources and privileges of public office enable incumbents to publicize themselves and build support through the positions they take and the decisions they make. Incumbents are better known than challengers and they have built-in ways of reaching the voters. Incumbent members of Congress stay in contact with their constituents through newsletters, surveys of constituent opinion, special targeted mailings, news releases, radio and television tapes, and meetings with constituent groups. Skilled incumbents use the rights and duties of public office in a way that projects the image of caring and conscientious legislators fulfilling their obligations to constituents. Voters often see these newsletters, office hours in the district, casework to help constituents having problems with the federal bureaucracy, and advocacy of programs to benefit the constituency as instances of members of Congress merely performing their official duties. By contrast, voters see challengers as "politicians" or "campaigners" interested primarily in winning votes on election day. The self advertisement efforts of incumbent members of the House have meant that they are not only well known to their constituents, but they are thought of in positive terms. By contrast, most House challengers are not well known to the voters, who have difficulty making an evaluation of their qualifications.[32]

Incumbency is less of an advantage for senators than it is for House members. Senators normally are elected from more competitive constituencies than representatives. Incumbent senators can expect, because of the prominence of the office, that a major campaign will be run against them and that their opponents will receive substantial funding and free publicity. In the case of the House elections, voters frequently do not know much about the challengers because only a weak campaign is run on their behalf. Voters are, however, more likely to know the alternative choices before them in Senate elections.[33] The incumbent advantage of senators is, therefore, reduced.

The pomp and circumstance of the presidency is impossible for any challenger to match. President Reagan's visit to the beaches of Normandy to commemorate the fortieth anniversary of D-Day in World War II provided a dramatic and emotional setting for an incumbent president seeking reelection in 1984. His trip to China also gave him major publicity advantages over his rivals. Indeed, the advantages of the presidency are so great that some incumbents adopt a "Rose Garden" strategy of campaigning. This involves staying close to the White House and arranging events for television in the Oval Office and the Rose Garden which show the president performing his responsibilities for the nation, while his opponent is out campaigning. During the 1976 presidential campaign, President Ford's advisors made full use of this technique after they discovered that his ratings in the polls were higher when he stayed in the White House than when he was on the road campaigning. And in 1980, President Carter for a time stopped campaigning for reelection outside the White House on the pretext that the Iranian hostage crisis required his full time attention at the White House.

Incumbent executives, especially the president and governors, are also in a position to claim credit for all the positive things that have occurred during their tenure. Presidents Eisenhower and Reagan, therefore, were able to run on themes of peace and prosperity during their reelection campaigns of 1956 and 1984. Incumbency is, however, a two edged sword. Presidents can also be held accountable for the negative things that have happened while they have been in office. Presidents Ford and Carter found that the voters in 1976 and 1980 were unforgiving about a faltering economy and foreign policy setbacks. It makes little difference that presidents cannot control all aspects of our domestic and international condition. They are still likely to be held accountable.

Incumbent senators and representatives have fewer problems than presidents with being held accountable for adverse conditions in the nation and world. Members of the Congress tend to be judged by their constituents not on the basis of the record of the institution of which they are members, but rather upon their own individual records. Therefore, they are somewhat insulated from voter resentment about the state of the union, provided they have used their incumbency to build voter trust.

A further advantage of incumbency, especially in the case of legislative campaigns, is the ease incumbents have in raising money. Incumbents consistently have more money to spend on their campaigns than do challengers in both House and Senate races. This pattern is illustrated in Figure 7–6, which presents the mean expenditures in 1988 House races for incumbents and challengers of both parties. Incumbents had average expenditures that were more than $104,000 higher than those of challengers. Such summary numbers, however, mask the full extent of incumbent financial advantage in campaigns. Many challengers fall far below the average expenditure figure cited in Figure 7–6. For example, the 119 Democratic challengers, who failed to gain 40 percent of the vote, spent an average of only $85,414 on their campaigns, while their incumbent GOP opponents had mean expenditures of $352,394. Similarly, the average spending by a Republican challenger who lost to a Democratic incumbent who gained more than 60 percent of the vote, was $71,285, compared to a mean expenditure by the incumbent of $326,931.[34] Such financial advantages for incumbents affect the way they campaign. Incumbents are much more likely to have campaign staffs composed of paid professionals than are their opponents, who must rely more heavily on volunteer assistance.[35]

Figure 7–6: Mean Expenditures of U.S. House of Representatives Candidates, 1988.

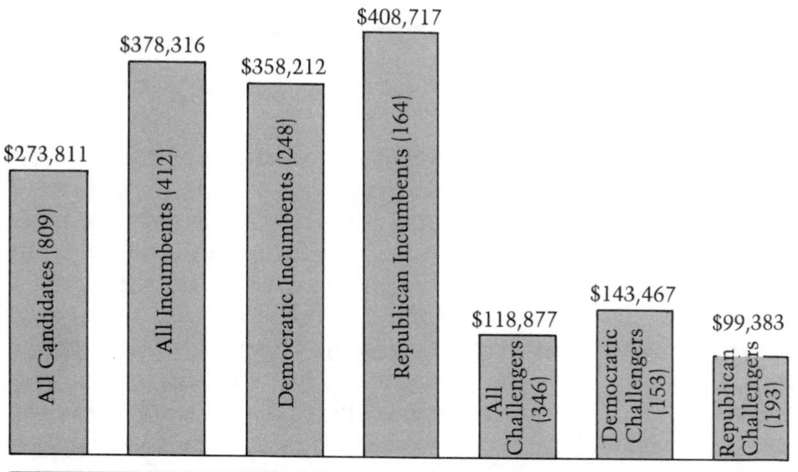

Source: Norman J. Ornstein, Thomas E. Mann, and Michael J. Malbin, *Vital Statistics on Congress, 1989–1990* (Washington, D.C.: Congressional Quarterly, 1990), pp. 71–72.

There is one particular set of candidates for whom incumbency has traditionally created severe difficulties. These are incumbent vice presidents seeking to succeed a president of their own party. Vice presidents running for president in their own right find themselves in a particularly restricted position in terms of campaign strategy. One of their claims to being qualified for the presidency is their service as vice president. Most claim that they were involved in the major decisions of the administration in which they served. The problem with such claims is that every administration after it has been in office for a time makes decisions that offend sizeable numbers of voters. This presents the vice president with a dilemma. If he gives unqualified support to the administration's policies, he risks losing the support of key voter groups. But if he suggests that he disagrees with some aspects of administration policy, he confesses to a lack of influence in the administration in which he claims to have been a key policy maker. And if he seeks to put distance between himself and the president, the vice president runs the risk of losing the support of the president's supporters. The liabilities inherent in the vice presidency were major problems for Richard Nixon in 1960 and Hubert Humphrey in 1968 as they sought the presidency. Walter Mondale found in 1984, four years after leaving office, that service in the vice presidency during the Carter Administration was a serious drawback for his campaign.

Even George Bush, who became the first incumbent vice president to be elected to the presidency since Martin Van Buren in 1836, had to endure and overcome charges that he was a "wimp" because of his reluctance to distance himself from Reagan administration policies.

Majority versus Minority Party Status

Candidates have customarily placed differing emphasis on partisan themes depending on whether they were the nominees of the majority or minority party. Majority party candidates have normally stressed party-type appeals and sought to rally the faithful to turn out and vote because if the faithful respond to the call, then the party's candidate is assured of victory. As the dominant party in terms of the electorate's party identification since the Great Depression of the 1930s, the Democratic party nationally has emphasized partisan Democratic appeals to the electorate. Past accomplishments of the party and its heroes have been stressed along with negative characterizations of the Republicans (e.g., "the party of the rich"). Because pro-Democratic voters groups have tended to have lower rates of turnout than Republican leaning voters, special efforts have been made to mobilize Democrats to get to the polls on election day. The Democratic candidates have stressed their party's label in campaign literature and advertising. Thus when Democrats were faced with the prospect of sizeable defections to the independent candidacy of John B. Anderson in 1980, they urged their supporters not to "waste" their votes and thereby help the Republicans through a vote for Anderson.

The minority party Republicans have faced since the 1930s a quite different strategic problem. Just holding their party together and turning out its affiliates on election day would not bring the GOP victory. They not only have needed to turn out their own vote, but they have also had to win over substantial numbers of independents and dissident Democrats. As a result, most Republican presidential campaigns have downplayed partisan Republican appeals. Instead, the party has often blurred the differences between the parties and sought to capitalize upon a more compelling cue than partisanship for voters to use in making their choice. The nomination of a World War II hero whose appeal transcended partisanship, Dwight D. Eisenhower, in 1952 and 1956 was a particularly effective tactic. Exploitation of major differences within the Democratic party, as in 1968 and 1972, has also proven effective. Less successful have been the "me-too" campaigns of the 1940s and 1960, which offered little in the way of differences between the Republicans and their Democratic opponents. The successful Reagan campaigns of 1980 and 1984 used a combination of all these minority party strategies. The candidate was an attractive and amiable former movie actor, who was fond of quoting Democratic stars like Franklin Roosevelt, John F. Kennedy, and Harry Truman, while also dramatizing major policy splits among Democrats.

As party identification has declined in importance as a basis for voter choice in presidential elections, the significance of majority-minority status in determining campaign strategy has been reduced. In addition, surveys conducted in the 1980s and 1990s have revealed that the two major parties were approaching parity in terms of the party identification of the voters. If this division between the parties continues within the electorate, it will further reduce the impact of majority-minority party status on campaign strategy.

Debates

Debates have now become a standard part of presidential campaigns and candidates debates or forums are common in contests for other offices. The debate format is not neutral in its impact. The presidential debates have generally worked to the advantage of the challenger or less experienced candidate. Debates elevate the challenger to equal status with the president by putting both individuals on the same stage and making both respond to the same questions and to each other. The aura of the presidency tends to be temporarily removed from the incumbent as he faces his opponent one-on-one on a sparsely furnished stage. The incumbent's claims about the importance of experience tend to be diminished when the challenger acquits himself reasonably well against the president. A clear example of this occurred in 1976 when Gerald Ford, the experienced national politician, met Jimmy Carter, who had held no federal office. Carter was reasonably effective in the debates, but Ford's campaign suffered a serious setback because he left the mistaken impression that in his opinion Eastern Europe was not under the domination of the Soviet Union.

As an incumbent in 1980, President Carter found that debates carried serious risks. Recognizing that third party candidate John B. Anderson potentially could drain millions of needed votes away from Carter, the president's strategists adamantly refused to participate in a debate format that included Anderson. They were fearful that permitting Anderson into the debates with Carter and Reagan would enhance Anderson's status and strengthen his appeal to normally pro-Democratic voters. However, Carter did finally agree to debate Reagan alone later in the campaign. It appears that, on balance, Reagan was helped by the debate, even though he may have lost the debate according to the high school debate scoring rules. He made no serious errors in the debate and, more important, he projected an amiable and nonthreatening image that was the exact opposite of Carter's depiction of him as a dangerous reactionary. Reagan, too, suffered a temporary loss of campaign momentum in 1984 because of a less than effective performance in his first of two debates with Walter Mondale. Reagan's inarticulate responses to some questions raised questions in the press in the days following the first debate about his capacity to serve as president while in his seventies. Mondale's public image, by contrast, was temporarily enhanced by his debate performance. The second debate between the two men, however, tended to neutralize the adverse effects of the first debate for Reagan.

While debates provide an opportunity for the underdog candidate to stage a comeback, they can also work to the advantage of the frontrunner. For example, in the first Bush–Dukakis debate of 1988, polls showed Dukakis scoring a narrow win. This gave a temporary and much needed boost to the badly wounded Democratic ticket. However, Dukakis failed in the second debate to deliver a decisive blow to the Bush candidacy. Indeed, polls showed viewers believed that Bush had won decisively and his lead in the polls rose.

On balance, the experience of incumbents and frontrunners has demonstrated that they have much more to lose in debates than do their challengers. The debates also demonstrate that it is not so much the substance of what is said that matters as it is the image of the candidates that is conveyed. The press tends to judge the debates in terms of winners and losers and press judgments affect the public's assessment. Voters in general do not follow the content of the debates carefully and do not normally have great confidence in their ability to make judgments concerning the substance of the debates. They, therefore, tend to rely rather heavily on media commentaries on the debates. As a result, immediately after the event, there is frequently a rather even split between the candidates in the viewers' minds about who won the debate. However, after several days of press commentary there is usually a shift by the public in the direction of the verdict rendered by the press. A dramatic example of this tendency occurred in 1976 when viewers by a two-to-one margin said that Ford had won the second debate. After heavy press coverage of Ford's gaffe regarding the Soviet domination of Eastern Europe, public opinion shifted two-to-one to Carter's advantage.[36] Similarly in the 1984 debates, there was a strong shift in the voters' judgment about who won the first Reagan–Mondale debate between the night of the debate and two days later. After extensive media discussion of Reagan's lackluster performance, the percent of voters saying he won the debate dropped from 34 to 17 percent and those saying Mondale won went from 43 to 66 percent.[37]

The longer term impact of the debates is that for partisans the major effect of the debates is to confirm and solidify their support for their party's candidate. For example, in 1984 the second Reagan–Mondale debate seems to have had the effect of reassuring the president's supporters after his subpar performance in the first debate and of helping Mondale demonstrate that he could hold the allegiance of most Democrats.[38] For weaker partisans and independents the debates can stimulate their interest in the campaign, color their perceptions of the candidates, and even change perceptions. For example, Kennedy in 1960 through his debate with Nixon was able to overcome some of the perception that he was the less experienced and knowledgeable of the two; and in 1980 Reagan used the debates to combat a common perception that he was doctrinaire and less knowledgeable than Carter.[39]

Issues

Throughout the years from the Great Depression in the 1930s until the 1980 election, Democratic party candidates have had a clear advantage over the Republicans when dealing with domestic issues. Through their sponsorship and expansion of a vast array of government programs, which Republicans frequently opposed, the Democrats have been in a position to seek support from virtually every major group in American society. The party has also had a favorable image on economic issues. When asked which party they believed was best for the economy, employment, and jobs, voters from the 1930s to 1980 consistently favored the Democrats. As a result, in elections when pocketbook issues were salient (e.g., 1960, 1976), the Democrats were at a distinct advantage. Indeed, during much of this period, Republican candidates sought to downplay domestic issues and emphasize foreign policy concerns (1952—"Bring the boys home from Korea"; 1968—"End the war in Vietnam") or the general management of the government (1948—"the mess in Washington"). The public's perceptions of the parties changed significantly during the Carter Administration and the 1980 campaign. For the first time since the 1930s, voters began to view the GOP candidate as best for the economy, no doubt reflecting the double digit inflation, rising unemployment, and high interest rates of the later years of the Carter Administration.[40] The Republicans lost their economic policy advantage during the serious 1981–1982 recession that occurred during the first Reagan Administration. However, an improved economy during

1984 and 1988 enabled the Republicans to achieve a favorable rating from the electorate in terms of their ability to handle the economy. As in 1980, the Republicans were able to stress economic issues—a tactic that had not been open to them prior to 1980. The long-term consequences of this change in partisan strategy are indeed significant. For the Democrats, it means that they no longer can count on economic issues to work in their favor. In all likelihood, Republicans cannot expect that the voters will consistently prefer them on economic issues. But perhaps the Republicans have at long last dispatched their image as the party of the Depressions, which burdened them after the Hoover Administration.

The Republicans' traditional disadvantage in domestic issues was partially offset by an advantage they carried regarding foreign policy. Voters during the period from World War II through 1972 tended to perceive the GOP as the party best for peace, though the party temporarily lost this advantage during the 1964 campaign.[41] As a result, Republicans tended to be advantaged when foreign policy issues were highly salient, as during the Korean War in 1952 and the Vietnam War in 1968. Foreign policy issues also helped the GOP in 1972, when the Democratic nominee, Senator George McGovern (D–S.D.), and his policies of quick withdrawal from Vietnam, opposition to continued military support for the government of Vietnam, sharp cuts in defense spending, and a willingness to beg North Vietnam for release of American POWs caused deep divisions within the Democratic ranks.

The Republicans' historic advantage of foreign policy issues was lost to the Democrats during the 1976–1984 elections. During this period, voters perceived the Democratic party ahead of the GOP in terms of being best for peace (though the Republicans came out ahead on the party best for maintaining a strong defense). In 1988, the Republicans regained their advantage over the Democrats as the party whom voters perceived as best for handling nuclear arms agreements, dealing with the Soviet Union, dealing with international terrorism, and maintaining national security.

A third cluster of issues involves social issues such as crime, traditional morality, law and order, abortion, race relations, and school prayer. These are issues that often stir deep emotions. In the presidential elections of the 1980s, these issues tended to work to the advantage of Republicans and enabled the party to make effective appeals to traditionally Democratic voter groups like Catholics and union members. The impact on the parties of social issues is, however, subject to rapid changes depending upon their salience with the public. In 1989 gubernatorial races in New Jersey and Virginia, abortion became a major issue and the pro-choice stance of Democratic candidates contributed to their victories. However, by 1990 in the midst of the Middle East crisis created by Iraq's invasion of Kuwait, major White House-congressional battles over taxes, and fears of looming recession, abortion faded as a major election issue.

Candidate Image

There are no hard and fast rules to guide candidates in terms of how to conduct their campaigns to achieve a favorable personal image, though homilies abound—appear decisive, don't appear trigger happy, the best defense is a strong offense, carry the attack to your opponent. Personal characteristics that voters believe are important tend to vary depending upon the condition in which the country finds itself. Thus Jimmy Carter's outsider, non-Washingtonian, peanut farmer, righteous image had substantial appeal to a nation reeling from the traumas of the Vietnam War and Watergate. Throughout the 1976 presidential campaign, Carter stressed these images to a public anxious for a president who radiated honesty and religious conviction. In the changed circumstances of 1980, as the country faced severe economic problems and foreign policy setbacks, effective leadership became the personal quality voters sought in a president. And effective leadership was what voters thought they were not getting from Carter, while they perceived Ronald Reagan to be a stronger leader. Again in 1984 and 1988 leadership was the top rated presidential quality for the voters. In both elections, the Republicans gained substantial electoral advantage from the experience factor. Thus in 1988, CNN–*Los Angeles Times* exit polls showed 34 percent of the voters citing "more experience" as the basis for their vote choice, with 97 percent favoring Bush and only 3 percent favoring Dukakis. Dukakis was also hurt by the Bush campaign's portrayal of him as a liberal.[42]

Clearly, both Reagan and Bush were aided in the 1984 and 1988 campaigns by their images of experienced leadership and being associated with relatively good economic conditions and a lessening of international tensions. Too much attention can be attached, however, to developing a favorable candidate image that is right for the times.

To a significant degree elections are about performance, as the voters render a verdict on an incumbent and the incumbent's party's record in office. That is, elections involve retrospective voting on the part of the citizenry. Abramson, Aldrich, and Rohde after analyzing National Election Study data between 1976 and 1988, emphasize this point when they concluded:

> The 1976 election, with its razor-edge for Carter, was a very narrow rejection of Ford's incumbency, and 1980 was clear and strong rejection of Carter's. In 1984, Reagan won in large because he was seen as having performed well. . . . Bush won in large because Reagan was seen as having performed well—and people thought Bush would stay the course, but such evaluations . . . were less positive than four years earlier. Hence the vote was closer in 1988 than in 1984.[43]

The Campaign and Governance

Although candidates can vary their campaign strategies and can hire experts to devise the seemingly most effective strategy, all are restricted by conditions over which they have little or limited control—election laws, the state of the economy, international conditions, campaign resources, public images of the parties, and the partisan division of the electorate between Republicans and Democrats. Candidates, therefore, must tailor their campaigns to fit conditions or run the risk of defeat or a serious decline in electoral support.

The impact of the campaign, however, goes well beyond its importance in terms of influencing voter decisions (the topic of Chapter 8). The campaign also affects the behavior of public officials after the election. Perceptions of the public, of societal problems, and of important interest groups that must be accommodated are influenced by campaign experiences. Obligations to the public in terms of campaign pledges to key constituency groups often mean that public officials feel honor bound to pursue particular policies once in office. Many elected officials recruit key staff personnel from their campaign organizations. But most importantly, the outcome of the campaign determines which party will control the government and by how large a margin. Which party holds power influences the direction of public policy.

Suggestions for Further Reading

Abramson, Paul R.; Aldrich, John H.; and Rohde, David W. *Change and Continuity in the 1988 Elections*. Washington, D.C.: CQ Press, 1990.

Asher, Herbert B. *Presidential Elections and American Politics: Voters, Candidates, and Campaigns since 1952*, 4th ed. Homewood, Ill.: Dorsey Press, 1987.

Herrnson, Paul S. *Party Campaigning in the 1980s*. Cambridge, Mass.: Harvard University Press, 1988.

Jackson, Brooks. *Honest Graft: Big Money and the American Political Process*. New York: Knopf, 1988.

Kessel, John H. *Presidential Campaign Politics*, 3d ed. Homewood, Ill.: Dorsey Press, 1988.

Magleby, David B., and Nelson, Candice J. *The Money Chase: Congressional Campaign Finance Reform*. Washington, D.C.: Brookings Institution, 1990.

Nelson, Michael (ed.), *The Elections of 1988*. Washington, D.C.: CQ Press, 1989.

Polsby, Nelson W., and Wildavsky, Aaron. *Presidential Elections: Strategies in American and Electoral Politics*. 7th ed. New York: Scribner's 1988.

Ranney, Austin. *Channels of Power: The Impact of Television on American Politics*. New York: Basic Books, 1983.

________, ed. *The American Elections of 1980*. Washington, D.C.: American Enterprise Institute, 1982.

________, ed. *The American Elections of 1984*. Washington, D.C.: American Enterprise Institute for Public Policy Research, published by Duke University Press, 1985.

Sabato, Larry J. *PAC Power: Inside the World of Political Action Committees*. New York: Norton, 1985.

________. *The Rise of the Political Consultants: New Ways of Winning Elections*. New York: Basic Books, 1981.

Salmore, Stephen A., and Salmore, Barbara G. *Candidates, Parties, and Campaigns*, 2d ed. Washington, D.C.: CQ Press, 1989.

Sorauf, Frank J. *Money in American Politics*. Glenview, Ill.: Scott, Foresman/Little, Brown, 1988.

Notes

1. Bruce A. Campbell, *The American Electorate: Attitudes and Action* (New York: Holt, Rinehart, and Winston, 1979), pp. 12–13.
2. *Smith v. Allright*, 321 U.S. 649 (1944).
3. *The Transformation of American Politics* (Washington, D.C.: Advisory Commission on Intergovernmental Relations, 1986), p. 152.
4. V.O. Key, Jr., *Politics, Parties, and Pressure Groups*, 5th ed. (New York: Crowell, 1964), p. 644.
5. Thomas B. Edsall, "Partners in Political PR Firm Typify Republican New Breed," *Washington Post*, April 7, 1985, p. A8.
6. Thad L. Beyle, "Governors," in Virginia Gray, Herbert Jacob, and Robert B. Albritton, eds, *Politics in the American States: A Comparative Analysis*, 5th ed. (Glenview, Ill.: Scott, Foresman/Little, Brown, 1990), p. 208.
7. Gary C. Jacobson, *The Politics of Congressional Elections* (Boston, Mass.: Little, Brown, 1983), pp. 101–102.
8. Derived from Federal Election Commission data on 1988 elections.
9. See Michael J. Malbin, "Looking Back at the Future of Campaign Finance Reform; Interest Groups and American Elections," in Michael J. Malbin, ed., *Money and Politics in the United States* (Chatham, N.J.: Chatham

House, 1984), pp. 232–276. For an analysis of the partisan conflict over campaign reform in 1990, see Chuck Alston, "Showdown on Spending Limits Moves Toward White House," *Congressional Quarterly Weekly Report*, Aug. 4, 1990, pp. 2478–2482.

10. Federal Election Commission data.
11. Richard L. Berke,"Realtors' Political Arm Offers Lessons on Strength of PACs," *New York Times*, June 29, 1989, p. 1,8Y.
12. Chuck Alston, "Republicans Seek to Reduce Labor's Clout at the Polls," *Congressional Quarterly Weekly Report*, March 31, 1990, p. 961.
13. Glen Craney, " 'Soft Money' in Big States Exceeded $28 Million," *Congressional Quarterly Weekly Report*, Dec. 9, 1989, p. 3389.
14. Ruth S. Jones, "Financing State Elections," in Malbin, *Money and Politics in the United States*, p. 198; see also Ruth S. Jones, "State Public Campaign Finance: Implications for Partisan Politics," *American Journal of Political Science*, 25 (May 1981): 342–361; and Ruth S. Jones, "State and Federal Legislative Campaigns: Same Song Different Verse," *Election Politics* 3 (Summer 1986): 11.
15. Jones, "Financing State Elections," p. 203.
16. Ibid., p. 202.
17. *Congressional Record* (daily edition, 89th Congress, 1st Session, April 4, 1967), pp. S4590–4592.
18. David E. Price, *Bringing Back the Parties* (Washington, D.C.: CQ Press, 1984), p. 243.
19. Ibid., pp. 244–245.
20. Ibid., p. 245.
21. Nelson W. Polsby and Aaron Wildavsky, *Presidential Elections: Strategies of American Electoral Politics*, 7th ed. (New York: Scribner's 1988), p. 276.
22. Ibid., pp. 278–280.
23. For further discussion of electoral college reform, see Lawrence D. Longley and Alan G. Braun, *The Politics of Electoral College Reform* (New Haven: Yale University Press, 1972); Wallace S. Sayre and Judith H. Parris, *Voting for President* (Washington, D.C.: Brookings Institution, 1970); Thomas E. Cronin, "The Direct Vote and the Electoral College: The Case of Meshing Things Up?," *Presidential Studies Quarterly* (Spring 1979), pp. 178–188; Alexander M. Bickel, *Reform and Continuity: The Electoral College, The Convention, and the Party System* (New York: Harper Colophon Books, 1971).
24. For an unusually thorough consideration of the impact of campaign decisions on elections, see Stephen A. Salmore and Barbara G. Salmore, *Candidates, Parties, and Campaigns*, 2nd ed. (Washington, D.C.: CQ Press, 1989).
25. Adam Clymer, "Poll Shows Iran and Economy Center among Late-Shifting Voters," *New York Times*, Nov. 16, 1980, pp. 1, 32.
26. Cornelius P. Cotter, James L. Gibson, John F. Bibby, and Robert J. Huckshorn, *Party Organizations in American Politics* (New York: Praeger, 1984), pp. 22–23.

27. Samuel Kernell, "A Primer on Demographic Targeting," *Election Politics* 1 (Winter 1983–84): 18.
28. Austin Ranney, *Channels of Power: The Impact of Television on American Politics* (New York: Basic Books, 1983), p. 114.
29. Ibid., p. 115.
30. Salmore and Salmore, *Candidates, Parties, and Campaigns*, pp. 157–158.
31. Paul Taylor, "Armed with Distortions, Candidates Attack," *Washington Post*, Sept. 21, 1990, pp. A1, A10.
32. Thomas E. Mann and Raymond E. Wolfinger, "Candidates and Parties in Congressional Elections," *American Political Science Review* 74 (Sept. 1980): 617–632.
33. Ibid., pp. 626–628; Barbara Hinckley, "The American Voter in Congressional Elections," *American Political Science Review* 74 (Sept. 1980): 641–650.
34. Norman J. Ornstein, Thomas E. Mann, and Michael J. Malbin, *Vital Statistics on Congress, 1989–1990* (Washington, D.C.: Congressional Quarterly, 1990), p. 78.
35. Edie N. Goldenburg and Michael W. Traugott, *Campaigning for Congress* (Washington, D.C.: CQ Press, 1984), p. 21.
36. Thomas E. Patterson. "Television and Election Strategy," in Gerald Benjamin, ed., *The Communications Revolution in Politics* (New York: Academy of Political Science, 1982), p. 31.
37. Kathleen A. Frankovic, "The 1984 Election: The Irrelevance of the Campaign," *P.S.* 18 (Winter 1985): 43.
38. Ibid.
39. Stephen J. Wayne, *The Road to the White House: The Politics of Presidential Elections*, 2nd ed. (New York: St. Martin's, 1984), p. 227.
40. William Schneider, "The November 4 Vote for President: What Did it Mean?" in Austin Ranney, ed., *The American Elections of 1980* (Washington, D.C.: American Enterprise Institute, 1981), p. 231: *Gallup Poll Index*, Report No. 181, Sept. 1980, p. 19.
41. *Public Opinion* 7 (Dec./Jan. 1985): 38.
42. "Explaining Their Vote," *National Journal*, Nov. 21, 1988, p. 2844.
43. Paul R. Abramson, John H. Aldrich, and David W. Rohde, *Change and Continuity in the 1988 Elections* (Washington, D.C.: CQ Press, 1990), p. 195.

CHAPTER 8

Political Parties and the Voters

Voter Turnout
Who Votes?
Is Nonvoting a Social Disease?
Party Identification
The Increase in Independents and the 1980s Resurgence of Partisanship
The Decline in Party Voting
Candidates and Issues
Social and Economic Bases of Partisanship and Voting
Economic and Class Differences
Religious Differences
Gender Differences
Regional Differences
Racial Differences
The Socioeconomic Composition of the Parties
Election Outcomes
Presidential Elections
Elections to the Senate
Elections to the House of Representatives
Gubernatorial and State Legislative Elections
Voters, Elections, and Control of Government

When the party nominating processes have narrowed the list of candidates and the campaign maneuverings have ended on election eve, it is the voter who decides the fate of the parties and their candidates. Parties cannot survive or exercise significant influence on the affairs of state without substantial voter support, because modern democratic governments derive their legitimacy through free elections. The nature of the party-in-the-electorate, therefore, is crucial to understanding the parties' role in the political process. Which voters will actually turn out and go to the polls on election day? How strong is the pull of partisanship in determining voter choices? Which party will benefit from the short term influences of current issues and candidates' images? The electoral fate of the parties is tied up in the answers to these questions, which are the focus of this chapter.

Voter Turnout

Although free elections are critical to the functioning of the republic, a relatively low proportion of the American electorate actually took advantage of its right to the franchise in 1988. The U.S. Bureau of the Census reported that in 1988, 50.2 percent of the eligible voters cast ballots.[1] This figure constituted a decrease of 2.9 percent over 1984 and continued a general downward trend in turnout since 1960.

Voter turnout varies significantly depending upon the timing of the election and the offices being contested. There is also substantial variation among the states in their rates of voter turnout.

Figure 8–1 demonstrates that voter turnout is substantially higher in presidential election years than it is in midterm elections for the House of Representatives. Presidential elections are characterized by saturation news coverage and intense campaigns. As a result, voters receive more stimuli to vote in these years than they do in midterm congressional elections. Since 1950, the fall-off in turnout from presidential elections to the next midterm congressional election has averaged − 13.1 percent. Turnout also varies between offices being contested. As is shown in Figure 8–1, there is a fall-off in voter participation between presidential balloting and voting for the House of Representatives in presidential election years.

Among the states, there are major differences in rates of turnout (see Table 8–1), with southern states having the lowest levels of voter participation. Political scientists have found that these varied turnout rates are related to both the political and the demographic characteristics of the states. Interparty competition is highly correlated with turnout: as the chances that either party may win goes up, the people are more likely to vote.[2] Turnout is also affected by the socioeconomic

Figure 8–1: Voter Turnout in Presidential and House Elections, 1932–1990 (Percentage of Voting Age Population)

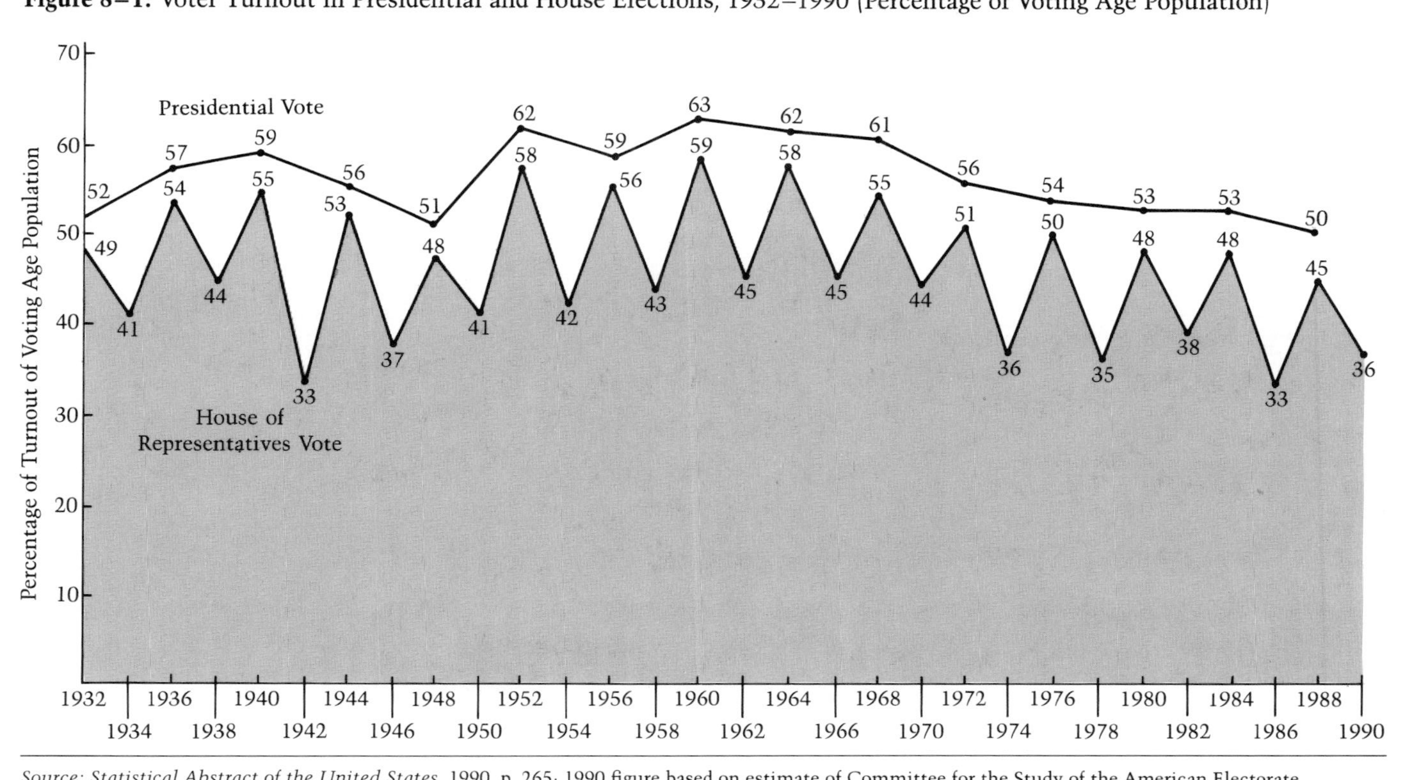

Source: Statistical Abstract of the United States, 1990, p. 265; 1990 figure based on estimate of Committee for the Study of the American Electorate.

Table 8–1 Mean Percentage of Voting Age Population Voting in Presidential, Gubernatorial, Senatorial, and House Elections, 1981–1988[a]

Rank	State	Overall	President	Governor	U.S. Senator	U.S. Representative
1	Montana	61.7	63.7	64.1	60.6	58.5
2	North Dakota	60.6	62.1	63.7	57.3	59.3
3	South Dakota	59.5	62.0	56.8	60.1	58.9
4	Minnesota	59.5	67.2	52.6	64.4	53.7
5	Maine	58.3	63.5	52.2	60.6	57.1
6	Utah	56.0	60.8	60.6	51.3	51.4
7	Idaho	55.9	59.1	52.4	57.2	54.9
8	Oregon	55.7	60.2	52.9	56.5	53.4
9	Alaska	54.7	55.6	55.3	54.1	53.8
10	Vermont	53.5	59.4	52.9	49.9	51.6
11	Iowa	52.6	60.8	46.3	51.8	51.8
12	Nebraska	52.0	56.2	47.8	52.6	51.5
13	Wisconsin	51.6	62.7	44.7	49.3	49.7
14	Missouri	51.4	56.0	56.9	45.3	47.3
15	Washington	51.0	56.3	58.5	42.4	46.8
16	Indiana	50.7	54.6	55.0	45.2	47.7
17	Connecticut	49.9	59.5	43.4	46.9	49.8
18	Massachusetts	49.8	57.8	42.3	53.5	45.5
19	Kansas	49.7	55.6	44.7	50.4	48.3
20	Rhode Island	49.7	54.4	48.5	50.5	45.3
21	Delaware	49.6	53.2	53.2	47.6	44.3
22	Wyoming	49.5	51.8	47.2	50.5	48.5
23	Colorado	48.8	55.1	43.0	49.6	47.4
24	Michigan	48.4	56.0	41.3	51.1	45.4
25	Ohio	47.8	56.7	40.9	45.8	47.7
26	Illinois	47.1	55.2	40.5	46.7	46.0
27	West Virginia	46.5	49.2	52.2	45.2	39.2
28	New Jersey	45.2	54.3	38.2	47.3	41.2
29	New Hampshire	45.2	53.9	41.7	42.0	43.1
30	Mississippi	44.6	51.6	39.9	46.1	40.5
31	Arkansas	44.5	49.4	46.4	45.7	36.4
32	New Mexico	44.3	49.3	40.2	45.7	42.2
33	Pennsylvania	44.3	52.0	39.4	41.8	43.9
34	North Carolina	43.2	45.4	48.5	41.2	37.6
35	California	42.8	48.5	40.0	40.7	42.2
36	Alabama	42.7	47.8	40.9	44.3	37.7
37	Oklahoma	41.9	50.4	37.5	43.5	36.1
38	Hawaii	41.8	43.7	42.7	40.7	40.2
39	Maryland	40.3	50.3	34.3	37.5	39.1
40	New York	40.3	49.6	36.1	37.3	38.1
41	Tennessee	39.9	46.9	35.1	42.2	35.2
42	Virginia	39.8	49.5	31.7	42.5	35.4
43	Louisiana	39.6	52.9	51.0	37.3	17.3
44	Nevada	39.1	43.2	36.2	38.6	38.6

Table 8–1 *(continued)*

Rank	State	Overall	President	Governor	U.S. Senator	U.S. Representative
45	Arizona	38.9	45.1	34.9	37.6	37.8
46	Kentucky	38.1	49.5	33.3	36.4	33.4
47	Texas	36.7	45.7	29.1	39.2	32.6
48	Florida	36.4	46.5	35.0	37.4	26.5
49	South Carolina	34.7	39.8	30.0	35.3	33.9
50	Georgia	32.8	40.4	27.7	33.7	29.5

a. In some states the vote may be understated because election returns are not reported in uncontested races.

Source: Virginia Gray, Herbert Jacob, and Robert B. Albritton (eds.), *Politics in the American States: A Comparative Analysis*, 5th ed. (Glenview, Ill.: Scott, Foresman/Little, Brown, 1990), p. 89.

makeup of the state population. The following characteristics are associated with higher levels of election day turnout: high incomes, high status occupations, high levels of educational achievement, middle age, Jewish heritage, Catholicism, and being white. A recent study showed that more than half of the variation among the states in voter turnout was caused by differences in race, age, income and educational level.[3] Differences in state registration requirements can also cause differential turnout rates. The restrictiveness of these regulations varies tremendously. For example, North Dakota has no registration requirements; Wisconsin requires registration only in urban areas; Maine, Minnesota, and Wisconsin permit registration at the polls; eighteen states have so-called "motor-voter" registration, which automatically registers an individual when they obtain a driver's license; twenty states permit registration by mail. Most states, however, require advance, in-person registration. States also have different deadlines for registration ranging from election day to fifty days in advance of the election. It has been estimated that if every state had registration laws as permissive as those in the most permissive states, turnout would rise by 9 percent.[4]

Who Votes?

Demographic characteristics. The two personal characteristics that are most closely related to voter turnout are *age* and *education* (see Table 8–2). As age increases, so does turnout until age sixty-five. Young people tend to have a low rate of turnout—only 18.6 percent of persons eighteen to twenty reported voting in 1986 compared to a participation rate of 60.9 percent for those in the over-sixty-five age bracket. The low rate of turnout among eighteen to twenty year olds

Table 8–2 Participation in National Elections, 1986

Characteristic	Percent of Persons Reporting That Voted 1986
Male	45.8
Female	46.1
White	47.0
Black	43.2
Spanish origin	24.2
Age	
18–20	18.6
21–24	24.2
25–34	35.1
35–44	49.3
45–64	58.7
65+	60.9
School years completed	
8 years or less	32.7
High school	
1–3 years	33.8
4 years	44.1
College	
1–3 years	49.9
4 years or more	62.5
Employed	45.7
Professional, technical unemployed	31.2
Not in labor force	48.2

Source: Statistical Abstract of the United States, 1990, p. 202.

has undoubtedly contributed to the decline in overall turnout that occurred in the 1970s, because the extension of the franchise to these persons significantly expanded the pool of eligible voters. This pattern of abstaining from voting reflects the unsettled character and mobility of young people's lives. Registration requirements, residency rules, military service, and moving all create hurdles to political participation among the young. It should be noted, however, that by age thirty-five most people have become at least occasional voters and that only a small portion of the middle aged and older public remain outside the voting public. It is estimated that only 5 percent of the electorate could be classified as habitual nonvoters.[5]

Education is the most important influence on voter turnout. The higher one's level of educational attainment, the greater the likelihood of voting. Better educated persons are more likely to vote because they tend to be better able to see the relevance of politics in their lives and the things they care about, are more interested in politics, and more skilled in dealing with registration requirements. Higher levels of educational attainment are associated with better paying jobs. However, income has only slight impact on turnout when other factors such as education, age, race, sex, and region are held constant.

There are also racial differences in turnout rates. A higher proportion of whites than blacks votes, and blacks are more frequent voters than Hispanics. The lower turnout rates of blacks and Hispanics tend to reflect the lower age and educational levels of these minorities. There are no significant differences in the turnout rates of men and women, though older women vote less than older men. This pattern reflects the fact that older women were socialized to politics in an era before participation in politics by women was widely accepted and the fact that women have a longer life expectancy than men and, therefore, are more apt to live socially isolated lives in old age.

Partisan implications. Voters are generally of a higher socioeconomic level than nonvoters; they are also more apt to be better educated, middle aged, and white. In partisan terms, this pattern of turnout means that Republicans are slightly more likely to turn out and vote than are Democratic voters. As a result, get-out-the-vote campaigns aimed at maximizing turnout have been a standard emphasis of Democratic campaigns. Increased voter turnout, however, is not necessarily advantageous for the Democrats. In 1988, for example, nonvoters probably held down Bush's margin of victory in the popular vote. A *New York Times*/CBS survey showed nonvoters preferred Bush by a 50–34 percent margin.[6]

The role of personal attitudes. Legal impediments, such as restrictive registration laws, can hold down participation in elections. To make voting easier and more convenient, some have even suggested making election day a national holiday. Although 50 percent of nonvoters in a recent survey reported that they would be likely to vote if it were done on a holiday, there is reason to doubt their good intentions. If these persons are not now sufficiently interested in politics to vote, there is every reason to believe that they would take a holiday from both work and voting if given the opportunity.[7] Nonvoting is not primarily a matter of legal impediments; it is rather caused by personal attitudes—a lack of interest, low sense of civic obligation, and weak feelings of partisan affiliation. Nonvoters are also more likely than voters to believe that elections do not make a difference. The importance of these attitudes can be seen in an ABC News Poll which compared persons likely to vote with those who rarely vote (see Table 8–3). Likely voters are more apt to

Table 8–3 Attitudes toward Voting and Politics

	Percent Agreeing	
Question	**Likely Voters**	**Persons Who Rarely Vote**
Aligned with a party	80%	54%
There are important differences between the parties	85	65
I'd feel guilty if I didn't vote	71	31
Politics/government so complicated I can't understand it	50	77
Public officials don't care about people like me	39	60
It's a waste of time to vote	12	41

Source: Jeff Alderman, ABC News Poll, Survey 0080. Conducted June 29–July 13, 1983.

be partisans and to see a difference between the parties. They also have a sense of civic obligation and feel guilty if they do not participate in elections. Likely voters also have a greater sense of confidence in their ability to understand politics and the willingness of public officials to pay attention to the wishes of the people.

The impact of voter mobilization. One of the problems with the research findings that have been summarized to this point is that they make it appear that voter turnout is a deterministic function of the personal characteristics of voters or the demographic properties of electorates. There are, of course, differences in the propensities of various subgroups of the population to vote, but the extent of electoral participation is also influenced by such factors as the amount of campaign spending, the level of interparty competition, and the intensity of the campaign. Political parties and candidate organizations through their campaign activities are able to influence turnout as they mobilize the electorate.

When the outcome of an election is a foregone conclusion with one party or candidate assured of election, voter participation is apt to be adversely affected. A clear example of this tendency for an absence of competition to depress turnout occurred in the South, where the entrenched Democratic party was assured of general election victories. As a result, voter turnout tended to be lower in the noncompetitive general elections than in the primaries, where meaningful contests for the Democratic nomination were likely to occur. However, as the Republican party has become a force in southern politics and contested the general elections, turnout in general elections has increased substantially.

An indicator of the intensity of a campaign is the level of spending in which the parties and candidates engage to mobilize voters. Studies of campaign spending in gubernatorial and state legislative races have demonstrated that spending increases electoral involvement, but that, after a certain threshold is reached, additional increments of spending produce increasingly smaller payoffs in terms of voter turnout.[8]

Is Nonvoting a Social Disease?

A commonly expressed view is that America's seemingly high rate of nonvoting is symptomatic of a civic disorder that endangers the republic. Unfavorable comparisons between turnout rates in the United States and other Western democracies are frequently cited as evidence of decay in the American body politic. It is necessary, however, when considering these cross-national comparisons to keep in mind that other nations compute turnout rates as a percentage of registered voters going to the polls. By contrast, American turnout rates are normally calculated as a percentage of the voting age population. As a result, most of the free world can boast of higher turnout rates than the United States. However, when turnout in the United States is computed on the basis of registered voters, instead of voting age population, the Census Bureau estimates the 1988 rate at a more respectable 71 percent.[9] In addition, Americans have more opportunities to vote than do citizens of other democracies because of the frequency and varied types of elections in the United States—primaries and general elections for national, state, and local offices, state and local referenda, and recall elections. British political scientist Ivor Crewe emphasized this point when he observed:

> Turnout rates provide only a limited perspective on the amount of electoral participation. Turnout cannot measure the frequency of elections. Although turnout in the United States is below that of most other democracies, American citizens do not necessarily do less voting; in fact, they probably do more. No country can approach the United States in frequency and variety of elections. Only one other country—Switzerland, can compete in the number and variety of local referendums. Only Belgium and Turkey hold party "primaries" in most parts of the country.[10]

There is no compelling evidence to indicate that America's relatively low rate of turnout results in distortions of the citizenry's will. In general, nonvoters have candidate preferences much like those of voters. Indeed, an analysis of the 1988 election by political scientists Abramson, Aldrich, and Rohde concluded that "there is no reasonable scenario under which increased turnout would have altered the outcome of the presidential election. . . . The problem for the Democrats is not low turnout but low levels of support." They found that even if two groups that voted heavily Democratic, blacks and Hispanics, had turned out at the same rate as whites, Michael Dukakis would have received 2.6 million additional votes, far fewer than George Bush's 7 million vote margin of victory. It should also be noted that the conditions that would be likely to stimulate higher rates of turnout among blacks and Hispanics also would, in all probability, cause higher turnout among whites.[11]

Americans' lower turnout rates do not appear to be caused by dissatisfaction with the political system. Americans have a higher level of confidence in their armed forces, legal system, educational system, churches, press, labor unions, major companies, civil service, and legislature than the European countries surveyed by Seymour Martin Lipset and William Schneider in their book, *The Confidence Gap.*[12] Americans also surpass Europeans in attitudes that are conducive to voting, such as a belief in their ability to influence political developments. The level of nonvoting in the United States may well reflect the confidence Americans have that the next election will not bring in its wake dangerous or threatening circumstances. Both major parties tend to be middle of the road and share a consensus on the nature of the political order and economic system that make election outcomes much less threatening than in nations where party differences are sharp and a change of regimes could result in an abrupt shift in governmental policy. Everett Carll Ladd has observed that the United States

> as a stable democracy that has operated under the same constitutional structure for two centuries . . . has a political system that is not so stress-filled [as such nations as France or Britain], and many Americans feel they can afford the luxury of not voting.[13]

Party Identification

Voters' electoral choices reflect the interaction of enduring attitudes and beliefs and more transitory factors such as current issues and candidate images. The most important long-term influence is *party identification*—a feeling of attachment to and sympathy for a political party.[14] It is considered a long-term and continuing influence on voter choice because one's party identification is not likely to undergo frequent changes in response to changing events or life circumstances. Unlike issues and candidate images which vary from year to year, a voter's party identification is quite stable.

Party identification is measured in public opinion surveys by asking voters a question such as the following: "Generally speaking, do you think of yourself as a Republican, Democrat, or Independent?" Scholars also attempt to probe voters to determine the strength of voters' partisan commitments and have developed the following seven point scale.

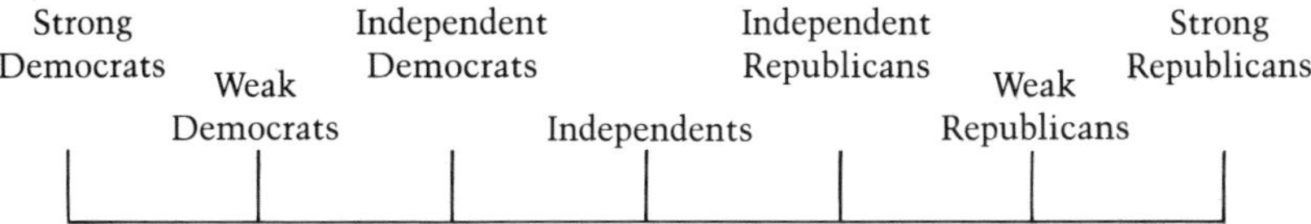

Table 8–4 shows that between 1952–1988 approximately three-fourths to two-thirds of the American electorate held a partisan identification, with the Democrats maintaining a consistent advantage over the GOP.

Party identification tends to be acquired at an early age. Studies of grade school children have shown that by fourth grade most students have a partisan preference.[15] This sense of partisanship is usually devoid of an informational or policy content—that is, young children know little about the candidates and issue differences between the parties. Children's sense of partisan affiliation is usually acquired through their families; they tend to imitate the behavior of their parents when the adults are not actively seeking to persuade their children to adopt their viewpoints. Learning party identification is not, therefore, a conscious activity; it is an informal family centered process. As Herbert Asher has noted, "One reason why the family is so crucial is that other agents of political learning, such as teachers and school curricula, studiously avoid getting enmeshed in partisan questions."[16]

Although partisanship is normally learned in childhood, there is substantial stability in most people's party affiliations.[17] Changing life circumstances and real-world events, however, can cause some voters to change their party preference. For example, President Reagan's popularity in 1981 coincided with an increase in Republican identifiers. A downturn in the economy in late 1981 and 1982 produced a decline in the president's popularity and a shift to the Democrats among party identifiers. Then, during 1984–85, the surging popularity of the president and an improved economy produced an increase in the proportion of voters identifying with the GOP. Clearly, party identification does respond to short-term influences,

Table 8–4 Party Identification in the United States, 1952–1988 (percents)

	1952	1956	1960	1964	1968	1972	1976	1980	1982	1984	1988
Strong Democrats	22	21	20	27	20	15	15	18	20	17	18
Weak Democrats	25	23	25	25	25	26	25	23	24	20	18
Leaning Democratic	10	6	6	9	10	11	12	11	11	11	12
Independent	5	9	10	8	11	13	15	13	11	11	11
Leaning Republican	7	8	7	6	9	11	10	10	8	12	13
Weak Republicans	14	14	14	14	15	13	14	14	14	15	14
Strong Republicans	14	15	16	11	10	10	9	9	10	12	14
Apolitical	3	4	3	1	1	1	1	2	2	2	2
Total	100	100	100	100	100	100	100	100	100	100	100

Source: National Election Study Surveys.

though the dominant pattern has been one of relative stability in individuals' party orientation.

The strength of party identification is related to both voters' patterns of turnout and loyalty to their parties. As the strength of commitment to a party increases, so does the likelihood that a person will turn out and vote. Strong partisans, therefore, have higher rates of turnout than weak partisans, who in turn are more likely to vote than independents.[18] As would be expected, independents and weak partisans are less likely to support one party consistently than are strong Republicans and Democrats, who have a high degree of party loyalty.[19] Democratic defection rates—especially among weakly committed Democrats—since 1952 have tended to be higher than those of Republicans (1964 was an exception when substantial numbers of Republicans deserted the Goldwater-Miller ticket to vote for Johnson and Humphrey). These high levels of Democratic defections have played a major role in enabling the minority Republicans to win five of the last six presidential elections. For example, CBS/*New York Times* exit polls on election day showed that in 1980 and 1984, 26 percent of Democrats had voted for the Republican candidate, Ronald Reagan. In the closer 1988 election, Democratic defections to the GOP were much lower—17 percent. By contrast, the Republican ranks held relatively firm: 15 percent defected in 1980 (11 percent to Democrat Jimmy Carter and 4 percent to John Anderson); only 7 percent went over to the Mondale-Ferraro ticket in 1984, and 8 percent voted for Michael Dukakis.[20]

The Increase in Independents and the 1980s Resurgence of Partisanship

A significant change in the partisan preferences of the electorate occurred during the mid-1960s through the mid-1970s. An increased proportion of the electorate came to consider themselves independents. The University of Michigan's Center for Political Studies has documented a rise from 22 percent of the voters saying they were independents in 1952 to 38 percent in 1976. This growth in the proportion of voters considering themselves to be independents is, however, less impressive when independents who lean toward one or the other of the major parties are treated as partisans (independent leaners have demonstrated higher levels of party loyalty on election day in some elections than weak partisans). The decline in partisanship that was detected in the 1960s and 1970s was particularly prevalent among young voters. For example, between 1964 and 1972, twenty-one to twenty-four year olds moved from being 33 percent to 50 percent independents, while those over sixty-five recorded only a 10 percent gain among independents (from 14 to 24 percent).[21] The 1980s have seen a reversal of the trend toward voters declaring themselves to be independents and a modest resurgence of partisanship even among younger voters.[22]

Although there has been a strengthening of partisanship among the voters in the 1980s, this does not necessarily mean that party is going to play a larger role in determining how people will vote. For example, defections to opposition party candidates by party identifiers was up substantially over 1976 among both Republican and Democratic partisans in 1980, even though the proportion of party identifiers in the electorate had increased. Partisan defections continued at high levels in 1984 among Democrats and then receded in 1988. This evidence of a weakening of the influence of partisanship on voter choice coupled with the presence in the electorate of substantial numbers of voters without strong partisan attachments has contributed to the volatility of American electoral politics. Short-term factors such as current issues, candidate images, and the ability of the parties to engage in successful voter mobilization efforts have taken on heightened importance.

The Decline in Party Voting

Studies consistently have demonstrated that party identification is a major determinant of how people vote. However, there is substantial evidence that partisanship is having a reduced impact on voters' decisions. Voters are engaging in ticket splitting with increased frequency—that is, voting for one party's candidate in one race, but voting for the other party's candidates in contests for different offices. Table 8–5 shows that at the turn of the century, ticket splitting between presidential and congressional candidates was unusual, but that by the 1960s it was commonplace for almost one-third of the nation's congressional districts to have split outcomes between the presidential and congressional outcomes.

Further evidence of a decline in partisan voting has been compiled from the surveys of individual voters done between 1952 and 1980 by the University of Michigan's Center for Political Studies. These surveys reveal that between 1952 and 1980 the percentage of voters reporting that they had:

- voted for different parties' presidential candidates in the various elections of the period rose from 29 to 34 percent.
- split their tickets between presidential and House candidates rose from 12 to 34 percent.

Table 8–5 Congressional Districts with Split Results for President and U.S. Representative, 1900–1988

Year	Districts[a]	Districts with Split Results[b]	
		Number	Percentage
1900	295	10	3.4
1904	310	5	1.6
1908	314	21	6.7
1912	333	84	25.2
1916	333	35	10.5
1920	344	11	3.2
1924	356	42	11.8
1928	359	68	18.9
1932	355	50	14.1
1936	361	51	14.1
1940	362	53	14.6
1944	367	41	11.2
1948	422	90	21.3
1952	435	84	19.3
1956	435	130	29.9
1960	437	114	26.1
1964	435	145	33.3
1968	435	139	32.0
1972	435	192	44.1
1976	435	124	28.5
1980	435	143	32.8
1984	435	196	45.0
1988	435	148	34.0

a. Before 1952 complete data are not available on every congressional district.

b. Congressional districts carried by a presidential candidate of one party and a House candidate of another party.

Source: Norman J. Ornstein, Thomas E. Mann, and Michael J. Malbin, *Vital Statistics on Congress, 1984–1985 Edition* (Washington, D.C.: Congressional Quarterly, 1990), p. 62.

- split their tickets between Senate and House candidates increased from 9 to 31 percent.
- split their tickets between state and local candidates went up from 27 to 59 percent.[23]

These data indicate that while approximately two-thirds of the electorate between 1952 and 1980 continued to profess a party identification, many voters did not vote consistently in accord with their partisan preference.

The declining impact of party identification on voter choice can also be seen in the frequently changing ratios of Democrats to Republicans in the electorate as a whole during the 1980s. From the 1950s through the 1970s, the Democrats held a consistent advantage in the 3:2 to 2:1 range. Yet, in spite of this Democratic advantage, the GOP won four of seven presidential elections between 1952 and 1976.

As is shown in Table 8–4, the Democratic advantage in party identifiers declined in the 1980s during the Reagan presidency. If independents who lean toward a party are counted as partisans, the percentage of Republicans rose from 33 percent in 1980 to 41 percent in 1988, and the Democratic advantage declined from almost 20 percent to less than 10 percent.[24]

The permanence of the partisan balance between Republican and Democratic identifiers is, of course, difficult to assess. There is a strong probability, however, that it will endure because it reflects realignments in the partisanship of major population groups—the erosion of Democratic strength among white southerners and Catholics—and the declining size of unions in society.

While studying the shifts in party identification that have occurred during and after presidential campaigns, Seymour Martin Lipset has identified a pattern of voters shifting their party identification to bring it into harmony with their vote preference. These voters who shift in response to candidate preference (20 percent of the electorate in 1984), plus the sizeable proportion of citizens claiming to be independents documents "that a large part of [the electorate] can be easily moved from one party to another."[25] The American electorate, therefore, is increasingly volatile, susceptible to mobilization by either party, and subject to the impact of short-term influences like candidate appeal and issues.

Candidates and Issues

Party identification has been a long-term and enduring influence upon voter choices, but its impact can be modified by the short-term and changing influences of candidates and issues. Candidate images are especially important when the candidates' personalities, political styles, backgrounds, and physical appearances are given a high level of media coverage, as in presidential elections. In the 1950s, Dwight Eisenhower was a candidate with exceptional personal appeal that increased the Republican percentage of the vote substantially. During most of the elections since 1952, candidate appeal has been a plus factor for Republican presidential tickets (1964 was the exception). In 1980, doubts about both candidates—Carter for his record as president, Reagan because of uncertainty about him as a president—meant that candidate image was of negligible effect.[26] However, in 1984, Reagan's standing as a strong leader added to the pulling power of the Republican ticket.[27] In 1988, the Republican nominee, George Bush, also benefited from a more positive image than his opponent.

In some elections a candidate gains a major advantage over an opponent because the opponent is extremely unpopular. This was true in the 1964 election when Republican Barry Goldwater was widely perceived to be "trigger happy" and impulsive. Senator George McGovern's low personal standing with the public gave Richard Nixon a major advantage in 1972. Only one-third of the public thought McGovern sufficiently trustworthy to be president, while 60 percent gave a trustworthy rating to Nixon.[28] In 1988, Dukakis's weakness as a candidate is believed to have contributed to Bush's victory margin. A CNN-*Los Angeles Times* exit poll on election day showed that voters rated Bush 54 percent positive to 39 percent negative, while Dukakis had a much less favorable voter assessment: 46 percent positive to 46 percent negative.[29]

The impact of issues on voter choice varies depending upon conditions and the candidates. In the 1964–1972 period—a time of controversial candidates, the civil rights movement, and Vietnam war—there was an increased correlation between attitudes on issues and vote choice.[30] In the 1980s, however, the issue positions of presidential candidates had a lesser impact on voters.[31] There are characteristics of electoral behavior that work against issues determining voter decisions. Widespread lack of knowledge concerning the stands taken by candidates on various issues exists within the electorate. Some voters, therefore, project to their favored candidate their own personal issue positions, irrespective of the actual issues stands of the candidate. Some voters may adopt an issue position because their preferred candidate has taken that position. In addition, voters may not feel intensely about some issues, even though they are subject to substantial debate during the campaign. Voters' ability to cast their ballots based upon issues is also affected by the campaign strategies of the candidates, who may or may not engage in issue oriented campaigns. As Flanigan and Zingale have pointed out, there are several factors that need to be present for issues to have an impact on voters: (1) voters must be informed and concerned about an issue; (2) the candidates must be distinguishable from each other on this issue; and (3) the voters must perceive the candidates' stands in relationship to their own issue position.[32]

The 1972 presidential election was an instance in which voter perceptions of candidate positions on issues appeared to play a significant role in voter choices. The National Election Study conducted by the University of Michigan revealed that voters saw Nixon as being closer to their own personal issue positions than was McGovern on eleven of fourteen issues. There was also a close correlation between the voters' perception of which candidate was closest to them on the issues and their actual vote choice.[33] The 1972 election also illustrates how candidate images can become intertwined with issue concerns of the voters and how these images of candidates can make the impact of issues more pronounced. McGovern's issue problems were compounded by his general image. His ideas were thought by 75 percent of the people to be "far out" and "impractical." He was perceived as liberal by 31 percent of the voters and as radical by another 31 percent, while only 17 percent considered themselves liberal and only 1 percent thought of themselves as radical. Peter Natchez has summarized how McGovern's image affected perceptions on his issues positions.

> His "indecisiveness" and "extremism" fed on each other; his indecisiveness created an aura of impracticality around the issue positions he was trying to develop; his search for the right issues made him seem indecisive.[34]

Another way of viewing issue voting is in terms of voters rendering a verdict on the past performance of the candidates and their parties, rather than in terms of candidates' promises for the future. This type of retrospective voting is especially important when an incumbent is running for reelection.[35] In 1980, for example, President Jimmy Carter was widely perceived to have been less than effective as president—particularly with regard to his handling of the economy, but also in foreign affairs (e.g., the Iranian hostage crisis). For many voters this was a more salient concern than their closeness to the candidates on various issues. The essence of retrospective issue voting was captured by candidate Reagan during his debate with President Carter when he asked the voters if they were better off than they had been four years before. In contrast to the negative verdict rendered on the performance of the Carter Administration in 1980, the voters were more positive about the record of the Reagan Administration in 1984. Voters gave Reagan a 58 percent positive to 46 percent negative rating for his handling of the economy and 86 percent of those giving him a positive rating also voted for him. In 1988, the Republicans again benefited from a favorable assessment of Reagan's stewardship of the economy. The GOP margin of victory was narrower, however, because Reagan got somewhat less positive marks in his second term and Bush had lower ability to win the support of those approving of Reagan's performance.[36]

The relative importance of various issues to the voters is subject to dramatic changes from election to election (see Table 8–6). In the 1950s,

Table 8–6 The Changing Public Perception of the Country's Most Important Problem: Presidential Election Years, 1936–1988

Year	Most Important Problem Facing the Country
1936	Unemployment
1940	Keeping out of war
1944	Winning war
1948	Keeping peace
1952	Korean war
1956	Keeping peace
1960	Keeping peace
1964	Vietnam, race relations
1968	Vietnam
1972	Vietnam
1976	High cost of living, unemployment
1980	High cost of living, unemployment
1984	Unemployment, fear of war
1988	Economy

Source: The Gallup Report, No. 208, Jan. 1983, p. 5; Report No. 220/221, Jan./Feb. 1984, p. 29; and Report No. 277, Oct. 1988, pp. 6–7.

foreign affairs was the most salient issue for America because of the Korean war and the cold war. During the early 1960s issues of race relations gained prominence. The Vietnam War pushed foreign policy concerns to the fore again in the mid-1960s along with the so-called social issues of urban riots, campus unrest, drugs, and law and order. During the mid-1970s and the 1980s, an unsteady economy made economic issues the most salient. Issue saliency is extremely important in elections because a candidate to be effective must be perceived favorably by the voters on the issues that are currently important to them. It does little good for a candidate to be well perceived on an issue of modest importance to the voters if that candidate is viewed unfavorably on the issue that is really on their minds. For example, in the 1988 presidential election, economic issues were most salient. Therefore, it did the Democrats little good to be perceived more favorably than the Republicans on such social welfare issues as developing policies that are fair to all Americans, protecting Social Security, and promoting education.[37]

The short-term influences of candidate image and issues can work either to reinforce partisan inclinations of voters or cause them to defect from their party. For example, dissatisfaction with the performance of the Ford Administration on the economy tended to reinforce the loyalty of Democrats to their party in 1976. But in 1984, Democrats defected in large numbers because of approval of the state of the economy and Reagan's favorable candidate image.

Table 8–7 Voting Patterns of Socio-Economic Groups, 1984–1988

	Percent of Vote by Party				Change	
	1984		1988		1984–1988	
	Dem.	**Rep.**	**Dem.**	**Rep.**	**Dem.**	**Rep.**
Party						
Democrat	74	26	83	17	+9D	−9R
Republican	7	93	8	92	+1D	−1R
Independent	36	64	43	57	+7D	−7R
Sex						
Male	38	62	42	58	+4D	−4R
Female	42	58	49	51	+7D	−7R
Age						
18–29	41	59	47	53	+6D	−6R
30–44	42	58	46	54	+4D	−4R
45–59	39	61	42	58	+3D	−3R
60+	36	64	49	51	+13D	−13R
Occupation/Union Membership						
Professional/Management	37	63	40	60	+3D	−3R
White collar	40	60	42	58	+2D	−2R
Blue collar	46	54	51	49	+5D	−5R
Union household[a]	52	48	55	43	+3D	−5R
Nonunion household[a]	36	64	40	59	+4D	−5R
Income						
Under $12,500	54	46	63	37	+9D	−9R
$12,500–24,999	42	58	51	49	+9D	−9R
$25,000–34,999	40	60	43	57	+3D	−3R
$35,000–49,999	32	68	43	57	+11D	−11R
$50,000–100,000	—	—	39	61	—	—
Over $100,000	—	—	33	67	—	—
Religion						
Protestant	31	69	40	60	+9D	−9R
Catholic	44	56	47	53	−3D	−3R
Jewish	67	33	65	35	−2D	+2R
"Born Again" white Protestants[a]	20	80	29	71	+9D	−9R
Education						
Less than high school	50	49	56	43	+6D	−6R
High school	39	60	49	50	+10D	−10R
Some college	37	61	42	57	+5D	−4R
College graduate or more	41	58	43	56	+2D	−2R
Race/Ethnicity						
White	34	66	40	60	+6D	−6R
Black	91	9	87	13	−4D	+4R
Hispanic	66	34	70	30	+4D	−4R

Table 8–7 *(continued)*

	Percent of Vote by Party				Change	
	1984		1988		1984–1988	
	Dem.	Rep.	Dem.	Rep.	Dem.	Rep.
Race/Ethnicity						
German/Austrian[b]	32	68	40	60	+8D	−8R
English/Scot/Welsh[b]	29	71	37	63	+8D	−8R
Italian[b]	41	59	49	51	+8D	−8R
Scandinavian[b]	38	62	47	53	+9D	−9R
Ideology						
Liberal	71	29	82	18	+11D	−11R
Moderate	46	54	51	49	+5D	−5R
Conservative	18	82	19	81	+1D	−1R
Region						
East	47	53	49	51	+2D	−2R
Midwest	38	62	47	53	+9D	−9R
South	36	64	41	59	+5D	−5R
West	38	62	47	53	+9D	−9R

a. Cable News Network/*Los Angeles Times* Exit Polls reported in *National Journal*, Nov. 12, 1988, p. 285.

b. ABC News and ABC News/Washington surveys reported in *Public Opinion*, Jan./Feb. 1989, p. 32.

Source: CBS/*New York Times* surveys compiled by *Public Opinion*, Jan./Feb.1989, pp. 24–32.

Social and Economic Bases of Partisanship and Voting

In the United States, lines of partisan conflict tend to cross-cut social and economic cleavages in society. The parties tend, therefore, to be broad coalitions embracing a wide variety of interests. Indeed, both parties draw significant levels of electoral support from virtually every major socioeconomic group in society. The only significant exception is black voters, who since 1964 have voted Democratic in overwhelming proportions (87 percent in 1988). Although both parties can expect at least some backing from just about every socioeconomic group, the two parties do not gain equal proportions of support from each group. There are distinctive patterns in the voting behavior of various groups, and the Republicans and Democrats have different bases of support.

Economic and Class Differences

As income, education, and occupational status go up, the likelihood of an individual's voting Republican increases (see Table 8–7). Lower income persons, blue-collar workers, and people from labor union households have constituted a traditional base of Democratic support, while professional/managerial personnel, college educated and nonunion household members have tended to be Republicans. While these patterns have been present in presidential elections since the New Deal realignment of the 1930s, it is important to note that a significant proportion of the voters in each of these categories consistently depart from their group's normal partisan inclination. For example, Republicans can normally expect to receive slightly less than 40 percent of the labor union household vote,[38] and Democrats customarily gain 33–40 percent of the professional/managerial voters and the college educated.

Since 1952, analysts have observed a decline in class based differences between the parties. This long-term decline in a relationship between class and voting behavior was reflected in the 1988 presidential vote. Democratic nominee Michael Dukakis directly appealed to working-class white voters by claiming to be "on your side" and made a stronger showing with these voters than with middle class voters. However, he did not receive a majority of the white working-class vote. At the same time, according to the CBS/*New York Times* exit poll, Dukakis did make a strong (40 percent) showing among professionals and managers. Abramson, Aldrich, and Rohde have argued that this pattern of Democrats being able to attract substantial voter support from both upper and lower socioeconomic groups reflects the party's ability to appeal to disadvantaged Americans on the basis of economic policies while better educated Americans may reject the traditional values emphasized by Republicans in recent elections. One of the likely reasons that Dukakis was not able to do better among working-class whites was the effective appeal Republican George Bush made to these voters on social issues like patriotism, support for the death penalty, and charges of Dukakis being soft on crime. Income based differences in voting behavior are much more pronounced when the analysis is expanded to include both white and black voters, because blacks are relatively poorer than whites and because they vote overwhelmingly for Democratic candidates.[39]

Although class based voting seems to be on the decline in the nation as a whole, this is not true in the South, where a quite different pattern is emerging. Through the 1950s, virtually all southerners, irrespective of their socioeconomic status, were Democrats. Since that time, the middle class has become increasingly Republican, while the working class, especially the black working class, has remained strongly Democratic. As a result, class based voter alignments in the South have been intensified, while they have been reduced in the North. In both regions, however, class based voting is relatively weak.[40]

Religious Differences

Religion, like class, has been a traditional basis of partisan alignment since the New Deal period. Catholics have tended to be Democrats and white Protestants to be Republicans. John Petrocik and Frederick Steeper have estimated that the normal white Anglo-Saxon-Protestant vote is 70 percent Republican—approximately the percentage won by Reagan in 1984.[41] Catholic support of Democratic presidential candidates, however, has declined in recent elections with the GOP actually carrying the Catholic vote in 1972, 1980, 1984, and 1988.

Like regionally based party loyalties, those which are religiously based frequently have their roots in historical circumstances. Prior to 1928, Catholics were less apt to vote Democratic than in succeeding years. But in 1928, Governor Al Smith of New York became the first Roman Catholic to be nominated for president by a major party. The 1928 campaign featured an intense anti-Catholic backlash that helped convert many Catholics to the Democratic cause. Religious cleavages were again activated in 1960 with the nomination of an Irish Catholic, John F. Kennedy, as the Democratic standard-bearer. In that election, 80 percent of Catholic voters voted Democratic, compared to the 50 percent that had cast ballots for the Democratic nominee, Adlai Stevenson, in 1956. Economic and educational status does affect the extent to which Catholics prefer the Democratic party. Higher status Catholics are less likely to be Democrats than lower status Catholics, but the two parties have a differential appeal to Catholics and Protestants that rests upon historical events interacting with cultural differences. The tendency of Catholics to be more Democratic than Protestants is not simply a reflection of class differences.[42]

Jewish voters have been overwhelmingly Democratic since the New Deal era. The allegiance of Jewish voters to the Democratic party has held firm even though substantial proportions of the Jewish population have achieved middle and upper-middle-class status. Antisemitism and discrimination against Jews have tended to cause them to identify with the less advantaged and be supportive of liberal social welfare policies. This type of policy orientation has made them pro-Democratic, irrespective of income, class, or educational attainment. In the 1980s, Jewish voters' Democratic proclivities were further encouraged by the appeals of Reagan and Bush to fundamentalist Christian groups like the Moral Majority and their endorsement of these groups' positions on issues of social policy (e.g., support for prayer in public schools).

Gender Differences

Gender has not been a source of partisan division in the United States until recently. In the elections of the 1980s, both Reagan and Bush received a plurality of the votes of men and women. However, women were more likely to support the Democratic presidential nominee than were men. Although a great deal of publicity has been given to the fact that the Democratic party has embraced most of the positions of the organized feminist movement, survey research indicates that gender based differences in voting behavior are more closely linked to women being less supportive of the use of force in foreign affairs, more supportive of government efforts to reduce the income gaps between rich and poor, and more supportive of environmental protection measures.[43] These attitude differences between the sexes indicate that the "gender gap" is likely to be an enduring feature of American politics in the 1990s. The "gender gap" is, however, a two-edged sword in terms of its consequences for the Republicans and Democrats. Whatever advantage the Democrats derive from their appeal to women is substantially offset by Republican pluralities among men.

Regional Differences

Periodically, major issues have emerged in American political history that have pitted one section of the country against another. These conflicts have had a lasting impact on party loyalties and voting habits. Because the first Republican president led the Union during the Civil War and a Republican Congress forced Reconstruction upon the South, the region became overwhelmingly Democratic in its political sympathies after the Civil War and up until the latter half of the present century.

In the South, the small town, white, Protestant, middle-class conservatives that in other regions could have been expected to provide the core of support for the Republican party were Democrats. They elected Democrats to Congress and supported virtually every Democratic presidential nominee from the post-Reconstruction period until the 1950s. An exception occurred when the Democrats nominated Governor Al Smith of New York, whose Catholicism pushed southerners into the Republican camp for one election. Starting in the 1950s, however, the GOP began to win significant proportions of the southern vote for president and since 1968 the Republicans have won a plurality of the white southern vote in every presidential election. Even a southern moderate, Jimmy Carter of Georgia, failed to carry the white southern vote in his two bids for the presidency in 1976 and 1980.

The change in the voting patterns of the South has been caused by the in-migration of middle class northerners who have carried their Republicanism with them. These transplanted Republicans are particularly evident in the growing suburban areas of cities such as Dallas, Houston, and Atlanta. Another factor creating a change in the partisan orientation of the South is the declining support for the Democratic party among young white southerners, who are less influenced by the traditions of the South than older generations. Despite the dramatic change that has occurred in southern voting patterns for president and Congress, the Democrats remain in control of most state and local offices and have an edge over the GOP in party identification.

The Plains states and the Mountain states have also shown a distinctive partisan orientation. These regions have tended to be the core areas of Republicanism, particularly in recent presidential elections. Through most of their history they have been predominantly rural and characterized by relatively high economic and cultural homogeneity. William Schneider has described Nebraska and Kansas as archetypal Farm Belt states

> overwhelmingly agricultural and white Anglo-Saxon Protestant, and not marked by major class or cultural stratification. For example, the largest foreign-stock group in Nebraska, Kansas, and the Dakotas is German, but the Germans in these states are mostly Protestants, whose culture is close to that of their Protestant neighbors.[44]

Schneider has also observed that the Farm Belt and Mountain states never experienced the same level of internal class conflict as did the Northeast, South, and Progressive states during the late nineteenth and early twentieth centuries. These areas have not been immune to protest movements (e.g., Populism), but a leftward leaning class constituency never developed because protest movements were confined to a native-stock agrarian milieu. However, there is a sense of sectional protest in the Farm Belt and Mountain states that tends to be directed against the federal government (e.g., the recent "sagebrush rebellion" protesting federal control of undeveloped western lands). Republicans have successfully appealed to the powerful anti-Washington sentiment of the western states.[45]

Racial Differences

After the Civil War and before the 1930s, black Americans were overwhelming Republican. They supported the party of Lincoln. During the Depression and New Deal era, they shifted toward the Democrats.

Their support for Republican candidates remained substantial, however, as Eisenhower received 39 percent of the black vote in 1956 and Nixon gained 25 percent four years later. In the 1964 presidential election between Barry Goldwater and President Lyndon Johnson, the images of the parties became sharply differentiated on civil rights issues, with the Democrats clearly perceived as the more liberal of the parties. In that election, blacks voted overwhelmingly for the Democratic candidate and have continued to do so in succeeding elections. It is estimated, for example, that even though Ronald Reagan scored a landslide victory in the country as a whole in 1984, he won only 9 percent of the black vote. A growing black population, higher levels of voter turnout, and massive support for Democratic candidates have meant that blacks constitute an expanding and increasingly important share of the Democratic vote. Strong black support is now essential for Democratic electoral victories in national, state, and most local contests.

Voters of Spanish heritage also show a strong but less pronounced tendency to support Democratic candidates. Whereas Bush lost the black vote 87–13 percent in 1988, his losing margin among Hispanic Americans was 70–30 percent. There are significant differences among Hispanics in their political preferences. Mexican-Americans tend to be Democrats, but Cuban-Americans, who have done relatively well economically in this country, tend to be Republicans for economic as well as foreign policy reasons. Because Hispanics are one of the fastest growing segments of the population, their political impact on elections, especially in the Southwest, is likely to be profound and results in both parties investing resources to win their allegiance.

Another growing population group is Asian-Americans, who doubled their population in the United States between 1970 and 1980 and are expected to do so again by 1990. Thus far this new Asian immigrant group has been disproportionately professional, educated, and socially active. In 1984, they voted 72–28 percent in favor of Republicans. The emergence of new racial voter groups, such as the Asian-Americans, plus the prominence of black and Hispanic voting blocks means that American politics will have significant racial dimensions into the foreseeable future. Interestingly, these groups are likely to manifest highly distinctive voting patterns at the very time that European ethnicity has declined as an important force in American politics, as the later European immigrant populations have been assimilated.[46]

The Socioeconomic Composition of the Parties

Although both parties have significant levels of support among virtually every major socioeconomic group in American life, there

Table 8–8 Party Preferences of Socioeconomic Groups, 1952–1972

Groups Rank Ordered from Most Republicans to Most Democrats	Percent Rep.	Percent Ind.	Percent Dem.	Party Advantage
Very high status Protestants	56	27	17	39 Rep.
Middle and high status Protestants	51	27	13	38 Rep.
Northern farmers	44	20	37	7 Rep.
Lower status Protestants	37	29	34	3 Rep.
Deep South immigrants	35	31	35	—
High status Catholics (non-Irish and Polish)	28	36	36	8 Dem.
Middle and upper status border state southerners	27	25	48	21 Dem.
Union members	20	29	51	31 Dem.
Lower status border state southerners	23	19	48	35 Dem.
Middle and lower status Catholics (non-Irish and Polish)	18	23	53	35 Dem.
Polish and Irish Catholics	13	29	58	45 Dem.
Deep South middle and lower status natives	11	28	61	50 Dem.
Jews	8	34	58	50 Dem.
Deep South lower status natives	13	20	67	55 Dem.
Blacks	11	20	69	58 Dem.

Source: Adapted from John R. Petrocik, *Party Coalitions: Realignments and the Decline of the New Deal Party System* (Chicago, Ill.: University of Chicago Press, 1981), p. 70.

are clear differences in the extent to which these groups support the Democrats and Republicans. John R. Petrocik has analyzed these patterns of party preference using surveys conducted during the elections between 1952 and 1972 (see Table 8–8). While the party preferences of major socioeconomic groups revealed in Table 8–8 will surprise few informed observers, they do highlight the extent to which partisanship in the United States cross-cuts various social, economic, religious, regional, ethnic and racial cleavages in society.

There are, however, significant changes occurring in the partisanship of the various elements of the population. Table 8–9 shows the extent of Republican voting among key socioeconomic groups between 1960 and 1988. These data demonstrate that while Republican voting by white Protestants has held steady at the approximately 70 percent level, support for Democratic candidates has declined among key support groups—Catholics, union members, white southerners, and Jews. The only exception to this trend is the increased level of Democratic voting by blacks. Probably more significant than these patterns of presidential voting are the changing profiles of the Republican and Democratic coalitions based upon avowed party identification (see Table 8–10). The three largest elements of the Democratic coalition in the late 1950s were northern union members, white southerners, and Catholics, with blacks contributing 9 percent of the party's core support and Jews 4 percent. The core of the Republican vote was white Protestants living outside the South. The parties had developed a new look by the late 1970s. The Democrats had become less southern and more black and northern union members were a smaller proportion of the party's support. Blacks had moved from 9 percent of the party's identifiers in the 1950s to 22 percent by 1988.

By 1988 black Republicans became even more rare and southerners constituted 25 percent of the identifiers compared to only 15 percent in the late 1950s. As Petrocik and Steeper have observed, "What had once been the party of Northern white Protestants was transformed into a national party by virtue of its growing Southern constituency."[47]

Clearly, the electoral landscape of the 1990s is significantly changed from that of the 1930s through the 1950s. Whereas in the New Deal years, women and men voted almost identically, today they show significant differences in party preferences. The New Deal Democratic coalition has been seriously undermined, particularly by the defections of white southerners and to a lesser degree by defections among Catholics and labor union households. Northern white protestants remain strongly Republican, with "born again Christians" joining their ranks. Black voters have come to constitute an enlarged and especially loyal base of Democratic voters and at the same time, the growing Hispanic population remains heavily Demo-

Table 8–9 Republican Voting among Key Voter Groups, 1960–1988

	Percent Republican in Election Years:							
	1960	**1964**	**1968**	**1972**	**1976**	**1980**	**1984**	**1988**
Northern white Protestants	79	51	75	77	64	66	76	72
Catholics	19	27	41	67	48	57	65	53
White northern union households	37	18	51	60	41	43	48	51
White southerners	53	42	65	78	57	60	69	67
Jews	11	11	7	31	29	37	31	23
Blacks	29	1	3	13	5			
Total Republican vote	49	39	44	61	49	51	59	52

Source: John R. Petrocik, "Issues and Agendas: Electoral Coalitions in the 1988 Election," a paper presented at the annual meeting of the American Political Science Association, Aug. 31–Sept. 3, 1989.

Table 8–10 Profiles of Democratic and Republic Party Coalitions, 1950s–1988

	Democrat Party Identifiers (Percent)					
	1950s	**1960s**	**1970s**	**1980**	**1984**	**1988**
White Protestants	18	20	17	16	17	15
Catholics	14	16	17	14	14	14
Northern union households	22	16	19	17	16	14
White southerners	31	26	23	23	22	23
Jews	4	4	3	5	3	4
Blacks	9	13	16	18	17	22
Hispanics	1	2	2	3	7	5
All others	2	2	3	4	5	3
Total	100	100	100	100	100	100
	Republican Party Identifiers (Percent)					
	1950s	**1960s**	**1970s**	**1980**	**1984**	**1988**
White Protestants	51	50	43	37	38	37
Catholics	10	12	12	14	14	16
Northern union households	16	11	14	16	12	12
White southerners	15	21	23	22	25	25
Jews	1	1	1	1	1	2
Blacks	5	2	2	3	2	4
Hispanics	0	—	1	2	4	2
All others	2	3	3	5	5	3
Total	100	100	100	100	100	100

Source: John R. Petrocik, "Issues and Agendas: Electoral Coalitions in the 1988 Election," a paper presented at the annual meeting of the American Political Science Association, Aug. 31–Sept. 3, 1989.

cratic. These significant changes in socioeconomic group party preferences and the demonstrated ability of the Republicans to win the presidency in five of the last six elections indicate that the era of the normal Democratic majority in presidential elections is now past.[48]

Election Outcomes

The discussion of voting behavior has dealt thus far with the forces influencing individual voter choices and the patterns of voting by socioeconomic groups. Elections, however, are played out as contests for specific offices, in different constituencies, at various times. Office, constituency, and timing factors, therefore, combine to produce diverse patterns of election outcomes.

Figure 8–2: Republican and Democratic Percentage of Popular Vote for President, 1956–1988

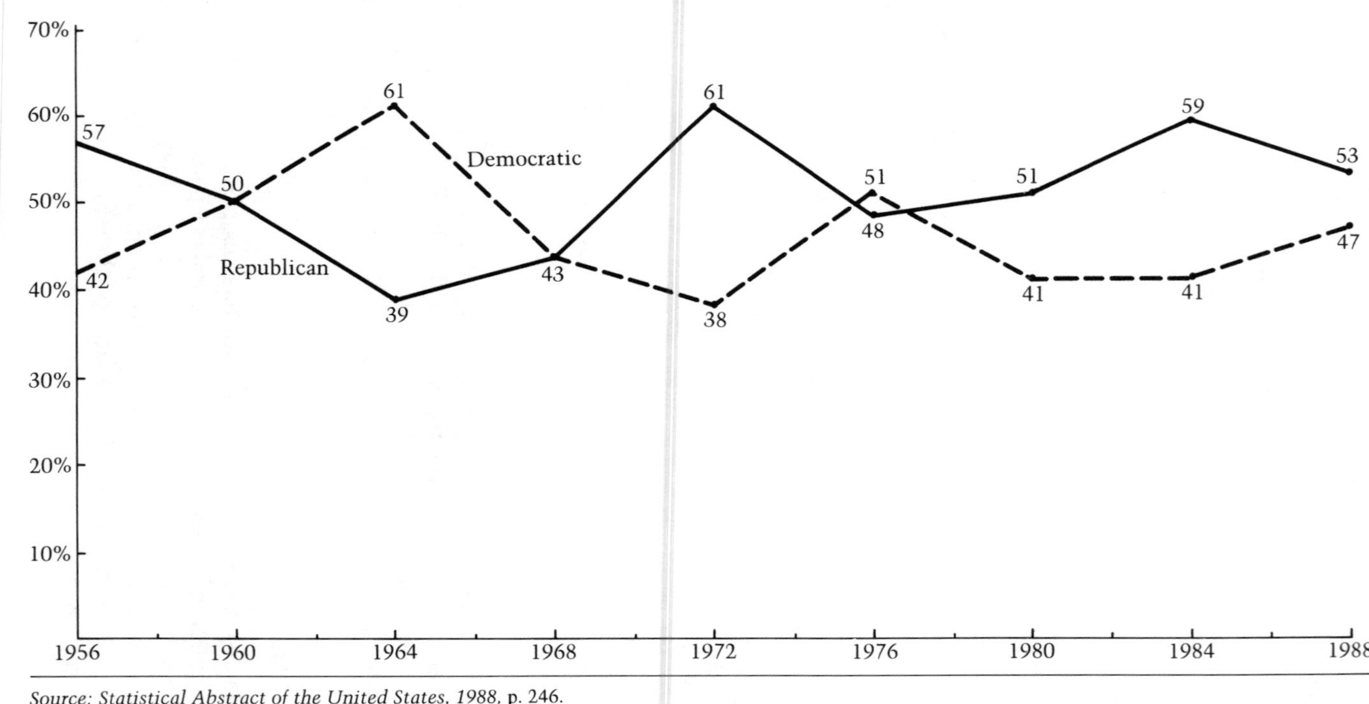

Source: Statistical Abstract of the United States, 1988, p. 246.

Presidential Elections

Despite the fact that Democrats have enjoyed a substantial advantage in party identification in the period of 1956–1988, the Republicans have been most successful in capturing the presidency (see Figure 8–2). In nine presidential elections held during this period, the Republicans have won six times and the Democrats three. The GOP has been victorious in five of the last six presidential contests. Obviously, short-term factors of candidate image, issues, and party image have overriden the normal Democratic advantage in party identifiers to produce this pattern of Republican dominance in presidential elections. Among the most dramatic aspects of this pattern is the changing allegiance of the South in presidential elections.

In 1952 and 1956 the Democratic nominee's strongest region was the South. Indeed, the only states carried by Adlai Stevenson against Dwight Eisenhower were states of the Old Confederacy or border states. The South was also critical for John F. Kennedy's election in the 1960s. However, none of these Democratic candidates was able to win all the states of the Confederacy, as had been the pattern in the 1930s and 1940s. In 1968 only one southern state, Texas, was carried by the Democratic ticket as the third party candidacy of Alabama Governor George Wallace swept five deep South states and Nixon won the balance. In his 1972 bid for reelection, Nixon carried every southern state for the GOP. Jimmy Carter, a native southerner, was the last Democratic nominee to carry this region and he accomplished this feat in 1976 without majority support of white southerners. In 1980 Ronald Reagan carried every southern state but Carter's native Georgia, and in 1984 and 1988 the GOP swept all the states in the region.

The twenty-one nonsouthern states west of the Mississippi have also shown a strong proclivity to vote Republican. Since 1968, the Republican candidate has never carried fewer than sixteen of these states and in 1984 Reagan won all but Walter Mondale's home state of Minnesota.

In each of its presidential victories since 1956, the Republicans have been beneficiaries of major internal splits within the dominant Democratic party. Democrats are divided on such matters as affirmative action, crime, abortion, school prayer, and national defense issues that have become more important than they were in the 1940s through the early 1960s. At the same time, the old New Deal agenda of national government responsibility for the social welfare of individuals and the regulation of the economy has either lost its salience or the perceived "superiority" of the Democrats on these issues for the party's traditional voters has become less obvious.[49] These changes have given the GOP the opportunity to compete effectively in presidential elections. At the same time, the declining importance of partisanship for most voters has eased the difficulty for the minority party in mobilizing an electoral majority.

The decline of partisanship within the electorate, however, presents opportunities for the Democrats as well as the GOP. A less partisan electorate is a volatile electorate that is capable of mobilization by either party, provided it has the right mix of conditions, issues, and candidates working in its favor. With the Democrats and Republicans approaching a rough parity in surveys of party identification, and party considerations playing a diminished role in voter choices, claims that there now exists a Republican majority in presidential elections would appear to be questionable. Clearly, the Democratic loss of the South has meant that the party has lost its normal majority, but that loss is not the same as saying there is now a Republican presidential majority.

Elections to the Senate

Whatever advantages the Republicans have had in presidential contests have been substantially offset by Democratic domination of the Congress since the mid-1950s. The GOP has not controlled both Houses of Congress since the 1952 election. Only the Senate has been in Republican hands (1981–1986) since the GOP surrendered control of Congress in the 1954 elections (see Figure 8–3).

Regional patterns. Some of the same regional patterns that are detectable in presidential elections are also present in senatorial elections. In state-wide elections for the Senate, the GOP is now competitive with the Democrats in the South and dominates the once Democratic delegations from Mountain and Pacific Coast states.

Democratic control of the Senate as recently as 1960 was anchored by the party's dominance of southern politics which enabled it to control all twenty-two seats in states of the Old Confederacy. As a result, southerners constituted the largest regional bloc within the Senate Democratic party in 1960—making up 33.8 percent of the party membership (see Table 8–11). The next largest group of Democratic senators were from the Mountain states (twelve seats; 18.5 percent). The party was, therefore, a strongly southern and western oriented party. The Republicans, by contrast, drew strength mainly from Plains, Middle Atlantic, and New England areas. In the thirty

Figure 8–3: Republican and Democratic Percentage of Senate Seats, 1956–1990

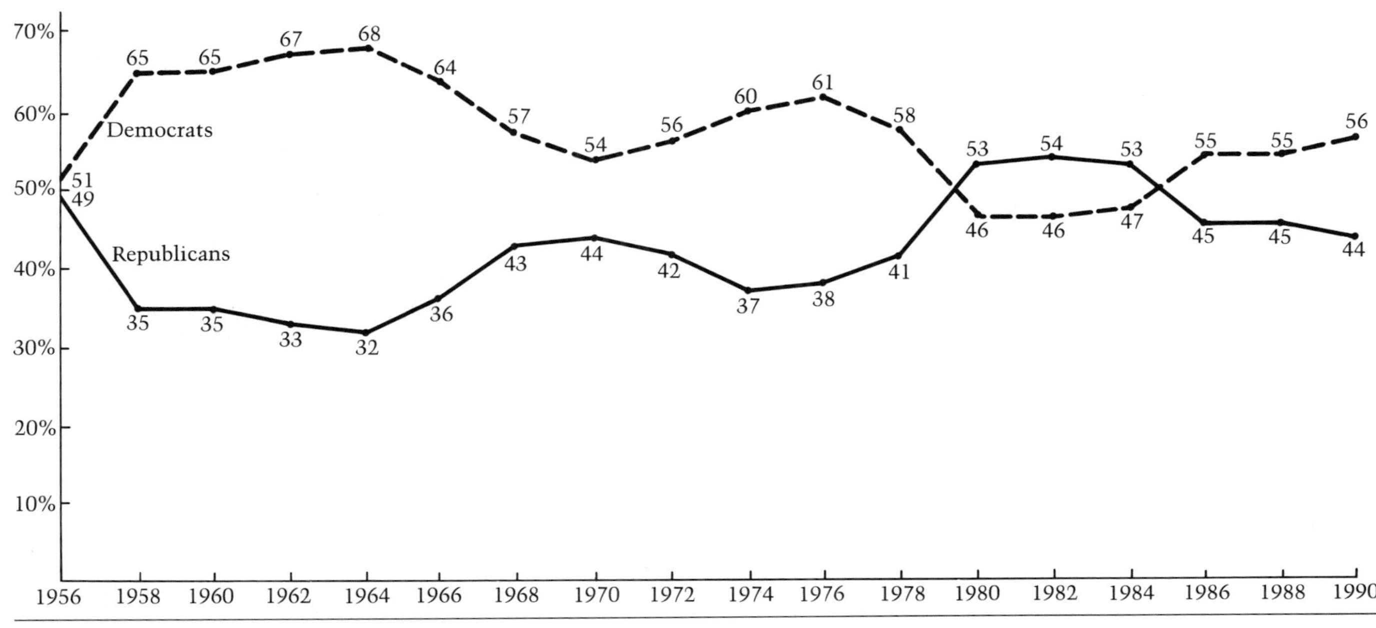

Source: Statistical Abstract of the United States, 1990, p. 250.

Table 8–11 Composition of Republican and Democratic Parties in the U.S. Senate, by Region, 1960–1990

		Republicans		**Democrats**	
Region	**Year**	**Seats Held**	**% of Party Membership in Senate**	**Seats Held**	**% of Party Membership in Senate**
South	1960	0	0	22	33.8
	1990	7	15.9	15	26.8
Border	1960	4	11.4	6	9.2
	1990	4	9.1	6	10.1
New England	1960	7	20.0	5	7.7
	1990	5	11.4	7	12.5
Mid Atlantic	1960	6	17.1	2	3.1
	1990	4	9.1	4	7.1
Midwest	1960	3	8.6	7	10.8
	1990	3	6.8	7	12.5
Plains	1960	9	25.7	3	4.6
	1990	5	11.9	7	12.5
Mountain	1960	4	11.4	12	18.5
	1990	10	22.7	6	10.7
Pacific Coast	1960	2	5.7	8	12.3
	1990	6	13.6	4	7.1

Sources: Norman J. Ornstein, Thomas E. Mann, and Michael J. Malbin, *Vital Statistics on Congress, 1989–1990* (Washington, D.C.: Congressional Quarterly, 1990), p. 13; *Congressional Quarterly Weekly Report*, Nov. 10, 1990, p. 3826.

years between 1960 and 1990, the senatorial parties have been transformed.

After the 1990 elections, the Senate Democratic party was substantially less southern and western in membership. Southern states constituted about a third of the party's membership and Mountain state senators were but 10.7 percent. Whereas in 1960, these two regions had elected a majority (52.3 percent) of the Democratic senators, by 1990 they were electing less than one-fifth (17.9 percent). By contrast, the Senate GOP membership clearly reflected the party's growing strength in the South and Mountain regions. Almost 40 percent of GOP senators in 1990 represented either southern or Mountain states.

Incumbency. Senate incumbents can generally be expected to be reelected. In the elections held (see Table 8–12) between 1960 and 1990, on average 80 percent of the incumbents seeking reelections were winners. The incumbent reelection rate for senators, however, is substantially below that of members of the House of Representatives. This was particularly true during the 1976–1980 period when less than 65 percent of incumbents were successful in retaining their seats. The relatively high levels of incumbent senator defeat reflect: (1) the generally higher levels of interparty competition that exist in state-wide constituencies as compared to the smaller and more demographically homogeneous House districts; (2) the higher levels of campaign resources plowed into challenger races for the Senate; and (3) the higher visibility of Senate contests. A substantial proportion of Senate incumbents, however, are normally elected by wide margins. In the elections from 1980 through 1988, 54 percent of the incum-

Table 8–12 Senatorial Incumbent Reelection Rates, 1946–1990

		Sought Reelection				
Year	**Retired**	**Total**	**Defeated in primaries**	**Defeated in general election**	**Total reelected**	**Reelected as percentage of those seeking reelection**
1946	9	30	6	7	17	56.7
1948	8	25	2	8	15	60.0
1950	4	32	5	5	22	68.8
1952	4	31	2	9	20	64.5
1954	6	32	2	6	24	75.0
1956	6	29	0	4	25	86.2
1958	6	28	0	10	18	64.3
1960	5	29	0	1	28	96.6
1962	4	35	1	5	29	82.9
1964	2	33	1	4	28	84.8
1966	3	32	3	1	28	87.5
1968	6	28	4	4	20	71.4
1970	4	31	1	6	24	77.4
1972	6	27	2	5	20	74.1
1974	7	27	2	2	23	85.2
1976	8	25	0	9	16	64.0
1978	10	25	3	7	15	60.0
1980	5	29	4	9	16	55.2
1982	3	30	0	2	28	93.3
1984	4	29	0	3	26	89.6
1986	5	28	0	7	21	75.0
1988	6	27	0	4	23	85.2
1990	3	32	0	1	31	96.9

Source: Norman J. Ornstein, Thomas E. Mann, and Michael J. Malbin, *Vital Statistics on Congress, 1989–1990* (Washington, D.C.: Congressional Quarterly, 1990), p. 57; *New York Times*, Nov. 8, 1990, Y A16.

bents gained at least 60 percent of the popular vote in their states, and in 1984 an unusually high proportion of incumbents (18 of 29—62.1 percent) compiled a 60 + percent margin.

Presidential elections and Senate outcomes. Senate election outcomes show substantial independence from presidential results. It is not unusual for states to have split outcomes between their presidential and senatorial votes. For example, in 1988, 30 percent of the states had split results between the presidential and senatorial elections. The tendency of voters to split their tickets between presidential and senatorial candidates has meant that the party winning the presidency is frequently unable to register a net gain of Senate seats. In four of the ten presidential elections since World War II, the party of the winning presidential candidate has actually lost Senate seats (see Table 8–13). The most dramatic postwar instance of presidential coattails occurred in 1980 when the Republicans picked up twelve seats and secured control of the upper chamber for the first time since 1954.

The outcome of Senate elections, of course, is conditioned by the fact that only one-third of the Senate is up for election in any presidential year. The extent to which national trends assist the party of the winning presidential candidate, therefore, is influenced by which one-third of the Senate is up for election that year. For example, the opportunities for the GOP to pick up seats in 1980 were enhanced by the fact that the Democrats were defending twenty-four seats and the Republicans only ten and those ten were relatively safe because they had survived the strong swing to the Democrats during the Watergate election of 1974. Some of these Democrat incumbents, therefore, were vulnerable in 1980 because they had benefited from the unusually heavy Democratic vote in 1974. The Constitution's requirement of staggered terms of senators makes unlikely a consistent pattern of gains in the Senate for the party of the winning presidential candidate.

Senatorial elections at midterm. As in the case of House elections, the president's party customarily loses seats during midterm elections (see Table 8–13). This pattern of outcomes, however, is less pronounced in the case of Senate elections than it is for House elections. In about one-third of the Senate midterm elections since the Civil War, the president's party has actually gained seats. The outcome at midterm is influenced not only by national political trends and the state of the economy, but by which particular set of senators is up for election. An important factor influencing the extent to which there is a net shift of seats from one party to the other is the number of seats each party is defending as it goes into the election. If

Table 8–13 Party Gains/Losses in Senate Seats in Presidential and Midterm Elections, 1946–1990

Year	Party Winning Presidency	New Seats Win/Lost
1946	(Democrat elected in 1944)	−9 Dem.
1948	Democrat	+9 Dem.
1950		−6 Dem.
1952	Republican	+1 Rep.
1954		−6 Rep.
1956	Republican	+1 Dem.
1958		−13 Rep.
1960	Democrat	+2 Rep.
1962		+3 Dem.
1964	Democrat	+1 Dem.
1966		−4 Dem.
1968	Republican	+6 Rep.
1970		+2 Rep.
1972	Republican	+2 Dem.
1974		−5 Rep.
1976	Democrat	No Change
1978		−3 Dem.
1980	Republican	+12 Rep.
1982		+1 Rep.
1984	Republican	−2 Rep.
1986		−8 Rep.
1988	Republican	No Change
1990		−1 Rep.

Source: Norman J. Ornstein, Thomas E. Mann, and Michael J. Malbin, *Vital Statistics on Congress, 1989–1990* (Washington, D.C.: Congressional Quarterly, 1990), p. 49.

the president's party is defending a relatively small number of seats, the likelihood of major losses by his party is reduced. For example, in the 1982 senatorial midterm elections, there were twenty-one seats being defended by the Democrats and twelve by the GOP. These circumstances, plus careful targeting of national party resources to races where incumbents were seriously threatened, enabled the Republicans to emerge from the election with a net gain of one seat rather than the customary midterm loss for the president's party.

Elections to the House of Representatives

Consequences of the single member district-plurality system. The single member district-plurality system of election has meant that a party's percentage of the House membership will not necessarily be proportionate to its national popular vote for Congress. If one party's voters tend to be concentrated in districts that it wins overwhelmingly and if the opposition party tends to win most of the marginal districts by narrow margins, then the composition of the legislative chamber is not apt to reflect accurately the share of the total vote received by either party. A disparity between popular votes and a party's share of the legislative seats is an inevitable consequence of the uneven manner in which adherents of the two parties are scattered across the country and the way boundary lines are drawn. Of course, overt gerrymandering of congressional district lines designed to enhance the advantage of one party or the other can magnify the disparity between seats won and a party's share of the national two party vote.

Table 8–14 Popular Vote for the House of Representatives and Percentage of Seats Won, 1946–1990

	Democratic Candidates		Republican Candidates		Difference between Democratic percentage of seats and votes won
Year	**Percentage of all votes**	**Percentage of seats won**	**Percentage of all votes**	**Percentage of seats won**	
1946	44.3	43.3	53.5	56.7	−1.0
1948	51.6	60.6	45.4	39.4	+9.0
1950	48.9	54.0	48.9	46.0	+5.1
1952	49.2	49.1	49.3	50.9	−0.1
1954	52.1	53.3	47.0	46.7	+1.2
1956	50.7	53.8	48.7	46.2	+3.1
1958	55.5	64.9	43.6	35.1	+9.4
1960	54.4	60.0	44.8	40.0	+5.6
1962	52.1	59.4	47.1	40.6	+7.3
1964	56.9	67.8	42.4	32.2	+10.9
1966	50.5	57.0	48.0	43.0	+6.5
1968	50.0	55.9	48.2	44.1	+5.9
1970	53.0	58.6	44.5	41.4	+5.6
1972	51.7	55.8	46.4	44.2	+4.1
1974	57.1	66.9	40.5	33.1	+9.8
1976	56.2	67.1	42.1	32.9	+10.9
1978	53.4	63.7	44.7	36.3	+10.3
1980	50.4	55.9	48.0	44.1	+5.5
1982	55.6	61.8	42.9	38.2	+6.2
1984	52.1	58.2	47.0	41.8	+6.1
1986	54.5	59.3	44.6	40.7	+4.8
1988	53.3	59.8	45.5	40.2	+6.5
1990	52.9	61.4	45.0	38.4	+8.5

Source: Norman J. Ornstein, Thomas E. Mann, and Michael J. Malbin, *Vital Statistics on Congress, 1989–1990* (Washington, D.C.: Congressional Quarterly, 1990), pp. 47–48; *Congressional Quarterly Weekly Report*, Feb. 23, 1991, p. 487.

Table 8–15 Popular vote for the House Compared to Percentage of Seats Won in Selected States, 1988

	Democrats			Republicans		
State	**Percent of Popular Vote for Congress**	**Percent of Seats Won**	**No. of Seats Won**	**Percent of Popular Vote for Congress**	**Percent of Seats Won**	**No. of Seats Won**
Arkansas	58	75	3	42	25	1
California	53	62	28	46	38	17
New Hampshire	41	0	0	59	100	2
New Jersey	48	57	8	51	43	6
Oklahoma	53	67	4	47	33	2
South Carolina	55	67	4	44	33	2
Texas	59	70	19	39	30	8
West Virginia	77	100	4	23	0	0

Source: Republican Almanac, 1989 (Washington, D.C.: Republican National Committee, 1989).

Table 8–14 shows the extent to which disparity exists between the national popular vote for Congress and the partisan distribution of seats within the House. Since the 1950s, it has been the Democrats that have been consistently advantaged by the single member district-plurality system of election. Even more dramatic disparities can exist between a party's percentage of the state popular vote for House candidates and the share of the seats it wins in a state's congressional delegation. Examples of instances in which both the Democrats and Republicans have benefited from this disparity are shown in Table 8–15. The alternative to a single member district-plurality system is a system of proportional representation using multimember legislative districts. Under proportional representation a party receives a share of legislative seats from a given constituency that corresponds to its percentage of the vote. Proportional representation, however, provides incentive to develop a multiplicity of parties because each is assured of some legislative representation if it can meet some minimum threshold requirement to qualify for electing legislators. The single member district system tends to give one party a majority in the national legislature, whereas proportional representation frequently leads to situations in which no party has a legislative majority and cross-party coalitions must be formed to organize a government.

Regional patterns. Changes in regional voting patterns are reflected in the makeup of parties in the House just as they are with the Senate parties. In 1960 almost 40 percent of the House Democratic membership came from the South (see Table 8–16). By 1990, southern Democrats constituted only 28.8 percent of the membership and Midwestern and Pacific Coast contingents had become more important. As southern influence in the House Democratic party has declined, it has grown significantly among the Republicans. Southern Republicans moved from being an insignificant segment of the party (3.5 percent) in 1960 to the largest regional contingent after the 1990 elections. This shift was symbolized in 1980 by the election of Trent Lott of Mississippi to be the Republican whip, the second ranking leadership post within the House GOP and Georgian Newt Gingrich's election to succeed him in 1989. Further evidence of the rising importance of the South in the House Republican party is the fact that Florida had one of the largest Republican state delegations after the 1990 elections. The Florida GOP delegation (ten members) was outranked only by those from California (seventeen), New York (thirteen) and Pennsylvania (twelve). The rise of the South in the House Republican party has been accompanied by a significant decline in the proportion of the party membership coming from the Midwest, Midatlantic, and Plains regions.

Incumbency. The pattern of incumbents gaining reelection is stronger in the House than in the Senate. Normally, over 90 percent of the House incumbents gain reelection. In 1986 the figure reached a postwar high of 98.5 percent. House incumbents benefit from the relatively homogeneous nature of their districts when compared to the larger and more socially diverse state-wide constituencies of senators. The distinctive socioeconomic character of individual House districts frequently gives a clear advantage to the candidate of one party or the other (e.g., predominantly black inner city districts are safely Democratic as are most big city districts with concentrations of blue collar workers of eastern and southern European heritage; middle and upper middle class suburban/small town districts are normally strongly Republican).

Incumbents are in a position to engage in extensive self-advertisement (e.g., mass mailings, constituent surveys, press releases, radio and television tapes, constituent service, town hall meetings) designed to project a favorable image. Of particular benefit to incumbents is the fact that major campaign efforts are not normally made on behalf of their challengers. Through skillful use of the advantages of public office, incumbents in most House districts are able to make their constituencies relatively safe for themselves for extended periods of time. Major struggles for control of the House, therefore, are fought out in the small proportion of districts in which incumbents are considered electorally vulnerable and in open seats, where no incumbent is seeking

Table 8–16 Composition of the Republican and Democratic Parties in the U.S. House of Representatives, by Region, 1960–1990

		Republicans		Democrats	
Region	Year	Seats Won	% of Party Membership in House	Seats Won	% of Party Membership in House
South	1960	6	3.5	98	37.5
	1990	39	23.4	77	28.8
Border	1960	6	3.5	32	12.3
	1990	11	6.6	23	8.6
New England	1960	14	8.2	14	5.4
	1990[a]	7	4.2	17	6.4
Mid Atlantic	1960	44	25.7	43	16.5
	1990	31	18.6	41	15.4
Midwest	1960	51	29.3	35	13.4
	1990	32	19.2	48	18.0
Plains	1960	25	14.6	6	2.3
	1990	12	7.2	12	4.5
Mountain	1960	4	2.3	11	4.2
	1990	15	9.0	9	3.7
Pacific Coast	1960	21	12.3	22	8.4
	1990	25	15.0	38	14.2

a. Indepedendent elected in Vermont.

Sources: Norman J. Ornstein, Thomas E. Mann, and Michael J. Malbin, *Vital Statistics on Congress, 1989–1990* (Washington, D.C.: Congressional Quarterly, 1990), pp. 11–12; *New York Times*, Nov. 8, 1990, Y A 16–17.

reelection. The advantages of incumbency are illustrated by the fact that between 1980 and 1990, the average House incumbent received 65.9 percent of the vote. These healthy reelection margins which House members in the aggregate pile up tend to mask the fact that a large proportion of the representatives have had at least one close election in their congressional careers. In the 101st Congress (1988-1990), 52 percent had had an election in which they won by 55 percent or less of the vote.[50] The sense of electoral insecurity which such elections can generate causes most members to work constantly to maintain a relationship of trust with their constituents.[51]

Presidential elections and House outcomes. Normally the party winning the presidency registers a net gain of House seats in presidential election years. Post World War II exceptions to this pattern of the

Table 8–17 Party Gains/Losses in House Seats in Presidential and Midterm Elections, 1946–1990

Year	Party Winning the Presidency	Net Seats Won/Lost
1946	(Democrat elected in 1944)	−55 Dem.
1948	Democrat	+75 Dem.
1950		−29 Dem.
1952	Republican	+22 Rep.
1954		−18 Rep.
1956	Republican	+2 Dem.
1958		−48 Rep.
1960	Democrat	+22 Rep.
1962		−4 Dem.
1964	Democrat	+37 Dem.
1966		−47 Dem.
1968	Republican	+5 Rep.
1970		−12 Rep.
1972	Republican	+12 Rep.
1974		−48 Rep.
1976	Democrat	+1 Dem.
1978		−15 Dem.
1980	Republican	+34 Rep.
1982		−26 Rep.
1984	Republican	+14 Rep.
1986		−5 Rep.
1988	Republican	−2 Rep.
1990		−8 Rep.

Sources: Norman J. Ornstein, Thomas E. Mann, and Michael J. Malbin, *Vital Statistics on Congress, 1989–1990* (Washington, D.C.: Congressional Quarterly, 1990), p. 49; *Congressional Quarterly Weekly Report*, Nov. 10, 1990, p. 3801.

party winning the presidency not picking up House seats occurred in 1956 and 1988 (net GOP loss of two seats in both elections) and 1960 (net Democratic loss of twenty-two seats). (See Table 8–17.) The advantages of incumbency and the tendency of voters to split their tickets between presidential and congressional races have reduced the likelihood of major shifts in the partisan composition of the House after a presidential election.

A much commented upon aspect of the 1984 presidential election landslide for Republican Ronald Reagan was the inability of the GOP to make large scale gains in the House (the Republicans scored a net gain of only fourteen seats). Obviously, the president's coattails did not have sufficient pulling power to bring into office with him significant numbers of additional Republican representatives. Many voters split their tickets between presidential and House elections. In

Alabama, for example, all five Democratic incumbent representatives won reelection by at least 60 percent of the vote, while Reagan was carrying the state for president by a 60 percent margin. The growing independence of presidential and House election outcomes (see Table 8-17) reflects the declining importance of partisanship as a decisional cue for voters in House races.

Congressional elections expert Gary Jacobson has concluded that a necessary condition for long presidential coattails is that "serious congressional candidates of the president-elect's party anticipate a good year well in advance and so position themselves to take advantage of the electoral benefits that later flow from the top of the ticket."[52] This clearly occurred in 1980 as GOP strategists anticipated a good year and succeeded in recruiting strong candidates for races in Democratic-held districts. The prospects of a strong showing for Republican candidates enabled them to raise substantial campaign warchests and mount major campaign efforts. Strong candidates with sufficient campaign resources were the key to the GOP gain of thirty-four House seats in the Reagan presidential victory of 1980. Jacobson's analysis reveals that only six House seats would have shifted to the Republicans in 1980 "if every Republican had enjoyed merely the average vote swing from 1978 to 1980 of three percentage points" in favor of the GOP. Victorious Republican challengers instead averaged an increase of 13 percent over the vote that candidates of their party had received in 1978.[53] Without the strong campaigns of these GOP challengers, the Reagan coattails in 1980 would in all likelihood have been virtually undetectable.

In 1984, the Republicans had greater difficulty taking advantage of the national trend which favored their party. The party's inability to dislodge incumbent Democrats in the 1982 midterm elections produced a lingering "bad memory" for some potentially strong GOP challengers who decided to bypass the 1984 House elections. Republican recruitment efforts were also hampered by the uncertain state of the recession racked economy during 1983, when most serious candidates had to make their decisions about whether to enter House election contests. The GOP also had difficulty recruiting strong challengers to Democratic incumbents for the 1988 House elections because of the decline in President Reagan's popularity due to the Iran-Contra affair, an uncertain economy in 1987, and polls in early 1988 showing the Democrats ahead of the Republicans. In addition, the Republicans have been hurt in recent elections by the shortage of Democratic open seats, which normally provide the best opportunity for a party to take seats away from the opposition.[54] Clearly, a large number of attractive, well-funded challengers and a substantial number of open seats are necessary conditions for major gains in House elections during presidential years.

Presidential coattails are also encouraged if congressional candidates are able to give voters a reason to connect the presidential vote and the congressional vote. This occurred in the presidential landslides of 1980 and 1964. In 1980, Republican congressional candidates were able to tap the public discontent with the general drift of political life as they joined Reagan in asking voters to "Vote Republican, for a change!" Similarly, Democratic candidates in 1964 campaigned on the theme of completing the agendas of the New Deal, John F. Kennedy, and Lydon B. Johnson. They also exploited the unpopularity of Barry Goldwater's policies by linking Republican congressional candidates with their party's presidential nominee. In both of these elections, the winning party gained landslide presidential victories with substantial coattails while advocating major changes in national policy.

By contrast in the presidential reelections of 1956, 1972, 1984, and 1988 there was an absence of coattails. Each election took place during a period of relative prosperity and improved international conditions. The emphasis of the winning campaigns, therefore, was upon continuity not change. Campaigns which stress continuity, however, give little rhetorical advantage to challengers seeking to dislodge incumbents. In 1984 and 1988 for example, Republicans seeking to oust Democrats had great difficulty blaming their opponents for obstructing progress, and Democrats sought to claim some of the credit for the good times. Thus the nature of the campaign themes and the issues which are salient to the voters also have a bearing on the extent of presidential coattails.[55]

House elections at midterm. Since the Civil War, in every midterm election except the one in 1934, the president's party has lost House seats. The one exception to this pattern occurred in the midst of the realignments of the early New Deal Era. A variety of explanations have been offered for the tendency of the president's party to lose House seats in midterm elections.

One factor influencing the extent of loss by the president's party in the House is that of the strength of the president's coattails in the previous election.[56] If a president sweeps a large number of candidates from his party into office with him, there is apt to be a sizeable bloc who will face difficult reelection bids at midterm when the president is not on the ballot. Those who are highly vulnerable are likely to fail in reelection. Thus in 1964, the Lyndon Johnson Democratic landslide coincided with a net gain of thirty-seven Democratic seats in the House. In the 1966 midterm election, many of these newly elected

Democrats lost their seats as the GOP registered a major net gain of forty-seven seats. However, if the presidential candidate lacks coattails and fails to carry House members of his party into office with him, the president's party is likely to suffer only minimal losses at midterm because few incumbents owe their previous election to presidential coattails. Such a pattern occurred in 1960 when John F. Kennedy ran behind most of his party's House candidates and the Democratic party actually lost twenty-two seats. As a result, few Democrats seeking reelection in 1962 owed their election to presidential coattails and Democrats sustained a loss of only four seats in the 1962 midterm elections.

The extent of midterm losses by the president's party also involves more immediate influences than the strength of presidential coattails in the previous election. Two such influences are presidential popularity and the state of the economy. Edward Tufte has analyzed the relationship of these factors to the vote received by candidates of the president's party in House midterm elections.[57] He discovered that both a decline in presidential popularity and a downturn in the economy correlated strongly with a fall-off in the popular vote for the president's party. While presidential popularity and economic conditions have significance for House elections at midterm, these kinds of aggregate national statistical analyses do not take fully into account the fact that House elections are decided by voters making choices among specific candidates in various congressional districts. Thus in 1982, the Republicans were able to hold their losses in the House to twenty-six seats, even though the depressed state of the economy and President Reagan's declining presidential popularity would have predicated a loss of a much more substantial magnitude. The inability of aggregate statistics to explain the extent of loss at midterm by the president's party has led political scientists to explore the consequences of strategic decision making by political activists.

Gary Jacobson and Samuel Kernell have suggested that economic conditions and the state of presidential popularity have their impact on the outcome of House races twelve to eighteen months in advance of the election when political leaders in both parties are making key decisions that will affect the outcome of specific House contests.[58] It is during this time that candidates make decisions about whether to run or not. If circumstances seem adverse for a party, promising challengers may conclude that they should wait and run when circumstances seem more likely to yield victory. Similarly, incumbents may elect to retire rather than face tough races when conditions are not favorable to their party. Or if conditions look good for a party, its incumbents are apt again to stand for reelection and it is easier to recruit strong challengers to run in districts held by the opposition. Contributors make similar calculations about the worth of investing in campaigns based upon assumptions concerning the possibility of a winnable race. Over a year in advance of an election, therefore, decisions are made about who the candidates will be, whether they will be well funded, and whether the party should adopt an offensive strategy designed to win seats from the opposition or adopt a defensive strategy that seeks to channel resources into retaining the party's existing seats. These decisions by political leaders go a long way toward determining the types of contests that will be waged in congressional districts across the nation.

An example of the effects of strategic decisions by political leaders on midterm elections can be seen in 1982. Democrats, anticipating a lagging economy and downturns in the president's popularity, mounted an effective campaign to recruit strong challengers to GOP incumbents and had little difficulty convincing their incumbent members to seek another term. By contrast, the GOP, confronted with adverse political circumstances, was forced into a defensive posture that sought to protect past gains in 1980 and could give less attention to races where the party was seeking to unseat incumbent Democrats.

Gubernatorial and State Legislative Elections

Democratic dominance. Despite setbacks in presidential politics, the Democratic party has dominated gubernatorial and state legislative elections. Between 1956 and 1990, the GOP has controlled a majority of the nation's governorships for only a brief two year period following the 1968 elections (see Figure 8–4) and the party never controlled both state legislative chambers in a majority of the states. The recent pattern of Republican presidential victories coupled with Democratic dominance of gubernatorial and state legislative elections (as well as House elections) has led to America having a two-tiered electoral system. This pattern of Republican presidential dominance and Democratic hegemony below the presidential level reflects the voters' differing expectations for governmental institutions and their perceptions of which party is best able to operate those institutions. A majority of the electorate appears to expect the presidency to protect broad national interests, and there has been a perception that the Republicans do this most effectively. At the same time, voters seem to expect the House of Representatives and state officials to protect specific government programs from which they derive benefits. To protect their government benefits, voters tend to believe

Figure 8–4: Party Control of Governorships (Percent)

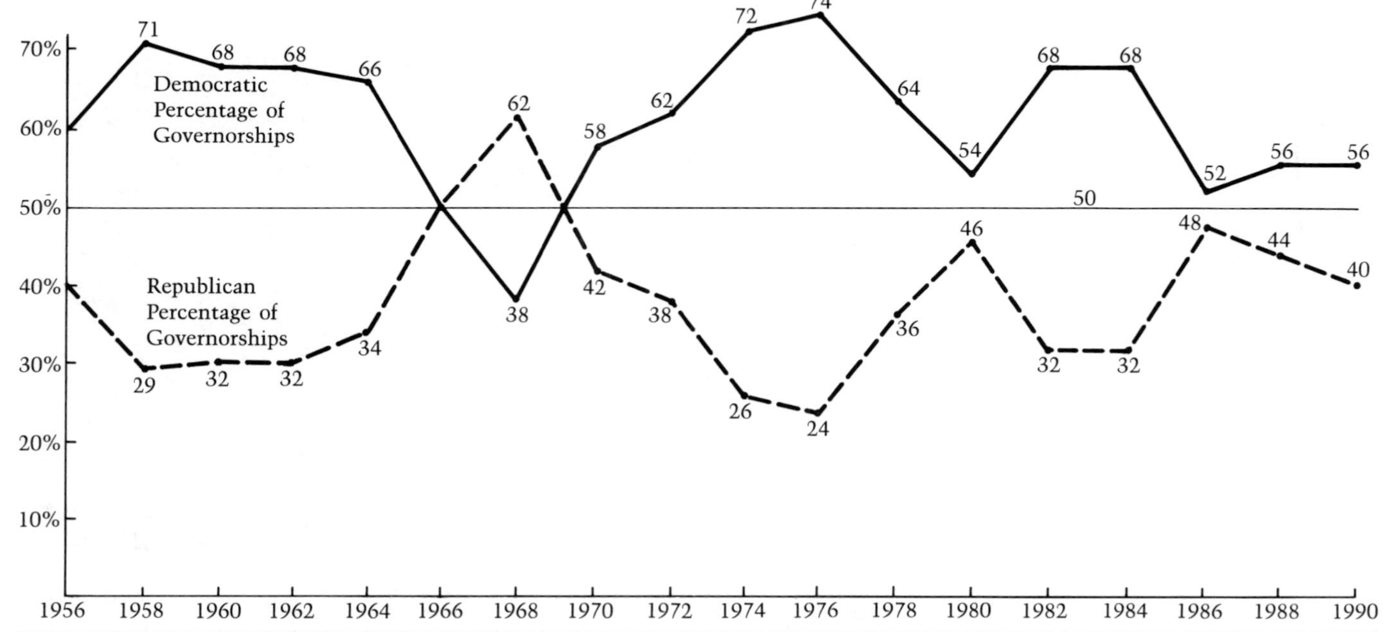

Note: In 1990, independents were elected in Alaska and Connecticut.

Sources: Statistical Abstract of the United States, 1990, p. 258; *Congressional Quarterly Weekly Report,* Nov. 10, 1990, p. 3838.

Table 8–18 Party Control of Governorships by Region, 1960–1990

	1960		1970		1980		1990		
Region	**Rep.**	**Dem.**	**Rep.**	**Dem.**	**Rep.**	**Dem.**	**Rep.**	**Dem.**	**Ind.**
New England	4	2	4	2	1	5	4	1	1
Mid Atlantic	1	3	3	1	3	1	1	3	0
Midwest	0	5	3	2	5	0	4	1	0
Plains	4	2	1	5	5	1	3	3	0
South	0	11	2	9	4	7	3	8	0
Border	0	5	2	3	1	4	1	4	0
Mountain	5	3	3	5	1	7	3	5	0
Pacific Coast	2	3	3	2	3	2	1	3	1
Totals	16	34	21	29	23	27	20	28	2

Sources: Statistical Abstract of the United States, 1990, p. 258; *New York Times,* Nov. 8, 1990, p. Y A13.

that Democrats will do a better job than the GOP.[59] Other explanations for America's two-tiered electoral system emphasize the advantages of incumbency, partisan gerrymandering, and the long term Democratic advantages in party identification.

Regional patterns. With the exception of Democrats in the South, there has been no consistent pattern of regional party dominance of governorships. Rather, party fortunes within regions have shown substantial variation over relatively short periods of time (see Table 8–18). For example, Republican control of the five midwestern governorships has ranged from zero to five between 1960 and 1980 and stood at four after the party gained two seats in 1990. Even the South has not escaped the rising tide of interparty competition. Every southern state but Georgia and Mississippi has elected at least one Republican governor since 1966 and it is now commonplace for southern Democratic governors to win elections with less than 55 percent of the vote.

One of the most interesting patterns of regional voting during the Reagan-Bush era has been the ability of the Democrats to win governorships in the Mountain states, one of the GOP's areas of greatest strength in presidential elections. Between 1980 and 1990 the Democrats have never held less than five of the eight governorships in this region and after the 1982 elections they held eight. Clearly, Democratic governors have been able to differentiate themselves from their national party and effectively appeal to the voters of this region.

The most distinctive pattern of regional voting for state legislative elections exists in the South, which has been overwhelmingly dominated by the Democrats. Whereas the Republicans have been able to compete effectively for governorships in most of the South since the mid-1960s, their progress toward competitiveness in state legislative elections has been much slower. There is, however, a growing GOP presence in southern state legislatures. Following the 1990 elections, the Republican party had one-third of the membership in the lower houses of Florida, Tennessee, Texas, and Virginia and was in a position to influence gubernatorial-legislative relations in veto situations. And in six of the southern states, the GOP held over 30 percent of the lower house seats. If these GOP gains continue, the traditional "nonpartisan" politics (i.e., intra-Democratic politics) of some southern state legislatures is likely to change to more conventional two party politics. True two party legislative politics in the South, however, is still a long way off, because the Republicans hold few seats in most of the region's state senates (e.g., four in Arkansas and six in Louisiana after the 1990 elections).

Incumbency. Incumbent governors tend to be more vulnerable to defeat than are United States senators or representatives. While incumbent representatives are returned at a 90 percent rate and senators at approximately the 80 percent level, governors since the 1950s have been reelected at an over 70 percent level. The higher level of gubernatorial vulnerability arises from the fact that governors are normally central figures in every controversial policy dispute within their states. There is also a public perception that governors have extensive power and are capable of handling state problems. Governors are likely, therefore, to be held accountable for the state of their states, especially when conditions become less than favorable.

Evidence is emerging that incumbency is becoming a major advantage for state legislators.[60] As state legislatures have developed into more professionalized institutions—annual sessions, higher pay, larger staffs, fewer voluntary retirements—the job of the legislator has become virtually a full time job in many states. Full time legislators have extensive opportunities to engage in self advertisement through use of their perquisites of office and normally have a much easier time raising campaign funds. In addition, they often enjoy the support of party caucus staffs and aggressive legislative campaign committees. As a result, defeating incumbent legislators has become more difficult. The National Conference of State Legislatures has reported that from 25 to 65 percent of the incumbent legislators in many states run unopposed in both the primary and general elections. In many states, incumbent legislators' reelection rates rival the 90+ percent level now prevalent in the U.S. House of Representatives. In Wisconsin, for example, State Assembly incumbents achieved an average reelection rate of 96 percent in 1986, 1988, and 1990; and, in 1988, 100 percent of incumbent state senators won reelection. If this trend toward incumbent advantage continues it may substantially retard partisan shifts in control of state legislative chambers.

Although incumbency carries with it significant advantages, its influence is not as pervasive in gubernatorial and state legislative elections as it is in congressional and senatorial elections. In state contests, the extent of partisan strength in the electorate and the capacities of the parties and their candidates to mobilize their supporters through campaign spending and other voter mobilization activities are important factors in determining the share of the vote each party receives. The Republicans, who have been the minority party in most states, can generally increase their share of the vote in gubernatorial races through higher levels of spending. By contrast, the electorally stronger Democrats quickly reach a point of diminishing returns from campaign spending.[61] In state legislative elections, challengers in both parties tend to benefit more than incumbents through increased expenditures.[62]

Presidential elections and state election outcomes. Gubernatorial elections have shown a marked independence from national trends in presidential years. In five of the ten elections since 1950, the party of the winning presidential candidate has actually lost governorships (1956, 1960, 1964, 1972, and 1988). Even in landslide years, such as 1964 and 1972, the party of the successful presidential candidate has sustained a loss of governorships (see Table 8-19). Similarly, in the 1988 Republican presidential victory for Bush the party lost two governorships. These data evidence the increased incidence of ticket splitting between presidential and gubernatorial elections since the turn of the century.

In the period 1896–1908, presidential and gubernatorial results within the states coincided in 89.5 percent of the elections.[63] This pattern continued into the 1920s. For example, in 1920 the Republicans won the governorship in each of the twenty-eight nonsouthern states carried by their presidential nominee, Warren G. Harding. By contrast, only 65 percent of the results coincided in the presidential elections from 1976 to 1988. Recently, the Democrats have been the least effective in capturing governorships while winning the presidency. Between 1952 and 1988, the party scored a net gain in governorships only once, in 1976. The GOP, by contrast, has more frequently registered gubernatorial gains when it was also winning the presidency (though the party's average gain has been only one governorship—see Table 8-19).

Table 8–19 Results of Gubernatorial Elections in Presidential and Midterm Election Years, 1950–1990

Year	Party Winning Presidential Election	Governorships at Stake				Republican Percent of Major-Party Vote	Election Result			Gains/Losses	
		Total	Rep.	Dem.	Ind.		Rep.	Dem.	Ind.	Rep.	Dem.
1950		33	15	18	0	53.1	25	23	0	+6	−6
1952	Rep.	31	15	16	0	47.0	30	18	0	+5	−5
1954		33	23	10	0	47.2	21	27	0	−9	+9
1956	Rep.	30	15	15	0	46.8	19	29	0	−2	+2
1958		33	13	20	0	44.1	14	35	0	−5	+6
1960	Dem.	27	12	15	0	46.5	16	34	0	+2	−1
1962		35	14	21	0	50.0	16	34	0	No change	
1964	Dem.	25	7	18	0	45.2	17	33	0	+1	−1
1966		35	14	21	0	53.1	25	25	0	+8	−8
1968	Rep.	21	8	13	0	47.3	31	19	0	+6	−6
1970		35	24	11	0	48.6	21	29	0	−10	+10
1972	Rep.	18	8	10	0	49.7	19	31	0	−2	+2
1974		35	11	24	0	43.6	13	36	1	−6	+5
1976	Dem.	14	6	8	0	50.8	12	37	1	−1	+1
1978		36	9	26	1	47.8	18	32	0	+6	−5
1980	Rep.	13	3	10	0	50.0	23	27	0	+5	−5
1982		36	16	20	0	45.6	16	34	0	−7	+7
1984	Rep.	13	7	6	0	51.7	16	34	0	+1	−1
1986						46.6	24	26	0	+8	−8
1988	Rep.	12	8	4	0	50.6	22	28	0	−2	+2
1990		36	16	20	0	44.9	20	28	2	−2	No change

Summary

Midterm elections
  Average number of governorships lost by:
    President's party 4.5
      Republicans 4.4
      Democrats 4.8

Presidential election years
  Average gain/loss for party of winning presidential candidate +1.0
  Average gain/loss when winning presidential party is Republican +1.6
  Average gain/loss when winning presidential party is Democratic −0.33

Sources: John F. Bibby, "State Elections at Midterm," in Thomas E. Mann and Norman J. Ornstein, eds., *The American Elections of 1982* (Washington, D.C.: American Enterprise Institute, 1983), p. 115; John F. Bibby, "State Elections: What 1984 Means for 1986," *Public Opinion* 8 (Feb./March, 1985): 52–54; *National Journal*, Nov. 12, 1988, pp. 2884–2885; *New York Times*, Nov. 9, 1990, p. Y A13.

State legislative elections are affected by presidential coattails. James Campbell has demonstrated that the presidential vote within a state consistently and positively influences the percentage of legislative seats gained by the party winning the presidency.[64] However, when partisan control of state legislative chambers is analyzed, it is apparent that there is substantial variation across the states in the impact of presidential campaigns. It is not unusual for the party of the winning presidential candidate to fail to gain control of additional legislative chambers or to actually lose control of chambers in presidential years. In six of the ten elections since 1950, the party winning the presidency has failed to achieve a net gain in legislative chambers and in five instances the winning party actually sustained a net loss. (See Table 8-20.)

State elections at midterm. Midterm gubernatorial elections are highly susceptible to national trends. Indeed, proportionate changes in partisan control of governorships are likely to be greater at midterm than switched party control of seats in the Congress. There is a consistent pattern of the president's party losing governorships during midterm elections. In every midterm election between 1950 and 1990, the president's party has lost governorships, except 1962 and 1986. The average midterm loss has been 4.5 governors, with the Republicans and Democrats both averaging a loss of four to five seats (see Table 8-19).

The sole instance of the president's party gaining governorships in the post World War II era occurred in 1986 when the GOP scored a net gain of eight governorships. With President Reagan riding a wave of popularity, the economy relatively strong, and an absence of foreign policy disturbance, local issues and candidate images dominated the 1986 elections. The Republicans in these circumstances were advantaged because they were defending only nine governorships while the Democrats were forced to defend twenty-seven. In addition, fifteen Democratic governors were not seeking reelection, thereby removing the Democrats' incumbent advantage factor.

One irony of the normal pattern of presidential party losses at midterm is that elections for governor seem more susceptible to national trends than do elections to the United States House of Representatives. A further irony in this pattern is that reformers have succeeded in shifting most gubernatorial elections from presidential to midterm years on the grounds that state elections should be fought on state issues rather than be contaminated by national issues and trends. It is apparent from the data presented in Table 8–19 that voters have

Table 8–20 Party Control of State Legislatures, 1950–1990

Year	Republicans Control Both Houses	Split Control	Nonpartisan Legislature	Democrats Control Both Houses	Net Number of Chambers Gained/Lost	
					Republicans	Democrats
1950	22	4	2	20	+9	−9
1952	26	2	2	18	+2	−2
1954	20	6	2	20	−8	+8
1956	17	6	2	23	−6	+6
1958	7	8	2	32	−18	+18
1960	14	5	2	29	+9	−9
1962	18	6	2	24	+9	−9
1964	7	9	2	32	−19	+19
1966	17	7	2	24	+18	−18
1968	20	8	2	20	+7	−7
1970	16	8	2	24	−8	+8
1972	16	8	2	24	No change	
1974	4	8	1	37	−24	+24
1976	4	10	1	35	+2	−2
1978	11	8	1	30	+12	−12
1980	15	5	1	29	+5	−5
1982	11	5	1	33	−8	+8
1984	11	10	1	28	+5	−5
1986	10	11	1	28	−3	+3
1988	7	13	1	29	−4	+4
1990	5	13	1	31	−4	+4

Summary

Midterm elections[a]	
Average number of chambers lost by:	
President's party	11.0
Republicans	10.4
Democrats	12.0
Presidential election years[b]	
Average gain of chambers for:	
Party of winning presidential candidate	1.1
Republicans	.5
Democrats	2.7

a. In each midterm election since 1950 the president's party lost control of legislative chambers.

b. In four of eight presidential election years the winning presidential candidate's party did *not* have a net gain in legislative chambers.

Sources: John F. Bibby, "State House Elections at Midterm," in Thomas E. Mann and Norman J. Ornstein, eds., *The American Elections of 1982* (Washington, D.C.: American Enterprise Institute, 1983), p. 123; National Conference of State Legislatures data.

foiled the reformers' objective. Instead, national trends appear to have a greater impact on midterm gubernatorial elections than on those occurring simultaneously with presidential elections.

The reason for this pattern is that in presidential years, gubernatorial candidates are not the most prominent persons on the ballot. But at midterm, they are the most visible candidates seeking public office. Governors, as has been noted, are widely perceived to be powerful officials involved in their states' major policy conflicts and are likely to be held accountable for conditions within their states. As the candidate at the top of the ticket, the governor stands exposed as the most readily available target of voter discontent, since the president is not on the ballot. The pattern of governors of the president's party being blamed for adverse conditions was particularly apparent in the 1982 midterm elections when the GOP sustained a net loss of seven governorships. Republican candidates that year found themselves constantly on the defensive because of the depressed state of the national economy as Democratic candidates focused their campaigns upon the adverse effects of the recession on their states[65]

Midterm elections for state legislatures also show a consistent pattern of the president's party losing legislative seats and suffering a net loss in control of state legislative chambers[66] (see Table 8–20). On average, the president's party has lost eleven legislative chambers in the midterm elections since 1950. As is true of gubernatorial elections, shifts in partisan control of legislative chambers tend to be greater in midterm elections than in presidential elections.

Voters, Elections, and Control of Government

Election results reflect the decisions of voters influenced by long-term affiliations with either the Republican or Democratic party and more short-term considerations relating to candidates and issues. The voters' electoral choices produce a wide array of different patterns of partisan control over governmental offices. These patterns of party control mirror the effects of regional diversity, incumbency, economic conditions, campaign effort, and the timing of elections. Those who assume governmental office as a result of elections constitute the party-in-government. It is these partisan leaders who carry major responsibility for the enunciation of party policy and for shaping the public's image of the party. They are also responsible for the content of governmental policies that affect the nation and the world. The role of the party-in-government and its impact on policy making are the concerns of the following chapter.

Suggestions for Further Reading

Abramson, Paul R.; Aldrich, John H.; and Rohde, David W. *Change and Continuity in the 1988 Elections*. Washington, D.C.: CQ Press, 1990.

Asher, Herbert B. *Presidential Elections and American Politics* 4th ed. Chicago, Ill.: Dorsey Press, 1988.

Campbell, Angus; Converse, Phillip E.; Miller, Warren E.; and Stokes, Donald E. *The American Voter*. New York: Wiley, 1960.

Flanigan, William H. and Zingale, Nancy H. *Political Behavior of the American Electorate,* 7th ed. Washington, D.C.: CQ Press, 1991.

Jacobson, Gary C. *The Electoral Origins of Divided Government*. Boulder, Colo.: Westview Press, 1990.

Nie, Norman; Verba, Sidney; and Petrocik, John R. *The Changing American Voter.* Cambridge, Mass.: Harvard University Press, 1976.

Wattenberg, Martin P. *The Decline of American Political Parties,* 1952–1988. Cambridge, Mass.: Harvard University Press, 1989.

Wolfinger, Raymond E. and Rosenstone, Steven J. *Who Votes?* New Haven, Conn.: Yale University Press, 1980.

Notes

1. *Statistical Abstract of the United States*, 1990, p.269.
2. C. Richard Hofstetter, "Interparty Competition and Electoral Turnout: The Case of Indiana," *American Journal of Political Science* 17 (Aug. 1973): 351–366.
3. Jae-On Kim, John R. Petrocik, and Stephen Enokson, "Voter Turnout among the American States: Systematic and Individual Components," *American Political Science Review* 69 (March 1975): 107–123.
4. Raymond E. Wolfinger and Steven J. Rosenstone, *Who Votes?* (New Haven, Conn.: Yale University Press, 1980), p. 41. For a cross-national analysis of factors influencing turnout, see G. Bingham Powell," American Turnout in Comparative Perspective," *American Political Science Review*, 80 (March, 1986): 17–43.
5. William H. Flanigan and Nancy H. Zingale, *Political Behavior of the American Electorate*, 6th ed. (Boston, Mass.: Allyn and Bacon, 1987), p. 14–20. For a multi-election analysis of turnout, see Lee Sigelman, Philip W. Roeder, Malcolm E. Jewell, and Michael A. Baer, "Voting and Nonvoting: A Multi-Election Perspective, *American Journal of Political Science*, 29 (Nov. 1985): 749–765.
6. Reported in *Congressional Quarterly Weekly Report*, Jan. 21, 1989, p. 138. See also Paul R. Abramson, John H. Aldrich, and David W. Rohde, *Change and Continuity in the 1988 Election* (Washington, D.C.: C Q Press, 1990), pp. 108–113.
7. Jeff Alderman, ABC News Poll, Survey 0080, conducted June 29–July13, 1983.
8. Gregory A. Caldeira and Samuel C. Patterson, "Contextual Influences on Participation in U.S. State Legislative Elections," *Legislative Studies*

Quarterly 7 (Aug. 1982): 359–381; Samuel C. Patterson and Gregory A. Caldeira, "Getting Out the Vote: Participation in Gubernatorial Elections," *American Political Science Review* 77 (Sept. 1983): 675–689; see also Gregory A. Caldeira, Samuel C. Patterson, and Gregory A. Markko, "The Mobilization of Voters in Congressional Elections," *Journal of Politics* 47 (May 1985): 490–509.

9. *Statistical Abstract of the United States, 1990*, p. 263. Others have estimated the turnout of registered voters at 87 percent. See David Glass, Peverill Squire, and Raymond Wolfinger, "Voter Turnout: An International Comparison," *Public Opinion* 6 (Dec./Jan., 1984): 52.
10. Ivor Crewe, "As the World Turns Out," *Public Opinion* 4 (Feb./March, 1981): 52.
11. Abramson, Aldrich, and Rohde, *Change and Continuity*, p. 111. See also Austin Ranney, "Nonvoting Is Not a Social Disease," *Public Opinion* 4 (Oct./Nov., 1983): 17.
12. Seymour Martin Lipset and William Schneider, *The Confidence Gap* (Washington, D.C.: American Enterprise Institute, 1983), p. 410.
13. Everett Carll Ladd, *The American Polity* (New York: Norton, 1985), p. 397.
14. A classic statement of the concept of party identification is contained in Angus Campbell, Phillip E. Converse, Warren E. Miller, and Donald E. Stokes, *The American Voter* (New York: Wiley, 1960); see especially pp. 121–128.
15. Fred I. Greenstein, *Children and Politics* (New Haven, Conn.: Yale University Press, 1965), p. 71.
16. Herbert B. Asher, *Presidential Elections and American Politics*, 4th ed. (Homewood, Ill.: Dorsey Press, 1988), p. 70
17. Ibid., pp. 70–75.
18. Flanigan and Zingale, *Political Behavior*, p. 47; Asher, *Presidential Elections* p. 86.
19. Asher, *Presidential Elections*, pp. 87–89.
20. CBS/*New York Times* Surveys, *New York Times*, Nov. 9, 1980, Nov. 8, 1984, Nov. 16, 1988.
21. Asher, *Presidential Elections*, pp. 78–79.
22. J. Merrill Shanks and Warren E. Miller, "Policy Direction and Performance Evaluation: Complementary Explanations of the Reagan Elections," a paper prepared for delivery at the Annual Meeting of the American Political Science Association, New Orleans, Aug. 29–Sept. 1, 1985, pp. 12–15.
23. Martin P. Wattenberg, *The Decline of American Political Parties, 1952–1988* (Cambridge, Mass.: Harvard University Press, 1990), p. 20.
24. For more detailed analyses, see Abramson, Aldrich, and Rohde, *Change and Continuity in the 1988 Elections*, pp. 203–205.
25. Seymour Martin Lipset, "The Elections, The Economy and Public Opinion," *P.S.* 18 (Winter 1985): 35.
26. Asher, *Presidential Elections*, pp. 113, 156, 163–164.
27. William Schneider, "An Uncertain Consensus," *National Journal*, Nov. 10, 1985, p. 2131.

28. Flanigan and Zingale, *Political Behavior*, pp. 123–124.
29. William Schneider, "Solidarity's Not Enough," *National Journal*, Nov. 12, 1988, p. 2854.
30. Norman Nie, Sidney Verba, and John R. Petrocik, *The Changing American Voter* (Cambridge, Mass.: Harvard University Press, 1976), ch. 10.
31. J. Merrill Shanks and Warren E. Miller, "Policy Direction and Performance Evaluation: Complementary Explanations of the Reagan Elections," a paper presented at the annual meeting of the American Political Science Association, Aug. 29–Sept.1, 1985.
32. Flanigan and Zingale, *Political Behavior of the American Electorate*, pp. 134–140; for analysis of issue voting in 1988, see Abramson, Aldrich, and Rohde, *Continuity and Change in the 1988 Elections*, ch. 6.
33. Arthur H. Miller, Warren E. Miller, Alden S. Raine, and Thad A. Brown, "A Majority Party in Disarray: Policy Polarization in the 1972 Election," *American Political Science Review* 70 (Sept. 1976): 760.
34. Peter B. Natchez, "Issues and Voters in the 1972 Elections," in *University Programs Modular Studies* (Morristown, N.J.: General Learning Press, 1974), p. 5. See also Asher, *Presidential Elections*, pp. 146–147.
35. Arther H. Miller and Martin P. Wattenberg, "Throwing the Rascals Out: Policy Performance Evaluations of Presidential Candidates," *American Political Science Review* 79 (June 1985): 359–373. See also Morris Fiorina, *Retrospective Voting in American National Elections* (New Haven, Conn.: Yale University Press, 1981).
36. Abramson, Aldrich, and Rohde, *Continuity and Change in the Elections of 1988*, pp. 190–191.
37. John R. Petrocik, "Issue and Agenda: Electional Coalitions in the 1988 Elections," a paper prepared for the annual meeting of the American Political Science Association, Aug. 31–Sept. 3, 1989.
38. John R. Petrocik and Frederick T. Steeper, "Realignment and 1984: New Coalitions and New Majorities?," *Election Politics* 2 (Winter 1984–1985): 5.
39. Abramson, Aldrich, and Rohde, *Continuity and Change in the 1988 Elections*, pp. 128–130.
40. Flanigan and Zingale, *Political Behavior*, pp. 63–64.
41. Petrocik and Steeper, "Realignment and 1984," p. 5.
42. John R. Petrocik, *Party Coalitions: Realignments and the Decline of the New Deal Party System* (Chicago, Ill.: University of Chicago Press, 1981), pp. 65–66.
43. For an analysis of gender based differences on issues, see *Public Opinion*, April/May 1982, pp. 27–31.
44. William Schneider, "Democrats and Republicans, Liberals, and Conservatives," in Seymour Martin Lipset, *Party Coalitions in the 1980s*, pp. 203–204.
45. Ibid., p. 204.
46. Nathan Glazer, "The Structure of Ethnicity," *Public Opinion* 7 (Oct./Nov. 1984): 5.
47. Petrocik and Steeper, "Realignment and 1984," p. 7.

48. Everett Carll Ladd, "The 1988 Elections: Continuation of the Post-New Deal System," *Public Opinion Quarterly* 104 (Spring 1989): 1–18.
49. Petrocik and Steeper, "Realignment and 1984," p. 8.
50. Norman J. Ornstein, Thomas E. Mann, and Michael J. Malbin, *Vital Statistics on Congress*, 1989–1990 (Washington, D.C.: Congressional Quarterly, 1990), p. 60.
51. See David R. Mayhew, *Congress: The Electoral Connection* (New Haven, Yale University Press, 1984) ch. 2; Richard Fenno, Jr., *Homestyle* (Boston, Mass.: Little, Brown, 1978).
52. Gary C. Jacobson, "Congress: Politics after a Landslide without Coattails," in Michael Nelson, ed., *The Elections of 1984* (Washington, D. C.: CQ Press, 1985), p. 217.
53. Ibid.
54. Gary C. Jacobson, "Congress: A Singular Continuity," in Michael Nelson, ed., *The Elections of 1988* (Washington, D.C.: CQ Press, 1989), pp. 128–131; on the Republican difficulty in recruiting strong challengers and in winning open seats, see Gary C. Jacobson, *The Electoral Origins of Divided Government*, 1946–1988 (Boulder, Colo.: Westview Press, 1990), ch. 3 and 4.
55. Jacobson, "Congress: Politics after a Landslide," pp. 220–221.
56. Barbara Hinckley, "Interpreting Midterm Elections," *American Political Science Review* 59 (Sept. 1967): 694–700.
57. Edward Tufte, "Determinants of the Outcome of Midterm Congressional Elections," *American Political Science Review* 67 (Sept. 1975): 812–826.
58. Gary C. Jacobson and Samuel Kernell, *Strategy and Choice in Congressional Elections* (New Haven, Conn.: Yale University Press, 1981).
59. Jacobson, *The Electoral Origins of Divided Government*, ch. 6; see also Byron E. Shafer, ed., *The End of Realignment* (Madison: University of Wisconsin Press, 1991), ch. 3.
60. Malcolm E. Jewell and David Breaux, "The Effect of Incumbency on State Legislative Elections," *Legislative Studies Quarterly* 13 (Nov. 1988): 477–494.
61. Samuel C. Patterson, "Campaign Spending in Contests for Governor," *Western Political Quarterly* 35 (December 1982): 469–474; see also Samuel C. Patterson and Gregory A. Caldeira, "The Etiology of Partisan Competition," *American Political Science Review* 78 (Sept. 1984): 691–707.
62. Gregory A. Caldeira and Samuel C. Patterson, "Bringing Home the Votes: Electoral Outcomes in State Legislative Races," *Political Behavior* 4 (1982): 33–67).
63. Larry Sabato, *Goodbye to Good-time Charlie: The American Govenorship Transformed*, 2nd ed. (Washington, D.C.: CQ Press 1983), p. 139.
64. James E. Campbell, "Presidential Coattails and Midterm Losses in State Legislative Elections," *American Political Science Review*, 80 (March 1986): 45–63.

65. The impact of the national economy on gubernatorial and legislative elections is analyzed by John E. Chubb, "Institutions, the Economy and the Dynamics of State Elections," *American Political Science Review* 82 (March 1988): 133–154.
66. Campbell, "Presidential Coattails"; John F. Bibby, "State House Elections at Midterm," in Thomas E. Mann and Norman J. Ornstein, eds., *The American Elections of 1982* (Washington, D.C.: American Enterprise Institute, 1983), pp. 121–125.

CHAPTER 9

Parties in the Government

In national and state government, Republicans and Democrats "make the major decision about who pays and who receives."[1] Only leaders of these two major parties have occupied the Oval Office in the White House since the Civil War; only an occasional independent ever gains election to the House or Senate, and those that do quickly associate themselves with one of the major parties for organizational purposes and committee assignments; since 1942 only three people have been elected to governorships as third party candidates or independents (James Longley of Maine in 1974, Walter Hickel of Alaska and Lowell Weiker of Connecticut, both in 1990); and following the 1988 elections only one state senator and three state representatives were elected as independents or minor party candidates (not including the nonpartisan unicameral legislature of Nebraska). American government is organized on a partisan basis. Presidents and governors customarily appoint fellow members of their party to key posts within their administrations and to judicial vacancies. In Congress and most state legislatures, key leadership posts go to members of the majority party and committees are aligned to give the dominant party numerical control. Partisans and partisanship pervade American government. Even so, American parties face major obstacles in guiding the policy making machinery.

The party-in-government must operate within a constitutional order that was designed to make coordinated and cooperative action difficult. Federalism and separation of powers were conceived as checks and balances on organized factions, not as facilitators of cooperation. American parties are divided geographically by federalism, which creates thousands of separate constituencies in which elected officials can operate with relative autonomy. Separation of powers divides the parties functionally and reduces the need for cooperation among party leaders in the executive and legislative branches. In a parliamentary system, legislators who fail to support their party's prime minister run the risk of forcing the cabinet to resign and the calling of new parliamentary elections. American legislators, however, are not required to support the policies of a president or governor of their party in order to maintain partisan control of the executive branch or to preserve their own positions in the legislature. Separation of powers assures executives of fixed terms of office irrespective of which party controls the legislature, and imposes no special obligations of loyalty to the executive's policies upon the party's legislators.

Within America's separation of powers system, there exists a "*separation of party organizations*"[2] as well. When President George Bush is called the leader of the Republican party, or President Jimmy Carter was said to be the leader of the Democratic party, there is an implication that these men head a single organizational entity. But American parties are not of this type. There is a "presidential party" composed of presidential appointees to the executive branch, national convention delegates, the national committee, and the president's personal campaign organization. There is also a "congressional party" with fully organized structures in both chambers that operates quite autonomously from the presidential party. In addition, there are gubernatorial and legislative parties in the states.

The separateness of these organizations is particularly noticeable in terms of nominations. Presidents play no significant role in the selection of party nominees for the House and Senate. Rather, they are chosen by their districts and states in primary elections. Presidents may encourage particular individuals to seek party nominations, but they cannot prevent others from running nor guarantee the nomination to their favorite candidates.

In a similar manner, representatives and senators have only the most limited influence upon presidential nominations. The largest proportion of national convention delegates are selected by presidential primaries in which congressional endorsements are of scant value. Nor are congressional leaders in a strong position to win presidential nominations for themselves. Winning a presidential nomination requires virtually full time campaigning for two to four years—time that is not available to a senator or representative with major congressional leadership responsibilities. As Austin Ranney has observed, members of Congress have about "as little power over whom their party nominates for the presidency as the president has over whom his party nominates for the House and Senate."[3] The separateness of the presidential and congressional parties stemming from the lack of centralized control of the nominating process was cogently stated by Richard E. Neustadt.

> What the Constitution separates, our political parties do not combine. The parties are themselves composed of separate organizations sharing public authority. The authority consists of nominating powers. Our national parties are confederations of state and local institutions, with a headquarters that represents the White House, more or less, if the party has a President in office. These confederacies manage presidential nominations. All other public offices depend upon electorates confined within the states. All other nominations are controlled within the states. The President and congressmen who bear one party's label are divided by dependence upon different sets of voters. The differences are sharpest at the stage of nomination. The White House has too small a share in nominating congressmen, and Congress has too little weight in nominating Presidents for party to erase their constitu-

> tional separation. Party links are stronger than is frequently supposed, but nominating processes assure the separation.[4]

Presidents have even less influence over the selection of congressional leaders than they do over nominations. Congressmen and senators strongly resent presidential intrusion into their leadership selection processes. As a result, even expressions of support by presidents are rare and there are no verified instances of presidents seeking to oust a speaker, floor leader, or whip.[5] Just as presidents do not influence selection of congressional party leaders, representatives and senators do not exert significant influence upon the organization of the White House staff which normally consists of principal and closest advisors to the president.

The existence of a separate and distinct "presidential party" alongside a "congressional party" has, in the words of Theodore J. Lowi, provided the basis for a "*real* separation of powers" within the government. That is, the separation of organizations within the parties reinforces and makes meaningful the separation of powers created by the writers of the Constitution.[6]

The separateness of the presidential and congressional parties at the national level is replicated in most of the states, where distinct gubernatorial and legislative party structures normally exist. Just as the national constitutional provisions for separation of powers make a unified party difficult to achieve, similar provisions in state constitutions cause party fragmentation. Yet for all their diffuseness, American parties do have a center of gravity. They tend to be executive centered coalitions.[7] The president is the only party leader with a truly national constituency and it is his nomination and general election campaigns that are the chief activities of the national party. His visibility makes him and his policies the symbols of the party to the mass electorate. The leverage derived from his visibility and mass support enhance the ability of the president to lead the government and persuade others in public office to support his policies. Even with all the difficulties that confront any president seeking to exert party leadership, his position is infinitely stronger than that of any competing party leader. In state government, governors tend to enjoy a similar level of prominence to that of presidents in national politics.

The President as Party Leader

Presidential leadership involves exerting influence over the national party organization, the Congress, the executive branch, and even the judiciary. In his relations with each of these institutions, the resources of the president are substantial, but he operates under severe constraints imposed by the Constitution and the party system.

The President and the National Party

A president needs to assert dominance over his party's organizational structure lest it become an independent power center during his administration or be used by rivals working against his policies and renomination. Of particular importance is controlling the national committee. It is the most inclusive party organization in the country because its membership includes representatives of all the state parties and key party constituencies. It operates a year-round headquarters, staffed by professionals in contact with political leaders around the country, and it has resources that can be used to underwrite White House political activities—polls, fund-raising expenses, and presidential travel. The national committee also exerts substantial influence over presidential nominations through its role in developing national party rules, administering those rules, and handling the arrangements for national conventions. These activities require that presidential interests be protected within the national committee.

Although he has no formal role in the national committee, the president's informal influence over the selection of the national chairman is nearly total. His "recommendations" are customarily accepted without dissent. For example, even with the Watergate scandals washing over the Nixon Administration and about to sink it, the president was able to designate George Bush as Republican National Committee chairman.

Presidents are anxious to have the national committee chairman act as the president's man rather than as the committee's man with an agenda and constituency of his own. The fate of two recent Republican National Committee (RNC) chairmen is illustrative. After the GOP lost the 1976 elections, William Brock, a former Tennessee senator, was elected by the RNC to be its chairman. His tenure is widely viewed as one of the most successful in the party's history as the RNC instituted an impressive array of fund raising, candidate recruitment, and candidate and state party support programs that are credited with helping the party achieve major gains in the 1978 and 1980 elections. Brock, however, was viewed during the 1980 presidential primaries as something less than a Reagan enthusiast by the candidate's key advisors, who sought Brock's ouster as national chairman. While Ronald Reagan, himself, declined to have Brock dismissed, the Reagan dominated national convention in 1980 adopted a rules change requiring that the national committee officers be elected immediately after the convention and in January of each odd numbered year thereafter. Although the Reagan forces permitted Brock to be reelected after the 1980 convention, they installed as RNC deputy chairman and chief operating officer, Drew Lewis, the Reagan campaign chairman in Pennsylvania. And in January, 1981, the White House passed the word that Nevada state GOP chairman, Richard Richards was the presidential choice for RNC chairman. Richards was duly elected without opposition. (Brock, however, was given the cabinet rank post of United States Trade Representative and later appointed Secretary of Labor in the Reagan Administration.)

After two years on the job and amidst rumors of White House dissatisfaction with his performance, Richards was replaced in a major overhaul of the national party that was dictated by the White House. The president wished to have his friend and confidant Senator Paul Laxalt (Nev.) head the national committee. RNC rules, however, required that the RNC chairman serve in a full time capacity—something that was impossible for Laxalt because of his Senate duties. To overcome this obstacle, the White House arranged for Laxalt to assume the newly created post of party General Chairman, while having the RNC elect Frank Fahrenkopf, the state chairman in Nevada, to the national chairmanship.

President George Bush, like his predecessor, has controlled the selection of GOP national chairmen. His first chairman was Lee Atwater (1989–1991), a close political advisor who managed Bush's presidential campaign in 1988. When Atwater developed a fatal illness and was forced to resign, Bush in 1991 tapped Secretary of Agriculture Clayton Yuetter to replace him. Since Yuetter had had relatively little campaign experience, it was clear that he was expected to serve as a spokesperson for the administration and to follow White House direction.

Democratic presidents have also controlled the selection of Democratic National Committee (DNC) leaders. John F. Kennedy installed his ally, John Bailey, the state chairman of Connecticut, as DNC chairman after his election. Jimmy Carter designated former Governor Kenneth Curtis (Me.) to be his first national party chairman; when Curtis resigned in frustration at the Carter White House's lack of interest in party building activities, the president designated his Deputy Secretary of Agriculture, Texan John White, to be his successor.

For the party controlling the presidency, national committee subordination to the White House is almost complete, as presidential interests are given priority. For example, the Carter White House in 1977 substantially revamped the reform commission appointed in 1975 by National Chairman Robert Strauss to examine the causes and consequences of the proliferation of presidential primaries. The size of the commission was doubled and faithful Carter supporters were appointed "to make sure that the commission did not exercise its enlarged mandate to review the party's national convention delegate selection rules in any way that might make Carter's renomination more difficult in 1980."[8] The report of the Commission demonstrated that the White House goal was achieved.

The leadership of the national committees customarily finds it necessary to work under the supervision of White House aides charged with responsibility for protecting the president's political interests. In the Reagan White House, this responsibility was formalized by the designation of one of the president's key aides as the Assistant to the President for Political and Government Affairs. Edward Rollins, who held this post during most of Reagan's first term, left the White House staff temporarily to manage the president's renomination and general election campaigns and then reassumed his White House post after the 1984 election. President Bush has relied more on the RNC to handle political business (especially while Lee Atwater was RNC chairman), but he has maintained a White House Office of Political Affairs, and the influence of Chief of Staff John Sununu on the RNC has been substantial.

White House personnel and political operatives have also assumed responsibility for handling administration patronage appointments. This reflects an unwillingness on the part of presidents and their supporters to place their executive appointments at the disposal of the party organization for purposes of party building. There is instead an emphasis on building a personal organization supportive of the president. The creation of personnel and political offices in the White House, operating with substantial autonomy from the national committees, is a departure from past practice when the national committees were the chief patronage dispensing agents. Until 1953, when Dwight Eisenhower stopped the practice, the national party chairman had frequently served simultaneously as postmaster general and handled the vast patronage available to the party within the postal system.[9] The reform of the postal service in the 1970s has removed the agency from the patronage system and precluded national committee involvement in its hiring practices.

National committees have also seen their presidential campaign roles restricted since the 1960s. National party chairmen formerly served as the campaign managers of presidential reelection campaigns and the campaigns were run out of the national committee headquarters. The last national chairman charged with responsibility for a presidential reelection campaign was Leonard Hall, who as RNC chairman managed the 1956 Eisenhower campaign. Since then incumbent presidents have set up their own personal campaign organizations and relegated the national committee to a supportive role. The Federal Election Campaign Act encourages this separation of the national committee from the presidential campaign committee responsible for the receipt and expenditure of funds, while also permitting separate national committee spending on presidential campaigns that are receiving public financing.

The assumption of traditional party functions by the White House staff and the subordination of the national committee to the White House have made being national chairman of the president's party a frequently frustrating experience. Based on his experiences as RNC chairman under President Richard Nixon in 1972, Senator Bob Dole (R-Kans.) commented, "When your party's in power, the chairman doesn't have any decision-making role." Kenneth Curtis, Carter's first DNC chairman, in announcing his resignation described the party chairmanship as "this lousy job" and Reagan's first chairman, Richard Richards, expressed similar sentiments of frustration when he announced in 1982, amidst rumors that he was being pushed out, that he would not seek a second term. He also complained about the White House staff acting as a buffer between the president and the party. "If I had my choice, I would not have a political shop in the White House," he stated.[10]

While the president and his chief aides exercise impressive influence over their party's national committee, national committees do have an element of autonomy in their operations. The programs of assistance that they operate for the benefit of state parties and candidates develop constituencies that expect continued support. This is particularly true within the Republican party which because of its superior financial resources has developed a wide range of support programs for state parties. It is doubtful that any president could discontinue these RNC activities now that they are well established without seriously undermining his position with his party. It is interesting to note, for example, that even though key Reagan supporters wanted Bill Brock removed as national chairman as soon as Reagan won the GOP nomination in 1980, the Reagan dominated RNC continued and even expanded programs of support for state parties and candidates that were initiated by Brock.

There is also an expectation that national chairmen will conduct their operations in a fair manner when handling national convention arrangements in instances when an incumbent president is being challenged for his party's nomination. When President Gerald Ford was challenged in 1976 by Ronald Reagan and President Jimmy Carter faced opposition from Senator Edward Kennedy in 1980, Mary Louise Smith of the RNC and John C. White of the DNC both sought to convey an image of neutrality in national committee operations relating to the convention, even though both were acknowledged supporters of their incumbent presidents.

As we noted in Chapter 4, governors frequently exert influence over their state party committees which is at least as pervasive as that of the president over the national committee. Like presidents, governors work to prevent their state committees from becoming competing or hostile centers of power within the party. Unlike the national committee-presidential relationship, however, there have periodically been instances of alienation and conflict between governors and state party committees. The most common pattern, however, has been for governors to play a substantial role in the selection of state chairmen, to be consulted on state party issues, and to assist the party in such activities as fund raising and candidate recruitment.

Presidential Nominations and the Building of Governing Coalitions

The pattern of national committee subordination to the president and his staff and the tendency of presidents to set up their own personal political operations within the White House is a reflection of the changed process of coalition building involved in gaining presidential nominations. As was noted in Chapter 6, winning a presidential nomination involves intense personal campaigning and an organization equipped to contest presidential primaries and party caucuses which are open to almost any interested citizen. It is no longer a process of forging a coalition from amongst state and local party leaders, governors, senators, congressmen, mayors, and interest groups aligned with the party. Prior to the 1970s, candidates for presidential nominations were required to build electoral coalitions around party leaders and elected officials. In the process of their negotiations with these leaders, presidential candidates became well acquainted with many of the people who would be important to them once they entered the Oval Office. In effect, presidents began to forge a governing coalition while they sought their party's nomination. The changes in the nominating process, which have substantially diminished the power of party and elected officials, have had the effect, according to Austin Ranney, of separating "the process of building the coalition needed for the nomination from the process of building the coalition needed for governing."[11] Presidential leadership of the government, already made difficult by the constitutional restrictions of federalism and separation of powers, is made even more difficult by the nature of the nomination process. *Washington Post* columnist David Broder noted the consequences of the changed nominating process for governance while comparing the experiences of John F. Kennedy and Jimmy Carter.

> Kennedy ran in four contested primaries in 1960. Contrast four with the thirty-four that await anyone who wants the nomination in 1980. After Kennedy won West Virginia, he still had to persuade the leaders of his party—the governors, the mayors, the leaders of allied interest groups—particularly organized labor—that they could stake their reputations on his qualities as the best man to be the standard bearer for the party. Contrast that with Jimmy Carter, who never had to meet, and in fact, in many cases, did not meet, those similar officials until after he had achieved the Democratic nomination.
>
> The significance of the difference for the presidency is that in one case, a man, if he is elected, comes with the alliances that make it possible for him to organize the coalitions and support necessary to lead a government.
>
> In the present nominating system, he comes as a fellow whose only coalition is whatever he got out of the living rooms of Iowa [precinct caucuses]. If there is one thing that Jimmy Carter's frustration in office ought to teach us, it is that the affiliation and commitment that is made on Iowa caucus night and New Hampshire primary day is not by itself sufficient to sustain a man for four years in the White House.[12]

The difficult leadership position in which an American president finds himself upon entering the White House is quite different than that of most chief executives in other Western style democracies. In the United Kingdom, for example, the leader of the opposition party is in an officially recognized governmental position. The opposition leader stands ready to assume the prime ministership in the event the cabinet is forced to resign or his party wins a national election. His governing coalition is already in place and he is, therefore, in a stronger position than an American president to exert leadership over the government. American presidents, by contrast, only assume leadership of their party upon winning a presidential nomination and they continue to hold the leadership only if they can win the general election.[13]

The Party, the President, and Congress

The president's policy making powers are shared with the Congress even in areas like international relations and national security. Much of what a president can accomplish in terms of policy-making requires the cooperation of the Congress. In gaining policy influence with the Congress, presidents are constantly required to use the kinship which they share with fellow party members in the legislature. These partisan ties, however, are not of a binding character and tensions always exist between the president and Congress.

Sources of Presidential-Congressional Differences

Electoral bases. The circumstances of elections to the Congress and presidency carry the seeds for conflict between the president and his fellow partisans on the Hill. As noted previously, presidents are nominated and elected without the development of mutual obligations between the president and the congressional party. He owes them nothing for his victory. But by the same token, members of the Congress also perceive that they got there largely through their own efforts. With the president having no real control over his party's congressional nominations, presidential leverage with legislators is fractured early in the electoral process.

Nor does the president derive substantial influence over members of Congress from the general election process. Presidential coattails are becoming rather threadbare as voters increasingly split their tickets in presidential and congressional contests.[14] This has weakened the position of the president vis-à-vis the Congress because it has diminished the perception among members that they owe their election at least in part to the president's popularity and that they should, therefore, support his policies. The pattern of diminished presidential coattails was reversed in the 1980 elections when the GOP achieved a net gain of twelve Senate and thirty-four House seats. Congressional perceptions of public support for President Reagan and his policies (reduced domestic spending, tax cuts, and increased military expenditures) assisted the president in winning congressional approval for his major policy initiatives during the first year of the administration. However, the unified support provided to President Reagan by Republican senators and representatives later diminished as members began to worry about their own reelections in 1982. With the president constitutionally barred from seeking a third term and having had only weak coattails in 1984, GOP defections continued in 1985–1989.

In 1988, the pattern of weak presidential coattails continued, with the GOP losing two House seats while its presidential nominee, George Bush, was winning the presidency. After a year and a half of soaring support ratings in the polls, Bush's popularity suffered a sharp drop in mid-1990 as he backed off from his "Read my lips: no new taxes!" campaign pledge and engaged in a lengthy and highly charged controversy with Congress over the budget. With midterm elections close at hand and the president's popularity falling, a majority of Bush's Republican colleagues in Congress deserted him and failed to support a budget agreement for fiscal year 1991 he and his aides had negotiated with congressional leaders of both parties.

The differing constituencies of members of Congress as compared to presidents and the timing of elections also creates differing perspectives. Legislators are ultimately responsible to the constituents in their states or districts. No matter how pressing national problems may be, reelection requires attention to local or state interests. Representatives and senators have few electoral incentives to view issues from a national perspective. By contrast, the president has a national constituency and is forced to take a more comprehensive view of issues than is required of legislators. Further tension is introduced into presidential-congressional relations by the staggered timing of elections. Because senators are elected for six year overlapping terms, only one-third of the senators are ever elected simultaneously with the president. Those that are elected with the president know their next reelection campaign will be fought during a midterm election when the president is not on the ballot. House members, of course, are also on a different election schedule than presidents. Their two year terms require them to run without the president on the ballot during midterm elections. The staggered timing of elections means that the president, senators, and representatives must confront the voters at different times and under divergent circumstances. They are, therefore, apt to view their electoral mandates quite differently.

Institutional bases. Complementing the electoral bases for differences between the president and Congress are institutional sources of tension. The executive branch is organized on a relatively hierarchical basis with the president in charge and held accountable for its actions. Presidents with their sweeping responsibility for policy development and implementation are forced to consider the trade-offs that must be made among various policies and to take a comprehensive national view of policy. The hierarchical character of the executive gives the president greater ability to propose policies that are comprehensive and consistent in character.

By contrast, the Congress is structured in a highly decentralized manner. Major decision-making responsibilities are delegated to committees and subcommittees, which often have memberships that are not particularly representative of their parent chambers. Senators and representatives tend to gravitate toward committees which have special significance for their constituencies (e.g., westerners to the Interior committees, farm state legislators to the Agriculture committees, and urban legislators to the Banking or Education and Labor committees). Committees, therefore, often become centers of narrower interest concerns than are found among leaders of the executive branch. Differences between the branches are further encouraged because Congress considers issues serially—one at a time—rather than in a comprehensive manner. That is, Congress often considers issues with little reference to other related policies. The decentralized power structure of Congress and its reliance on the committee/subcommittee system for detailed review of policy proposals make it almost impossible for the institution to consider policies in as integrated and comprehensive a manner as the executive branch.[15]

The relatively hierarchical structure of the executive branch and the decentralized character of Congress also cause the president and legislators to have a different sense of accountability to the voters.[16] Because presidents are so visible and responsible for the development and implementation of a full range of policies, they are held accountable for the performance of the government as a whole. The representatives and senators are substantially less visible and the decentralization of power within Congress makes it virtually impossible to hold any of its members accountable for the actions of the Congress, let alone the national government. Legislators, therefore, are evaluated on the basis of their own records, not the performance of the government as a whole. This frees them to engage in activities that will enhance their standing with constituents, irrespective of the national implications of those actions. Many even campaign by running against the Congress and its record, knowing full well that individually they will not be judged by Congress' institutional record.[17] This difference in public accountability between presidents and legislators means that presidents normally have a much greater sense of urgency for dealing with national problems than do members of the Congress. Presidents know that they will be held accountable for national ills, but legislators find themselves less likely to be held responsible.

Presidents also operate on a different time perspective than do legislators. Whereas the president's term in office is fixed and he has a limited time to accomplish his objectives and establish his place in history, representatives and senators normally think in terms of lifetime careers in the Congress. Presidents are concerned about problems of the moment—passing proposals that are of high priority. Congressmen, instead, worry about how to advance their long term influence in the chamber, promote the policies to which they attach importance, and maintain electability within their constituencies.[18]

Presidential leadership of Congress is also made more difficult because of the separation of powers system which makes possible divided partisan control of the presidency and Congress. Indeed, in the years since the first Eisenhower election in 1952, divided government has been more common than single party control (see Table 9–1). Except during Eisenhower's first two years in office, Republican presidents have consistently had to face a Congress in which at least one chamber was controlled by the Democrats. Democratic presidents have been more fortunate. There have been Democratically controlled congresses during each Democratic administration since Harry Truman's election in 1948. Separation of powers has had similar consequences for state government. Between 1952 and 1990 only two states (Georgia and Mississippi) did not experience divided government at least once. In some states, it has been a common occurrence (e.g., Illinois, Michigan, New York, Ohio). Following the 1990 elections twenty-six states had divided partisan control between the governor and at least one house of the state legislature.

Party Loyalty as a Basis for Presidential-Congressional Cooperation

While the tensions between the president and Congress are substantial, the extent of conflict can be overstated. Partisanship does provide a basis for cooperation and for keeping inevitable conflicts within reasonable bounds. The claims of party loyalty are important within the Congress. Studies of roll call voting have consistently found that the best single predictor of the way members of Congress will vote is their party affiliation.[19] With major portions of the congressional agenda determined by presidential policy initiatives, the party membership that the president shares with congressional colleagues is of substantial importance in promoting cooperation between the executive and legislature. Table 9–2 presents evidence of the extent of support received by presidents from their congressional party members and the opposition. In the thirty years between 1954 and 1990, presidents have been able to count upon their party members in Congress supporting them at least two-thirds of the time, and periodically the level of support reached the 80 percent range (see Ta-

Table 9–1 Single Party versus Divided Control of the National Government, 1952–1991

Single Party Control of Government	Divided Government
Republican President, Senate and House	*Republican President/ Democratic Senate and House*
1953–54 Eisenhower	1955–56 Eisenhower
	1957–58 Eisenhower
Democratic President, Senate and House	1959–60 Eisenhower
1961–62 Kennedy	1969–70 Nixon
1963–64 Kennedy/Johnson	1971–72 Nixon
1965–66 Johnson	1973–74 Nixon/Ford
1967–68 Johnson	1975–76 Ford
1977–78 Carter	1987–88 Regan
1979–80 Carter	
	Republican President and Senate Democractic House
	1981–82 Reagan
	1983–84 Reagan
	1985–86 Reagan
	Republican President Democratic Senate and House
	1987–88 Reagan
	1989–90 Bush
	1990–91 Bush
Total Years of Single Party Control of Government: 14	*Total Years of Divided Party Control of Government:* 28

ble 9–2). Presidential influence can even cause legislators of the president's party to alter their previous voting patterns on roll calls. This is particularly noticeable in the area of foreign policy. A study of House votes on foreign aid legislation by Herbert Asher and Herbert Weisberg for the period 1949–1972, for example, revealed that Republicans were likely to increase significantly their support for foreign aid under GOP presidents and that southern Democrats increased their support slightly for these measures when there was a Democratic president. Republicans have also been found to be more supportive of increasing the national debt limit[20] and of activist federal domestic policies when a Republican has been in the White House.[21]

In seeking to influence the Congress, presidents tend to work closely with the elected party leadership of their party in the House and Senate. Party leaders on the Hill are normally quite supportive of presidential policy initiatives because they have a stake in his legislative successes. If the president fails in gaining adoption of his legisla-

Table 9–2 Average Level of Congressional Support for the President's Position, 1954–1990 (Percent)

		Members of the President's Party			Members of the Opposition Party		
Years	**President**	**Party**	**House**	**Senate**	**Party**	**House**	**Senate**
1954–60	Eisenhower	Rep.	68%	80%	Dem.	54%	52%
1961–63	Kennedy	Dem.	83	75	Rep.	41	47
1964–68	Johnson	Dem.	81	71	Rep.	49	56
1969–74	Nixon	Rep.	73	73	Dem.	53	50
1974–76	Ford	Rep.	65	72	Dem.	41	48
1977–80	Carter	Dem.	69	74	Rep.	42	52
1981–89	Reagan	Rep.	68	79	Dem.	33	44
1989–90	Bush	Rep.	69	82	Dem.	36	55

Sources: Norman J. Ornstein, Thomas E. Mann, and Michael J. Malbin, *Vital Statistics on Congress, 1989–1990* (Washington, D.C.: Congressional Quarterly, 1990), pp. 196–197; *Congressional Quarterly Weekly Report*, Dec. 30, 1989, p. 3540, and Dec. 22, 1990, p. 4184.

tive program, they also fail. Through acting as presidential spokesmen on Capitol Hill and as conduits for communication between the White House and the Capitol, party leaders gain influence and leverage with their congressional colleagues. They, therefore, zealously guard their prerogatives as the principal presidential contact persons within the Congress. Presidents also benefit from working through the party leadership in Congress. As David Truman has pointed out:

> The clock provides no hours for the cultivation of rank-and-file legislators which direct leadership of the Congress would require. . . . If the agenda . . . [the President] . . . sets is to emerge in a product he favors, he must have the information and means for day-to-day assessment, if not actual guidance of Congressional activity. The elective leaders wield no monopoly here, but standing as strategic communications points, they are, for the President as much as for their legislative associates, an important source of intelligence, entirely aside from their capabilities as facilitators or obstructors of his program. . . . Relations with the leaders of the Congressional party can be supplemented . . . but no substitutes have appeared on which he can rely with equal confidence. To the degree that the mechanism of the Congressional party is relied upon, however, it must be taken as it is, with the leaders it has produced.[22]

Although the presidential-congressional leader relationship is in Truman's words "collaborative and mutually useful," it is not necessarily smooth. The most important constituency of congressional party leaders is not the president, but their legislative colleagues. To hold their leadership positions, they must protect the interests of their congressional colleagues. Thus it was widely reported that Robert Dole (R–Kan.) was selected by Senate Republicans to replace Howard Baker (R–Tenn.) as majority leader in 1984 because his GOP colleagues considered him sufficiently independent and tough minded to stand up to presidential and White House staff pressures. Dole's willingness to criticize publicly the Reagan and Bush White House and initiate policy proposals not necessarily blessed by the president demonstrates that this confidence was not misplaced. He has also sought to mediate the administration and senatorial policy differences. More frequently, however, Dole has been a party loyalist actively defending and mobilizing senatorial support for White House policy.

In seeking to influence Congress, recent presidents have expanded the resources of the White House. Eisenhower created an Office of Congressional Relations in the White House to complement the formal party structures. Since then, this office has become one of the key units in the White House. It has a contingent of personal presidential lobbyists, who are dispatched daily to the Capitol to win votes for the Administration's program. The Office of Congressional Relations also seeks to coordinate its activities with those of the congressional liaison personnel in each of the agencies of the executive branch.

More recently, starting with the Nixon Administration, an Office of Public Liaison has been set up within the White House. Under the leadership of Anne Wexler during the Carter Administration, this office became an effective mobilizer of grass roots constituency and interest group pressures on Congress. This practice was intensified under the Reagan Administration. For example, during the 1981 struggle to enact the president's budget, business groups were mobilized to contact contributors to Democratic House members. These contributors were in turn activated to urge representatives whom they had supported to back the president's budget. Similarly, the White House helped activate the network of state Reagan-Bush campaign committees in 1981 to urge their senators to support the administration's plan to sell AWACS reconnaissance aircraft to Saudi Arabia.

As the numbers in Table 9–2 demonstrate, presidents can rarely expect nearly unanimous support for their programs from party colleagues in Congress. Even if such support were forthcoming, it could be insufficient to pass legislation, because the president's party does not necessarily control the Congress. It is, therefore, often necessary for presidents to build bipartisan legislative coalitions. The recurring need for support on both sides of the aisle tends to dampen partisan conflict and forces bipartisan consultation on the formulation of legislation. It also permits members of both parties to claim credit for policy initiatives that are popular within the president's coalition.[23] The experience of the Reagan Administration provides recent proof of even a popular president's need for cross-party coalitions in the Congress. The major policy changes contained in the 1981 budget and tax bills were possible only because he was able to win the support of substantial numbers of Democratic representatives. Similarly, the massive tax reform act of 1986 was the product of White House cooperation with a bipartisan congressional coalition.

Of course, the need for bipartisan support may create difficulties for the president within his own party. To the extent that he negotiates and makes deals with the opposition party in order to build legislative majorities, the president runs the risk of alienating his loyal supporters. Loyalists in the president's party often perceive that White House largesse seems to be flowing toward members of the opposition party, whom they view as less deserving than themselves. But if the president fails to accommodate some elements in the opposition, he is likely to leave his governance responsibilities unfulfilled. Balancing the need for both party loyalty and bipartisanship support is a constant juggling act which presidents are compelled to perform.[24]

The Party, the President, and the Executive Branch

For a president to influence the direction of national policy requires more than influence with the Congress. He must also exert influence *within* the executive branch because it is here that policy initiatives are developed and implemented. Government organization charts often depict the president at the pinnacle of the executive branch with direct control over the far-flung departments and agencies. Most presidents, however, have found organizational chart depictions of their power illusionary. A multitude of factors contribute to making it difficult for presidents to exercise effective control over the executive establishment.

Each agency and department has a separate congressionally enacted statutory mandate governing its organizational structure, policies, and budgets. Presidents and their appointees within the agencies must operate within the constraints imposed by these statutes. In addition, each agency has its own permanent civil service staff. These persons are committed to the mission of the agency and often have developed a policy orientation and style of operation—a bureaucratic culture—that even presidents find almost impossible to alter. Conservative presidents are normally highly suspicious of bureaucrats who administer liberal programs and insist on maintaining these programs when the president sees no need for them. Liberal presidents often complain about the bureaucracy for different reasons. They see the bureaucracy as being unwilling to break out of its traditions and move in new directions. President John F. Kennedy, for example, in a mood of frustration is said to have once referred to the State Department as a "fudge factory." The federal bureaucracy is, however, essential for the successful administration of presidential policies. Presidents of either ideological stripe must, therefore, reconcile their style of operation with this relatively independent force within their administrations.[25] The programs administered by the various agencies develop a clientele of beneficiaries who have ties to the civil service and to the congressional committee members involved in passing agency authorizations and appropriations. These clientele groups are normally prepared to mobilize political influence to protect their interests within the agency. Therefore, cabinet secretaries charged with carrying out presidential policies are confronted frequently with having to cope with the combined influence of their department's bureaucracy, clientele groups, and attentive congressmen and senators. Since any of these forces has the political resources to make the life of a cabinet officer difficult in the extreme, there is a tendency on the part of many department heads to come to an accommodation with these interests. However, to the extent that they become responsive to these so-called "iron triangles," the president loses influence over his cabinet officers. Presidents and White House staff are constantly concerned that cabinet secretaries will become more responsive to pressures arising within their departments than they are to presidential initiatives. The cross-pressures operating upon department heads were once captured in somewhat exaggerated form by President Coolidge's vice president, Charles Dawes, who quipped that "the members of the Cabinet are a President's natural enemies."[26]

Presidential leadership of the executive branch has become more difficult in recent decades because of what Hugh Heclo calls "policy congestion." As the involvement of the government in society and the world has expanded, the policy concerns of the government have become more complex. One government program has implications for another and one issue impinges on another. This interaction of federal programs is now pervasive and results in overlap and layering. In domestic programs, overlap results because federal assistance to state and local governments, profit and nonprofit groups, and individuals is administered by a variety of agencies, and recipients may receive assistance from several agencies. But no one is responsible for supervising the cumulative effects of each agency's programs. The layering stems from attempts to impose crosscutting requirements on all programs (e.g., rules against discrimination based on race, sex, or age). With each of these crosscutting requirements administered by a different agency, there is no one department responsible for supervising their cumulative effect. The interrelatedness of issues, Heclo notes, is illustrated by the ways in which consideration of highway policy has changed since the 1950s when Eisenhower proposed building the interstate highway system. At that time, it was debated and then executed as a highway program with only modest attention given to nonhighway type concerns. Today if such a program were proposed anew, the implications of the interstate system for a whole range of nonhighway uses would be considered, e.g., private car versus mass transportation, energy conservation, economic development, minority hiring of construction workers, and urban development.[27]

"There are," Heclo concludes," more issues to be coordinated affecting any given agency, and there are more agencies in need of coordination for any given issue." As a result, the president, "rather than simply deciding on the government agenda, is increasingly involved in sorting out relationships among agendas—for economic management, international affairs, social policy, intergovernmental relations, and so on."[28] The end product of his synthesis is apt to appear diffuse and unfocused. Presidents operate within a system in which

> one unrelinquishable value interferes with another and . . . no final choice can be made between the environment and profitability, between social compassion and economic competition, or between the risks of peace and those of war.[29]

As a result, the executive branch cannot speak with one voice and presidents who seek to balance these conflicting values often appear ambiguous and undecisive.

The massive expansion of governmental programs in the 1960s and 1970s has also spawned additional organized interests capable of political mobilization to protect their special policy interests. They range from grass-roots neighborhood organizations, to state and local government officials who administer federal programs, to Ralph Nader's Raiders, to conservative public interest law firms, to high priced Washington lawyers maneuvering to protect their client's interests.

There are now more interests to be reconciled by a president seeking to coordinate governmental policy.

A traditional means used by presidents to exercise some control over the sprawling executive branch has been the appointment of fellow partisans to policy-making positions. John F. Kennedy, for example, installed Democrats in 63 percent of positions he filled and appointed Republicans in only 10 percent of the cases (the balance of the appointees were unaffiliated with a party). Reagan was even more partisan in his appointments: 83 percent of those appointed in 1981–1982 were Republicans and only 3 percent were Democrats.[30] When members of the opposition party are appointed, they are normally on the same ideological wavelength as the president—such as Reagan's former United Nations Ambassador Jeane Kirkpatrick or disarmament negotiator Max Kampelman.

Given the loose nature of American parties, appointment of fellow partisans does not assure a president that his appointees will be inclined to follow faithfully his policy initiatives. As previously noted, cabinet members often find it necessary to make an accommodation with their staffs, clientele groups, and congressional committees. In addition, prominent party leaders appointed to the cabinet have their own networks of supporters and are likely to be inclined toward periodic spells of independence.

White House staff personnel operate in a quite different environment than do presidential appointees to the departments and agencies. In the White House, the president and his key aides reign supreme. Actions taken to facilitate presidential objectives bring rewards, not responsiveness to Congress, interest groups, or the civil service. Presidents have, therefore, tended to expand the size of the White House staff as a mechanism to monitor and supervise the rest of the executive branch. Of course, increasing the size of the White House staff in itself creates problems of control and the potential for elements of the staff to get off the reservation periodically. For Republican presidents, the Office of Management and Budget (OMB) has been a key control and coordinating agency. Democratic presidents, who have had a greater interest in expanding governmental programs, have tended to rely more heavily on the domestic policy staff at the White House.[31] In both Republican and Demcratic administrations, however, there is heavy reliance on the domestic and foreign policy staffs in the White House because of their responsiveness to presidential concerns. The creation of policy development and evaluation staffs within the White House, of course, creates tensions between the senior officials of the departments and their counterparts in the White House. Conflicts over policy and scrambling for influence with the president became so intense during the Carter Administration that Secretary of State Cyrus Vance resigned after many disputes with National Security Advisor Zbigniew Brzezinski. Though less dramatic, the Bush Administration too has seen its share of conflicts between White House staffers and agency heads. Gaining particular media attention have been the policy differences between White House Chief of Staff John Sununu and the head of the Environmental Protection Agency, William Reilly.

Heclo reports that during his first term Ronald Reagan had unusual success in controlling his administration and attributes it to four factors. First, he and his key staff members drastically limited their policy priorities. Although there were intrusions caused by foreign policy crises (e.g., in the Middle East and Central America), the focus of the administration was on economic issues. The president was, therefore, perceived as rising above the policy congestion with a clear agenda for action. Second, the Reagan Administration entered the White House with a program. It was, however, not so much a party program as it was a program developed by conservative policy activists. The Heritage Foundation, a conservative, Washington based think tank, for example, produced a 1080 page compilation of 1270 policy recommendations for the administration. After the first year of the Reagan Administration, the Foundation claimed that 61 percent of its recommendations had been acted upon.

A third factor in the administration's management strategy was finding a body of likeminded people to staff the executive branch. Loyalty to Reagan and to his conservative philosophy were essential prerequisites for appointment. For example, John Kessel's comparative study of White House personnel has revealed that Reagan appointees were not only highly conservative, but they showed a greater level of agreement with each other than did the staffs of Presidents Nixon and Carter.[32]

Unlike Presidents Nixon and Carter, who allowed their department heads to have a free hand in filling subordinate positions, job applicants in the Reagan Administration were checked out by the White House personnel office for their loyalty to the president's objectives. Conservative policy networks that had helped generate the presidential program also provided or helped identify the manpower for the administration. The problems of Margaret Heckler, Reagan's Secretary of Health and Human Services, illustrate how difficult life can be for an appointee whom the White House staff view as less than committed to the administration's policy agenda. She encountered great difficulty in getting her designatees for posts in the department cleared through the White House personnel office and an organized effort removed her from the cabinet by shunting her off to be ambassador to Ireland.[33] In 1990, the Bush White House also forced the resignation of a cabinet secretary, Lauro Cavazos of the Department of Education, when he failed to fulfill White House expectations.

The final factor contributing to presidential control of the executive branch during the Reagan Administration was a concerted effort to reinforce central rather than department loyalties among leaders of the executive branch. Initial policy proposals for the various departments were developed by transition teams of conservative activists from outside the government. The newly appointed heads, therefore, were given little time or opportunity to try and develop their own policy directives. In addition, much of the negotiation with the Congress on key issues was handled by White House staff personnel, not the various department heads. The administration also made extensive use of the cabinet councils—policy groups composed of cabinet members dealings with related policy matters and key White House staff members (e.g., the cabinet council on economic affairs). For a time, the president's counselor, Edwin Meese, even considered housing the cabinet secretaries next door to the White House in the Executive Office Building in an attempt to reinforce their loyalty to the White House and reduce their tendency to identify with the departments and their respective staffs, clienteles, and congressional supporters.[34]

Most other modern presidents, including George Bush, have had less centralized administrations, less ideologically oriented personnel policies, and more diffuse policy objectives than the Reagan Administration. In all administrations, however, the party in the executive branch is used primarily for purposes of governing and not for the building up of the party organizations. The party in the executive, of course, is also a resource that can be used to help secure the president's renomination and reelection. It is not, however, an institution over which the party organization exerts substantial influence.

The Party, the President, and the Judiciary

The president and his White House staff can exert direct pressure upon the Congress and the executive branch. Party and presidential influences upon the judiciary, however, follow a much more indirect route—largely through the process of appointing federal judges. Presidents normally select approximately 90 percent of their judicial nominees from within the ranks of their own party. The impact of these appointments on judicial policy-making can be profound. Together, Ronald Reagan and George Bush, between 1981 and 1992, will have appointed 70 percent of all the federal judges. This is an impact on the federal judiciary exceeded only by Franklin Roosevelt, who appointed 75 percent of the federal judges. During the Reagan and Bush administrations, therefore, the federal bench was transformed from being predominantly Democratic to one with a Republican majority. The Justice Department, which handled the screening of candidates for judicial appointments, demonstrated an unusually high level of concern for appointing judges who shared Reagan's and Bush's conservative judicial philosophy.[35] One of the lasting legacies of the Reagan and Bush presidencies, therefore, has been a conservative Republican influence on the federal bench.

In making federal district and court of appeals appointments, presidents are forced to share power with their party's senators. The practice of senatorial courtesy enables senators of the president's party to block federal appointments within their own states if they disapprove of the nominee. To a significant degree, therefore, the initial screening of judicial candidates is done by senators of the president's party from the state in which the appointment is to be made. Because federal judicial appointments are among the most prized patronage plums at the disposal of a president and his party, there is often substantial jockeying for influence among home state senators of the president's party, the Justice Department, White House staff, concerned interest groups, bar associations, state party organizations, and presidential supporters from the state where the appointment will be made. The ultimate decision on a judicial nomination is a presidential prerogative. There were a significant number of cases during the Reagan Administration in which candidates recommended by their home state senators were rejected by the White House on the grounds that they were too liberal or unqualified. A particularly striking example of intraparty conflict between Republican senators and the Reagan Justice Department occurred in Pennsylvania. Six federal judgeships were left vacant for two years because the persons recommended by the state's two GOP senators were deemed too liberal by the Reagan administration.[36]

In those states in which there is no senator of the president's party, presidents normally give substantial weight to the recommendations of congressmen of the president's party, governors, and campaign officials. To a significant degree, any administration is dependent upon knowledgeable people within the states in making judicial appointments because the Justice Department and the White House staff do not have detailed knowledge of the legal fraternity in the various states.

In selecting nominees for the Supreme Court, the president has substantially more leeway than in making appointments to the federal district courts or the courts of appeals. The practice of senatorial courtesy does not operate in the confirmation process, though it is essential for presidents to nominate candidates capable of securing the necessary votes for confirmation by the full Senate. The direction of national judicial policy can be dramatically changed through Supreme Court appointments. The reliable liberal majorities that existed on the Warren Court have ceased to exist, because since 1969 Presidents Nixon, Ford, Reagan, and Bush have been able to appoint a majority of the justices.

Because of the Supreme Court's potential to affect controversial public policy issues like abortion, affirmative action, and presidential war powers, it is not surprising that Court appointments can become an issue in presidential campaigns. Reagan's ideological approach to Court appointments and the likelihood that the president elected in 1984 would have several vacancies to fill (five justices were over 75 years of age!) caused the presidential campaign to be sprinkled with rhetoric about Court appointments. While President Reagan pledged to continue filling judicial posts with conservatives, his opponent, Walter Mondale, gave the convention of the National Association for the Advancement of Colored People the following warning: "Don't let Mr. Reagan get his hands on the Supreme Court," and later raised the specter of Moral Majority leader Reverend Jerry Falwell picking Supreme Court nominees in a second Reagan Administration. The controversy over the policy implications of future appointees to the Supreme Court caused judicial process analyst Sheldon Goldman to observe that the Reagan Administration

> is furthering its goals [through judicial appointments]. It may not be your goals or my goals, but that's why we have elections. When we elect a president, we're electing a judiciary.[37]

Parties in Congress

The congressional environment is not conducive to high levels of party unity or strong policy leadership by the parties. The party leadership of Congress has been forced to adapt to the fact that members of the House and Senate are individually responsible for their own renomination and reelection. Since the congressional party organizations can guarantee members neither safe seats nor extensive campaign resources in return for loyalty on roll call votes, members frequently assume a highly independent orientation when voting on the House and Senate floor. They must protect themselves with their constituents, irrespective of party policy positions.

As was noted previously, the separation of powers systems further reduces the incentives for party loyalty within the party of the president. Unlike a parliamentary system, members of Congress who desert their president on key votes do not risk losing control of the executive branch or the calling of new congressional elections. The Constitution assures both the president and members of Congress fixed terms in office, even when presidential programs lack congressional support.

The parties of Congress also have to contend with the committee/subcommittee system, which has major responsibility for the development of policy proposals. Strong congressional committees and subcommittees result in power over various aspects of public policy being scattered among hundreds of House and Senate subcommittees and committees. With each committee and subcommittee zealously guarding its jurisdiction and prerogatives, policy development and coordination by congressional party leaders is extremely difficult. Each committee has too much autonomy and control over its particular subject matter jurisdiction to permit parties to dictate policies.

Although electoral forces and institutional arrangements operate to frustrate party influence within Congress, evidence of partisanship abounds in the organizational structure, decision making, and social life of the Congress. It is not, however, an all pervasive or disciplined type of partisanship. Rather, it is an ever present influence—a relatively undemanding mistress to the average member.

Evidence of Partisanship

Congress is organized on a highly partisan basis. Members of the majority party hold the key leadership posts—Speaker of the House, Majority Floor Leader of the Senate, and all committee and subcommittee chairmanships in each chamber. By holding these positions, the majority party maintains procedural control of the Congress. This enables the majority leadership to determine which bills will be scheduled for action, as well as when they will be on the agenda and under what conditions. With majority status there are other benefits—additional staff assistance to facilitate action on policies supported by the members of the party, and committee ratios of Democrats to Republicans that assure the majority party of at least a numerical advantage in each committee and subcommittee. In the House, for example, the majority party has set the ratio of majority to minority members of key committees, such as Rules, Ways and Means, Appropriations, and Energy and Commerce, at a level that assures the Democrats a comfortable majority on most issues. These majority party advantages often make life in the minority a frustrating experience. In recent years, these frustrations have surfaced among a group of young Republican members who have decided to forego attempts to win minor concessions from the majority Democrats through cooperation and compromise. Instead, they have adopted a highly confrontational style on the House floor designed to raise issues that can be used in the next election. A leader of these aggressive and highly conservative Republicans explained their actions as follows.

> There is . . . a sense of trying to force confrontation as a . . . permanent way for the Republican minority to operate. More confrontation rather than cooperation. . . . Another way to put it from our perspective would be that we receive absolutely none of the benefits for helping you guys [Democrats] pass your bills. We're never going to be committee chairmen as long as we're in the minority. We're never going to move up, we're never going to be subcommittee chairmen, and as long as we don't have that option, we'll confront instead of cooperate.[38]

The parties tend to loom large in the minds of junior members because it is through the congressional party organizations that members receive their committee assignments. Assignment to preferred committees is often essential, especially in the House, if members are to achieve such congressional career goals as reelection, power in the chamber, or policy influence.[39] During the days immediately after their first election and before they have even taken the oath of office, members-elect must campaign among their senior party colleagues for support in gaining good committee assignments. Thus at the beginning of their life in the Congress, they are confronted with the importance of partisanship. Often the leadership will impress upon members the importance of loyalty before granting assignment to a key committee.

The party leadership is also important as a source of needed information—the legislative schedule, the expected outcome of a roll call, the position of the president on a key amendment, the strategy of interest groups on an issue, and the electoral consequences of a yea or nay vote. The party leaders are obviously not the only source of information on such matters, but with their larger staffs and wide range of political contacts, they are an important source of political intelligence for rank and file members. The leadership can also be extremely useful in helping members acquire the financial resources for reelection campaigns.

The social contacts of a member of the Congress tend to be

within their own party. The physical layout of the two chambers encourages this. The House and Senate floor arrangements feature a center aisle with the Democrats on one side, the Republicans on the other. One's seatmates, with whom one shares information, political gossip, and small talk are fellow partisans. The same pattern holds true in the committee and subcommittee meetings rooms, where the seating arrangement divides the members of the two parties. Even the cloakrooms off the House and Senate floors are segregated along party lines. Republicans go to the Republican cloakroom and Democrats to the Democratic cloakroom when they wish to get a cup of coffee, make a phone call, or just relax. The social life of the Congress, therefore, tends to reinforce the organizational partisanship of the institution.

Partisanship is also encouraged because of the ideological bonds that exist among party members in Congress. Most national legislators share strong ideological affinities. Through their political socialization processes, fellow partisans come to develop compatible ideological orientations. They are also likely to have a common interest in supporting similar voter groups and interest groups.

The extent of partisanship in the Congress may also be seen in member voting patterns on House and Senate roll calls. Figure 9–1 shows the percentage of time between 1954 and 1988 that a majority of voting Republicans have aligned themselves against a majority of voting Democrats on roll call votes in the House and Senate. The percentage of party votes in the two chambers has ranged between a high of 56 percent in the 1986 House to just 27 percent in the House during 1970 and 1972. When viewed in historical perspective, this level of partisan division constitutes a significant decline from the period around the turn of the century when over 70 percent of House roll calls involved a majority from each party voting on opposite sides.[40] Similarly, the current levels of partisan voting in Congress appear low when compared to the more intense partisanship found in other Western democracies. However, with each chamber holding between 800 to 1,000 roll calls during each Congress (a two year period) and with many of the bills being of a minor or noncontroversial character, the data in Figure 9–1 give evidence of substantial partisan division within the House and Senate.

The extent of partisanship in Congress can be explored further by examining the degree of party unity on those roll calls which pit a majority of Democrats against a majority of Republicans. Figures 9–2 and 9–3 show the percentage of Republicans and Democrats voting in agreement with a majority of their party colleagues on issues that divided the two parties. These 1954–1988 data reveal that average party unity scores for a session of the Congress have rarely dipped below 70

Figure 9–1: Party Votes in the Congress, 1954–1988 (Percent of All Roll Calls)

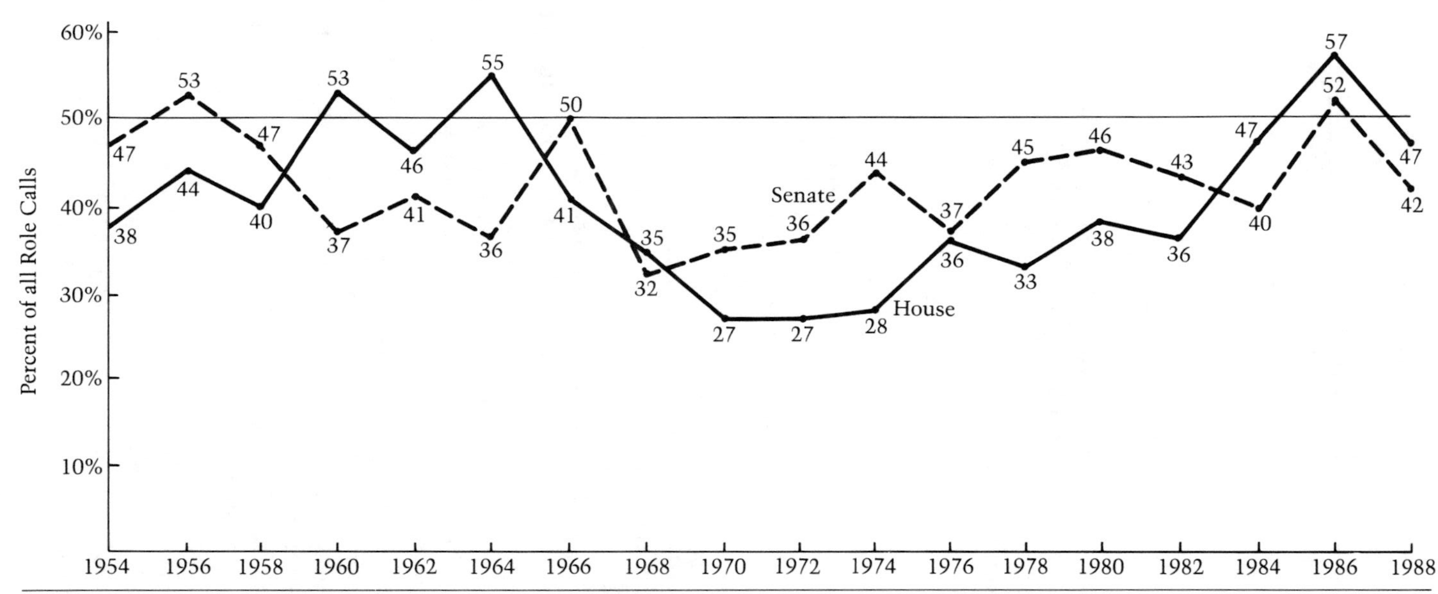

Note: Data indicate the percentage of recorded votes on which a majority of voting Democrats opposed a majority of voting Republicans.

Source: Norman J. Ornstein, Thomas E. Mann, and Michael J. Malbin, *Vital Statistics on Congress, 1989–1990* (Washington, D.C.: Congressional Quarterly, 1990), p. 198.

percent and frequently have climbed into the +80 percent range. Like the data on the extent of partisan roll calls, the party unity scores can be viewed from different perspectives. On the one hand, the data show substantial evidence of partisanship and party loyalty. But at the same time, the data also demonstrate that the parties are far from unified and that substantial divisions exist within both parties.

The extent of these internal party cleavages are portrayed in Table 9–3, which uses scales of liberalism/conservatism developed by the *National Journal* to rate members of the House and Senate. These data derived from roll call votes in 1990 show that eastern and western Democrats are substantially more liberal than their southern colleagues and slightly more liberal than midwestern Democrats. There are also significant intraparty differences among the Republicans. Eastern Republicans are much less conservative than their colleagues from the South and West, with the midwestern GOP members occupying a more centrist position within the party. Clearly the two parties are anything but monolithic in their policy orientations.

The internal cleavages within the congressional parties and the resulting lack of party unity mean that legislative majorities must frequently be forged with bipartisans coalitions. One of the most influential and enduring cross-party coalitions in the postwar years has been the so-called conservative coalition of Republicans and conservative southern Democrats. Table 9–4 shows the frequency with which this coalition has appeared since 1957 as well as its success rate. When it has appeared, the coalition normally scored legislative victories. It was a critical factor in President Reagan's successful push for major budgetary reductions and tax law changes during his first year in office and it continued to be important on foreign and defense policy issues during his second term.

Although the cross-party conservative coalition has in the past been a major force in congressional decision making, the data in Table 9–4 show that by the late 1980s it had become a shadow of its former self. It now appears much less frequently than in the 1960s and 1970s. The decline of the conservative coalition reflects heightened party unity and increased intensity of partisan conflict divisions since the late 1980s within Congress (see Figures 9–2 and 9–3).

This increase in party line voting in Congress has been caused by more policy oriented Democratic congressional leaders and the divisiveness of such issues as the budget, defense versus social program spending, and social issues. These and other issues have increasingly pitted a Republican president and his party colleagues in Congress against Democratic legislators. Intensified partisan conflict also reflects the changing composition of the two parties in Congress. As par-

Figure 9–2: Party Unity in the House of Representatives, 1954–1990

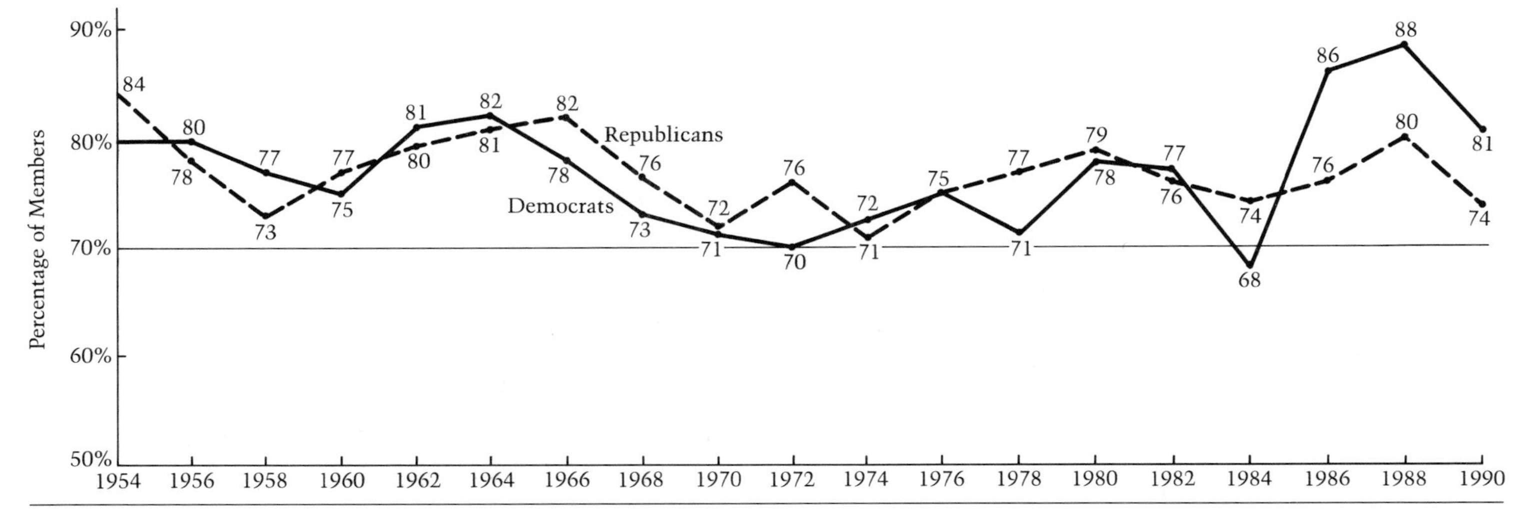

Note: Data show percentage of members voting with a majority of their party on roll call votes on which a majority of voting Democrats oppose a majority of voting Republicans.

Source: Norman J. Ornstein, Thomas E. Mann, and Michael J. Malbin, *Vital Statistics on Congress, 1989–1990* (Washington, D.C.: Congressional Quarterly, 1990), p. 199.

Figure 9–3: Party Unity in the Senate, 1954–1990

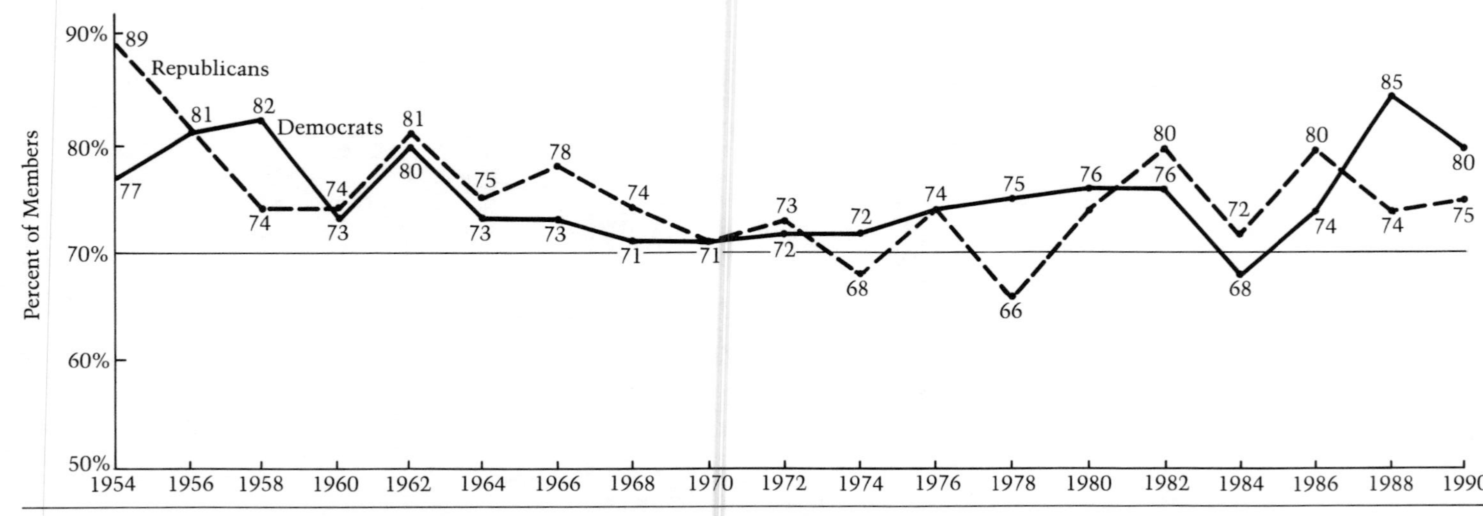

Note: Data show percentage of members voting with a majority of their party on roll calls on which a majority of voting Democrats oppose a majority of voting Republicans.

Source: Norman J. Ornstein, Thomas E. Mann, and Michael J. Malbin, *Vital Statistics on Congress, 1989–1990,* (Washington, D.C.: Congressional Quarterly, 1990), p. 199.

Table 9–3 Ideological Profiles of the Congressional Parties, 102nd Congress, 2nd Session, 1990

Party/Region	**On average are more *conservative* than . . . % of their *House* Colleagues**	**On average are more *liberal* than . . . % of their *House* Colleagues**
Western Democrats	77	19
Eastern Democrats	74	22
Midwestern Democrats	71	26
Southern Democrats	52	47
Eastern Republicans	35	62
Midwestern Republicans	20	77
Western Republicans	16	79
Southern Republicans	13	81
	On average are more *liberal* than . . . % of their *Senate* Colleagues	**On average are more *conservative* than . . . % of their *Senate* Colleagues**
Eastern Democrats	79	12
Western Democrats	71	23
Midwestern Democrats	66	28
Southern Democrats	57	39
Eastern Republicans	38	58
Midwestern Republicans	22	75
Western Republicans	19	76
Southern Republicans	12	82

Note: Scores reflect member voting records on economic, social, and foreign policy issues identified by the *National Journal.*

Source: Richard E. Cohen and William Schneider, "Partisan Patterns," *National Journal,* Jan. 19, 1991, pp. 137, 139. Copyright © 1990 by National Journal Inc. All Rights Reserved. Reprinted by permission.

tisan realignment has occurred among southern voters, Republicans have won an increasingly larger share of the region's House and Senate seats. This has meant that the Republican membership has become more southern and more conservative. At the same time, the Democratic membership has become less southern, and those Democrats elected from the South are often heavily dependent upon black voters and less likely to be conservatives (often dubbed "Boll Weevils"). Further contributing to the intensified partisanship of Congress is the growing number of Republicans from generally conservative western state constituencies. The net effect of these membership changes has

Table 9–4 Conservative Coalition Appearances and Victories in Congress, 1957–1990 (percent)

	House		Senate	
Year	Appearances	Victories	Appearances	Victories
1957	16	81	11	100
1958	15	64	19	86
1959	13	91	19	65
1960	20	35	22	67
1961	30	74	32	48
1962	13	44	15	71
1963	13	67	19	44
1964	11	67	17	47
1965	25	25	24	39
1966	19	32	30	51
1967	22	73	18	54
1968	22	63	25	80
1969	25	71	28	67
1970	17	70	26	64
1971	31	79	28	86
1972	25	79	29	63
1973	25	67	21	54
1974	22	67	30	54
1975	28	52	28	48
1976	17	59	26	58
1977	22	60	29	74
1978	20	57	23	46
1979	21	73	18	65
1980	16	67	20	75
1981	21	88	21	95
1982	16	78	20	90
1983	18	71	12	89
1984	14	75	18	94
1985	13	84	16	93
1986	11	78	20	93
1987	9	88	8	100
1988	8	82	10	97
1989	11	80	12	95
1990	10	74	11	95

Note: Appearances refers to the percentage of all roll call votes in the House or Senate on which a majority of voting southern Democrats and a majority of voting Republicans opposed a stand taken by a majority of northern Democrats.

Sources: Norman J. Ornstein, Thomas E. Mann, and Michael J. Malbin, *Vital Statistics on Congress*, 1989–1990 (Washington, D.C.: American Enterprise Institute, 1989), p. 200; *Congressional Quarterly Weekly Report*, Dec. 30, 1989, p. 3551, and Dec. 22, 1990, p. 4218.

been to make each party's membership more homogeneous ideologically and thereby to sharpen partisan divisions within Congress.[41]

The ideological profiles of the congressional parties contained in Table 9–3 show that Democrats are clearly more liberal on the whole than the Republicans. The difference between the two parties is not the difference between Tweedledee and Tweedledum. Even the most conservative element of the Democratic party, its southern representatives and senators, are more liberal than the most liberal group in the GOP—the eastern Republicans. There are, of course, individual examples of highly conservative Democrats (e.g., Senators James Exon of Nebraska and Howell Heflin of Alabama) and relatively liberal Republicans (e.g., Senators James Jeffords of Vermont and John Chafee of Rhode Island). But clearly, the general tendency of the two parties diverges rather sharply. Party is, therefore, an extremely important element in congressional decision making. The parties, however, have to compete with other interests—the administration, interest groups, and constituency interests—for member votes. In this competition, the parties do not necessarily prevail on every issue. Party influence on most members, however, is substantial.

The special character of the congressional party was captured by political scientist David B. Truman. After identifying the distinctive voting patterns of the members of the two parties as well as deep intraparty schisms, he concluded that congressional parties were *mediate groups*. He wrote:

> The party labels do distinguish different patterns of attitude and value and different systems of interaction. . . . Moreover, they have a marked degree of stability and structure. . . . Yet, the degree of cleavage . . . in both parties indicates that the parties constitute a different and perhaps special type of group. They have a vitality and persistence as organizations despite internal divisions which in most other groups would be a prelude to dissolution, secession, or ostracism. . . . [The congressional party] is mediate and supplementary in function. That is, from the viewpoint of the members it does some things of importance, and its failures may be of considerable consequence to them. On the other hand, retention of their status as senators [and representatives] is not so completely dependent upon it—unlike the management of a corporation, the members of a labor union, or the components of a military organization—that its risks are entirely their risks or its failures necessarily theirs.[42]

Party Organization in the House

Because of its large size (435 members), the House has rules that strictly regulate the processing of legislation and limit the effectiveness of dilatory tactics. These rules, which bring an element of order to the chamber and enable it to fulfill its legislative responsibilities, also have the effect of severely limiting the power of individual members. In the House, the majority is in a position to work its will on most issues and individual members have only the most restricted powers of delay and obstruction. These procedural rules strengthen the position of the party leaders, especially the Speaker

Table 9–5 Key Leadership Positions in the 102nd Congress, 1991–1992

House of Representatives	
Speaker: Thomas Foley (D-Wash.)	
Majority Party (Democrats)	*Minority Party* (Republicans)
Floor Leader: Richard Gephardt (Mo.)	Floor Leader: Robert Michel (Ill.)
Whip: David Bonier (Mich.)	Whip: Newt Gingrich (Ga.)
Caucus Chairman: Steny Hoyer (Md.)	Conference Chairman: Jerry Lewis (Calif.)
Steering and Policy Committee Chairman: (also serves as Democratic Committee on Committees) Thomas Foley (Wash.)	Policy Committee Chairman: Mickey Edwards (La.)
Chief Deputy Whips: John Lewis (Ga.), Butler Derrick (S.C.), and Barbara Kennelly (Conn.)	Committee on Committees Chairman: Robert Michel (Ill.)
Democratic Congressional Campaign Committee Chairman: Vic Fazio (Calif.)	Chief Deputy Whips: Steve Gunderson (Wis.); Robert Walker (Pa.)
	National Republican Congressional Committee Chairman: Guy Vander Jagt (Mich.)
Senate	
President Pro Tempore: Robert Byrd (D–W. Va.)	
Majority Party (Democrats)	*Minority Party* (Republicans)
Floor Leader: George Mitchell (Maine)	Floor Leader: Bob Dole (Kans.)
Whip: Wendell Ford (Ky.)	Whip: Alan Simpson (Wyo.)
Caucus Chairman: George Mitchell (Maine)	Conference Chairman: Thad Cochran (Miss.)
Policy Committee Chairman: George Mitchell (Maine)	Policy Committee Chairman: Don Nickles (Okla.)
Co-Chairman: Tom Daschle (S. Dak.)	Conference Secretary: Robert Kasten (Wis.)
Conference Secretary: David Pryor (Ark.)	Committee on Committees Chairman: Larry Pressler (S. Dak.)
Steering Committee Chairman: George Mitchell (Maine)	National Republican Senatorial Committee Chairman: Phil Gramm (Tex.)
Democratic Senatorial Campaign Committee Chairman: Charles Robb (Va.)	

and majority floor leader, who tend to dominate the setting of the House agenda.

The Speaker of the House. The most prominent and influential member of the House is its Speaker, who serves as both its presiding officer and the leader of the majority party. Early in this century, the Speaker was a substantially more powerful leader than he is in the 1990s. The speakership was brought to the zenith of its power by the legendary and autocratic Joseph G. Cannon ("Uncle Joe"), an Illinois Republican, who served as Speaker from 1903 to 1911. He dominated his party and the House through his extensive formal powers, which he used aggressively to assure that his faction of the Republican party controlled the House. These powers included serving as presiding officer of the House, control of member committee assignments, designation of committee chairmen, whom he both appointed and removed, and regulation of the work schedule of the House through his chairmanship of the Committee on Rules. Cannon, however, lost his majority on procedural issues within the House during 1910 and 1911. In a revolt of Progressive Republicans and Democrats, the Speaker was stripped of his position as chairman of the Rules Committee, his power to make committee assignments, and some of his powers to recognize members on the floor. The modern Speakers, lacking as extensive formal powers as those that were available to Cannon, must lead their parties and the House by relying primarily upon informal means—persuasion, bargaining, and negotiation.

In the 1970s, the Democrats did make a series of rules changes that vested some renewed formal power in the Speaker. The Speaker was made chairman of the Steering and Policy Committee, which makes committee assignments for Democratic members. This gives the Speaker the ability to exert a significant impact on the careers of rank and file members and to influence the composition and therefore the policy orientation of committees. The Speaker was also given authority to name Democratic members of the Rules Committee and through the Rules Committee to control the flow of the legislation to the floor as well as the procedures under which bills will be considered by the House. In addition, the Speaker was given special powers to make multiple referrals of bills to committees and in this way influence the substance and timetable for committee decisions on legislation. As the presiding officer of the House, the Speaker is also in a position to make strategically important parliamentary rulings. Backed by a relatively cohesive party membership, these formal powers in the hands of an aggressive speaker, like Jim Wright

(D.–Tex., 1986–1989), provide the bases for strong and policy oriented party leadership.[43]

As significant as these powers are, the Speaker operates in an arena where power is relatively decentralized. Members recognize that party loyalty will not guarantee them reelection and they, therefore, act with substantial independence. The feeling of independence was recently summarized by a Democratic member who observed:

> I don't even think about the leadership in the sense of a threat. I've voted against the leadership's position on some very key issues. . . . the Speaker made an impassioned plea . . . and the majority leader made a strong plea for the Chrysler bailout [guaranteed loans to save the company from bankruptcy], and I . . . voted against their position. . . . I didn't consider whether or not this was going to cause any problems for me with the leadership.[44]

In addition, the committees and subcommittees operate within their own subject matter jurisdictions with substantial autonomy from the Speaker and each other. The Speaker's powers do not extend to controlling the work of the committees and subcommittees, which have grown in influence and autonomy since a series of committee reforms were instituted in the 1970s. Operating with limited formal powers in an environment of widely dispersed power, the Speaker must rely on his skills at building personal ties and loyalties that can be used to achieve his party policy objectives. When Speaker Thomas P. ("Tip") O'Neill (D.–Mass., 1977–1985) was asked about the sources of his power, he candidly stressed their informal nature.

> You ask me what are my powers and my authority around here? The power to recognize on the floor, little odds and ends—like men get pride out of the prestige of handling the Committee of the Whole, being named Speaker for the day; those little trips that come along—like those trips to China, trips to Russia, things of that nature; or other ad hoc committees or special committees, which I have assignments to; plus the fact that there is a certain aura and respect that goes with the Speaker's office. He does have the power to pick up the telephone and call people. And Members often times like to bring their loyal political leaders or a couple mayors. And often times they have problems from their area and they need aid and assistance, either legislativewise or administrativewise. We're happy to try and open the door for them, having been in town for so many years and knowing so many people. We do know where a lot of bodies are and we do know how to advise people. . . . Rare is the occasion when a man has a personal fund-raiser or being personally honored that I don't show up at it. I've made . . . personal

> appearances and visited areas if they believe I can help them. I'm always accessible. These are part of the duties and the obligations of the Speaker, and it shows the warm hand of friendship.[45]

The floor leaders. Within the majority party, the Speaker's principal associate is the floor leader. He normally acts as the key party spokesman and strategist on the House floor. With the Speaker, he helps to plan the legislative schedule of the House. He carries major responsibilities for persuading his colleagues to support party leadership positions on House votes and must also spend time talking with his colleagues to gauge members' sentiments on various issues.

The minority floor leader is the highest ranking position within his party. He is responsible for serving as party spokesman and defender on the floor, developing legislative strategy to advance the minority goals, building bridges to dissident members of the opposition, and keeping in touch with the sentiments of his party colleagues. When his party controls the presidency, the minority leader has the responsibility of acting as a spokesman for the White House and for advancing its legislative program. Republican Leader Robert Michel of Illinois has often found that serving the needs of the White House and his colleagues is extremely difficult. On the one hand, it has frequently been necessary to make concessions to the majority Democrats in order to fashion a majority on the House floor. But such concessions frequently are not well received by his own hard core partisans who are seeking confrontations with the opposition to develop issues for the next election. The minority leader with the president of his party is constantly torn by his party's obligations to govern, thereby downplaying partisanship, and the party's desire for majority status.

The whips. Both parties have assistant leaders known as whips. The term derives from the English hunt, where the job of the whip was to keep the dogs together. Similarly, the duty of the party whips is to encourage party discipline. The whips do not have the formal authority to "whip" their colleagues into line. Rather, they are responsible for conveying to rank and file members the party position on issues, persuading them to support it, and making advance nose-counts to determine the likelihood for success of a leadership position on the floor. Each party has an elaborate whip organization composed of a deputy whip and regional whips responsible for contacting and persuading their colleagues. Just before key party votes and during the roll calls, whips can be seen roaming the floor rounding up votes for their side and standing by the doors of the chamber signaling members how to vote as they enter the House chamber from their offices and committee rooms.

The policy committees. Party policy committees function as agencies to gauge party sentiments and to identify the party position on issues before they come to the House floor for a vote. For example, if there is substantial disagreement within a policy committee concerning what should be the party's position on an issue, this absence of a consensus will probably cause the leadership not to take a formal party position on an issue. On the other hand, policy committee endorsement of a position on a bill tends to strengthen the leadership's position in winning party members' support for their viewpoint. The policy committees play a role of providing policy guidance to members, but they do not have the power to bind members to support their positions. Nor do the policy committees customarily seek to involve themselves in the deliberations of the standing committees. The policy committees instead enter the process at the stage when legislation has emerged from committee and is being scheduled for floor action. Therefore, they are not agencies for the development of a party program. The Congress and its parties are too decentralized for them to play such a role.

In addition to its policy role, the Democratic Steering and Policy Committee acts as the party's committee on committees in the House. This is the committee which makes committee assignments for Democratic members and nominates members for committee chairmanships. These nominations must be confirmed by the full Democratic membership or caucus. Because committee assignments are so critical to members, this power adds significantly to the influence of the committee. The Republican Policy Committee does not handle committee assignments. Rather, a separate Committee on Committees, chaired by the floor leader and composed of representatives from every Republican state delegation, dispenses committee assignments and nominates persons for ranking minority member positions on committees. These recommendations must be ratified by the Republican membership of the House, or Conference.

Party caucuses and conferences. Party caucuses or conferences include all the members of the party in a chamber. The most important work of the party caucuses is done at the beginning of a new Congress when they meet to organize their parties in the House. It is at these meetings that party leaders are elected and party rules are adopted. In addition, these organizational meetings customarily ratify decisions of the committee on committees concerning committee assignments and chairmanships or ranking minority member positions on the committees. Major intraparty struggles periodically erupt over the selection of leaders, which can affect the future course of the party. House Democrats have been less inclined to have contested elections for leadership positions than the Republicans. Democratic leaders have tended to move through a series of subordinate positions before becoming Speaker. For example, Thomas Foley served apprenticeships as whip and majority leader before being elected to the Speakership upon the retirement of Jim Wright (D.–Tex.) in 1989. By contrast, the minority Republicans have had a series of revolts that have toppled the minority leaders—e.g., Gerald Ford (Mich.) ousted Charles Halleck (Ind.) after the election debacle of 1964, and Halleck successfully challenged Joseph Martin (Mass.) after a similar GOP electoral disaster in 1958.

Party caucuses are held periodically throughout a congressional session to allow members to express their sentiments on issues facing the House and to rally partisan support for leadership positions on key votes.[46] Like the policy committees, however, the caucuses do not make decisions that are binding on their members in terms of how they shall vote on the floor. Only rarely have the caucuses in recent years sought to instruct committee members concerning action on legislation being considered by a committee. Every member of the caucus is also a member of at least one standing committee and, therefore, has a stake in maintaining the autonomy and power of the committees. Strong expressions of sentiment in the caucus can, however, affect the actions and strategy of the party leadership. In 1985, just prior to the August recess, for example the Democratic leadership pulled a major Defense Department authorization bill off the House schedule because of objections expressed in the Democratic caucus about the level of expenditures contained in the bill.[47]

The Democratic caucus has played a major role in reshaping the procedures of the House of Representatives. Through changes in party and House rules initiated in the caucus during the 1970s, the seniority system for selection of committee chairmen was modified, members were restricted to one subcommittee chairmanship, subcommittees gained substantial autonomy from full committee chairmen, the Steering and Policy Committee gained the power to make committee assignments from the Democratic members of the Ways and Means Committee, the Speaker acquired the power to nominate Democratic members to the Rules Committee, and had his power to refer bills to committee strengthened. As a consequence of the committee reforms, the power and independence of committee chairmen were significantly weakened, particularly for conservative committee chairmen who were out of step ideologically with a majority of their party colleagues. In addition, legislative decision-making power was dispersed to approximately 150 subcommittees. In spite of these power-fragmenting effects, the net impact of the 1970s rules changes has been to strengthen significantly the party leadership and to centralize power within the House.

Informal party groups. In addition to the regular party organizational structure that has just been described, there also exists within the House a series of informal party groups which can work under some circumstances to reinforce party unity and at other times to cause fragmentation. An important set of groups within each party are the state party delegations which vary in size and in the formality of their organizations. Some meet regularly to discuss their position on legislation and to share information. As communications networks, state delegations can be used by both the leadership and dissident factions to line up support for floor votes. State delegations are particularly active during the time early in a Congress when committee assignments are being made. The various delegations lobby to get their members on key committees and often engage in complicated multidelegation bargaining schemes in order to secure the best possible assignments for their members.

Within both parties there are class clubs which are organized on the basis of the Congress or year in which a member was first elected. Freshmen class clubs are the most active as they seek to promote junior members' interests with the leadership and assert some influence through coordinated actions. As members gain seniority and positions of influence in the committee system and party organizations, however, they normally find the class clubs of limited usefulness.

There are also a series of ideologically oriented groups within each party which seek to pressure their parties' leadership to adopt policies compatible with the groups' views. The most successful and oldest of these ideologically oriented groups is the Democratic Study Group (DSG). It is a liberal group of Democrats that is virtually a party organization within a party organization. It has its own fund raising mechanism, whip system, research operation and staff. The much smaller and conservatively oriented Democratic Forum ("Boll Weevils") seeks to combat DSG's influence and make the leadership conscious of the role conservative southern Democrats play in enabling the party to retain its majority status in the House. The much smaller size of the Forum and its rather informal organizational structure have severely limited its influence in the House Democratic party. An additional and increasingly important faction within the Democratic party is its Black Caucus, which furthers liberal positions and black interests.

The Republicans also have policy oriented subgroups. There is the Republican Study Committee, a group of conservative Republicans who have patterned their operations after the DSG. Their aggressiveness has made them an important force within the House GOP, although they do not constitute as large a share of the Republican membership as the DSG does of the Democratic membership.

The Republicans also have several informal clubs to which membership is gained by invitation only. These organizations carry substantial prestige and include the party's influential members. The most important of these clubs are the Chowder and Marching Society and S.O.S. Although these organizations have their social dimension, their weekly meetings are also important as intraparty communications forums and agencies for testing out policy proposals and strategy. There are no comparable organizations on the Democratic side of the aisle. Their existence among the Republicans may reflect the party's long term minority status and the need of the members for additional outlets for their energies since the regular avenues to House influence are largely closed to them.

Party Organization in the Senate

Whereas the average member of the House is a relatively anonymous figure, except in his or her own constituency, senators are much more visible and are frequently national figures. They represent major commonwealths. Most importantly, there are only 100 senators. The smaller size of the Senate means that it can function with rules that permit the individual senators much greater leeway and influence. As a result, the average senator has significantly more formal power than the average representative. For example, much of the work of the Senate is done under unanimous consent agreements developed and negotiated by the majority leader. By refusing to agree to a unanimous consent request, an individual senator can hold up the work of the Senate until concessions are made to him. Senators also have available to them the filibuster or its threatened use as means of gaining leverage with their colleagues. The Senate's closure rule requires the votes of sixty senators to cut off debate. This means that a determined band of senators can often block action on legislation to which they are strongly opposed or at least gain concessions in return for dropping their filibuster. In comparison to the House, influence is more widely dispersed in the Senate and each member is more equal in power. Formal leadership positions (e.g., majority or minority floor leader, committee chairmanships) are important, but they are less important in the modern individualistic Senate than in the more hierarchical House.[48]

Unlike the House, the Senate's presiding officer is not a key party leader. The vice president is constitutionally empowered to preside, but he rarely does so except when his vote may be needed to break a tie or when he may be called upon to make an important parliamentary ruling. As a nonmember of the Senate and a figure with limited power in the White House, the vice president is not normally an important factor in Senate decision making. Nor is the position of president pro tempore an influential position. By tradition this post is awarded to the majority party's most senior member in terms of Senate service. Senator Robert Byrd (D.–W.Va.) became president pro tempore in 1989. Senator Byrd's Senate influence stems, however, not from his position as president pro tempore, but from his chairmanship of the Appropriations Committee. Like the vice president, the president pro tempore rarely presides over the Senate. This task is instead delegated to freshman senators as an apprenticeship task. It is not an onerous duty because the Senate rules are relatively simple, unlike the complex House rules which give substantial advantage to the party controlling the presiding officer.

The floor leaders. The key leaders of the Senate are the party floor leaders.[49] The majority floor leader is responsible for the Senate schedule, which he handles mainly through negotiated unanimous consent agreements. This procedural prerogative gives the leader some bargaining advantage with colleagues. He also acts as his party's chief spokesman and legislative strategist. But much more than in the House, the leader has only limited formal powers. His influence rests upon his ability to find a compromise position and then persuade a majority of the senators to support his position. The minority floor leader serves his party in a capacity similar to that of the majority leader, except he has no responsibility for developing the schedule of Senate business.

Senate floor leaders are also responsible for steering presidential programs through the Senate when their party controls the presidency. This normally involves juggling the interests of fellow party members in the Senate and the concerns of the White House, while keeping lines of communication open to opposition party senators whose votes may be needed to build a majority. With senators on a different reelection schedule and often holding different policy priorities than the president, the majority leader can easily become ensnarled in intraparty and institutional rivalries. In addition he must negotiate with the House leadership, whose views are apt to depart from those of the Senate or president. For example, GOP Floor Leader Robert Dole, as a spokesman and strategist for the Senate GOP, on occasion has found himself at odds with Presidents Reagan and Bush, White House staff, and Democratic and Republican House leaders over how to effect substantial reductions in the federal budget deficit.

The whips. Each party has a whip who serves as an assistant floor leader. In the Democratic party, the whip appoints a series of deputy whips to work with him in counting votes prior to key roll calls, persuading members to support the party position, and communicating leadership positions to the membership. The Republican whip does not operate with a deputy whip organization.

The policy committees. Senate policy committees do not make policy for the parties. The Republican policy committee meets on a weekly basis for luncheon to discuss matters of mutual interest, but not to take position on issues. It also has a staff which does research for the leadership and individual members, but it is not involved in the development of party policy. The Democratic Policy Committee has been used as an advisory body to the floor leader and has assisted him in scheduling Senate business when the party was in the majority.

The committees on committees. Each party has a committee on committees (called the Steering Committee in the Democratic party) to handle member committee assignments. In making these appointments, the Republicans have tended to rely heavily upon seniority as a criterion for selection, while the Democrats have had a more open process in which candidates for committee posts waged campaigns to secure coveted assignments. Compared to the House, a larger share of Senate issues are resolved on the floor than in committee. As a result, the committee assignment process is of somewhat less importance to the individual senators than it is for House members. Senate rules permit each senator substantial opportunities to have an impact on floor deliberations, whereas the restrictive House rules do not permit rank and file members equivalent chances to influence the decisions of the full House.

The conferences. The party conferences in the Senate are used primarily to organize the parties at the beginning of each new Congress. At these meetings the leadership is elected and party rules are adopted. Senate party conferences meet much less frequently than in the House, but as in the case of the House, they are not used to develop party policy or to intervene in the work of the standing committees.

Congressional Parties and National Party Organizations

The congressional parties operate with substantial autonomy from their national committees. The principal constituencies of the national committees are the state party organizations and the president, when a party holds the White House. Congressional party leaders, especially when the party does not control the presidency, zealously guard their prerogatives as policy spokesmen for the party and show little deference to, or interest in, the work of the national committees. When out-party national chairmen have set up policy advisory committees to develop party positions on issues, these committees have been most successful when they were dominated by congressional leaders, as was true of the Republican Coordinating Committee of the period between the 1964 and 1968 elections.[50] However, when policy advisory committees have sought an independent policy development role, they have often been treated with disdain or ignored by the party leadership of Congress. Thus Speaker Sam Rayburn and Senate Majority Leader Lyndon B. Johnson of Texas paid little heed to the activities of the Democratic Advisory Council appointed by Democratic National Chairman Paul Butler after the 1956 elections. Further evidence of the distance between the national committees and the congressional party members was the decision of several key Democrats (including House Caucus Chairman Richard Gephardt and Senators Sam Nunn of Georgia and Lawton Chiles of Florida) after the 1984 presidential election defeat to form a policy advisory council in direct competition to that appointed by DNC Chairman Paul Kirk.[51]

The national committee's separation from the congressional parties is also revealed by the existence in both parties of autonomous House and Senate campaign committees. Conscious that their constituency is members of the House and Senate, the congressional and senatorial campaign committees go about their business of seeking to elect representatives and senators, and leave presidential election politics and aid to state candidates to the national committees.

Nor do the congressional and senatorial campaign committees seek to enforce party loyalty or ideological purity by bestowing their campaign support only on incumbents who have adhered to the party line on roll call votes, or to nonincumbents who have pledged to do so. Rather, the campaign committees have granted aid to candidates on strictly electoral criteria: Which candidates are the strongest? Which races does the party have the best chance of winning? Which incumbents are in tough reelection contests? Given the diversity of viewpoints represented in the congressional and senatorial parties, it would be almost impossible for the campaign committees to enforce party discipline without causing bitter and counterproductive intraparty disputes. The campaign committees, therefore, function principally as candidate recruiters, fund raisers, and campaign professionals rather than as party policy makers or enforcers of party discipline.

Parties and Policy in the Congress

Political parties are the most inclusive institutions within the Congress. As such, they constitute Congress' strongest integrating and centralizing influence. For members of the president's party, this integrating force is often reinforced by the influence of the White House and its legislative program. But even with the parties' very substantial influence, the policy-making process of Congress cannot be characterized as party government, where disciplined parties with agreed upon programs confront each other.

Congressional parties operate in an environment in which forces of decentralization are intense. Strong standing committees and their relatively autonomous subcommittees create multiple centers of influence over specific aspects of public policy. The centralizing influence of the parties is further weakened by the fact that most representatives and senators are what might be termed independent political entrepreneurs. They are personally responsible for the well-being of their own political enterprises. The party organization and the congressional parties did not get them nominated and elected, though they may have helped. Members are, therefore, unwilling to submit to any kind of party discipline that might jeopardize their electoral positions and their careers. If the congressional parties are relatively weak, it is, as David Mayhew has noted, because that is the kind of parties that the members want. They want parties that will be of assistance to them, but which will not impose burdens of discipline to party policy line that could cost them the support of their constituents.[52]

The party leadership of Congress recognize their colleagues' need for substantial freedom in making policy decisions. They also appreciate the power realities of the committee/subcommittee system. Lacking extensive formal authority, the party leaders seek through informal means to build legislative majorities one issue at a time. Occasionally they can enlist the support of outside forces like the administration or interest groups to reinforce party unity (though these same outside forces can also be an influence for party disunity). And frequently they must seek votes on the other side of the aisle to forge a majority. It is an endless process of bargaining, negotiation, and compromise. Party loyalty alone is frequently insufficient to carry the day on a key vote in the House and Senate.

Many have lamented the absence of strong and disciplined parties in the Congress on the grounds that it prevents the voter from being able to hold a party responsible at the polls for the policies of the government. It should be noted, however, that the relatively low level of party unity in Congress mirrors the lack of unity that also exists in the party-in-the-electorate. The electoral coalitions that elect Republicans and Democrats are diverse and contain conflicting and contradictory elements. Furthermore, the American constitutional system of separation of powers, which permits divided party control of the government, would be extremely difficult to operate if the parties were highly unified and disciplined. In a circumstance in which one party controlled the White House and another held the Congress, disciplined parties could be a prescription for stalemate and deadlock. Weak parties introduce an element of flexibility into the system and permit the government to act, even though neither party controls the government.

A Party Influenced Government, But Not a Party Dominated Government

The political parties' role in government is a paradoxical one. On the one hand, party influence is pervasive in the organizing of both the executive branch and the Congress, and partisan considerations are constantly in evidence in the selection of federal judges. In addition, shared partisanship between members of the Congress and the president does much to facilitate cooperation and bridge the gap created by a constitutional separation of power. Party affiliation has also been shown to be the single best predictor of how representatives and senators will vote on congressional roll calls. Despite this evidence of party influence, there also exists evidence of the parties' limited capacity to control American governmental institutions. Presidents have consistently found it difficult to maintain effective control over the far-flung executive establishment, including the White House staff, even though key policy-making posts are occupied by persons from the president's party. In Congress, the absence of party discipline has been shown to be even more pronounced. American government and policy making, therefore, is party influenced, but it is not party dominated. The looseness of the American party system gives governmental officials substantial flexibility and independence in shaping public policy.

Suggestions for Further Reading

Bailey, Christopher, J. *The Republican Party in the U.S. Senate.* Manchester, Eng.: University of Manchester Press, 1989.

Dodd, Lawrence C., and Oppenheimer, Bruce I., eds. *Congress Reconsidered.* 4th ed. Washington, D.C.: CQ Press, 1989.

Edwards, George C., III. *At the Margins: Presidential Leadership of Congress.* New Haven, Conn.: Yale University Press, 1989.

Edwards, George C., III. *Presidential Influence in Congress.* San Francisco, Cal.: W.H. Freeman, 1980.

Epstein, Leon D. *Political Parties in the American Mold.* Madison: University of Wisconsin Press, 1986. Ch. 3 and 4.

King, Anthony, ed. *Both Ends of the Avenue: The Presidency, the Executive Branch, and Congress in the 1980s.* Washington, D.C.: American Enterprise Institute, 1983.

Mackaman, Frank H., ed. *Understanding Congressional Leadership.* Washington, D.C.: CQ Press, 1981.

Polsby, Nelson W. *Congress and the Presidency,* 4th ed. Englewood Cliffs, N.J.: Prentice-Hall, 1986.

Sinclair, Barbara. *Majority Leadership in the U.S. House.* Baltimore, Md.: Johns Hopkins University Press, 1983.

Sinclair, Barbara. *The Transformation of the United States Senate.* Baltimore, Md.: Johns Hopkins University Press, 1989.

Notes

1. Sarah McCally Morehouse, *State Politics, Parties and Policy* (New York: Holt, Rinehart and Winston, 1981), p. 29.
2. Austin Ranney, "President and His Party." in Anthony King, ed., *Both Ends of the Avenue: The Presidency, the Executive Branch, and Congress in the 1980s* (Washington, D.C.: American Enterprise Institute, 1983), p. 137.
3. Ibid., p. 138.
4. Richard E. Neustadt, *President Power: The Politics of Leadership* (New York: Wiley, 1960), pp. 33–34.
5. Ranney, "President and His Party," p. 139.
6. Thedore J. Lowi, "Party, Policy, and the Constitution in America," in William Nisbet Chambers and Walter Dean Burnham, eds., *The Ameri-*

can Party Systems: Stages of Development (New York: Oxford University Press, 1975), p. 248; see also Leon D. Epstein, *Political Parties in the American Mold* (Madison: University of Wisconsin Press, 1986), pp. 80–89.

7. Frank J. Sorauf, *Party Politics in America*, 5th ed. (Boston: Little, Brown, 1984), p. 375; Epstein, *Political Parties*, pp. 80–89.
8. Ranney, "President and His Party," p. 134.
9. Cornelius P. Cotter, "Eisenhower as Party Leader," *Political Science Quarterly* 98 (Summer 1983): 261. The development and extent of White House control over executive branch appointments is analyzed by C. Calvin Mackenzie, "Partisan Presidential Leadership: The President's Appointees," in L. Sandy Maisel, ed., *The Parties Respond: Changes in the American Party System* (Boulder, Colo.: Westview Press, 1990), ch. 13.
10. David Broder, "At White House Order," *Washington Post*, Jan. 1, 1991, p. A17; *New York Times*, Oct. 5, 1982, p. A24; Paul Taylor and Lou Cannon, "RNC's Embattled Richards Quits; Timing and Performance Questioned," *Washington Post*, Oct. 10, 1982, p. A5.
11. Ranney, "President and His Party," p. 143.
12. *Choosing Presidential Candidates: How Good Is the New Way*, John Charles Daly, moderator, AEI Forums (Washington, D.C.: American Enterprise Institute, 1979), p. 7. Used with permission.
13. Ranney, "President and His Party," pp. 141–142.
14. See John A. Ferejohn and Randall L. Calvert, "Presidential Coattails in Historical Perspective," *American Journal of Political Science* 28 (Feb. 1984): 127–146; Randall L. Calvert and John A. Ferejohn, "Coattail Voting in Recent Presidential Elections," *American Political Science Review* 77 (June 1983): 407–419.
15. George C. Edwards, III, *Presidential Influence in Congress* (San Francisco: W.H. Freeman, 1980), pp. 42–45.
16. Ibid., p. 45.
17. Richard F. Fenno, Jr., "U.S. House Members in Their Constituencies: An Exploration," *American Political Science Review* 71 (Sept. 1977): 914.
18. Nelson W. Polsby, *Congress and the Presidency*, 4th ed. (Englewood Cliffs, N.J.: Prentice-Hall, 1986), pp. 193–194.
19. For classic studies of the importance of party in roll call voting, see Julius Turner, *Party and Constituency: Pressures on Congress* (Baltimore, Md.: Johns Hopkins University Press, 1959); David B. Truman, *The Congressional Party* (New York: Wiley, 1959); See also Samuel C. Patterson and Gregory A. Caldeira, "Party Voting in the United States Congress," *British Journal of Political Science* 18 (Jan. 1988): 111–131.
20. Herbert B. Asher and Herbert F. Weisberg, "Voting in Congress: Some Dynamic Perspectives of an Evolutionary Process," *American Journal of Political Science* 22 (May 1978): 406–409.
21. Aage R. Clausen and Carl E. Van Horn, "The Congressional Response to a Decade of Change," *Journal of Politics* 39 (Aug. 1977): 637–640.
22. Truman, *Congressional Party*; pp. 297–298.

23. Polsby, *Congress and the Presidency*, p. 207.
24. Ibid., pp. 194–196.
25. Francis E. Rourke, "The Presidency and the Bureaucracy: Strategic Alternatives," in Michael Nelson, ed., *The Presidency and the Political System* (Washington, D.C.: CQ Press, 1984), p. 340.
26. Quoted in Neustadt, *Presidential Power*, p. 39.
27. Hugh Heclo, "One Executive Branch or Many?" in Anthony King, ed. *Both Ends of the Avenue*, pp. 32–33.
28. Ibid., pp. 33–34.
29. Ibid., p. 34.
30. Roger G. Brown, "The Presidency and the Political Parties," in Nelson, *The Presidency and the Political System*, p. 323.
31. David E. Price, *Bringing Back the Parties* (Washington, D.C.: CQ Press, 1984), p. 176.
32. John H. Kessel, "The Structures of the Reagan White House," *American Journal of Political Science* 28 (May 1984): 235.
33. Gerald M. Boyd, "Reagan Requests Heckler to Yield Her Cabinet Post," *New York Times*, Oct. 1, 1985, pp. 1, 15.
34. Heclo, "One Executive Branch?" pp. 42–47.
35. See David M. O'Brien, "The Reagan Judges: His Most Enduring Legacy," in Charles O. Jones, ed., *The Reagan Legacy* (Chatham, N.J.: Chatham House, 1988), p. 62; Ruth Marcus, "Bush Quietly Fosters Conservative Trend in Courts," *Washington Post*, Feb. 18, 1991, pp. A1, A4, A6.
36. Ibid., p. 70.
37. Howard Kurtz, "Reagan Transforms the Federal Judiciary," *Washington Post*, March 31, 1985, p. A4.
38. Quoted in John F. Bibby, *Congress Off the Record: The Candid Analyses of Seven Members* (Washington, D.C.: American Enterprise Institute, 1983), p. 29.
39. For the most thorough analysis of member goals and committee politics, see Richard F. Fenno, Jr., *Congressmen in Committees* (Boston, Mass.: Little, Brown, 1983).
40. David Brady, Joseph Cooper, and Patricia Hurley, "The Decline of Party in the U.S. House of Representatives, 1887–1968," *Legislative Studies Quarterly* 4 (Aug. 1979): 383–386; see also Melissa Collie and David W. Brady, "The Decline of Partisan Voting in the House of Representatives," in Lawrence C. Dodd and Bruce I. Oppenheimer, eds., *Congress Reconsidered*, 3d ed. (Washington, D.C.: CQ Press, 1985), pp. 272–287.
41. For a concise analysis of the reasons for the increased partisanship within Congress, see Barbara Sinclair, "The Congressional Party: Evolving Organizational, Agenda Setting, and Policy Roles," in Maisel, ed., *The Parties Respond*, ch. 11.
42. Truman, *Congressional Party*, p. 95.
43. See Sinclair, "The Congressional Party." See also Lawrence C. Dodd and Bruce I. Oppenheimer,"Consolidating Power in the House: The Rise of a New Oligarchy," in Lawrence C. Dodd and Bruce I. Oppenheimer, eds., *Congress Reconsidered*, 4th ed. (Washington, D.C.: CQ Press, 1989), ch. 2.

44. Quoted in Bibby, *Congress off the Record*, p. 26.
45. Quoted in Michael J. Malbin, "House Democrats Are Playing with a Strong Leadership Lineup," *National Journal* (June 18, 1977), p. 942.
46. See Diane Granat, "Democratic Caucus Renewed as Forum for Policy Questions," *Congressional Quarterly Weekly Report* (Oct. 15, 1983), pp. 2115–2119.
47. Margaret Shapiro, "House Leaders Delay Vote on Defense Budget," *Washington Post*, July 31, 1985, p. A4.
48. On the highly individualistic nature of the modern Senate, see Alan Ehrenhalt, "In the Senate of the '80s, Team Spirit Has Given Way to the Rule of the Individual," *Congressional Quarterly Weekly Report* (Sept. 4, 1982), pp. 2185–2192; see also Sinclair, "The Congressional Party."
49. For an up-to-date account of the role of party leaders in the Senate, see Roger H. Davidson, "The Senate: If Everybody Leads, Who Follows?" in Dodd and Oppenheimer, *Congress Reconsidered*, pp. 275–305.
50. See John F. Bibby and Robert J. Huckshorn, "Out-Party Rebuilding Strategy: Republican National Committee Rebuilding Politics, 1964–1968," in Bernard Cosman and Robert J. Huckshorn, eds., *Republican Politics, The 1964 Campaign and Its Aftermath for the Party* (New York: Praeger, 1968), pp. 218–223.
51. Phil Gailey, "Dissidents Defy Top Democrats; Council Formed," *New York Times*, March 1, 1985, pp. 1, 9.
52. David R. Mayhew, *Congress: The Electoral Connection* (New Haven, Conn.: Yale University Press, 1974), pp. 97–105.

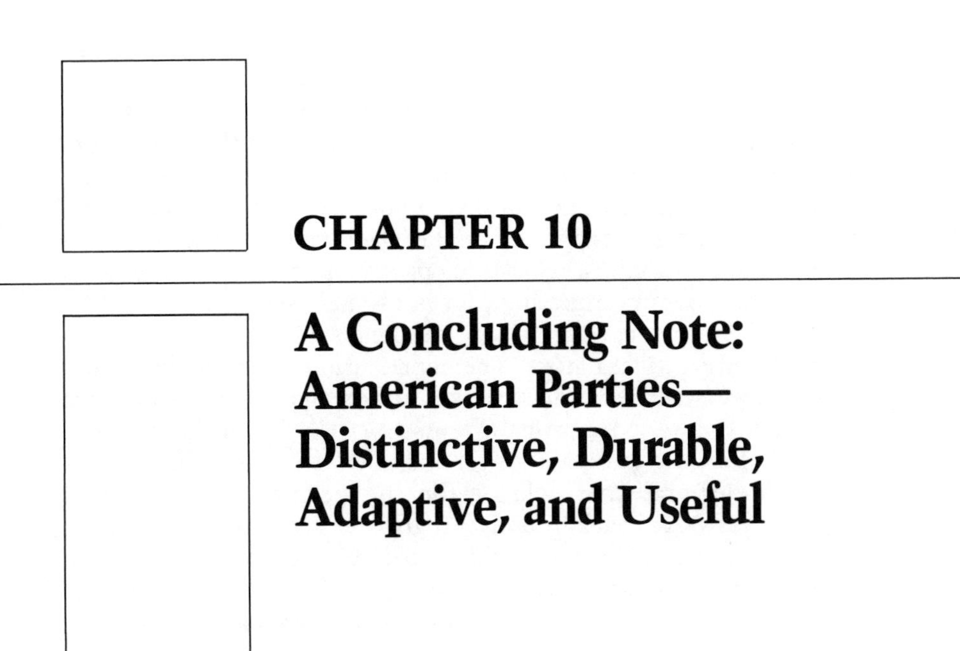

CHAPTER 10

A Concluding Note: American Parties—Distinctive, Durable, Adaptive, and Useful

Throughout this brief exploration of American political parties, four strands of thought have consistently been a part of the discussion. American parties are distinctive, durable, adaptive, and useful to the republic.[1] These parties are unlike any others in Western democracies—they are organizationally weaker, lacking in substantial internal cohesion, without a mass dues paying membership, unable to control their own nominating processes, and heavily regulated by statute. They operate under severe handicaps—obstacles of a constitutional and political nature. The constitutional barriers of separation of powers and federalism make unified and disciplined parties extremely unlikely. Historical events (e.g., Civil War, Depression, patterns of immigration and migration) have created partisan loyalties in the electorate that meld together in the same party elements of disparate views and backgrounds. Progressive reforms like the direct primary have weakened the parties' capacity to control nominations, and civil service reforms have taken away much of the patronage that was used to sustain them. Competing political organizations such as interest groups, candidate organizations, campaign consultants, and PACs have gained seemingly increased influence both in campaign politics and governmental decision making. At the same time, voters seem less inclined to make their choices on election day on the basis of partisan considerations.

In the changing patterns of American party politics, many have perceived a general pattern of party decline, and a few have even envisioned an age of partyless politics in the near future.[2] Others see signs of party revival in such phenomenon as the increased strength of the national party organizations.[3] Of course, it is dangerous to predict the future and determine whether the revivalists or the seers of decline are correct. However, based upon past history, it is probably safe to predict that American parties will maintain their record of proven durability and adaptibility to changing and even hostile conditions.

The evidence of their durability and adaptability is striking. For over 130 years the same two parties—the Republicans and Democrats—have dominated electoral politics. This is a record of durability unmatched in any other Western style democracy. Remarkably, these two parties compete against each other across the nation, despite the obstacles of regional diversity and federalism. They have adapted to the Progressive era reforms which stripped them of control over nominations and patronage; and they have adapted to the more recent reform environment of public funding of presidential elections and some state elections. The rise of political action committees has not put parties out of business. Instead, the parties have sought to coordinate and channel PAC contributions. As campaigns became more professionalized, technical, and expensive, the parties increased their fund-raising potential through such techniques as direct mail and hired their own technical experts to provide in-kind services to candidates. At both the national and state levels there is evidence of increased party organizational strength compared to that which existed in the 1960s.[4]

Party identifiers continue to constitute approximately two-thirds of the voters, and the decline in party identifiers seems to have stabilized since the mid-1970s. Parties organize the Congress, state legislatures, the White House, and state administrations. They exert substantial influence on the decision making processes at the national and state levels.

But if American parties have a record of adaptability and durability, they also have a record of only modest strength. Defection rates among party identifiers in elections are frequently high—over 20 percent. Party organizations are insufficiently strong to nominate preferred candidates and then run their campaigns. The party-in-government is often fragmented and unable to hold together enough to enact a coherent program. The American system is not one of party government like that of the British. It should be noted, however, that the Congress took on a much more partisan tone in the late 1980s as party unity increased, particularly between the northern and southern wings of the Democratic party.

The picture of political parties in America that emerges, therefore, is a contradictory one—durability and adaptability combined with modest organizational strength, declining voter commitment, and lack of internal cohesion among public office holders. The political parties of the United States constitute a unique response to the American constitutional system, demography, culture, and historical events. But for all their acknowledged weaknesses, parties remain and are likely to remain the principal agents for recruiting leaders, making nominations, contesting elections, bridging the gulf created by separation of powers, and providing a link between the citizenry and their government.

Notes

1. The distinctiveness of American political parties and their persistence are major themes of Leon D. Epstein's comprehensive and insightful analysis of the American party system. See Leon D. Epstein, *Political Parties in the American Mold* (Madison: University of Wisconsin Press, 1986).
2. Walter Dean Burnham, *Critical Elections and the Mainsprings of American Politics* (New York: Norton, 1970). See also David Broder, *The Party's*

Over (New York: Harper and Row, 1972); and William Crotty, *Parties in Decline* (Boston: Little, Brown, 1984).

3. See, for example, Paul S. Herrnson, *Party Campaigning in the 1880s* (Cambridge, Mass.: Harvard University Press, 1988); and Xandra Kayden and Eddie Mahe, *The Party Goes On* (New York: Basic Books, 1985).
4. Cornelius P. Cotter and John F. Bibby, "Institutional Development of Parties and the Thesis of Party Decline, *Political Science Quarterly* 95 (Spring 1980):1–28; Kayden and Mahe, *The Party Goes On;* and Cornelius P. Cotter, James L. Gibson, John F. Bibby, and Robert J. Huckshorn, *Party Organizations in American Politics* (New York: Praeger, 1984).

INDEX TO REFERENCES

INDEX